COLLECTED STUDIES SERIES

Culture and Spirituality
in Medieval Europe

For Paul Meyvaert
on his seventy-fifth birthday

Giles Constable

Culture and Spirituality
in Medieval Europe

VARIORUM
1996

This edition copyright © 1996 by Giles Constable.

Published by VARIORUM
Ashgate Publishing Limited
Gower House, Croft Road,
Aldershot, Hampshire GU11 3HR
Great Britain

Ashgate Publishing Company
Old Post Road,
Brookfield, Vermont 05036
USA

ISBN 0–86078–609–9

British Library CIP Data

Constable, Giles, 1929–
Culture and Spirituality in Medieval Europe. (Variorum Collected
Studies Series; CS541).
1. Europe–History–476–1492. 2. Europe–Religion–History.
3. Europe–Social conditions–To 1492. 4. Europe–Church history–
600–1500.
I. Title.
940. 1' 7

US Library of Congress CIP Data

Constable, Giles.
Culture and Spirituality in Medieval Europe / Giles Constable.
p. cm. – (Collected Studies Series; CS541).
Includes index (cloth / alk. paper).
1. Spirituality–Catholic Church–History. 2. Europe–Church
history–600–1500. 3. Civilization, Medieval. 4. Civilization,
Medieval–12th century. 5. Catholic Church–Doctrines–History.
6. Eleventh century. I. Title. II. Series: Collected Studies; CS541.
BR270. C65   1996   96–15495
274' .04–dc20   CIP

The paper used in this publication meets the minimum requirements of the
American National Standard for Information Sciences – Permanance of Paper
for Printed Library Materials, ANSI Z39.48–1984. ∞ ™

Printed by Galliard (Printers) Ltd, Great Yarmouth, Norfolk, Great Britain

COLLECTED STUDIES SERIES C541

CONTENTS

Preface

This volume contains viii + 318 pages

PREFACE

I am particularly glad to have an opportunity to reprint these articles because two of them (numbers IV and XI) were originally published with a number of misprints, especially in the notes, which have been corrected here. The present versions of these articles, therefore, are to be preferred to the original publications. Some minor errors and misprints have also been corrected in the other articles.

One of the wholesome (and somewhat humbling) aspects of bringing together a volume like this is to discover one's own repetitions and inconsistencies, of which several showed up in the course of compiling the index, such as Adrian and Hadrian IV, Hildebert of Lavardin and Le Mans, and Wibald of Corvey and Stavelot. Most striking is Honorius *Augustodunensis*, who for a time in the late 1980s I was convinced came from Augsburg. It looks as if he in fact came from Regensburg, but I have taken refuge (as he did) in the ambiguity of *Augustodunensis*.

GILES CONSTABLE

Institute for Advanced Study, Princeton, New Jersey
February 1996

PUBLISHER'S NOTE

The articles in this volume, as in all others in the Collected Studies Series, have not been given a new, continuous pagination. In order to avoid confusion, and to facilitate their use where these same studies have been referred to elsewhere, the original pagination has been maintained wherever possible.

Each article has been given a Roman number in order of appearance, as listed in the Contents. This number is repeated in each page and is quoted in the index entries.

Corrections noted in the Addenda and Corrigenda have been marked by an askerisk in the margin corresponding to the text to be amended.

I

Forgery and Plagiarism in the Middle Ages[*]

Forgery and plagiarism are subjects of endless fascination. Their types and forms may vary from age to age, and the moral judgments concerning them may differ, but they always hold up a mirror to the period in which they were created. Fraud is the special vice of man for Dante: 'Frode è de l'uom proprio male.'[1] According to an old saying, *Mundus vult decipi, ergo decipiatur:* 'The world wants to be deceived, let it therefore be deceived.'[2] Each generation creates its own deceptions and looks back with a combination of scorn and amusement, not always unmixed with admiration, on the deceptions of the past. The secret of successful forgers and plagiarists is to attune the deceit so closely to the desires and standards of their age that it is not detected, or even suspected, at the time of creation. The passage of time alone shows up many forgeries[3], whereas authentic works, which are less bound to a particular standard,

---

[*] This article was first given as a lecture to the 11th annual meeting of the Midwest Medieval Conference in Milwaukee in 1973. It was given in translation in Paris in 1975, and later that year at Marburg, where Professor Dr. Heinemeyer generously offered to publish it in the *Archiv für Diplomatik*. It has benefitted from the comments of several critics who heard it presented orally, including Professors Bautier, Guenée, and Lemarignier in Paris, and now appears in a substantially revised and enlarged version. It still preserves, however, some of the form and expressions imposed by its original presentation as a lecture, including examples chosen from the literature of my own university and from popular sources. When possible, medieval sources are cited in translation.

[1] *Inferno*, 11.25.
[2] De Thou attributed this saying to Cardinal Caraffa, but it is certainly older: see Gilbert Bagnani, 'On Fakes and Forgeries,' *Phoenix*, 14 (1960) 228 and n. 43. It is paralleled by the saying attributed by Acton to Fénelon: 'He who fears excessively to be duped deserves to be duped, and he nearly always does get grossly duped:' cited by G. G. Coulton, *Fourscore Years: An Autobiography* (Cambridge, 1944) 348.
[3] They may therefore be embraced under the motto *Veritas filia temporis*, which expresses the idea of the progressive discovery or revelation of truth: see Fritz Saxl, 'Veritas filia Temporis,' *Philosophy and History: Essays Presented to Ernst Cassirer*, ed. Raymond Klibansky and Herbert J. Paton (Oxford, 1936) 197–222, esp. 200, n. 1.

may be in a real sense timeless. The *Libri Carolini* were once thought to be a forgery, and the authenticity of the plays of Hrotswitha was doubted when they were first published in 1501 precisely because at that time no one believed that a nun at Gandersheim in the tenth century could have written plays imitating Terence[4]. Forgeries and plagiarisms, on the other hand, follow rather than create fashion and can without paradox be considered among the most authentic products of their time[5]. They therefore deserve attention not only in order to distinguish them from those works which are considered original and authentic but also to assess their own value as historical sources[6].

To the historian the most interesting questions about forgeries and plagiarisms are not who made them or how they were discovered, fascinating as these are, but why they were made and, if successful, accepted[7]. The subject of this paper, therefore, is deceptions made in the Middle Ages in order to take in people at that time, not later forgeries or imitations of documents or works of art in the medieval style, made as a rule for mercenary motives. Among medieval forgeries, I shall be concerned less with those made for obvious institutional or personal reasons than with problematical forgeries, often made by respectable, even prominent, members of society for reasons that are now not always clear. Many forgeries were made for altruistic, even noble, purposes, or for obscure personal motives. 'For all born forgers,' according to Berenson, 'forging is its own reward.'[8] And Trevor-Roper remarked on the subtle temptation leading the forger from 'disinterested craftsmanship, through a positive delight in his own virtuosity, to the exquisite private satisfaction of

---

[4] Max Manitius, *Geschichte der lateinischen Literatur des Mittelalters* (Handbuch der Altertumswissenschaft, IX.2.1–3; Munich, 1911-31) I, 632, n. 3.

[5] A full classification of types of forgeries, including some types that might not generally be considered forgeries, is given by Ernst Bernheim, *Lehrbuch der historischen Methode,* 5th–6th ed. (Leipzig, 1908) 331-76.

[6] The value of forgeries as historical sources in their own right was recognized by Marc Bloch, *The Historian's Craft,* tr. Peter Putnam (New York, 1953) 93: 'Above all, a fraud is, in its way, a piece of evidence.' See also A. von Brandt, *Werkzeug des Historikers,* 2nd ed. (Urban-Bücher, 33; Stuttgart, 1958) 124 and, in the area of artistic forgeries, W. M. Ivins, Jr., 'Some Notes on Fakes,' *Magazine of Art,* 41.5 (May 1948) 168-71, who stressed the importance of fakes and museum restorations as guides to the history of taste (171).

[7] Geoffrey Grigson, reveiwing two books on the forger Tom Keating in the *Times Literary Supplement* (July 15 1977) 852, described four parties to forgery: the forger, situation, deceived, and unmasker.

[8] A letter on 'Art Forgeries' published in the *Times* April 4 1903 and reprinted in *The First Cuckoo: A Selection of the Most Witty, Amusing and Memorable Letters to the Times, 1900–1975,* ed. Kenneth Gregory (London, 1976) 43.

deceiving the elect.'[9] Like miracles, visions, and other works of social imagination, forgeries served to justify profound social and personal needs and reflected the hopes and fears, the praise and criticism of people in the Middle Ages.

Before turning to these questions, however, we should consider what is meant by the terms forgery and plagiarism, which are less easy to define than may appear at first sight. The original meaning of to forge was simply to make or fabricate, but already in Middle English it took on the pejorative implication (which to fabricate now also has) of making something up, that is, of imitating falsely. To plagiarize is a more recent term in English, though it derives from the Latin word for a kidnapper or seducer, and refers to taking some one else's ideas or words and passing them off as one's own. In both terms the intention to deceive is as central as the actual deception. The falseness lies not in the words or object but in the intention of the creator or, occasionally, of the receiver[10]. The intention differs inasmuch as forgers attribute their own work to some one else and plagiarists pass off some one else's work as their own, but both intend to deceive. Neither term is commonly used for unintentional deceptions, nor as a rule for hoaxes of which the only purpose is foolery, though the line between forgeries and hoaxes is often very narrow. Honest copies and unconscious borrowings are not called forgeries or plagiarisms, any more than all verbal inaccuracies are called lies. There are infinite shadings between correction, revision, imitation, and falsification and, in works of art, between repair, restoration, reproduction, and copying. When does a letter drafted by a secretary or a painting finished by an assistant become a forgery? In common parlance, only when the writer's or artist's intent is falsified. An honest version or copy can be turned into a forgery either by ignorance or by design, however, as happened with a Renaissance bust of Caesar in the British Museum, which was believed to be ancient after it was cleaned in the eighteenth century[11], and as may happen with many modern museum reproductions, which will be taken, perhaps in good faith, to be originals. The falsifica-

---

[9] Hugh Trevor-Roper, *A Hidden Life: The Enigma of Sir Edmund Backhouse* (London, 1976) 287.

[10] Bernheim, *Lehrbuch*, 331, put the fault in the source: 'Wenn eine Quelle ganz oder zu einem Teile sich für etwas anderes ausgibt, als sie tatsächlich ist, . . . so haben wir mit Fälschung, bezw. partieller Fälschung oder Verunechtung zu tun; die Quelle ist gefälscht, bezw. verunechtet.' In reality, the deception is the work of the forger. The distinction is small, but not trivial.

[11] Bagnani, in *Phoenix,* 14.230-32.

tion may thus be the work of the receiver, who takes something to be what it is not.

The idea of truth and authenticity has long disturbed philosophers and moralists. Dr Johnson put the issue with his usual common sense when he said that, 'Physical truth, is, when you tell a thing as it actually is. Moral truth, is, when you tell a thing sincerely and precisely as it appears to you.'[12] Physical truth can be called objective, impersonal, absolute, amoral, or, in the classical language of philosophy, idealist or realist. Moral truth is subjective, personalist, relative, ethical, or pragmatic[13]. Physical truth depends upon abstractions; moral truth on persons. What is called fiction falls somewhere between the two, since by clothing truth with untruth it may come closer to truth than some non-fictions[14]. 'The distinction between fact and fiction is a late acquisition of rational thought,' according to Koestler[15], and one that is less clear in theory than it is in practice.

In an article entitled 'A Human View of Truth', Wilfred Smith deplored the loss in western society, as he saw it, of the personal quality of truth and the consequent divorce between truth and morality. He contrasted the current western idea of truth as inherent in propositions with the view found in many non-western societies, and in the West down at least until the Scientific Revolution, that truth exists in relation to people, and people in relation to truth. This view of truth still exists in Islam, which is in many respects closer than we are to the thought-world of the Middle Ages. There are three distinct words in Arabic referring respectively to the truth of things, of persons, and of statements. In the

---

[12] James Boswell, *Life of Johnson*, ed. G. B. Hill (New York, 1891–1904) IV, 7.

[13] William James, *Pragmatism* (New York, 1943), preface, where he contrasted the meaning of Truth for pragmatists ('something about the ideas, namely their workableness') and antipragmatists ('something about the objects'), and Lecture VI, where he again contrasted the pragmatist view that 'True ideas are those that we can assimilate, validate, corroborate and verify' with the rationalist view that 'Truth is a system of propositions which have an unconditional claim to be recognized as valid.' See also Leszek Kolakowski, 'Karl Marx and the Classical Definition of Truth,' in *Toward a Marxist Humanism* (New York, 1968) 38–66, contrasting the Marxist-positivist view of truth as 'the relation between a judgment or an opinion and the reality to which it refers' (38) and the Jamesian-pragmatic view that 'The truth of a judgment is defined as a practical function of the usefulness of its acceptance or rejection' (40).

[14] Franz H. Bäuml, 'Varieties and Consequences of Medieval Literacy and Illiteracy,' *Speculum*, 55 (1980) 237-65. Augustine recognized that a legend or fiction referring to a true meaning was not a lie but a way of presenting the truth: Klaus Schreiner, 'Zum Wahrheitsverständnis im Heiligen- und Reliquienwesen des Mittelalters,' *Saeculum*, 17 (1966) 162-63.

[15] Arthur Koestler, *The Act of Creation* (New York, 1964) 350.

Middle Ages all of these were embraced in the terms *verus* and *veritas,* which referred to truth not only in an objective but also in a subjective sense, including what would now be called honesty and trustworthiness[16].

People in the Middle Ages, though they were accomplished deceivers in both practical and moral affairs, were deeply concerned with truth and recognized its human element[17]. St Anselm in his treatise *De veritate,* while stressing that God is the single truth from Whom all truths derive, discussed the truth of statements, opinions, the will, actions, the senses, and the essence of things, concluding that the highest truth is rectitude, which he equated with justice[18]. 'A prayer is true,' he said, 'even when it says what is not,' if it signified what ought to be. Truth in actions 'is to do well, and to do well is to do rectitude.'[19]. Hugh of St Victor said that the truth of statements depended on the individual. Some one who speaks in order to deceive is a liar even if what he says is factually correct[20]. The thirteenth-century philosopher Grosseteste followed Anselm in saying that, 'All created truth can be perceived only in the light of the highest truth,' but he recognized that, since this perception varied from person to person, there were many degrees of perception of the truth[21]. Between three and five kinds of truth are defined in the late-

---

[16] Wilfred C. Smith, 'A Human View of Truth,' *Studies in Religion/Sciences religieuses,* 1 (1971) 6–24, who said that, 'Different civilizations and ages have had differing visions of truth'. Hans von Soden, 'Was ist Wahrheit?' *Vom geschichtlichen Begriff der Wahrheit* (Marburger akademische Reden, 46; Marburg, 1927) distinguished the Greek from the Jewish concept of truth, which embraced action as well as knowledge and had a specifically historical character (13–14). On Harvard's motto *Veritas* see Smith 20 and Aleksandr Solzhenitsyn, who said in his commencement address at Harvard in 1978, printed in the *Harvard Gazette,* June 8 1978, that we must concentrate on the pursuit of truth: 'Even while it eludes us, the illusion still lingers of knowing it and leads to many misunderstandings.'

[17] See Julian Pitt-Rivers, *The People of the Sierra,* 2nd ed (Chicago, 1971) xvi, for a modern parallel, referring to 'Simmel's great essay on secrecy and the lie'.

[18] Anselm of Canterbury, *Opera omnia,* ed. F. S. Schmitt (Edinburgh, 1946-61) I, 176-99. For other references to truth in Anselm's works see s.v. *Veritas* in the index in VI, 375-78.

[19] *Ibid.,* I, 178.

[20] Hugh of St Victor, *On the Sacraments of the Christian Faith,* I. 12. 15, tr. Roy J. Deferrari (Cambridge, Mass., 1951) 197.

[21] Robert Grosseteste, *De veritate,* in *Die philosophischen Werke des Robert Grossetestes,* ed. Ludwig Baur (Beiträge zur Geschichte der Philosophie des Mittelalters, 9; Münster, 1912) 134-38. His contemporary William of Auvergne defined six types of truth in the section of his *Magisterium divinale* entitled 'On the Universe', I. 3. 26, where he said that, 'Veritas secundum multas intentiones dicitur': William of Auvergne, *Opera omnia* (Paris, 1674) I, 794^{b}E, and, generally, 794-95 and 836^{a}E–836^{b}F.

medieval treatises on *insolubilia*, statements that could be considered true or false depending on the type of truth[22].

This view is also found in vernacular literature. The difference between the truths spoken by Beatrice and Piccarda was explained by Dante in terms of the absolute and mixed wills[23]. The term 'truth' in Old English meant 'faith' or 'trust' and still had an ethical implication in the works of Langland and Chaucer, who used it in the sense of 'fidelity'[24]. Its opposite was faithlessness and falseness in a personal as well as an objective sense. This subjective concept of truth still survives in common usage, and among perceptive observers of the world as it is. 'There is no "True",' wrote Flaubert toward the end of his life. 'There are only ways of perceiving.'[25] We speak of people as true to their word, Smith pointed out, and use the terms true, genuine, real, and authentic in a value-laden sense. According to William Perry, in an entertaining and perceptive essay on college examinations, facts without a frame of reference, which gives them moral value, 'are not even "true" at all.'[26]

A subjective sense also clings, as we have seen, to the modern concept of forgery and plagiarism in the element of intention, but there were important differences between the nature and types of forgery and plagiarism in the Middle Ages and today. Perhaps the most characteristic form of modern forgery, that of works of art, was unknown at that time. There were any number of adaptations, pastiches, and at times copies of works of art (the skill of which is shown by the fact that modern critics often disagree over their date)[27], but they were not put forward as origi-

---

[22] Paul V. Spade, *The Mediaeval Liar: A Catalogue of the 'Insolubilia'-Literature* (Pontifical Institute of Mediaeval Studies: Subsidia mediaevalia, 5; Toronto, 1975) 39, 70, 75-76.

[23] *Paradiso*, 4.14.

[24] Will Héraucourt, ' "What is trouthe or soothfastnesse?" ' *Englische Kultur in sprachwissenschaftlicher Deutung. Max Deutschbein zum 60. Geburtstage*, ed. Wolfgang Schmidt (Leipzig, 1936) 75–84, and, on Langland, Ruth M. Ames, *The Fulfillment of the Scriptures: Abraham, Moses, and Piers* (Evanston, 1970) 76: 'The Truth that is God is the same truth that is manifested by men who refrain from lying, or who do an honest day's work.' See also the unpublished dissertation on truth in Piers Plowman by Sister Mary C. Davlin, to whom I am indebted for these references and who stressed the need for love in truth.

[25] *The Letters of Gustave Flaubert, 1857–1880*, ed. and tr. Francis Steegmuller (Cambridge, Mass. – London, 1982) 266.

[26] William G. Perry, Jr., 'Examsmanship and the Liberal Arts: A Study in Educational Epistemology,' *Examining in Harvard College*, ed. Leon Bramson (Cambridge, Mass., 1963) 130. See also the passage by Huxley cited n. 118 below.

[27] See Hanns Swarzenski, 'The Role of Copies in the Formation of the Styles of the Eleventh Century,' *Studies in Western Art: Acts of the Twentieth International Congress of the History of Art*, I: *Romanesque and Gothic Art* (Princeton, 1963) 7–18 (and the review of

nals at the time they were made. The closest medieval parallel to modern forgery of art was the flourishing manufacture and trade in false relics, which were esteemed then much as works of art are now[28]. The most characteristic types of medieval forgery and plagiarism, however, are not found today, and their purpose and acceptance are often hard to understand. The obvious forgers who forged for personal gain, such as coiners, were dealt with in a summary fashion when they were detected; but the most interesting forgers, and those who have attracted the attention of scholars, forged for the advantage not of themselves but of a cause or institution, or for the sake of some high purpose. Some of these were great forgeries, which have influenced the course of history, like the Donation of Constantine and the Pseudo-Isidorian Decretals[29]. Others were little forgeries, sometimes affecting only a few words in an otherwise authentic document. But they have in common that they were of no personal advantage to the forger, and this was doubtless a factor in explaining the apparent tolerance with which they were regarded at the time they were made.

Historians have long discussed the purposes and results of these forgeries and have drawn some interesting conclusions concerning the causes and institutions they were created to serve. The Donation of Constantine promoted the independence and territorial claims of the papacy, but its precise purpose is still the subject of debate. It may have been created 'not to deceive the Frankish or Byzantine chancelleries or to assert the rights previously possessed by the pope and the clerics of his patri-

---

the same author's *Monuments of Romanesque Art* by Meyer Schapiro in the *Art News*, 54.5 (Sept. 1955) 44, 59–60); H. van de Waal, 'Forgery as a Stylistic Problem,' *Aspects of Art Forgery* (Strafrechteliche en criminologische Onderzoekingen, N.S. 6; The Hague, 1962) 3; and Madeline Caviness, ' "De convenientia et cohaerentia antiqui et novi operis": Medieval Conservation, Restoration, Pastiche and Forgery,' *Intuition und Kunstwissenschaft. Festschrift für Hanns Swarzenski* (Berlin, 1973) 205-21, esp. 213–18.

[28] See H. Silvestre, 'Commerce et vol de reliques au moyen âge,' *Revue belge de philologie et d'histoire*, 30 (1952) 721-39; Denis Bethell, 'The Making of a Twelfth-Century Relic Collection,' *Studies in Church History*, 8 (1972) 61–72; and Nicole Herrmann-Mascard, *Les reliques des saints. Formation coutumière d'un droit* (Société d'histoire du droit: Collection d'histoire institutionelle et sociale, 6; Paris, 1975) passim, esp. 364-87.

[29] See the new edition of the *Constitutum Constantini* by Horst Fuhrmann (Monumenta Germaniae historica: Fontes iuris germanici antiqui, 10; Hanover, 1968) and, on the Pseudo-Isidorian Decretals (which Haller called 'the greatest fraud in the history of the world') Horst Fuhrmann, *Einfluß und Verbreitung der pseudoisidorischen Fälschungen von ihrem Auftauchen bis in die neuere Zeit* (Monumenta Germaniae historica: Schriften, 24; Stuttgart, 1972-74), of which chap. 1 of vol I (65–136) is an enlarged version of his article on 'Die Fälschungen im Mittelalter,' *Historische Zeitschrift*, 197 (1963) 529-54, with three 'Diskussionsbeiträge' by Karl Bosl (555-67), Hans Patze (568-73), and August Nitschke (574-79) and a 'Schlußwort' by Fuhrmann (580–601).

archate' but simply to instruct the pilgrims who visited the Lateran Basilica[30]. The Pseudo-Isidorian Decretals were concerned with the diocesan bishops in Carolingian Gaul and their relations with Rome, but who wrote them, and when, where, and why are uncertain. The famous forgeries associated with the name of Lanfranc were probably made to support the superiority of Christ Church over the abbey of St Augustine, not of Canterbury over York, though they were later used to promote the primatial claims of Canterbury[31]. 'Primacy and exemption,' according to Brooke, 'demanded forgery.'[32]

Smaller forgeries are no less interesting. Those made for ecclesiastical institutions in France in the tenth and eleventh centuries were mostly concerned with privileges and property rights. The famous *falsarius* Guerno of St Médard at Soissons confessed on his deathbed in 1119/31 that in return for precious ornaments given to his abbey he had forged papal privileges for several monasteries in addition to his own, guaranteeing their spiritual rights and freedom from various payments, episcopal control, and royal officials[33]. The principal concern of many of the forgeries made for German monasteries in the twelfth and thirteenth centuries (which according to Mayer outnumbered those made in France by four to one) was to protect them from the claims of bishops, other monasteries, secular rulers, and advocates[34]. The apparently greater number of forgeries made in France and Germany than in Italy may have been owing to the greater emphasis on authentic written records there[35]. Why more forgeries were made for Monte Cassino than for Farfa, however, is

---

[30] N. Huyghebaert, 'Une légende de fondation: le Constitutum Constantini,' *Moyen Age,* 85 (1979) 208. On the influence of the Donation of Constantine, see Domenico Maffei, *La Donazione di Costantino nei giuristi medievali* (Milan, 1964).

[31] Margaret Gibson, *Lanfranc of Bec* (Oxford, 1978) 231-37.

[32] C. N. L. Brooke, 'Approaches to Medieval Forgery', in his *Medieval Church and Society: Collected Essays* (London, 1971) 114.

[33] *Literae Cantuarienses,* ed. J. B. Sheppard (Rolls Series, 85; London, 1887-89) III, 365-66; *Papsturkunden in Frankreich,* N.F., 7: *Nördliche Ile-de-France und Vermandois,* ed. Dietrich Lohrmann (Abhandlungen der Akademie der Wissenschaften in Göttingen, Phil.-hist. Kl., 3rd S., 95; Göttingen, 1976) 226, no. 1. See Wilhelm Levison, *England and the Continent in the Eighth Century* (Ford Lectures, 1943; Oxford, 1946) 207-23.

[34] Theodor Mayer, *Fürsten und Staat* (Weimar, 1950) 22–24, drew a contrast, with which not all scholars agree, between the types of forgeries made in France and Germany. Among the many interesting works on this topic, see Hans Hirsch, *Die Klosterimmunität seit dem Investiturstreit* (Weimar, 1913) 102, and Henri Dubled, 'L'avouerie des monastères en Alsace au Moyen Age,' *Archives de l'Eglise d'Alsace,* 26 (N.S., 10; 1959) 1–88, esp. 42–53.

[35] Both the premise and the conclusion here are open to question. A great deal of work still needs to be done on the regional distribution of forgery.

unclear. The vagaries of forgery can indeed often be explained only by individual circumstances, such as a particular dispute or the opportunity offered by the talents of Guerno, and they often throw light on the relations between ecclesiastical institutions and the local society in which they existed.

Canonical forgeries were especially common in the Carolingian period and during the Investiture Contest, when, according to Le Bras, they show 'the movement of ideas and the influence of the schools'[36]. They deal with subjects ranging from the independence of the church and position of the pope to the rights of monks to exercise pastoral responsibilities and to collect parish revenues[37]. Many found their way into canonical collections, including the authoritative *Decretum* of Gratian, which includes at least five hundred apocryphal texts. Theological forgeries range from minor revisions designed to insure the orthodoxy of a text to the reattribution of works in order to give them antiquity and authority. Among the most famous of these are the mystical writings attributed to Dionysius the Areopagite, the follower of St Paul. The variety of hagiographical forgeries was infinite. Some were designed to prove the authenticity of relics, even by fabricating tales of theft, since it was presumed that no one in their right mind would willingly dispose of anything as valuable as an authentic relic[38]. Others were to protect property, to attract pilgrims and their donations, to prove apostolic foundations, even to promote national causes. Ademar of Chabannes wanted to prove the

---

[36] Gabriel Le Bras, 'Les apocryphes dans les collections canoniques,' *La critica del testo. Atti del secondo Congresso internazionale della Società italiana di storia del diritto* (Florence, 1971) (I) 377. See also Horst Fuhrmann, 'Über den Reformgeist der 74-Titel-Sammlung (Diversorum patrum sententiae),' *Festschrift für Hermann Heimpel* (Veröffentlichungen des Max-Planck-Instituts für Geschichte, 36; Göttingen, 1971-72) II, 1101-21, esp. 1115-19, and, for a series of anti-reform forgeries made at Ravenna in the late eleventh century, Ian S. Robinson, '*Periculosus homo:* Pope Gregory VII and Episcopal Authority,' *Viator,* 9 (1978) 122-24.

[37] Charles Dereine, 'Le problème de la *cura animarum* chez Gratien,' *Studia Gratiana,* 2 (1954) 309-10. See also Giles Constable, *Monastic Tithes from their Origins to the Twelfth Century* (Cambridge Studies in Medieval Life and Thought, N.S., 10; Cambridge, 1964) 166, n. 3, and 304, n. 4, and 'The Treatise "Hortatur Nos" and Accompanying Canonical Texts on the Performance of Pastoral Work by Monks,' *Speculum historiale. Festschrift Johannes Spörl* (Munich, 1966) 569. Forged canons, like forged charters, are a valuable indication of the needs of ecclesiastical institutions, especially when they can be dated and localized.

[38] See in particular Patrick J. Geary, *Sacra Furta: Thefts of Relics in the Central Middle Ages* (Princeton, 1978); also Silvestre, in *Rev. belge,* 30. 731-39; Schreiner, in *Saeculum,* 17.165; Wolfgang Speyer, *Die literarische Fälschung im heidnischen und christlichen Altertum* (Handbuch der Altertumswissenschaft, I.2; Munich, 1971) 98-99; and Herrmann-Mascard, *Reliques,* 364-65.

apostolicity of St Martial[39], and the *Vita* of St Servatius was designed to sanctify the reign of Henry IV and to assert the independence of the bishops of Tongres by showing that their power derived directly from St Peter[40].

In cases such as these, the concept of forgery as intrinsic in things, which is linked with the propositional or objective idea of truth, loses much of its meaning. Even in dealing with more straight-forward forgeries, it is often impossible to distinguish clearly between the true, the false, and the fictional. Almost all forgeries include some authentic elements, and most authentic works include elements that by some standards could be considered false[41]. What should we call a fraudulent document found in an authentic register? Or an illegitimate claim inserted into a genuine charter?[42] Or even a text corrected by a scribe or redactor?[43] J. H. Round said that there were 'an indefinite number of stages between an absolutely genuine record and one that is a sheer forgery' and cited as examples documents made to replace ones that had been lost, stolen, or destroyed; authentic grants which were extended; and charters which were adapted, as he put it, by 'a systematic process of florid and grandiloquent adornment to a depraved monkish taste.' While clearly disapproving of this, Round denied that it sprang from any intention to deceive and compared it to embroidery or illumination[44]. Giry distin-

---

[39] See the succession of articles on Ademar by Louis Saltet in the *Bulletin de la littérature ecclésiastique*, 26 (1925) 117–139, 161-86, 279–302; 27 (1926) 145-60; and 32 (1931) 149-65 (of which I have seen all except the last), and his intro. to Antoine Bonal, *Histoire des évêques de Rodez*, ed. J.-L. Rigal (Rodez, 1935) I, xiii-xvi, and Robert Lee Wolff, 'How the News Was Brought from Byzantium to Angoulême; or, The Pursuit of a Hare in an Ox Cart,' *Essays Presented to Sir Steven Runciman* (Byzantine and Modern Greek Studies, 4; Oxford, 1978) 139-89.

[40] Friedrich Wilhelm, *Sanct Servatius* (Munich, 1910) xvi–xxi. See, generally, Hippolyte Delehaye, *The Legends of the Saints*, tr. Donald Atwater (New York, 1962) 77-78.

[41] Many scholars have remarked upon the problem of distinguishing rigidly between authentic and forged works of art and documents: see George Swarzenski, 'Art and Forgery,' *Magazine of Art*, 41.5 (May 1948) 164, and Hans Patze, commenting on the article of Fuhrmann cited n. 29 above, in *Historische Zeitschrift*, 197 (1963) 568-69.

[42] Alfons Becker and Dietrich Lohrmann, 'Ein erschlichenes Privileg Papst Urbans II. für Erzbischof Guigo von Vienne (Calixt II.),' *Deutsches Archiv für Erforschung des Mittelalters*, 38 (1982) 66–111.

[43] Alan Cameron, 'The Authenticity of the Letters of St Nilus of Ancyra,' *Greek, Roman, and Byzantine Studies*, 17 (1976) 181-96, suggested that the 'forger' may have been 'a rather unintelligent late admirer of Nilus whose purpose was merely to produce an edition of the great man's correspondence.' (194).

[44] J. H. Round, *Geoffrey de Mandeville* (London, 1892) 424. Round was not the type of scholar who was inclined to be lenient toward forgers. An even more severe critic, G. G. Coulton, while saying that, 'The audacity and the frequency of medieval forgeries are

I

guished between what he called forgeries and rewritten or surreptitious acts, and recent scholars have stressed the difference between intellectual forgeries, on the juridical level, and material forgeries, on the diplomatic level, and between formal forgeries which appear to be something they are not and substantive forgeries which actually distort the facts[45]. Indeed, one of the most important advances in the study of medieval documents in recent years has been a more sensitive approach to forgery, which has rescued a number of suspect documents from the hyper-criticism of earlier scholars[46].

If the intrusion of any fictional element into a document is considered the defining characteristic of a forgery, then indeed an enormous number of medieval charters can be said to have been forged. According to Bresslau, 50% of Merovingian, 15% of Carolingian, and 10% of later documents are forgeries[47], and Von Brandt estimated that two-thirds of all documents issued to ecclesiastics before 1100 are wholly or partially forged[48]. Of the 164 known charters attributed to Edward the Confessor, 44 (27%) are spurious, 56 (34%) are uncertain, and 64 (39%) are authentic[49]. Scholars disagree, however, over the precise rate and diffusion of forgery in the Middle Ages. As social and institutional conditions changed, so did forgery, which adapted to the needs of each new period, and almost every century has been called a high point of medieval forgery[50].

---

astounding,' also cited mitigating considerations: *Five Centuries of Religion, 3: Getting and Spending* (Cambridge, 1936) 310. Commenting on one of Bernard's sermons of which Mabillon and Dom de Sainte-Beuve had doubted the authenticity, Jean Leclercq said, 'Il y a plusieurs degrés ou, pour mieux dire, plusieurs formes d'authenticité,' depending on the degree to which Bernard took part personally in the redaction of his sermons: 'L'authenticité bernardine du sermon "In celebratione Adventus" ', *Recueil d'études sur saint Bernard et ses écrits*, II (Storia e letteratura, 104; Rome, 1966) 289.

[45] Arthur Giry, *Manuel de diplomatique* (Paris, 1894) 865-87; Georges Despy, *Les chartes de l'abbaye de Waulsort*, I (Académie royale . . . de Belgique: Commission royale d'histoire; Brussels, 1957) intro. 159; Von Brandt, *Werkzeug* (n. 6 above) 123-24. 'The bulk of forging was in the interests of perfectly genuine rights,' according to Adrian Morey and C. N. L. Brooke, *Gilbert Foliot and his Letters* (Cambridge, 1965) 133.

[46] See Despy's intro. to *Chartes de Waulsort*, 119-218.

[47] Harry Bresslau, *Handbuch der Urkundenlehre für Deutschland und Italien*, 2nd ed. (Leipzig-Berlin, 1912-31) I, 15, whose figures are cited Fuhrmann, in *Hist. Zs.*, 197.532 (= *Einfluß*, I, 68) and by R. C. van Caenegem and F. L. Ganshof, *Kurze Quellenkunde des westeuropäischen Mittelalters* (Göttingen, 1964) 65.

[48] Von Brandt, *Werkzeug*, 120.

[49] These figures, which are based on the lists in Peter H. Sawyer, *Anglo-Saxon Charters* (Royal Historical Society Guides and Handbooks, 8; London, 1968), are given by Michael T. Clanchy, *From Memory to Written Record: England, 1066–1307* (Cambridge, Mass., 1979), 14, 249.

[50] Fuhrmann, in *Hist. Zs.*, 197.551-52 (= *Einfluß*, 134).

Peter Brown said that the amount of forgery in the sixth century was 'a sure sign that the past had become cut off from the present, and had become a timeless, flat backdrop'[51]. Denis Bethell stressed the prevalence of relic forgery both in the eighth and again in the thirteenth century, after the fall of Constantinople to the crusaders[52]. The Carolingian period is distinguished in the annals of forgery not only by the Donation of Constantine and Pseudo-Isidorian Decretales[53] but also by a general archaism, primitivism, and desire for the *vita apostolica,* which created, according to Delaruelle, an atmosphere favorable to forgers: 'A people which relies on its past is tempted to invent one for itself, when history has nothing to say to it'[54]. The resurrection of the past in the tenth century, and its adaptation to the present, were cited by Dubois as factors promoting monastic forgeries 'aimed not solely at the often legitimate recovery of lands but also to justify present decisions by tradition'[55].

The golden age of medieval forgery, however, was by general consent the eleventh and twelfth centuries, when, as Morey and Brooke put it, 'Respectable men and respectable communities forged as they had not forged before and would never forge again. . . . Forgery was one of the elements in the common European culture of the twelfth-century renaissance.'[56] Among the factors promoting this flowering of forgery were

---

[51] Peter Brown, *The World of Late Antiquity, AD 150–750* (London – New York, 1971) 181.

[52] Bethell, in *Studies,* 8.71.

[53] Horst Fuhrmann, 'Fälscher unter sich: zum Streit zwischen Hinkmar von Reims und Hinkmar von Laon,' *Charles the Bald: Court and Kingdom,* ed. Margaret Gibson and Janet Nelson (BAR International Series, 101; Oxford, 1981) 237, citing Heinrich Brunner, *Deutsche Rechtsgeschichte,* 2nd ed. (Leipzig, 1906-28) I, 557, and Wilhelm Levison, 'Die Politik in den Jenseitsvisionen des frühen Mittelalters,' (1921) in his *Aus rheinischer und fränkischer Frühzeit* (Düsseldorf, 1948) 236, calling the ninth century 'eine Zeit großer Fälschungen'. See also the review by J. M. Wallace-Hadrill of Fuhrmann, *Einfluß,* in *English Historical Review,* 110 (1975) 116-18.

[54] Jean-Rémy Palanque and Etienne Delaruelle, 'La Gaule chrétienne à l'époque franque,' *Revue d'histoire de l'Eglise de France,* 38 (1952) 64.

[55] Jacques Dubois, 'Les moines dans la société du moyen âge (950–1350),' *Revue d'histoire de l'Eglise de France,* 60 (1974) 19.

[56] Morey and Brooke, *Foliot,* 127, 130, 137. See also Brooke in *The Letters of John of Salisbury,* I: *The Early Letters (1153–1161),* ed. W. J. Millor and H. E. Butler (Nelson's Medieval Texts; London – Edinburgh, 1955) 98, n. 5 (calling the twelfth century 'the golden age of medieval forgery') and in *Medieval Church* (n. 32 above) 100-20; Speyer, *Literarische Fälschung* (n. 38 above) 317; and Clanchy, *From Memory,* 248. Cf., however, Bethell, in *Studies,* 8.71, and Albert Brackmann, *Die Kurie und die Salzburger Kirchenprovinz* (Studien und Vorarbeiten zur *Germania Pontificia,* 1; Berlin, 1912) 76-77, who commented on the relatively small number of forgeries in the twelfth century in the province of Salzburg.

not only the appeal to tradition in an age of rapid change but also the shifting attitudes toward written evidence. Brooke cited the chaos of tenures in England after the Norman Conquest[57], and Eleanor Searle said that the first group of Battle Abbey forgeries, made in 1155–57, marked the end of 'an epoch in which oral tradition had had real force. . . . In a more document-minded age, among men who could not share their carefully preserved memory of the Conqueror's verbal commands, the monks of Battle defended their tradition by forgery.'[58] The number of forgeries in France at the same time reflected, according to Werner, a new confidence not only in written documents, especially royal charters, but also in the monarchy itself[59].

The spread of forgery in the twelfth century contained the seeds of its own decline, however, as the skill in forging was increasingly met with professionalism both in preventing and in detecting forgery. The improvements in the writing of documents and the keeping of records, especially in the second half of the twelfth century, reduced the need as well as the opportunity for the respectable forgers of the previous age[60]. Unwitnessed *scripta authentica,* according to Pope Alexander III (who apparently meant simply ancient by the term 'authentic' here), were without legal force 'unless they have been made by a public hand, so that they appear public documents, or have an authentic seal'[61]. A few years later Innocent III instituted his well-known measures to insure and enforce the authenticity of papal documents[62], which Gregory IX incorporated, with other papal decrees on the same subject, into the section of his Decretals entitled *De fide instrumentorum*[63]. The increased knowledge about the na-

---

[57] C. N. L. Brooke, *The Twelfth-Century Renaissance* (New York, 1970) 174.

[58] Eleanor Searle, 'Battle Abbey and Exemption: the Forged Charters,' *English Historical Review,* 83 (1968) 468.

[59] K. F. Werner, 'Königtum und Fürstentum im französischen 12. Jahrhundert,' *Probleme des 12. Jahrhunderts: Reichenau-Vorträge 1965–1967* (Vorträge und Forschungen, 12; Constance – Stuttgart, 1968) 219, tr. T. Reuter, *Medieval Nobility* (Leiden, 1978) 271.

[60] Brooke, *Renaissance,* 174, and in *Medieval Church* (n. 32 above) 110, 116.

[61] Gregory IX, *Decretales,* II. 22, 2, ed. Emil Friedberg, *Corpus iuris canonici* (Leipzig, 1879) II, 344. See the remarks of Jean-François Lemarignier, 'Le prieuré d'Haspres, ses rapports avec l'abbaye de Saint-Vaast d'Arras et la centralisation monastique au début du XIIe siècle,' *Revue du Nord,* 29 (1947) 263, n. 18: 'Le respect des *antiquitates* décroît et le pape cherche a renouveler les privilèges anciens pour en finir précisément avec ces textes plus ou moins suspects que produisaient toujours tant d'établissements religieux.'

[62] Reginald L. Poole, *Lectures on the History of the Papal Chancery* (Cambridge, 1915) 152-62. See also L. C. Hector, *Palaeography and Forgery* (St Anthony's Hall Publications, 15; London – York, 1959) 10; Peter Herde, 'Römisches und kanonisches Recht bei der Verfolgung des Fälschungsdelikts im Mittelalter,' *Traditio,* 21 (1965) 337; and Fuhrmann, in *Hist. Zs.,* 197.547 (= *Einfluß,* 123-27).

[63] Gregory IX, *Decretales,* II.22, ed. Friedberg, 344-54.

ture and history of documents now caught up with the forgers and forms in itself an important chapter in the history of scholarship[64]. It put many amateur forgers more or less out of business and marked the end of one of the most productive periods in the history of medieval forgery, just as the development of scientific techniques of detection may some day put a stop to forging works of art.

After about 1200 both ecclesiastical and secular courts not only developed better techniques for discovering forged documents but also relied increasingly on recent documents and reissues, so that the fabrication of alleged originals was no longer necessary. This may account for the fact, remarked upon by several scholars, that forgery was more prevalent in the old religious orders than in the new, whose privileges and records, being more recent, were in less need of improvement[65].

The late Middle Ages and early modern period saw the continuation and development of other types of forgery. The popularity of pilgrimage fostered the manufacture not only of false relics but also of fraudulent mobile and histrionic religious images[66]. The antiquarian interest of the fifteenth century was responsible for Ingulph's *History of Croyland*, which took in scholars down to the nineteenth century[67]. The age of humanism and the Renaissance, according to Speyer, ushered in 'a new epoch in the history of forgery', including pseudo-antique forgeries, literary forgeries, and faked works of art[68]. The Reformation likewise had its types of forgeries, as did later periods. The second half of the eighteenth century has been called 'the classical period of English literary forgeries', and the nineteenth century, according to Swarzenski, was peerless in the field of forgery, grasping at 'everything that did or could provoke interest'[69].

---

[64] Hector, *Palaeography*.

[65] J. Dubois, 'Quelques problèmes de l'histoire de l'ordre des chartreux à propos des livres récents,' *Revue d'histoire ecclésiastique*, 63 (1968) 30, and Jean-François Lemarignier, commenting on a paper by J. C. Dickinson, in *La vita comune del clero nei secoli XI e XII. Atti della settimana di studio: Mendola, settembre 1959* (Pubblicazioni dell'Università cattolica del Sacro Cuore, 3rd S.: Scienze storiche, 2–3; Milan, 1962) I, 299.

[66] Jonathan Sumption, *Pilgrimage: An Image of Mediaeval Religion* (London, 1975) 56, 313. A good example of a fraud of this type, which was brought to my attention by Herbert Kessler, is in *The Second Book of the Travels of Nicander Nucius of Corcyra*, ed. J. A. Cramer (Camden Society, 17; London, 1841) 55-57.

[67] T. F. Tout, 'Mediaeval Forgers and Forgeries,' in his *Collected Papers* (Manchester, 1932-34) III, 129-35, and Charles Gross, *A Bibliography of English History to 1485*, ed. Edgar Graves (Oxford, 1975) 294, no. 2163.

[68] Speyer, *Literarische Fälschung* (n. 38 above) 317.

[69] Zoltán Haraszti, *The Shakespeare Forgeries of William Henry Ireland: The Story of a Famous Literary Fraud* (offprint from *More Books;* Boston, 1934) 6, and G. Swarzenski, in *Magazine of Art*, 41 (5). 166. On the variety of types of nineteenth-century forgery, see

The twentieth century will doubtless be looked back upon as a prime period of forgery not only in the creative and scholarly arts – I am thinking of the Van Meegeren Vermeers, Cyril Burt's fraudulent statistics, and the Piltdown Man, who may have started as a hoax but ended up a forgery[70] – but also, and perhaps more important, in mass propaganda and advertising, which have carried the art of intentional deception to heights undreamed-of in the Middle Ages. The techniques of reproduction have reached a point which challenges the very concept of authenticity in works of art, and in literature we delight in a kind of spurious realism which may not fool us now but which may well puzzle the future[71]. Many fictional heroes take on a life and reality of their own. Letters seeking advice and help are still sent each year to Sherlock Holmes at 221B Baker Street; the *New York Times* published a two-column obituary, complete with portrait, of Hercule Poirot; and C. Northcote Parkinson's *Life and Times of Horatio Hornblower* leaves even professional historians with a lingering suspicion – perhaps a hope – that C. S. Forester's hero was based on fact[72]. The skill and detail of this work, which contains no indication that it is all made up, are such that it will surely be accepted in the future, long after Forester's novels are forgotten, as a piece of authentic naval history. There may be no harm in this. Parkinson is a learned historian, and his fiction may well be as accurate, in its overall picture as well as its details, as another scholar's facts. To admit this, however, is to slip into the standards of forgery in the Middle Ages and to forsake the professional credo of modern historians.

These examples are a reminder not to moralize about medieval forgery, though it has long been a favorite stick with which to beat the church and the Middle Ages generally[73]. Homicide was the characteristic crime of medieval knights, said T. F. Tout, and forgery of medieval cler-

---

the catalogue of the *L'exposition mondiale. Le faux dans l'art et dans l'histoire* (Grand Palais, Paris, June–July 1955).

[70] J. S. Weiner, K. P. Oakley, and W. E. Le Gros Clark, *The Solution of the Piltdown Problem* (offprint from *Bulletin of the British Museum (Natural History): Geology*, 2.3; London, 1953), calling it 'a most elaborate and carefully prepared hoax' (145), and Stephen J. Gould, 'Piltdown Revisited', in his *The Panda's Thumb* (New York – London, 1980) 108-24, who attributed the acceptance of the Piltdown Man to 'the imposition of strong hope upon dubious evidence', the 'reduction of anomaly by fit with cultural biases' and by matching fact with expectation, and the prohibition to touch the original and thus discover its falsity.

[71] On fictional 'pseudo-reality', see Bäuml, in *Speculum*, 55.257.

[72] C. Northcote Parkinson, *The Life and Times of Horatio Hornblower* (Boston – Toronto, 1970).

[73] Fuhrmann, in *Hist. Zs.*, 197.536-37 (= *Einfluß*, 76-79).

ics. 'Forgery ran rampant all through the Middle Ages. It was largely undetected, still more largely unpunished.'[74] The basic axiom of historical knowledge for positivist historians is the identity of human nature and behavior: the crimes of one age are the crimes of the next and people are restrained from performing the same deeds only by the law. Silvestre argued along these lines that the fabricators of relics and miracle stories were motivated not by profound psychological or sociological needs but by competition between rival ecclesiastical institutions. People would do the same today if they could get away with it, he said, but in the Middle Ages forgery was easier and, at least for clerics, safer[75].

This approach assumes that the amount of forgery in a society corresponds to the degree of disapproval and repression[76]. Forgery in the Middle Ages (as it is now) was indeed for the most part ahead of the means to detect and suppress it, but this cannot be attributed either to a lack of a sense of authenticity, when it was considered relevant, nor to an absence of desire to suppress forgery. Writers in the Middle Ages constantly experimented with ways to authenticate personal letters as well as legal intruments, including seals, subscriptions, signs, pictures, private references, keys, secret writing, and even literary style[77]. Bernard of Clairvaux wrote at the end of one of his letters that, 'My seal was not to hand, but the reader will recognize the style, since I dictated it myself.'[78] Later, the distinctive rhythmical style used by the scribes of the curia was recognized as a mark of authenticity in papal documents[79].

Medieval legislation against forgery, and the steps taken against known forgers and forgeries, also show the desire to prevent forgery. Forging was universally condemned in the medieval codes of both canon and

---

[74] Tout, *Papers*, III, 127. Morey and Brooke, *Foliot* (n. 45 above) 130, said that, 'If it was true that there was safety in numbers, then forgery was comparatively safe in the eleventh and twelfth centuries.'

[75] Hubert Silvestre, 'Le problème des faux au moyen âge,' *Moyen Age*, 66 (1960) 362-66.

[76] Fuhrmann, in *Hist. Zs.*, 197.593-95, in the 'Schlußwort' after the three discussions of his article on forgery, argued that the skill in detecting forgeries in the Middle Ages corresponded to the desire to do so. By this standard, modern society is at least as ready to accept forgery, at least in the areas I have mentioned, as the Middle Ages.

[77] Hartmut Hoffmann, 'Zur mittelalterlichen Brieftechnik,' *Spiegel der Geschichte. Festgabe für Max Braubach* (Münster, 1964) 141-70.

[78] Bernard of Clairvaux, Ep. 304, in *Sancti Bernardi opera*, ed. Jean Leclercq a.o. (Rome, 1957-77) VIII, 221. See Hoffmann, in *Spiegel*, 163, who also cites a case when Peter Damiani did not have his seal to hand.

[79] Poole, *Lectures* (n. 62 above) 94-97, 156.

civil law, which in this respect followed Roman legislation[80]. The late Roman laws on counterfeiting gold coins, which was considered a form of treason, were applied to all coining in the medieval West[81], and the Lombard kings Rothair and Liutprand in the seventh and eighth centuries decreed that falsifiers of documents should have their hands cut off[82]. The view of St Ambrose that Satan should receive a slave of Stilicho who made *falsas epistolas* was repeated by Eugippius in the *Vita* of St Severinus[83], and according to Gregory of Tours, Archbishop Giles of Rheims was declared a *fallax* after he presented some fraudulent documents[84]. There are countless references in medieval charters to the *crimen falsi, falsitas, falsarius, fallax, furtim,* and *fabricatus*. Many forgeries were in fact discovered and their makers punished. Pope Urban II on his visit to France in 1095 uncovered two cases, one involving the bishop of Limoges, who was duly deposed and disgraced, and the other concerning some property of the monks of St Orens[85]. Pope Innocent II at the Council of Rheims in 1131 ordered some of the forgeries made by Guerno of St Médard to be burned[86].

Lives of saints and relics were not always regarded without suspicion. Abbot Benedict of La Chiusa vigorously rebutted Ademar of Chabannes's claims for the apostolicity of St Martial, whom he called a *con-*

---

[80] Frederick Pollock and Frederic Maitland, *The History of English Law*, 2nd. ed. (Cambridge, 1898) II, 540-41, stressing that 'the making of a false document with intent to defraud' was not severely punished until the sixteenth century; Patze, in *Hist. Zs.,* 197.569; and, on the continuation of Roman legislation, Herde, in *Traditio,* 21.291-365.

[81] Philip Grierson, 'The Roman Law of Counterfeiting,' *Essays in Roman Coinage Presented to Harold Mattingly,* ed. R. A. G. Carson and C. H. V. Sutherland (Oxford, 1956) 255-56. For the condemnation by Pope Honorius III of the 'falsam . . . monetam' made by the abbot and monks of Ittebö, see Augustin Theiner, *Vetera monumenta historica Hungariam sacram illustrantia* (Rome – Paris – Vienna, 1859-60) I, 22-23, no. 37. See Dante, *Paradiso,* 19.118-20, 140-41.

[82] Franz Beyerle, *Leges Langobardorum 643–866* (Germanenrechte, N.F.; Witzenhausen, 1962) 64, c. 243, and 143, c. 91. See *The Lombard Laws,* tr. Katherine Fischer Drew (Philadelphia, 1973) 100, 184.

[83] Paulinus, *Vita Ambrosii,* c. 43, in *Pat. lat.,* XIV, 44D–45A, and Eugippius, *Vita s. Severini,* c. 36, ed. Pius Knöll (Corpus scriptorum ecclesiasticorum latinorum, 9.2; Vienna, 1886) 54.

[84] Gregory of Tours, *Historia Francorum,* X. 19, ed. Henri Omont and Gaston Collon, 2nd ed. by René Poupardin (Collection de textes pour servir à l'étude et à l'enseignement de l'histoire, 47; Paris, 1913) 443.

[85] *Cartulaires du chapitre de l'église metropolitaine Sainte-Marie d'Auch,* ed. C. Lacave La Plagne Barris (Archives historiques de la Gascogne, II. 3–4; Paris – Auch, 1899) 55, no. 56. See H. E. J. Cowdrey, *The Cluniacs and the Gregorian Reform* (Oxford, 1970) 99 (and 94 on Bishop Humbald of Limoges).

[86] *Lit. Cant.* (n. 33 above) III, 366, where the bishop of Evreux reported that he had burned the documents on Innocent's instructions.

trafactum apostolum and whose *Vita* he declared to be *totam falsam*[87], and Gocelin of St Augustine, Canterbury, defending the claims of his abbey to the relics of St Mildred against the assertions of two lost hagiographical works, declared that, 'Powerful and learned men may be deceived, but what is false cannot be true.'[88] Efforts to authenticate relics were revived in the eleventh century, after almost two centuries[89]. Alexander III forbade the public display and cult of relics without the approval of the pope, and the Fourth Lateran Council specifically forbade prelates to allow worshippers 'to be deceived by vain figments and false documents'[90]. Among the supernatural powers of St Juliana of Mont-Cornillon, in the mid-thirteenth century, was the ability to recognize, even from a distance, and to warn against false relics[91].

A critical attitude toward texts is likewise found in a few writers. Abelard warned against false ascriptions and textual corruptions in the writings of the saints[92], and Guigo of La Chartreuse, in his preface to the letters of St Jerome, based their authenticity, much like a modern editor, on considerations of style, content, and anachronism[93]. This is not to say that any number of fabulous lives of saints, faked relics, and falsely-attributed texts were not accepted as genuine in the Middle Ages, just as forged works of art are often accepted today, even by eminent critics, but this should not be considered as a sign either of a lack of concern over forgery or of an absence of critical sense.

There seems to have been a rising tide of concern over forgery in the twelfth century. The famous case of Nicholas of Montiéramey, the secretary of St Bernard who was accused of forging letters in his name and of

---

[87] *Pat. lat.*, CXLI, 91D and 92A. See the articles by Saltet and Wolff cited in n. 39 above and Klaus Schreiner, ' "Discrimen veri ac falsi": Ansätze und Formen der Kritik in der Heiligen- und Reliquienverehrung des Mittelalters,' *Archiv für Kulturgeschichte*, 48 (1966) 29–31.

[88] Marvin Colker, 'A Hagiographic Polemic,' *Mediaeval Studies*, 39 (1977) 83 (and comments on 63).

[89] Hermann-Mascard, *Reliques* (n. 28 above) 120-26.

[90] Gregory IX, *Decretales*, III. 45. 1–2, ed. Friedberg, II, 650. On the forging of relics, and efforts to discover it, see Peter Browe, *Die eucharistischen Wunder des Mittelalters* (Breslauer Studien zur historischen Theologie, N.F., 4; Breslau, 1938) 179-81, and Schreiner, in *Archiv für Kulturgeschichte*, 48. 1–53.

[91] *Vita s. Julianae*, I. 6 (42), in *Acta sanctorum*, April, I, 455A.

[92] Peter Abelard,' *Sic et Non*, ed. Blanche Boyer and Richard McKeon (Chicago – London, 1976-77) prologue (89–104).

[93] *Lettres des premiers Chartreux* (Sources chrétiennes, 88, 274: Textes monastiques d'Occident, 10, 274; Paris, 1962-80) I, 214 (Guigo, no. 8). A charter in *Cartulaires de l'église cathédrale de Grenoble*, ed. Jules Marion (Paris, 1869) 52, was declared false in 1095 on the basis of an anachronism.

making off with his seal[94], may have inspired the Cistercian legislation of 1157 defining the punishments for the falsifiers of charters and seals[95]. There are many references to forgers in the letters written by John of Salisbury for Archbishop Theobald of Canterbury in the 1150s. In one to Pope Adrian IV he mentioned a suspected case of forgery and asked for 'a ruling on the punishment to be inflicted on those who forge your letters'. In another, also to the pope, he referred to a forger who had been deprived of his office and benefice for forging some letters of Eugene III. And in yet another he asked Bishop Robert of Lincoln to capture 'a manifest forger and perjurer' and said that forgers should be punished 'as public enemies' and that to forge the pope's seal imperilled 'the universal church, since the mouths of all the pontiffs may be opened or closed by the marks of a single impress'[96]. Gerald of Wales accused the future Bishop Cadogan of Bangor of 'the crime of forgery' for falsely sealing a charter of Llewellyn making a grant 'that had never entered the prince's head'[97].

This awareness of the dangers of forgery in practical affairs doubtless stimulated the development of critical skills in authenticating documents, but the attitude was no different with regard to forgeries to

---

[94] Bernard, Ep. 284, ed. Leclercq, VIII, 199: 'Periclitati sumus in falsis fratribus, et multae litterae falsatae sub falsato sigillo nostro in manus multorum exierunt.' See also Ep. 298, *ibid.*, 214. See *The Letters of Peter the Venerable*, ed. Giles Constable (Harvard Historical Studies, 78; Cambridge, Mass., 1967) II, 326-28, with further references on Nicholas, who was evidently an accomplished mimic. C. S. Jaeger, 'The Prologue to the *Historia calamitatum* and the "Authenticity Question"', *Euphorion*, 74 (1980) 11–13, said that Nicholas's borrowings 'fall under the heading of literary imitation'.

[95] *Statuta capitulorum generalium ordinis Cisterciensis*, ed. J.-M. Canivez (Bibliothèque de la Revue d'histoire ecclésiastique, 9–14; Louvain, 1933-41) I, 67, c. 61.

[96] *Letters of John of Salisbury* (n. 56 above) 98, 109, 134, also 117, Epp. 57, 67, 73, 86. See Brooke, in *Medieval Church* (n. 32 above) 102. In a collection of letters appended to a mid-twelfth century Bolognese treatise on letter-writing there are two letters in which the patriarch of Ravenna told Pope Eugene III that he had imprisoned a forger 'qui, cum in curia uestra dictandi locum haberet, plurimas falsas litteras componere superba temeritate presumpsit'; and Eugene replied rejoicing that the forger had been caught and put in chains: Hermann Kalbfuss, 'Eine Bologneser Ars dictandi des XII. Jahrhunderts,' *Quellen und Forschungen aus italienischen Archiven und Bibliotheken*, 16 (1914) 18–19. Toward the end of the century Stephen of Tournai repeatedly denounced a nest of forgers in his letters to the pope and to the archbishop of Rheims: *Lettres d'Etienne de Tournai*, ed. Jules Desilve (Valenciennes – Paris, 1893) 283, 328, 337, 373, Epp. 227, 263, 269, 297; see J. Warichez, *Etienne de Tournai et son temps 1128–1203* (Tournai – Paris, 1937) 289-90.

[97] Gerald of Wales, *Speculum ecclesiae*, III. 7, in *Giraldi Cambrensis opera*, ed. J. S. Brewer a.o. (Rolls Series, 21; London, 1861-91) IV, 166. Walter Map, *De nugis curialium*, I. 25, ed. M. R. James, rev. C. N. L. Brooke and R. A. B. Mynors (Oxford Medieval Texts; Oxford, 1983) 106, accused the Cistercians of Heath of changing the number of acres in a grant from the Earl of Gloucester.

which the principle of *cui bono* could less easily be applied. The official attitude was one of disapproval, and neither the doctrine of *pia fraus* nor the view that concealing the truth was not to lie were ever officially endorsed, though both enjoyed a certain popular currency, as they do today[98]. It is better 'modestly to confess ignorance', declared Heriger in his *Lives* of the bishops of Tongres, Utrecht, and Liège, 'than irreverently to lie for the sake of piety.'[99] Dante put all types of defrauders in the two lowest circles of Hell, with falsifiers at the bottom of the eighth circle. Why then, we may ask, were so many frauds perpetrated and widely accepted in the Middle Ages? The answer should be sought not on the level of positivist morality, that people were less good or even that controls were less effective than they are now, but in terms of historical relativity. Various scholars have approached the subject through the medieval ideas of order, history, accuracy, and truth. I shall look briefly at each of these.

Among the first to seek a solution to the riddle of medieval forgery in the idea of order was the German historian Fritz Kern. He has a distinguished follower in Horst Fuhrmann, who came to the subject through his work on the Donation of Constantine and the Pseudo-Isidorian Decretals. They argue that many medieval forgeries, other than those made for manifestly selfish ends, were designed to realize God's plan on earth and thus to establish, or reestablish, things in their proper order. In the terms used by modern diplomatists, they were material or formal forgeries, in that they were not what they purported to be, but they were not intellectual or substantive forgeries, because in the deepest sense they were authentic and true. In a disordered world, as Fuhrmann put it, forgeries represented an effort to establish order[100], and the forgers were thus asserting and protecting rather than deforming truth and justice.

Another explanation of medieval forgery has been found in the medieval attitude toward the past which goes under the name of traditionalism, conservatism, or mythomania. It draws the past into the present and shapes it to meet the needs of the living rather than to depict the di-

---

[98] Fuhrmann, in *Hist. Zs.*, 197.537-39 (= *Einfluß*, I, 80–85); Schreiner, in *Saeculum*, 17. 162-67.

[99] *Pat. lat.*, CXXXIX, 1024C.

[100] Fuhrmann, in *Hist. Zs.*, 197.553 (apparently not in *Einfluß*). R. W. Southern, *Western Society and the Church in the Middle Ages* (Hardmondsworth, 1970) 93, followed a similar line of reasoning, saying that, 'Forgeries, like art, brought order into the confusions and deficiencies of the present.' See also Le Bras, in *Critica del testo* (n. 36 above) 832-33.

versity of the dead [101]. Justinian instructed Tribonian that if in compiling the *Corpus Iuris Civilis* he found any of the old laws and constitutions to be incorrectly written, he should correct them 'in order that what you choose and place there may appear to be true and the best and as if it had been written from the beginning' [102]. Many societies authenticate their patterns of behavior by an appeal to the past, embodied either in myth, history, or law, and bring it into conformity with the needs of society [103]. Even written constitutions are made by interpretation to uphold principles and serve ends that were far from the minds of their framers.

Legal and social historians have shown that customary law, far from being rigid, depends on social standards and memory and is constantly changing. With regard to the law, 'old' usually means 'good' rather than 'of long duration' [104]. Time is relative in traditional societies, and myth lies beyond the remembered past, which rarely goes back more than half a century [105]. Poets rather than historians are the remembrancers of society, and they deal in formulas rather than facts. The present thus throws its shadow back over the past, and distant origins and historical justifications are found especially for recent institutions, which are depicted as renewals or revivals [106]. 'By a curious paradox,' Bloch said, 'through the very fact of their respect for the past, people came to reconstruct it as

---

[101] See, among other works, Marc Bloch, *Feudal Society*, tr. L. A. Manyon (Chicago, 1961) 91-92, and *Historian's Craft* (n. 6 above) 90-95, where he wrote that, 'Periods which were the most bound by tradition were also those which took the greatest liberties with their true heritage,' and the works of Delaruelle (n. 54 above), Brown (n. 51 above), and Clanchy (n. 49 above) 119-20, who stressed that preoccupation with posterity, as well as with the past, may also promote falsification of the present.

[102] *Corpus iuris civilis*, ed. Paul Krüger and Th. Mommsen (Berlin, 1928-29) I, 8–9 (*Digesta*, intro.).

[103] See the stimulating article of Peter Munz, 'History and Sociology,' *Gesellschaft – Kultur – Literatur* (Festschrift Luitpold Wallach), ed. Karl Bosl (Monographien zur Geschichte des Mittelalters, 11; Stuttgart, 1975) 1–17.

[104] M. T. Clanchy, 'Remembering the Past and the Good Old Law,' *History*, 55 (1970) 167-72. See also Hans Martin Klinkenberg, 'Die Theorie der Verändbarkeit des Rechtes im frühen und hohen Mittelalter,' *Lex et sacramentum im Mittelalter*, ed. Paul Wilpert and Rudolf Hoffmann (Miscellanea Mediaevalia, 6; Berlin, 1969) 157-88, who stressed that law in the Middle Ages was less unchanging, in theory as well as fact, than was once thought.

[105] Bernard Guenée, 'Temps de l'histoire et temps de la mémoire au moyen âge,' *Bulletin de la Société de l'Histoire de France*, no. 487 (1976-77) 25–35.

[106] In addition to the works cited above of Silvestre (n. 75), and those by Saxer and Marrou cited by him, and of Southern (n. 100), see Walter Ullmann, 'The Papacy as an Institution of Government in the Middle Ages,' *Studies in Church History*, 2 (1965) 81, and Gérard Fransen's review of Fuhrmann, *Einfluß*, in *Revue d'histoire ecclésiastique*, 70 (1975) 778-86.

they considered it ought to have been'[107]. This dependence on the past in itself marked a break with historical reality and an unwillingness to accept the truth of change and development.

This tendency has been associated by some scholars with a general lack of concern for accuracy in medieval society. 'Everywhere there was fantasy, imprecision, inexactitude . . .,' wrote Lucien Febvre, who was, with Bloch, the founder of the *Annales* school of history. 'The masses abdicated every care for precision'[108]. In particular they lacked a strict sense of time, which has been associated by some scholars with the emergence of urban society[109]. People in the Middle Ages knew how to be precise when they wanted to be, however. Though a lack of accurate information on certain subjects, therefore, such as when papyrus ceased to be used for papal documents, may have contributed to the relative ease of forgery in the Middle Ages, as it does today, the widespread tolerance for forgeries cannot be attributed to a general lack of exactitude. There was nothing imprecise in the medieval attitude toward property, or toward theology, legal procedure, or church ritual. Fossier has indeed argued that there was 'a movement of precision' both of words and of numbers in the documents from Picardy in the eleventh and twelfth centuries, together with a growing sense of efficiency and profit[110].

The increasing reliance on written records rather than on memory was an important aspect of this concern for accuracy. Before the twelfth century documents were essentially aids to memory and at best supplementary to the evidence of personal witnesses[111]. Even an historian like Orderic Vitalis, writing in the first half of the twelfth century, still 'thought of the documents as part of a living tradition rather than as title deeds,'[112] and in 1181 the canons of St Furzy at Péronne lost a case not

---

[107] Bloch, *Feudal Society*, 92.

[108] Lucien Febvre, *Le problème de l'incroyance au XVIᵉ siècle* (Evolution de l'humanité, 53; Paris, 1942) 429-30.

[109] See Jacques le Goff, 'Merchants' Time and Church's Time in the Middle Ages', in his *Time, Work, and Culture in the Middle Ages*, tr. Arthur Goldhammer (Chicago – London, 1980) 29–42.

[110] Robert Fossier, *La terre et les hommes en Picardie jusqu'à la fin du XIIIᵉ siècle* (Paris – Louvain, 1968) I, 257-59, 455.

[111] In addition to the classic study of V. H. Galbraith, *The Literacy of the Medieval English Kings* (offprint from the *Proceedings of the British Academy*, 21; London, 1937), see those, already cited, of Bäuml (n. 14) and Clanchy (n. 49).

[112] Marjorie Chibnall, 'Charter and Chronicle: The Use of Archive Sources by Norman Historians,' *Church and Government in the Middle Ages*, ed. C. N. L. Brooke a.o. (Cambridge, 1976) 14. See also Pierre Gasnault, 'Les actes privés de l'abbaye Saint-Martin de Tours du VIIIᵉ au XIIᵉ siècle,' *Bibliothèque de l'Ecole des Chartes*, 112 (1954) 52-54 on the dispositive and evidentiary value of medieval charters.

because the judges put 'little or no faith' in the forged charters they produced but because the charters confirmed possession of property which the canons 'neither possessed or ever had possessed in the memory of modern man'[113]. Charters were not valid in themselves but insofar as they confirmed memory. Round's view that the concept of 'the sacredness of an original record . . . was wholly foreign to the men of the Middle Ages' is essentially correct[114]. The transfer in the late Middle Ages from a society based on memory and oral tradition to one based on authentic documents and records changed the role both of forgers and of forgery in society. No longer was a charter regarded as true only if it agreed with the way people thought things were, and the concept of truth started on its development away from people and toward propositions.

This brings us back to the medieval idea of truth, which, as we have seen, was subjective and personal rather than, as today, objective and impersonal. The personal element lingers in the stress on intention in defining the terms forgery and plagiarism, however, and recent research into scientific and legal evidence has shown that the distinction between what we desire and what we believe to be true is less clear than was once thought. Science has been called 'a human activity, motivated by hope, cultural prejudice, and the pursuit of glory'[115], and even the most careful scientific observations are influenced by the hopes and expectations of the researcher[116]. 'The tendency to see what we want or need to see has been demonstrated by numerous experiments,' according to Robert Buckhout in an article on eyewitness testimony, which he de-

---

[113] *Papsturkunden in Frankreich*, N.F., 4: *Picardie*, ed. Johannes Ramackers (Abhandlungen der Akademie der Wissenschaften in Göttingen, Phil.-hist. Kl., 3rd S., 27; Göttingen, 1942) 54-56, no. 1, and N.F., 7: *Ile-de-France* (n. 33 above) 523, no. 230 (where the editor suggests that the charters may in fact have been authentic) and *Charters of St-Fursy of Péronne*, ed. William M. Newman and Mary A. Rouse (Mediaeval Academy of America, Publ. 85; Cambridge, Mass., 1977) 19–21, nos. 1–2 (and p. viii, where their authenticity is denied). The claim was against the monks of Mont-St-Quentin, who showed that they had held the properties for over forty years. The canons lost the case through their failure to establish possession, not on the basis of the charters, whether or not they were forged.

[114] Round, *Geoffrey* (n. 44 above) 425, saying that 'the sacredness of an original record' had been recognized only 'in the present generation'. This was cited with approval by Charles Johnson, 'Some Charters of Henry I,' *Historical Essays in Honour of James Tait*, ed. J. G. Edwards a.o. (Manchester, 1933) 142. See Morey and Brooke, *Foliot*, 133-34, who also use the term sanctity in reference to the written word.

[115] Gould, *Panda's Thumb* (n. 70 above) 115-16.

[116] The influence of the researcher's views on the subject is known in experimental psychology as the experimenter effect.

scribed as 'sloppy and uneven, albeit remarkably effective in serving our need to create structure out of experience.'[117]

People in the Middle Ages also saw what they wanted and needed to see, and believed to be true what had to be true[118]. In all matters except those relating to God, the standard of truth varied according to the subject and the person. For Anselm and Hugh of St Victor, as we have seen, a correct statement made without sincerity was a lie, whereas a false statement made sincerely might be true[119]. Even the statement that the Father is the beginning of the entire Trinity, which derived from Augustine and Gennadius, was said by Simon of Tournai to be true 'not from the sense of the words, since He is not the beginning of divinity but rather divinity itself, but from the sense in which the words were made by the author'[120]. It was thus morally true though theologically incorrect.

Truth in this sense was the touchstone of authority and authenticity, what was felt to be right. Herveus of Bourg-Dieu called for a return to 'the pure truth as it was promulgated from the beginning by the evangelists and prophets,' and Bernard of Clairvaux told the monks of Montiéramey that it was fitting to hear in the liturgy 'not new and light but clearly authentic and ancient things'[121]. The dictum that the name

---

[117] Robert Buckhout, 'Eyewitness Testimony,' *Scientific American,* 231.6 (1974) 23, 26. According to another article in the same journal, 239.1 (1978) 72, 'A recent series of experiments [in quantum mechanics] addresses an even more perplexing issue arising from the theory: the possibility that the observer's knowledge or ignorance may have some influence on the state of the particle. The experiments seem to call into question the philosophical conviction that the world exists and has fixed properties independent of any observer.'

[118] Aldous Huxley, in *Point Counter Point,* ch. 27, said of one of his characters that, 'Her inability to distinguish between the testimony of her senses and that of her fancy had often resulted in her being punished for lying.' This is said of a child, but elsewhere (ch. 34) Huxley wrote: 'After all, the only truth that can be of interest to us, or that we can know, is a human truth. And to discover that, you must look for it with the whole being, not with a specialized part of it. . . . What the scientists are trying to get at is nonhuman truth. . . . This non-human truth that the scientists are trying to get at with their intellects – it's utterly irrelevant to the ordinary human being.'

[119] See nn. 18–20 above.

[120] *Les Disputationes de Simon de Tournai,* ed. Joseph Warichez (Spicilegium sacrum Lovaniense, 12; Louvain, 1932) 32 (Disp. V, 3). See Nikolaus M. Häring, 'Commentary and Hermeneutics,' in *Renaissance and Renewal in the Twelfth Century,* ed. Robert L. Benson and Giles Constable (Cambridge, Mass., 1982) 196, who cited the view attributed to Hilary of Poitiers that, 'Heresy flows not from the words used but from the user's intention or interpretation of the words.'

[121] Germain Morin, 'Un critique en liturgie au XIIe siècle. Le traité inédit d'Hervé de Bourgdieu *De correctione quarumdam lectionum,' Revue bénédictine,* 24 (1907) 43; Bernard, Ep. 398, ed. Leclercq, VIII, 378: 'non novella audiri decet vel levia, sed certe authentica et antiqua'. For Matthew of Vendôme, an *exempla authentica,* as contrasted with an *exempla*

of God was truth, not custom, inspired the reformers both of the eleventh and of the sixteenth century [122]. The sacramental and moral theology of the eleventh and twelfth centuries was permeated by an emphasis on the attitude of the believer. Hugh of St Victor said that faith was as powerful as the words of institution in the consecration of the sacraments. 'Where there is true faith', he wrote, 'the word of God cannot be absent, since the word itself is conceived by faith and operates through faith' [123]. Even improperly consecrated elements were valid for those who believed in them [124]. According to the canonist Hostiensis, God considers the faith of prayers offered in private (though not in public) even to an uncanonized person who is sincerely thought to be a saint [125]. Abelard and his followers went further in regarding all actions as deriving their moral value from the intention of the doer [126]. The same deed might be either good or evil depending on whether it was performed with good or bad intent.

Relics and miracles were also judged by a subjective standard. Guibert of Nogent in his treatise on relics emphasized the interior attitude of the venerator more than the external status of the relic. 'Veritas in the field of the cult of relics,' wrote Schreiner, 'not only meant the outer material truth (Sachwahrheit) of holy remains but also related to the inner truthfulness of those who relied on them to give the church real pledges of divine protection.' Even a false relic is thus genuine, or at least efficacious, for a pious person, whereas it is powerless for anyone who knows

---

domestica, was one derived from another writer and not invented by the author: Edmond Faral, Les arts poétiques du XII⁰ et du XIII⁰ siècle (Bibliothèque de l'Ecole des Hautes Etudes, 238; Paris, 1924) 156-57.

[122] Schreiner, in Saeculum, 17. 143, and n. 61, citing sources from Augustine to Luther. On truth as the test of authenticity in canon law, see Le Bras, in Critica del testo (n. 36 above) 387-88.

[123] Hugh of St Victor, Sacraments, II.9.1, tr. Deferrari (n. 20 above) 316.

[124] Rupert of Deutz, Liber de divinis officiis, II.9, ed. R. Haacke (Corpus christianorum: Continuatio mediaevalis, 7; Turnhout, 1967) 41-42. See also the anonymous Libellus adversus errores Alberonis sacerdotis Merkensis, II.8, in Veterum scriptorum . . . amplissima collectio, ed. E. Martène and U. Durand (Paris, 1724-33) IX, 1260A: 'Sacramenta a criminoso sacerdote confecta, nec defunctis nec vivis crimina sacerdotis scientibus, sed ignorantibus dumtaxat prodesse.' See R. I. Moore, The Origins of European Dissent (London, 1977) 188. The corollary to this teaching, that sinners received only bread and wine, was argued by some theologians: see Browe, Eucharistischen Wunder (n. 90 above) 113.

[125] Henry of Ostia (Hostiensis), In tertium decretalium librum commentaria (Venice, 1581) 172ᵛ (B).

[126] Among various works on intentionality in the twelfth century, the best is still Odon Lottin, Psychologie et morale aux XII⁰ et XIII⁰ siècles (Louvain – Gembloux, 1942-60), esp. vol. I.

it is false[127]. Peter the Chanter held that the efficacy of a miracle, unlike that of a sacrament, often depended on the merit of the performer[128]. By this standard, a forgery designed to promote truth and justice would not be considered a forgery, in the pejorative sense, at all.

It is in this concept of the personal character of truth and the stress on intention that the ideas of forgery and plagiarism met in the Middle Ages. In other respects they differed, since forgery involved primarily the fabrication of documents and objects and plagiarism the stealing of words and ideas. Plagiarism is therefore a peculiarly literary and academic vice, though it can be applied to the creative arts generally[129]. It is no accident that the term plagiarism first appeared in English in the seventeenth century, since it depends upon the distinctively modern concept of creativity and originality as the personal property of individuals[130]. The law of copyright, of which the purpose is to convert 'things of the mind into transferable articles of property'[131], dates in England from the beginning of the eighteenth century.

Today, plagiarism far more than forgery threatens our most cherished values[132], though it is often difficult to distinguish precisely between pla-

---

[127] Schreiner, in *Archiv für Kulturgeschichte*, 48.31-33, and in *Saeculum*, 17.148-52, 163, where the cited passage is found. See also Colin Morris, 'A Critique of Popular Religion: Guibert of Nogent on *The Relics of the Saints*,' *Studies in Church History*, 8 (1972) 55–60.

[128] Peter the Chanter, *Summa de sacramentis et animae consiliis*, ed. J.-A. Dugauquier, I (Analecta mediaevalia Namurcensia, 4; Louvain-Lille, 1954) 107 (De baptismo, 37).

[129] Both composers and painters can plagiarize, but the term is not commonly used for painters who either copy parts of others' paintings into their own or who pass off other people's paintings as theirs.

[130] Konrad Burdach, *Schlesisch-böhmische Briefmuster aus der Wende des vierzehnten Jahrhunderts* (Vom Mittelalter zur Reformation, 5; Berlin, 1926) 8: 'Was wir heute unter Originalität und schöpferischer Freiheit verstehen, das ist der gesamten Schriftstellerei und Dichtung des Mittelalters fremd.' See Schreiner, in *Saeculum*, 17.159-60 and, on plagiarism, W. A. Edwards, *Plagiarism: An Essay on Good and Bad Borrowing* (Cambridge, 1933); Etienne Gilson, 'Philosophie du plagiat,' *Académie royale de Belgique. Bulletin de la Classe des Lettres et des Sciences morales et politiques*, 5th S., 45 (1959) 556-72; and the symposium on plagiarism printed in the *Times Literary Supplement* (April 9 1982) 413-15. On the arts, see Van de Waal, in *Aspects* (n. 27 above) 4: 'Not until the seventeenth century did the idea appear that borrowing in the artistic field might be something improper.'

[131] John Sutherland, in *TLS* symposium, 415.

[132] The Dean of Harvard College, in his Report for 1980-81, said, 'It is commonplace to observe that plagiarism is the most fundamental academic violation; it misrepresents as one's own another's ideas and efforts and is thus a form of lying.' In the course of a discussion with some students about the legitimate scope of academic discipline, there was general agreement that a university had a right and duty to prohibit plagiarism, whereas theft was considered only partially under its jurisdiction, and fornication not at all. In a similar discussion in the Middle Ages, I suspect that the priorities would have been reversed: fornication would have been prohibited, theft for the most part, and plagiarism, in the sense of taking other people's ideas or words, not at all.

giarism, in the legal sense, and improvement, parody, and imitation. Unconscious and unintentional plagiarism may result from too good a memory, or too great a reliance on memory, rather than from an intent to deceive. Not every good idea is new, as Charlotte Brontë emphasized when she contrasted, in a letter concerning a lecture by Thackeray, 'freshness of treatment', which she considered originality, with mere novelty, 'the stimulus of an ever-new subject'[133]. T. S. Eliot is said to have quipped that, 'The immature poet imitates; the mature poet plagiarizes'[134].

These views would have struck a familiar chord in the Middle Ages, when writers were sometimes criticized for copying or compiling but not for what we call plagiarism, because there was no sense of literary or creative property. The modern system of licenced plagiarism, by which writers may take whatever they want so long as they say so in the footnotes, was almost unknown[135]. When sources were cited in medieval writings, they were to lend authority rather than to acknowledge indebtedness to other writers. Medieval writers, like medieval artists, sought an authoritative truth, an inner form, which was regarded as common property rather than the private possession of the first discoverer. Indeed, the definition of copyright cited above is almost exactly that of simony, the sale of spiritual gifts, which was regularly prohibited in the Middle Ages. According to Swarzenski, speaking of art, 'The achievement of a type, in an idol, image, or tool, was the essence; . . . not the "original" but the "example" characterizes the work'[136].

---

[133] E. C. Gaskell, *The Life of Charlotte Brontë* (New York, n.d.) 404: 'You do well to set aside odious comparisons, and to wax impatient of that trite twaddle about "nothing newness" – a jargon which simply proves, in those who habitually use it, a coarse and feeble faculty of appreciation; an inability to discern the relative value of *originality* and *novelty*; a lack of that refined perception which, dispensing with the stimulus of an ever-new subject, can derive sufficiency of pleasure from freshness of treatment.'

[134] Cf. Picasso's remark, cited by Cocteau in *Exposition mondiale* (n. 69 above) n.p., that, 'Il n'y a pas de faux parce qu'il n'y a que des faux.'

[135] George Eliot, *Romola*, ch. 5 (Penguin ed., 102) said that, 'Scholarship is a system of licensed robbery, and your man in scarlet and furred robe who sits in judgment on thieves, is himself a thief of the thoughts and the fame that belongs to his fellows.' According to Edward Epstein, in the *New York Times Book Review* (July 6 1980) 18, 'Plagiarism is not a legal concept but a matter of academic bargaining that defines the terms under which scholars may borrow material from other authors.'

[136] George Swarzenski, in *Magazine of Art*, 41(5).165. See also W. S. Heckscher, 'Relics of Pagan Antiquity in Mediaeval Settings,' *Journal of the Warburg Institute*, 1 (1937) 210: 'What the mediaeval mind chiefly sought in the remains of the past was – in contradistinction to modern romanticism – the permanent form, the opposite of ruin.'

St Bonaventura in his commentary on the *Sentences* of Peter Lombard said that there were four ways of making a book (*quadruplex modus faciendi librum*).

Someone may write the works of others (*aliena*), adding or changing nothing, and he is called simply a scribe. Some one may write the works of others, adding but not from his own work (*suo*), and he is called a compiler. Some one may write the works both of others and of himself, but with the works of others predominating, and his own added for support; and he is called a commentator, not an author. Some one may write both his own works and those of others, with his own predominating, and that of others added for confirmation, and such a writer should be called an author [137].

Bonaventura's contrast between *aliena* and *sua* and his recognition that all books contain the work of others are characteristic of the medieval point of view. He makes no reference to the possibility that a book could be entirely a writer's own work. For him, writers are ranked 'according to the degree of independence they enjoy in relation to existing books' [138].

The point at issue before the twelfth century was the balance between *aliena* and *sua*, since it was recognized that the author was in some way superior to the scribe, compiler, and commentator. Rabanus Maurus, who was one of the first exegetes on the continent to use the so-called catena method of commentary, by which 'chains' of passages from earlier commentators were used to elucidate verses of Scripture, was apparently accused of copying, not to say stealing, because he more than once defended himself with protestations that he had taken everything openly and had cited his sources [139]. In some manuscripts of his works, indeed, his references to the initials of the authors he used can still be found. In the prefatory letter to his commentary on Matthew he followed Bede in saying that he had been 'solicitous throughout lest I should be said to have stolen the words of greater men and to have put them together as if they were my own' [140], and in the preface to his commentary on Ezechiel

---

[137] Bonaventura, *Commentarius in I. Librum Sententiarum*, preface, in *Opera omnia* (Quaracchi, 1883–1902) I, 14b–15a.

[138] John Burrow in his review of John Trevisa, *On the Properties of Things*, in the *Times Literary Supplement* (May 1976).

[139] J. B. Hablitzel, *Hrabanus Maurus. Ein Beitrag zur Geschichte der mittelalterlichen Exegese* (Biblische Studien, 11.3; Freiburg-im-Br., 1906) 96-97, who associated the origins of the *Katenenmethode* with Alcuin and the school of Tours.

[140] *Monumenta Germaniae historica: Epistolae* (Berlin, 1887 ff.) V: *Epistolae Karolini aevi*, III (Berlin, 1898-99) 389. See also his Ep. 14 to Abbot Hilduin of St Denis, *ibid.*,

he faced his critics squarely, asking in what way he had sinned in judging the masters of the church worthy of veneration and in placing their sentences as they themselves produced them, together with notes of their names, at opportune places in my works? It seems to me healthier to lean upon the doctrines of the holy fathers, and to preserve my humility, than improperly to offer my own, through pride, as if I were seeking my own praise. . . . For those [of the Fathers] who sought praise and to be seen by men, dictated and wrote whatever they wished[141].

This attitude continued for a long time. Borrowings, unacknowledged as well as acknowledged, are found in most medieval writings and are both the bane and, when discovered, the joy, of textual editors. Still in the twelfth century no need was felt to cite sources, even by writers who clearly had no intent to deceive. John of Salisbury, whose warnings against forged documents were cited above, freely admitted in the *Policraticus* that he had taken whatever had been well said by others and incorporated it into his own work, 'sometimes in my own words, for brevity, and sometimes in another's words, for faith and authority'[142]. Nicholas of Montiéramey, an imitative writer whose works have long been confused with those of Peter Damiani, Bernard, and other writers, wrote in a letter to the count of Champagne accompanying a collection of his sermons that they were 'invented in my sense [and] dictated in my style, except for what I took over in a few places from other writers'[143]. Sermon-making has never been a very inventive art, and medieval sermons are filled with re-used material. Peter of Cornwall in his *Pantheologus,* which was written in the 1170s or 1180s, said that he had put together materials from the Fathers ('sometimes in their own words, sometimes with their prolixity pruned') in order to save preachers the trouble of writing their own sermons and to allow them 'to form an already-made sermon out of previously-invented sermons, placed before his eyes and ex-

---

402-3, saying that he had added in the margins the names of the writers whose words he had used, 'ubi vero sensum eorum meis verbis expressi aut ubi iuxta sensus eorum similitudinem, prout divina gratia mihi concedere dignata est, de novo dictavi.' The author of Ep. 4 in the appendix to Alcuin's letters, *ibid.,* IV: *Epp. Kar. aevi,* II, 491, denied that he was a 'compilator veterum'.

[141] *Pat. lat.,* CX, 498AB. See also the prefaces to his commentaries on the letters of Paul and the Book of Numbers, in *Pat. lat.,* CVIII, 587B-88A, and CXI, 1273-76.

[142] John of Salisbury, *Policraticus,* I, prol., ed. C. C. J. Webb (Oxford, 1909) I, 16. See Schreiner, in *Saeculum,* 17.159-60.

[143] Jean Leclercq, 'Les collections de sermons de Nicolas de Clairvaux,' in his *Recueil d'études sur Saint Bernard et ses écrits,* I (Storia e letteratura, 92; Rome, 1962) 50. On Nicholas, see n. 94 above.

plained'[144]. Preachers who used sermon-manuals such as this were not considered plagiarists in the Middle Ages, however, any more than they are today.

The confusion created by borrowing and imitation was compounded by the practices of anonymity and false attribution, which have been more studied in Antiquity and Late Antiquity than in the Middle Ages[145]. Many works circulated under no name or false names owing not only to ignorance but also to the desire of their real authors, who sought to conceal their identities, either out of humility, and a sense that all creative work was common property, or in order to give authenticity and authority to their writings[146]. Salvian wrote to Bishop Salonius that he had attributed his treatise *Ad ecclesiam* to the apostle Timothy because, 'He wished to be completely hidden and to keep out of the way, lest [his] writings, which contained many helpful things, might lose their force through the name of the author.' He chose the name of Timothy to do honor to this subject, not to deceive his readers[147]. Honorius *Augustodunensis* in the twelfth century wrote that

I have covered my name in silence lest consuming envy should bid its readers to neglect a useful work by scorning it. The only thing the reader should ask is that it [my name] be written in heaven, lest at some time it be deleted from the book of the living[148].

---

[144] R. W. Hunt, 'English Learning in the Late Twelfth Century,' in *Essays in Medieval History,* ed. R. W. Southern (London – Melbourne – Toronto, 1968) 119, 126. See Richard H. Rouse and Mary A. Rouse, '*Statim Invenire:* Schools, Preachers, and New Attitudes to the Page,' in *Renaissance and Renewal* (n. 120 above) 214-15, who also commented (209) on the general question of citation of sources by twelfth-century writers.

[145] See generally, in addition to works already cited, Wolfgang Speyer, 'Religiöse Pseudepigraphie und literarische Fälschung im Altertum,' *Jahrbuch für Antike und Christentum,* 8–9 (1965-66) 88–125; Bruce Metzger, 'Literary Forgeries and Canonical Pseudepigrapha,' *Journal of Biblical Literature,* 91 (1972) 3–24; and the collected essays in *Pseudepigraphie in der heidnischen und jüdisch-christlichen Antike,* ed. Norbert Brox (Wege der Forschung, 484; Darmstadt, 1977). On the Middle Ages esp., see Ernst Robert Curtius, *European Literature and the Latin Middle Ages,* tr. Willard R. Trask (New York, 1953) App. 18 (515-18): 'Mention of the Author's Name in Medieval Literature'.

[146] Abelard, in the prologue to the *Sic et Non,* ed. Boyer and McKeon (n. 92 above) 91, commented, 'Pluraque enim apocrypha ex sanctorum nominibus, ut auctoritatem haberent, intitulata sunt.' Generally, see, Eric J. Dobson, *The Origins of 'Ancrene Wisse'* (Oxford, 1976) 327-43, and Nikolaus M. Häring, 'Commentary and Hermeneutics', in *Renaissance and Renewal,* 174-80.

[147] Salvian, Ep. IX.16–17, in *Opera omnia,* ed. F. Pauly (Corpus scriptorum ecclesiasticorum latinorum, 8; Vienna, 1883) 221-22. See *The Writings of Salvian the Presbyter,* tr. Jeremiah F. O'Sullivan (New York, 1947) 260-62.

[148] Martin Grabmann, 'Eine stark erweiterte und kommentierte Redaktion des Elucidarium des Honorius von Augustodunum,' *Miscellanea Giovanni Mercati,* II: *Letteratura medioevale* (Studi e testi, 122; Vatican City, 1946) 247.

Theophilus, writing between 1110 and 1140, expressed a similar attitude   *
with regard to the arts in the preface to his *De diversis artibus.*

What God has given man as an inheritance, let man strive and work
with all eagerness to attain. When this has been attained, let no one
glorify himself, as if it were received of himself and not Another, but
let him humbly render thanks to God, from Whom and through
Whom all things are, and without Whom nothing is [149].

This became an increasingly conservative view as the twelfth century
progressed. Pächt in his introduction to the St Albans Psalter referred to
the traditional belief in the anonymity of medieval art as a dangerous
half-truth [150], and there is evidence that more and more artists after about
1100 signed their works [151]. Though the old habits of anonymity died
slowly in some artistic traditions, and in some regions, the growing practice of signing has been seen by many scholars as an indication of a sense
of artistic individualism and of personal talent. The pride of artistic
creation was clearly expressed by Dante in his references to the painter
Oderisi [152].

The same is true of literature in the twelfth century. 'In this period we
find unadulterated pride of authorship,' according to Curtius, who said
that he could find no example of suppression of an author's name at that
time [153]. A possible, though problematical, exception is the case of Peter
the Venerable's secretary Peter of Poitiers, who claimed that he had published under his own name the works of others, including Peter the Venerable himself, 'not out of pride, from which may God preserve me, but
by the devotion of obedience, especially since I know that many men of

---

[149] Theophilus, *De diversis artibus,* I, preface, ed. C. R. Dodwell ([Nelson's] Medieval
Texts; London – Edinburgh, 1961) 2. See Andrew Martindale, *The Rise of the Artist in the
Middle Ages and Early Renaissance* (London – New York, 1972) 66-67, and on the date
and provenience, Hubert Silvestre, in *Revue d'histoire ecclésiastique,* 71 (1976) 334-35.
[150] *The St. Albans Psalter (Albani Psalter),* ed. Otto Pächt, C. R. Dodwell, and Francis
Wormald (Studies of the Warburg Institute, 25; London, 1960) 172. See also Heinrich
Klotz, 'Formen der Anonymität und des Individualismus in der Kunst des Mittelalters
und der Renaissance,' *Gesta,* 15.1-2 (1976) 303-12, who questioned the contrast between
medieval anonymity and modern individualism, citing examples of medieval artists who
identified themselves.
[151] Meyer Schapiro, 'On the Aesthetic Attitude in Romanesque Art', in his *Selected Papers [I]: Romanesque Art* (New York, 1977) 22, and Martindale, *Artist,* passim.
[152] *Purgatorio,* 11.79-81.
[153] Curtius, *European Literature,* 517.

proven religion and humility have previously done the same thing with some of their writings'[154]. It is unknown why Peter the Venerable or other writers wanted their writings to appear under the name of Peter of Poitiers, which is a form of pseudonymous publication, but they were apparently not concerned by questions of plagiarism or originality.

The sense of literary individuality is reflected in the accusations of stealing that were increasingly brought against authors in the twelfth and thirteenth centuries. The related question of the extent of legitimate innovation was also raised. Rupert of Deutz, for instance, cited Genesis 26.18-22, where Isaac dug other wells, in order to justify his additions to the traditional commentaries on the Bible. It was proper, he argued, to 'dig other wells by the ploughshare of my own talent (*ingenium*), as long as I live, and we can find water'[155]. The issue of the theft of words was clearly involved in the Bridlington Dialogue, which dates from the middle of the twelfth century, for when the disciple urged the master to 'go through the spacious fields of Scripture, as is your wont' and to gather 'here and there the flowerets of thoughts' for a commentary on the Rule of St Augustine, he replied that, 'I see you want me to be derided and devoured. For because I have done this in some of my collections, those who return evil for good disparage me for doing this kindness for my friends, saying that I should be declared a thief and compiler of the words of others.' Encouraged by the disciple, however, he said that he would disregard these detractors, and he gave a long and interesting justification of his practice.

> For since 'every best gift and every perfect gift is from above, coming down from the Father of lights' (James 1.17), and the gift of understanding is one thing, and that of making known another, and each man has his own gift from God, the one in this way and another in that, those who have nothing [of their own] to make known do not act improperly if they receive from others and commit to memory what they receive, especially if this is required by ecclesiastical dispensation or fraternal request. For it is certainly useful that many become preachers of the truth, but not many masters, provided that they all

---

[154] *Bibliotheca Cluniacensis,* ed. Martin Marrier and André Duchesne (Paris, 1614) 604B.

[155] Rupert of Deutz, *Commentarium in Apocalypsim,* preface, in *Opera omnia* (Venice, 1748-51) III, 349. See also Rupert's prefatory letter, addressed to Abbot Cuno of Siegburg, to his *Commentaria in evangelium sancti Iohannis,* ed. R. Haacke (Corpus christianorum: Continuatio mediaevalis, 9; Turnhout, 1969) 1.

say the same thing as disciples of one master and 'there be no schisms among' them (1 Cor. 1.10). They should not be deterred by the prophet Jeremiah, through whom God rebukes those 'who steal His words every one from his neighbor' (Jer. 23–30). For those who steal take what belongs to another (*alienum*). But the word of God belongs (*non est . . . alienum*) to those who obey it. God therefore said that His words are stolen by those who pervert them, or those who wish to seem good because they speak the things of God while [really] they are bad because they do their own things. Whatever good things they say appear to be invented by their own talent (*ingenium*) but do not belong (*aliena sunt*) to their way of life. For they speak and do not act. If you study this carefully, these people in one way say and in another way do not say the good things they say. They speak with the mouth but they do not speak with the will or the deed.

He then ridiculed the idea that Jerome, Augustine, or Gregory should be called 'thieves of the words of others (*fures uerborum alienorum*)' because they borrowed from the writings of earlier Fathers, and he ended with Augustine's dictum that many books must be written in diverse forms but with one faith, Eusebius's statement that Mark wrote his Gospel from Peter's preaching, without his knowledge but with his later approval, and the quip of Terence that, 'No one can say anything that has not been said before.' He then called on his critics to stop cavilling[156].

This passage is of exceptional interest because it recognizes at the same time the diversity of individual talents (like the *ingenium* of Rupert of Deutz), the divine origin of all understanding, and the relativity of virtue. 'The word of God belongs to those who obey it.' To be fully good, words must be said with will and deed as well as with the lips. Truth depends on intention, not simply on factual accuracy. For someone to take the true words of earlier writers is not therefore stealing, so long as the intention is pure, but to take them in order to pervert them or to give an appearance of virtue, is stealing. The perversion, as it were, becomes theirs, while the truth remains another's. Mary of France expressed a similar view when she said that, 'One should believe when one sees the deed which reveals the truth'[157]. Alexander of Ashby,

---

[156] Robert of Bridlington, *The Bridlington Dialogue* (London, 1960) 12–14. On this work, see Marvin L. Colker, 'Richard of Saint Victor and the Anonymous of Bridlington,' *Traditio*, 18 (1962) 181–227.

[157] *Die Fabeln der Marie de France*, ed. Karl Warnke (Bibliotheca normanica, 6; Halle, 1898) 129 (Fable 37, *De leone et homine*, 11. 63-64).

writing about 1200, also said that, 'Only those who by the purity of
their lives adhere to the spirit in which Scripture was written and expounded purely and rightly understand the holy writings'[158].
The question of the nature of originality and legitimate extent of
copying attracted increasing attention in the second half of the twelfth century[159]. Gerald of Wales accused the future Bishop Cadogan of Bangor
not only of forgery, as we have seen, but also of reciting from memory
other preachers' sermons, 'more for ostentation than for the edification
of others', and he referred scornfully to modern theological works which
were patched together out of the works of others, simply with some
changes in wording and title, 'as if now newly made, whereas in truth artificially innovated'[160]. Peter of Blois protested indignantly that he had
been called a compiler because he used historical exempla and scriptural
authorities in his writings. After citing the example of the Fathers and
the authority of Macrobius and Seneca, who said that writers, like bees,
should gather flowers and transform them into a single flavor, Peter
went on to say that he would always emulate the writings of the
ancients, whatever his critics said. 'We are like dwarfs on the shoulders
of giants,' he said, using a famous twelfth-century metaphor for the relation of modern to ancient writers, 'by whose kindness we see further
than they do, when we adhere to the works of the ancients and arouse
into some newness of being their more elegant sentences, which age and
human neglect have let decay and become almost lifeless.' The apostles
borrowed words and sentences from the prophets, the doctors of the
church from the apostles, and other doctors from these doctors. Finally,
Peter said, the speed with which he wrote excluded the possibility that
he was simply compiling[161]. The work of composing was clearly quicker
and easier for Peter than that of compiling.

---

[158] Hunt, in *Essays* (n. 144 above) 115. See Alexander Murray, *Reason and Society in the
Middle Ages* (Oxford, 1978) 14, 403 on Alexander of Ashby.
[159] See the work of R. H. and M. Rouse cited n. 144 above.
[160] Gerald of Wales, *Spec. ecc.*, III.7, in *Opera* (n. 97 above) IV, 165. See also his *Speculum duorum or A Mirror of Two Men*, ed. Yves Lefèvre and R. B. C. Huygens (Board of
Celtic Studies, University of Wales: History and Law Series, 27; Cardiff, 1974) 172,
where Gerald commented on theological works 'quasi de novo nunc fabricata sed
verius quidem artificialiter innovata'. The canonist Albinus said in the autobiographical
preface to his *Digesta* that his sermons were put together 'de invento non de furto com-
positos': *Le Liber censuum*, ed. P. Fabre and L. Duchesne (Bibliothèque des Ecoles
françaises d'Athènes et de Rome, 2nd. S., 6; Paris, 1889–1952) II, 88.
[161] Peter of Blois, Ep. 92, in *Opera omnia*, ed. J. A. Giles (Oxford, 1847) I, 285-87, and
Pat. lat., CCVII, 290AC. On this letter, see Richard W. Southern, *Medieval Humanism
and Other Studies* (Oxford, 1970) 119, dating it about 1184, and Edouard Jeauneau,

The seriousness of the charge of copying in the early thirteenth century is shown by the behavior of the enemies of Master Boncompagno, who mutilated a copy of his *Quinque tabulae salutationum* in order to make it look old and then accused him of copying it[162]. Gottfried of Strasbourg launched an invective in his *Tristan,* written at about the same time, against an anonymous inventor of wild tales (commonly thought to be Wolfram von Eschenbach) who despoiled true stories and poached from the work of others[163]. Increasing recognition was given to the distinctive character of fiction, which was described by John of Garland as truth covered with the outward form of a story. Allegory, for John, was 'truth cloaked in the words of history'[164]. These techniques were even used by lawyers, who in fourteenth-century England gave fictitious 'color' to their pleading by supplying circumstances known to be incorrect but needed for the discussion in court. A plaintiff who had taken some property might thus be said to have believed that there was no heir, even though the real basis of his claim was known to be different[165]. Such color, though factually false, was true inasmuch as it served the ends of justice.

By this time the question of the relation between writers and their sources had taken on many of the implications it has today. It was of particular concern to Petrarch, who came back to it repeatedly in his writings. He had no desire to plunder the works of another writer, he wrote to Boccaccio in 1359, declaring that he would no more despoil some one else's talent (*ingenium alienum*) than he would their patrimony. In an-

---

' "Nani gigantum humeris insidentes." Essai d'interprétation de Bernard de Chartres,' *Vivarium,* 5 (1967) 91. With regard to Peter's remark concerning the speed of his composition, John of Salisbury, in the passage cited n. 142 above, also said that he used his own words 'ad compendium'. It was clearly regarded as more laborious to compile than to compose.

[162] Carl Sutter, *Aus Leben und Schriften des Magisters Boncompagno. Ein Beitrag zur italienischen Kulturgeschichte im dreizehnten Jahrhundert* (Freiburg-im-Br. – Leipzig, 1894) 49 (and 27 on the date).

[163] Gottfried von Strassburg, *Tristan und Isold,* ed. Friedrich Ranke, 11th ed. (Dublin – Zurich, 1967) 58 (ll. 4638-90), tr. Arthur T. Hatto (Baltimore, 1960) 105. I owe these references to Eckehard Simon.

[164] *The 'Parisiana Poetria' of John of Garland,* ed. Traugott Lawler (New Haven – London, 1974) 104-5. The idea of the *integumentum* or *involucrum* of words covering truth attracted considerable attention in the twelfth and thirteenth centuries; see Jon Whitman, 'From the *Cosmographia* to the *Divine Comedy:* An Allegorical Dilemma,' *Allegory, Myth, and Symbol,* ed. Morton Bloomfield (Harvard English Studies, 9; Cambridge, Mass., 1981) 79–80, with further references.

[165] Donald Sutherland, 'Legal Reasoning in the Fourteenth Century: The Invention of "Color" in Pleading,' *On the Laws and Customs of England: Essays in Honor of Samuel E. Thorne,* ed. Morris E. Arnold a.o. (Chapel Hill, 1981) 182-94.

other letter, also to Boccaccio, he warned that an imitation should be similar to but not identical with the model. The resemblance should be that of a son to a father, he said, not a perfect image[166]. He knew that all writers, including himself, had to imitate, but he stressed that what is imitated must be assimilated. Like the honey made by bees, what is well said belongs to the writer, not to the source, and he therefore bore with equinimity, he said, the destiny of his own talent[167]. The count made the same point during a long discussion on imitation in the *Libro del Cortegiano*, saying that

> There are many who want to judge style and discuss the rhythms of language and the question of imitation, but they cannot get me to understand what style and rhythm are, or what imitation consists of, nor why things taken from Homer or some one else read so well in Virgil that they seem improved (*illustrate*) rather than imitated[168].

Castiglione published this work in 1528, when the concept of originality and creativity as personal attributes was commonly accepted[169], but in this passage he still reflected the belief that imitation is inevitable and, if well done, desirable. The writer's real task is not to dream up new ideas but to put well, and thus truthfully, what has been said before.

The attitude of these writers toward the authors of the past is shown by their use of the metaphors of honey, bunches of flowers, and dwarfs and giants. Writers were often compared to bees, as were monks, who

---

[166] Petrarch, Ep. fam. XXII.2 and XXIII.19, ed. Vittorio Rossi and Umberto Bosco (Edizione nazionale delle opere di Francesco Petrarca, 10–13; Florence, 1933-42) IV, 106-7, 206. See Morris Bishop, *Letters from Petrarch* (Bloomington, Ind. – London, 1966) 183, 314.

[167] Petrarch, *De sui ipsius et multorum ignorantia*, ed. and tr. Pier Giorgio Ricci, in Francesco Petrarca, *Prose* (La letteratura italiana, 7; Milan – Naples, 1955) 760, and Ep. fam. I.8, ed. Rossi and Bosco, I, 39–40. See also Ep. fam. XXI.15, ed. Rossi and Bosco, IV, 96.

[168] Baldassare Castiglione, *Il libro del Cortegiano*, I.39, ed. Carlo Cordié (La letteratura italiana, 27; Milan – Naples, 1960) 68, and tr. George Bull (Harmondsworth, 1976) 85. I have followed Bull's translation in all except a few places, notably the last word (*imitate*), which Bull translated as 'plagiarized'. My wife drew this passage to my attention.

[169] In addition to the works cited nn. 130 above and 177 below, on the lack of such a concept in the Middle Ages, see Ernst Cassirer, *The Individual and the Cosmos in Renaissance Philosophy*, tr. Mario Domandi (New York, 1963) 164, stressing the slow emergence, after Galileo, of 'the principle that genius is the gift of nature'; Richard Douglas, 'Talent and Vocation in Humanist and Protestant Thought,' *Action and Conviction in Early Modern Europe: Essays in Memory of E. H. Harbison*, ed. T. K. Rabb and J. E. Seigel (Princeton, 1969) 261-98, esp. 266; and Gianni Mombello, *Les avatars de "Talentum"* (Biblioteca di Studi Francesi, 5; Turin, 1976).

were said by Cassian to gather honey from various sources[170]. Honey is both derivative and original, old and new, as is a bouquet of differently colored flowers, and these metaphors therefore expressed the sense of dependence felt by medieval writers toward their sources. The dwarfs on the shoulders of giants are more ambiguous, since they can be seen in a modernist sense, emphasizing that they can see further than the giants, or in an antiquarian sense, since the ancient giants are larger than the modern dwarfs. The image may have had some ambiguity even in the twelfth century, but the main emphasis was certainly on the greater stature of the giants than on the further vision of the dwarfs, and this is clearly what Peter of Blois had in mind when he used it to justify his borrowings from classical and patristic works[171]. The ambiguity is even more striking in the parallel dictum *quanto iuniores tanto perspicaciores*, which may be roughly translated, 'The younger we are the more perspicacious we have to be.' This seems to emphasize the superiority of the moderns to the ancients, but in the Middle Ages it meant, as my translation suggests, that modern people must be more perspicacious than people of Antiquity precisely because they are further from the fountain of truth[172].

The debt felt by medieval writers to the past was also expressed in the doctrine of the *translatio studii*. In the thirteenth and fourteenth centuries Latin culture was seen as coming from Greece, and to have declined in the process of moving[173]. Even the Greeks were by this time conscious of a sense of decline. The Emperor Manuel II Palaeologus acknowledged the inferiority of modern to ancient writing in a famous letter written in

---

[170] Cassian, *Institutiones*, V.4.2., ed. and tr. Jean-Claude Guy (Sources chrétiennes, 109: Textes monastiques d'occident, 17; Paris, 1965) 194. Among the writers cited above, it was used by both Peter of Blois (n. 161) and Petrarch (Ep. fam. I.8 and XXII.2). For other examples, see Tore Janson, *Latin Prose Prefaces: Studies in Literary Conventions* (Acta Universitatis Stockholmiensis: Studia latina Stockholmiensia, 13; Stockholm – Göteborg – Uppsala, 1964) 152-53: 'The writer has obviously tried to combine the images of picking flowers and gathering honey. With the surprising result that the bees now pick the flowers and store them in the hive.' It still appears on the seal of Phillips Academy in Andover.

[171] Jeauneau, in *Vivarium*, 5.79-99; Hubert Silvestre, ' "Quanto iuniores, tanto perspicaciores": Antécédents à la Querelle des anciens et modernes,' *Recueil commémoratif du Xe anniversaire de la Faculté de Philosophie et Lettres* (Publications de l'Université lovanium de Kinshasa, 22; Louvain – Paris, 1968) 251-55; and Brian Stock, 'Antiqui and Moderni as "Giants" and "Dwarfs": A Reflection of Popular Culture,' *Journal of Modern Philology*, 76 (1979) 370-74.

[172] Silvestre, in *Recueil*, 231-51.

[173] Among other works, see Beryl Smalley, *English Friars and Antiquity in the Early Fourteenth Century* (Oxford, 1960) 70-71.

1408/10 to the metropolitan of Thessalonica. The moderns must not give up writing, however, just because they are inferior to the ancients.

> Those who try their hand at writing should strive with all their might to look to those who have become perfect in the art and take them as their models. But they must also recognize very clearly that they are not attaining that level . . . . For the achievements of the past have flown beyond the grasp of the men of today[174].

In the view of these writers, it was vain to hope to equal and proud to attempt to surpass the writers of Antiquity, who were models of wisdom and inventiveness. In comparison, as the master in the Bridlington Dialogue said, many modern writers have nothing new to say and should be satisfied with disseminating established truths rather than trying to formulate specious novelties. The standard by which a writer's works was judged was not one of originality but of truth as established by antiquity and orthodoxy. The only moral obligation of writers with regard to their sources was therefore to choose them carefully. 'To copy second-rate authors indeed is immoral,' according to a modern critic[175]. The ancients likewise looked up to their predecessors. 'Every writing, like the truth it contained, was the property of the community, and everyone had a right to add to it, curtail it, or modify it in order to obtain a better definition of this truth.'[176] The four types of writers described by Bonaventura all looked backward, as did medieval students in their studies. According to Goldschmidt,

> We are guilty of an anachronism if we imagine that the medieval student regarded the contents of the books he read as the expression of another man's personality and opinion. He looked upon them as part of that great and total body of knowledge, the *scientia de omni scibili,* which had once been the property of the ancient sages[177].

---

[174] *The Letters of Manuel II Palaeologus,* ed. and tr. George T. Dennis (Corpus fontium historiae byzantinae, 8=Dumbarton Oaks Texts, 4; Washington, D. C., 1977) 52. On this attitude, see Ihor Ševčenko, 'Theodore Metochites, the Chora, and the Intellectual Trends of his Time,' *The Kariye Djami, IV: Studies in the Art of the Kariye Djami and its Intellectual Background,* ed. Paul Underwood (Bollingen Series, 70.4; Princeton, 1974) 44, and nn. 188-89.

[175] Harold Bloom, in *TLS* symposium (n. 130 above) 413.

[176] C. Charlier, *La lecture chrétienne de la Bible* (Maredsous, n.d.) 112, cited by Leclercq, in *Recueil,* I (n. 143 above) 261-62.

[177] E. Ph. Goldschmidt, *Medieval Texts and their First Appearance in Print* (Bibliographical Society's Transactions: Suppl. 16; London, 1943) 113. Frederic W. Maitland, *Select Passages from the Works of Bracton and Azo* (Selden Society, 8; London, 1894) xxvi-xxviii, defended Azo against the charge of plagiarism: 'A literary communism prevailed. There was no property in ideas or in sayings.'

The key to understanding plagiarism in the Middle Ages lies precisely in this attitude toward the past and toward the truth which it embodied. The term plagiarism should indeed probably be dropped in reference to the Middle Ages, since it expresses a concept of literary individualism and property that is distinctively modern. Likewise with regard to forgery, the term should be restricted to those deliberate falsifications and imitations which were intended to promote selfish ends and which were repeatedly prohibited and, when discovered, punished in the Middle Ages. To call the works attributed to Dionysius the Areopagite or the Donation of Constantine forgeries in this sense is to empty the term of historical meaning, just as if the average novel, political speech, or advertisement today were called a forgery, though they are often designed to deceive, and usually with the hope of personal gain. Rather than apply to the past our own definitions and criteria, we should try to enter into the world in which these works were created and to understand them in the light of the standards of truth and falsity at that time.

Let us, in conclusion, look at three examples drawn from the writing of history, where fact and fiction meet and the balance is held between the personal and impersonal views of truth. In the preface to the *Ecclesiastical History of the British People,* Bede said that, 'If history tells of good men and their good estate, the thoughtful listener is spurred on to imitate the good; if it records the wicked deeds of evil men, the devout and earnest listener is no less effectively kindled to eschew what is harmful and perverse.' A few pages later he defined the 'true law of history' as writing down whatever information he could gather[178]. Bede was probably not aware of any tension between the approaches to history expressed in these two passages, one ethical and personal, the other factual and objective. He simply selected his material and presented his history as best he could. This does not mean that he falsified the facts, but he brought a high religious sense to history, which he saw as something different from the material out of which it was constructed. 'We should consider with some care our own interpretation of what . . . Bede thought facts were for;' wrote Wallace-Hadrill, 'or, put another way, be sure of the level at which we choose to appreciate his history.'[179]

---

[178] Bede, *Historia ecclesiastica gentis Anglorum,* preface, ed. Bertram Colgrave and R. A. B. Mynors (Oxford Medieval Texts; Oxford, 1969) 2–3, 6–7. The translation of Colgrave has been revised in a few points.

[179] J. M. Wallace-Hadrill, 'Bede and Plummer,' in *Famulus Christi,* ed. Gerald Bonner (London, 1976) 375.

A parallel approach is found in the ninth-century history of the patriarchs of Ravenna by Agnellus, who said that

When I did not find a history or an account of the life [of an individual patriarch], either from old or ancient men or from a building, or from some authority, in order to avoid a gap in the series of holy bishops as they obtained the see one after another, I composed his life, with God's assistance through your prayers, and I believe that I did not lie, since they were preachers and chaste and charitable men and acquired the souls of men for God[180].

The gap between fact and fiction is wider here than in Bede, and Agnellus was clearly aware that he might be accused of lying, while denying that he in fact did so.

A more elaborate justification is found in the *Vita* of St Stephen of Obazine, which was completed about 1180 and was apparently criticized for, among other things, inaccuracy and prolixity. To the charge of inaccuracy the author replied that any change, reduction, or increase in the wording was attributable to 'the license of the writer not the falsity of the narrative.' He went on the draw a parallel between the historian and the translator, 'who transfers not from word to word but from sense to sense.' The variety of words used by the writers of the Gospels, he continued, 'did not introduce any falsity into the Holy Gospels, of which the venerable text is the foundation of all truth, since what is dissimilar in words is found in perfect agreement in sense and in the truth of the events'[181].

---

[180] Agnellus, *Liber pontificalis ecclesiae Ravennatis,* 32, in *Monumenta Germaniae historica: Scriptores rerum Langobardicarum* (Hanover, 1878) 297. The passage is well-known, and translations will be found in Charles W. Jones, *Saints' Lives and Chronicles in Early England* (Ithaca, N.Y., 1947) 63, and R. Ian Jack, *Medieval Wales* (Ithaca, N.Y., 1972) 39. On Agnellus, see Claudia Nauerth, *Agnellus von Ravenna. Untersuchungen zur archäologischen Methode des ravennatischen Chronisten* (Münchener Beiträge zur Mediävistik und Renaissance-Forschung, 15; Munich, 1974), who stressed Agnellus's use of inscriptions and effigies.

[181] *Vita s. Stephani Obazinensis,* II, preface, ed. and tr. Michel Aubrun (Faculté des lettres et sciences humaines de l'Université de Clermont-Ferrand: Publications de l'Institut d'Etudes du Massif Central, 6; Clermont-Ferrand, 1970) 94. This passage raises the interesting issue, which is not irrelevant to this paper, of the difference between translation from word to word and from sense to sense, on which see Peter Classen, *Burgundio von Pisa* (Sitzungsberichte der Heidelberger Akademie der Wissenschaften, Phil.-hist. Kl., 1974.4; Heidelberg, 1974) 62-65, showing the difficulties of Burgundio's method at translating (in 1171-73) 'de verbo ad verbum de greco in latinum' (85). See Häring, in *Renaissance and Renewal* (n. 120 above) 196, on 'the important distinction between the grammatical meaning of a word and the writer's intention,' citing Gilbert of Poitiers and Simon of Tournai.

Though the attitude of these writers toward history is different from that of scholars today, it would be absurd to call them liars or forgers. They saw their responsibility as not to the endless process of change and countless mutations of human experience that is today called history but to the larger truths which they sought to make clear through their work. Their intention, as Agnellus said, was to enlighten, not to deceive. Petrarch urged his friend Philip of Cabasoles not only to omit nothing in exposing a danger but also to add simulated facts if true ones were lacking. 'For when simulation is the assistant of truth,' he said, 'it should not be called lying'[182]. Historians today do much the same when they choose and present evidence to support various historical interpretations, but they are not called liars because their presentations differ. To dismiss as forgeries the works of Bede and Agnellus, or the life of Stephen of Obazine, or many of the other works mentioned in this paper, because they do not correspond to the modern view of historical scholarship is to condemn the Middle Ages in terms which would have been incomprehensible to people living at that time and to deprive ourselves of a precious source for understanding their real feelings and beliefs.

---

[182] Petrarch, Ep. fam. XXII.5, ed. Rossi and Bosco (n. 166 above) IV, 115. See the slightly different translation in Morris Bishop, *Petrarch and his World* (Bloomington, Ind., 1963) 314.

II

Forged Letters in the Middle Ages

I

Early in the year 250 Bishop Cyprian of Carthage received two letters from the clergy of Rome, one (which is lost) announcing the death of Pope Fabian at the hands of the Decian persecutors, and the other concerning the need to stand firm during the persecution[1]. This second letter raised some doubts in Cyprian's mind, since he wrote in his reply, 'There is no clear indication of either who wrote it or to whom it was written. And since both the writing and the contents and the sheet itself in this letter concerned me lest some of the truth was either removed or changed, I have returned to you the original letter so that you may examine whether it is the same one that you gave to the Subdeacon Crementius to carry. For it is a very serious matter for the truth of a cleric's letter to be corrupted by a lie or fraud. Examine whether both the writing and the subscription are yours, therefore, and write back to us what it is in truth so that we many know this'[2].

Over eight hundred years later, in 1076/7, Archbishop John of Rouen felt similar doubts about a letter ostensibly from himself, recommending a certain Robert known as 'the colt', to Lanfranc of Canterbury, who wrote that Robert had brought 'a letter signed with your seal, which is well known to me, asking me (if it was true) to receive him with honor, to recommend him as strongly as I could to Abbot Baldwin for [treating] his bodily infirmity, and to support [him] out of my own resources as the need might arise ... I am astonished if he

---

1) Cyprian, Ep. 8, ed. and tr. Louis BAYARD (Collection Budé, 1945–61) 1 p. 19–21, and tr. Rose Bernard DONNA (Fathers of the Church 51, 1964) p. 20–23. See Luc DU-QUENNE, Chronologie des lettres de S. Cyprien. Le dossier de la persécution de Dèce (Subsidia hagiographica 54, 1952) p. 114–20, and Henneke GÜLZOW, Cyprian und Novatian. Der Briefwechsel zwischen den Gemeinden in Rom und Karthago zur Zeit der Verfolgung des Kaisers Decius (Beiträge zur historischen Theologie 48, 1975) p. 25–46.

2) Cyprian, Ep. 9.2, ed. BAYARD, 1 p. 22–23, tr. DONNA, p. 24. See Hermann PETER, Der Brief in der römischen Litteratur (Abh. Leipzig 20.3, 1901) p. 176–177; DU-QUENNE, Chronologie p. 120; and GÜLZOW, Cyprian p. 20 and 51–52.

presented a false letter, for how could he have made his falseness convincing by getting the seal of such a man?'[3].

These letters show that the writers and receivers of letters in Late Antiquity and the Middle Ages were worried that their letters might be falsified. Cyprian thought that something had been removed or changed, and mentioned the possibility of 'some lie or fraud', and Lanfranc spoke of 'false letters' and 'falsity'. Both expressed a concern for truth, Cyprian referring to *veritas*, to *in vero*, and *ex vero* and Lanfranc asking whether the letter was 'true'. Today we should probably say 'genuine' or 'authentic', but Cyprian used *authenticus* (*in epistolam authenticam*) in the sense of 'the very same' to refer to the document he had received, which he returned to the writers in order to establish whether it was authentic in the modern sense[4]. Truth and falsity were broader terms in the Middle Ages than they are now, since they involved intention as well as fact, and they were central to the medieval concept of forgery[5]. The prompt punishment of a forger of *falsas epistolas*, whom Ambrose said should be delivered to Satan, was cited by Eugippius in his Life of Severinus[6]. And the decrees of the Lombard kings Rothair and Liutprand condemning the writer of 'a false written document or any parchment' to having his hand cut off, which were repeated in the Liber Papiensis in the eleventh century, show the desire to suppress forgery[7].

The terms *cartola* and *membraneum* in these laws probably meant documents of record rather than letters, which were more difficult to authen-

---

3) Lanfranc, Ep. 41, ed. and tr. Helen CLOVER and Margaret GIBSON (Oxford Medieval Texts, 1979) p. 136.

4) Albert BLAISE, Dictionnaire latin-français des auteurs chrétiens (1954) p. 108, s. v., citing this example. *Exemplum*, on the other hand, usually referred to a copy, and the phrase *eodem exemplo* meant 'with the same words'; see Christian HABICHT and Peter KUSSMAUL, Ein neues Fragment des Edictum de Accusationibus, Museum Helveticum 43 (1986) p. 143–144.

5) See Giles CONSTABLE, Forgery and Plagiarism in the Middle Ages, AfD 29 (1983) p. 1–41, esp. 4–7.

6) Paulinus, Vita Ambrosii 43, in MIGNE PL 14 col. 44 D – 45 A; Eugippius, Vita S. Severini 36, ed. Pius KNOELL (CSEL 9.2, 1886) p. 54, tr. George W. ROBINSON (1914) p. 90.

7) Edictus Rotharii 243, and Liutprandi leges 91 (XV 8), ed. Franz BEYERLE, Leges Langobardorum 643–866 (1962) p. 64 and 143, tr. Katherine Fischer DREW, The Lombard Laws (1973) p. 100 and 184. See Peter HERDE, Römisches und kanonisches Recht bei der Verfolgung des Fälschungsdelikts im Mittelalter, Traditio 21 (1965) p. 291–362, esp. 302–308.

ticate, since they lacked witnesses. Cyprian was disturbed by the lack of salutation and by apparent irregularities in the subscription, writing, and papyrus as well as by the contents. For Lanfranc the central issue was the seal, which he thought was genuine but might have been improperly used. For both him and Cyprian a key role was played by the bearer, since only Robert would have forged a letter in his own favor, and only Crementius could have tampered with a letter that he both carried and delivered[8].

Cyprian's letter also raises the questions of the definition of letters, and how they were collected, since we cannot study letters that were forged without knowing what made others genuine. The letter from the clergy of Rome looks like an exhortation or short tract. The only points which mark it as a letter are the request to distribute 'a copy of this letter (*harum litterarum exemplum*)', the *Bene valere* at the end, and above all its inclusion in the collection of Cyprian's letters. He himself referred to it twice as *litterae*, twice (indirectly) as *epistola*, and once, in another letter, as *scripta*[9]. In the first part of this paper I shall therefore look at the epistolary genre generally in order to ascertain the range of authentic letters, and the boundaries of forgery. I shall then look at some of the specific ways, including those which Cyprian and Lanfranc suggest, in which letters could be falsified, both in form and in content, so as to show the fragility of the genre and its susceptibility to forgery.

II

Letters in Antiquity and the Middle Ages, as they are today, were essentially personal communications over a distance of space and time, which scholars have described as 'the epistolary situation' ('Briefsituation')[10]; but the genre

---

8) GÜLZOW, Cyprian (as note 1) p. 36–37.

9) Cyprian, Ep. 20.3.2, ed. BAYARD (as note 1) 1 p. 55. See DUQUENNE, Chronologie (as note 1) p. 116–117.

10) See in particular Heikki KOSKENNIEMI, Studien zur Idee und Phraseologie des griechischen Briefes bis 400 n. Chr. (Annales Academiae scientiarum Fennicae B, 102.2, 1956) p. 53 and 155–200: 'Das Wichtigste bei der Briefsituation ist, daß die Korrespondenten räumlich voneinander getrennt sind' (p. 169); William G. DOTY, The Classification of Epistolary Literature, The Catholic Biblical Quarterly 31 (1969) p. 183–199, esp. 193; Klaus THRAEDE, Grundzüge griechisch-römischer Brieftopik (Zetemata 48, 1970) p. 3, who stressed the importance of friendship in the 'Briefsituation'. On medieval letters generally, see Giles CONSTABLE, Letters and Letter-Collections (Typologie

was broader and more difficult to define then than it is now, when there is a tendency to consider letters 'real' only when they are private and spontaneous expressions of a writer's personality and are actually sent from one person to another[11]. There is in this view an assumed spectrum of privacy and intimacy with real letters at one end and public pronouncements and treatises in epistolary form at the other, with unsent letters, business and official letters, letters to the editor, dedicatory letters, round-robins, newsletters, and the like somewhere in between, and with an invisible line dividing real from unreal letters[12]. There is a parallel spectrum of falsification running from innocent

---

des sources du moyen âge occidental 17, 1976), which overlaps in places with the material presented here.

11) See, for instance, the opinion of Lytton STRACHEY 'that no good letter was ever written to convey information, or to please the recipient . . .: its fundamental purpose was to express the personality of the writer', cited by Michael HOLROYD, reviewing Bernard Shaw, Collected Letters, 3 in the Times Literary Supplement, 31 May 1985 p. 595. Ruskin, who often used letters as a form of literary publication, stressed in a letter to F. W. Pullen in 1872 that letters, unlike lectures and treatises, should be personal and were written 'for persons who wish to know something of me': The Library Edition of the Works of John Ruskin, ed. Edward T. COOK and Alexander WEDDERBURN (1903 – 12) 37 p. 48. Mary Russell Mitford's letters 'came from her pen like balls of silvery down from a sun-ripened plant, and were wafted far and wide over the land to those she loved', according to W. H. HUDSON, Afoot in England, ch. 6 (1923) p. 72, who went on to say 'They are so spontaneous, so natural, so perfectly reflect her humour and vivacity, her overflowing sweetness, her beautiful spirit'.

12) Cyprian used *littera* and *epistula* interchangeably, and there is no evidence for a strict terminological distinction, but some scholars have used the terms to apply to the two ends of the spectrum suggested here. PETER, Brief (as note 2) p. 11 and 13, and especially Adolf DEISSMANN, Licht vom Osten (⁴1923) p. 194 – 196, distinguished private, personal, non-literary letters from public, artistic, and literary epistles: 'Der Brief ist ein Stück Leben, die Epistel ist ein Erzeugnis literarischer Kunst' (p. 195). See also Georg LUCK, Brief und Epistel in der Antike, Das Altertum 7 (1961) p. 77 – 84. This distinction was rejected as overly rigid by Otto ROLLER, Das Formular der paulinischen Briefe. Ein Beitrag zur Lehre vom antiken Briefe (Beiträge zur Wissenschaft vom Alten und Neuen Testament 58 [= 4. Folge, 6] 1933) p. 22 – 28; M. Monica WAGNER, A Chapter in Byzantine Epistolography: The Letters of Theodoret of Cyrus, Dumbarton Oaks Papers 4 (1948) p. 124; DOTY, Classification (as note 10) p. 183 – 185 (with a bibliography on the problem on p. 183, n. 4), whose classification runs from 'more private letters' to 'less private letters', which include official, public, 'non-real', discursive, and 'other special types' (amorous, poetic, inserted, consolation, dedication, introduction, and congratulation); THRAEDE, Grundzüge (as note 10) p. 1 – 3; and Paolo CUGUSI, Evoluzione e forme dell'epistolografia latina nella tarda repubblica e nei primi due secoli

foolery and joking, which was mostly a matter of ideas and feelings, through fictional and literary letters, of which the nature was understood by most readers, to deceits and falsifications which affected property and the conduct of public affairs. What is a joke or a legitimate literary device to readers who know and understand its nature may be a forgery to readers and scholars who are deceived by their own ignorance. Since the term forgery is now used primarily for intentional frauds perpetrated for personal or institutional gain, it is difficult to say at what point a letter which is not exactly what it appears to be should be called a forgery[13].

Cicero divided letters broadly into public and private, and in a letter to Curio, he said that, of the many types of letters, the most clearly established – 'for the sake of which the thing itself was invented' – was to let absent people know matters concerning themselves or the writer. His own letters were not of this type because Curio was well-informed about his own affairs and Cicero had no news, but, 'There are two other types of letters which greatly please me, one familiar and jocular, the other severe and serious'[14]. C. Julius Victor distinguished two types of letters: business (negotiales), which are concerned with serious affairs, and friendly (familiares), which should be brief and clear[15]; and Sidonius Apollinaris said at one point, speaking of his letters, that 'I have dictated some exhortations, many of advice, some of persuasion, a few in grief, and not a few jokes'[16]. Even the medieval masters of letter-writing, known as dictatores, found it easier to define letters in terms of what they were not than what they were. The author of the Summa prosarum dictaminis, written in the second quarter of the thirteenth century, said that the genre of missive letters was very general and subject to no strict rules. 'They confer no authority; they

---

dell'impero (1983) p. 105 – 125, who distinguished private from public letters, with many intermediary categories.

13) I am concerned here and elsewhere in this paper with forgeries made in the Middle Ages, not with modern commercial forgeries made to deceive collectors of autographs and documents.

14) Cicero, Ep. ad fam. 48 (II 4), ed. D. R. Shackleton BAILEY (1977) 1 p. 107 – 108. Bailey described these three types of letters as informatory, serious, and facetious (p. 348 – 349). In Ep. ad Quintum 1, 37, ed. D. R. Shackleton BAILEY (1980) p. 33, Cicero said illud, quod est epistulae proprium, ut is ad quem scribitur de eis rebus quas ignorat certior fiat, praetermittendum esse non puto. See CUGUSI, Evoluzione (as note 12) p. 27 – 31.

15) C. Julius Victor, Ars rhetorica 27: De epistolis, ed. Karl HALM, Rhetores latini minores (1863) p. 447 – 448.

16) Sidonius, Ep. VII 18, 2, ed. W. B. ANDERSON (Loeb Library, 1936 – 65) 2 p. 396.

convey no law; they occasion no necessity; they express and declare only the intention of the sender and the receiver'[17].

Perhaps the most important characteristic of ancient and medieval letters was their representative function. They were often called a *sermo absentium* and compared (as they still are today) to a conversation or dialogue between two or more people who were physically separated but whom the letter joined in a quasi-presence. Hugh of Bologna in his Rationes dictandi said that letters are sent to friends with whom we cannot talk viva voce and to whom we speak by a letter *quasi ore ad os*[18]. The soul of the writer and 'the face of the interior man' is imprinted in a letter. Sidonius, immediately before the passage cited above, said that his mind appeared in his book of letters 'like a face in a mirror'[19]. In a letter to a friend it was more important to reveal oneself than to

17) Ludwig ROCKINGER, Briefsteller und Formelbücher des eilften bis vierzehnten Jahrhunderts (Quellen und Erörterungen zur bayerischen und deutschen Geschichte 9, 1863) p. 260. Over fifty types of letters are listed in the index to this work.

18) ROCKINGER, Briefsteller, p. 55–56. On the illusion of conversation (quasi-colloquium) in Antiquity, see Francis Xavier J. EXLER, The Form of the Ancient Greek Letter: A Study in Greek Epistolography (1923) p. 15: 'The letter may be defined as a "written conversation"'; WAGNER, Byzantine Epistolography (as note 12) p. 131–132; KOSKENNIEMI, Studien (as note 10) p. 38–47; THRAEDE, Grundzüge (as note 10) p. 46; Carmen CASTILLO, La epístola como género literario: de la Antigüedad a la edad media latina, Estudios clásicos 18 (1974) p. 439–440; and CUGUSI, Evoluzione (as note 12) p. 73–74 and 105, who treated it as a topos. On the continuity of this view in the Middle Ages and Renaissance, see Adolf BÜTOW, Die Entwicklung der mittelalterlichen Briefsteller bis zur Mitte des 12. Jahrhunderts, mit besonderer Berücksichtigung der Theorien der 'ars dictandi' (Diss. Greifswald, 1908) p. 53–56 and Carol Dana LANHAM, *Salutatio* Formulas in Latin Letters to 1200: Syntax, Style, and Theory (Münchener Beiträge zur Mediävistik und Renaissance-Forschung 22, 1975) p. 103–104. On the illusion of presence (*quasi-praesentia, quasi-coram*), see THRAEDE, Grundzüge p. 46; CASTILLO, Epístola p. 440; in tenth-century Byzantine letters: Gustav KARLSSON, Idéologie et cérémonial dans l'épistolographie byzantine (Acta universitatis Upsaliensis. Studia Graeca Upsaliensia 3, ²1962) p. 34–40; Konrad KRAUTTER, Acsi ore ad os... Eine mittelalterliche Theorie des Briefes und ihr antiker Hintergrund, Antike und Abendland 28 (1982) p. 155–168; and Helene HARTH, Poggio Bracciolini und die Brieftheorie des 15. Jahrhunderts. Zur Gattungsform des humanistischen Briefs, in: Der Brief im Zeitalter der Renaissance, ed. Franz J. WORSTBROCK (Deutsche Forschungsgemeinschaft. Kommission für Humanismusforschung, Mitteilung 9, 1983) p. 88, stressing 'das dialogische Verständnis der Gattung' and citing Francesco Nigri that the reason for letters was *ut absentes amicos praesentes redderemus.*

19) Sidonius, Ep. VII 18,2, ed. ANDERSON (as note 16) 2 p. 396. See CASTILLO, Epístola p. 440–441; CUGUSI, Evoluzione (as note 12) p. 34; and, on the autobiographical

convey information. 'I really have nothing to write about', Cicero said in Letter 98 to Atticus, 'no commissions for you since nothing has been overlooked; no news to tell since there is none; and jokes are out of season, there are too many things on my mind'[20]. 'I do not speak true things', said Baldric of Bourgueil in the twelfth century, 'rather I make everything up', putting into people's mouths words of joy, grief, love, and hate[21]. Ficino wrote to Giovanni Cavalcanti in 1468 that 'There is always a reason for a letter to friends', even if they have nothing to say[22]. Letters look at the same time in and out and backwards and forwards, and the elements of truth and sincerity are often inextricably mixed with those that are fictional and derivative.

Second, letters were supposed to be brief. There are countless references in medieval letters to the brevity of the epistolary mode, and to its prohibition of prolixity, which was cited as an excuse for not explaining a matter more fully or giving further examples[23]. Gregory of Nazianzus said towards the end of the fourth century that letters should be concise, clear, and elegant[24]. These re-

---

character of letters as 'the mirror of the soul', Georg MISCH, Geschichte der Autobiographie (1944 – 62) 2.2 p. 415 – 464, and Colin MORRIS, The Discovery of the Individual, 1050 – 1200 (Church History Outlines 5, 1972) p. 79.

20) Cicero, Ep. ad Atticum 98 (V 5), ea. D.R. Shackleton BAILEY (1965 – 68) 3 p. 14 – 17.

21) Baldric of Bourgueil, CXLVII 35 – 38, ed. Phyllis ABRAHAMS (1926) p. 123. I have not seen the new edition of Baldric's poems by K. HILBERT. The author of a twelfth-century poetic love letter said that 'I direct my words to others, my intentions to you': Epistolae duorum amantium. Briefe Abaelards und Heloises?, ed. Ewald KÖNSGEN (Mittellateinische Studien und Texte 9, 1974) p. 11. He went on to say Sepe in verbis cado, quia cogitacio mea ab extranea est.

22) Marsilio Ficino, Ep. 34, anon. tr. 1 (1975) p. 74 – 75. This translation is based on MS Florence, Riccardiana 797 as well as the printed editions of Ficino's letters.

23) In addition to the references given in CONSTABLE, Letters (as note 10) p. 29, see Gertrud SIMON, Untersuchungen zur Topik der Widmungsbriefe mittelalterlicher Geschichtsschreiber bis zum Ende des 12. Jahrhunderts, AfD 5 – 6 (1959 – 60) p. 82 – 86; Ronald WITT, Medieval "Ars Dictaminis" and the Beginnings of Humanism: A New Construction of the Problem, Renaissance Quarterly 35 (1982) p. 13 n. 29; and CUGUSI, Evoluzione (as note 12) p. 74 – 75, who treated brevity under the heading of topoi.

24) George DENNIS, Gregory of Nazianzus and the Byzantine Letter, in: Diakonia: Studies in Honor of Robert T. Meyer, ed. Thomas HALTON and Joseph WILLIMAN (1986) p. 8 – 9. His own letters were described as 'laconic' by Basil of Caesaria, Ep. 19, ed. and tr. Roy J. DEFERRARI (Loeb Library, 1926 – 34) 1 p. 122. They are in an easy, unadorned style, lightened by occasional jokes and avoiding harsh words and unpleasant subjects.

mained the principles governing the writing of literary letters in both East and West throughout the Middle Ages[25]. The rhetorical excerpt 'On letters' in Ms. Paris, lat. 7530, gives as the first rule of letters that they should be clear (*delucidae*), brief, and meaningful[26]. For Poggio Bracciolini, the three features of letters were brevity, elegance, and pleasantness (*festivitas*)[27]. These rules, especially the law of brevity, were not always observed with equal success. Jerome referred to his long letters as *liber* or *libellus,* and Bernard of Clairvaux at the end of his treatise De praecepto et dispensatione, which he composed as a letter to the abbot of Coulombs, said that he had so exceeded the epistolary mode that the work could be called either a book or a letter[28]. The restrictions imposed by the nature of the genre were not therefore severe. Almost any work that met the requirement of the epistolary situation, and was not too long, too heavy in style, or too impersonal in subject-matter, could be called a letter. It is not therefore surprising that it was a popular literary genre among writers of many kinds of works.

The unpublished eighth book of Henry of Huntingdon's History of the English is in the form of three letters which are certainly fictional and might be considered forgeries if taken (as they often are) out of the context for which they were written[29]. After giving in the introduction to this book a brief sum-

---

25) DENNIS, Gregory p. 3–5, argued that a new type of personal literary letter appeared in the fourth century and was used in educated circles, both Christian and pagan.

26) HALM, Rhetores latini (as note 15) p. 589.

27) HARTH, Poggio (as note 18) p. 89.

28) Evaristo ARNS, La technique du livre d'après saint Jérôme (1953) p. 100, and Bernard of Clairvaux, De praecepto et dispensatione XX 61, ed. Jean LECLERCQ and others (1957–77) 3 p. 244. See the Ps-Bernardine letter or treatise, De baptismo (addressed to Hugh of St. Victor) III 15, in: Sancti Bernardi ... opera omnia (1839) 1 col. 1418 BC: *Multa sunt quae ad haec confirmanda concurrunt; sed modus epistolaris cuncta non patitur, nec opus est.* John of Salisbury referred to the *Institutio Traiani* both as a *libellus* and as an *epistola* and gave it an epistolary salutation: Policraticus V 1–2, ed. C. C. J. WEBB (1909) 1 p. 281–282 (see the paper of M. KERNER in the proceedings of this congress, vol. 1, p. 715–738).

29) Henry of Huntingdon, Historia Anglorum, ed. Thomas ARNOLD (Rolls Series 74, 1879) intro. p. xviii-xxiv. I have used MSS. London, British Library, Egerton 3668 (E) and Arundel 48 (A). Two of the letters have been published separately: that to Walter as an appendix to Henry of Huntingdon and the famous letter to Warin, based on Geoffrey of Monmouth, in Chronicles of the Reigns of Stephen, Henry II, and Richard I., 4: The Chronicle of Robert of Torigni, ed. Richard HOWLETT (Rolls Series 82.4, 1889) p. 65–75. See Antonia GRANSDEN, Historical Writing in England c. 550 to c. 1307 (1974) p. 194 and esp. 199–200 on the letter to Warin.

mary of English history, and a defense of the value of writing history, Henry wrote, referring to himself, that 'The author of this work has written a letter to King Henry concerning the series of most powerful kings who were throughout the world down to the present time. He wrote another letter concerning the origin of the kings of the Britons who ruled in this land up until the coming of Julius Caesar or of the English people. He also wrote a third [letter] to his colleague Walter concerning the desires of the world. To insert all these here is neither foreign nor useless. To read them is neither harmful nor burdensome'.

The three letters were addressed respectively to Henry I of England, to an otherwise-unknown Briton named Warin, and to a cleric named Walter, who may have been an archdeacon of Leicester. In each of them Henry referred to brevity, telling the king that he would learn the names and dates of former kings 'by the brevity of what is written below' and Warin, that he was sending excerpts 'very briefly, as it should be in a letter' from a work he had seen at Le Bec – Geoffrey of Monmouth's History of the Kings of England, to which this is one of the first known references –, and, at the end, that 'These are the things I promised you in brief form (*brevibus*), of which if you desire a full treatment (*prolixitatem*) you should consult the big book of Geoffrey of Arthur'. At the end of the letter to Walter, who had died in the meantime, Henry wrote, 'Now I cannot send you a letter, but a brief epitaph or monument must be written with tears'[30].

Henry apparently chose the epistolary mode to treat a type of topic – the high points of history (*De summitatibus rerum*), as he called them in the title of this book – which differed from the material in the other books of his History, and which he wanted to discuss in a serious yet brief and readable form, without having to go into excessive detail. He discussed the fate of earthly rulers in a letter to a king[31], the early history of Britain in a letter to a Briton, and contempt for the world in a letter to a cleric. These letters were certainly

---

30) E 113ᵛ, 113ᵛ–114ʳ, 123ᵛ, 128ʳ, and 134ʳ, and A 119ʳ, 119ᵛ, 130ʳ, 135ᵛ, and 142ᵛ. Some of these excerpts are published in Henry of Huntingdon, Historia p. xxi–xxiii and 319. The first writer to use the work of Geoffrey of Monmouth was Ordericus Vitalis: see his Ecclesiastical History, ed. Marjorie CHIBNALL (Oxford Medieval Texts, 1969–80) 1 p. 47 and 65 and 6 p. 380 n. 5.

31) At the end Henry wrote *Vide igitur rex sapientissime, uide et perpende, quam magnificorum, quam terribilium regum nomina ad nichilum deuenerint* [A: *deuenerunt*] (E 123ᵛ and A 130ʳ).

fictional, in that they were neither sent nor intended to be sent, and at least one of the addressees was made up and another not known personally to Henry, but in terms of his work and purpose, and the expectations of his readers, they are authentic examples of the epistolary genre.

The forging of letters in Antiquity and the Middle Ages must be seen as part of the larger problem of apocryphal and pseudepigraphical writings[32]. So many works at that time appeared anonymously or under false names, imitated other works, or sailed under some sort of false colours, that it may be wise to drop the terms forgery and fraud and to call them impostures or fictions[33]. Salvian said that his treatise To the Church was attributed to the apostle Timothy out of humility, since under his own name it would lose its power to help[34], and Abelard said in his Yes and No that 'Many apocryphal works are entitled with the names of saints in order that they may have authority'[35]. Whether such works are called frauds or fictions depends to some extent on the views and causes they promoted, some of which were less innocent and disinterested than others. The letters attributed to Alexander, Hannibal, and Philip of Macedon, for instance, had a political as well as a rhetorical and literary purpose[36], and scholars since the eighteenth century have devoted much time and effort to

---

32) Wolfgang SPEYER, Religiöse Pseudepigraphie und literarische Fälschung im Altertum, Jb. für Antike und Christentum 8–9 (1965–66) p. 88 (rp. in: Pseudepigraphie in der heidnischen und jüdisch-christlichen Antike, ed. Norbert BROX [Wege der Forschung 484, 1977]) and SPEYER, Die literarische Fälschung im heidnischen und christlichen Altertum (Handbuch der Altertumswissenschaft I 2, 1971) p. 13–15. Speyer's 'schematically ordered classifications' and 'tendency ... toward setting up strict categories' were criticized by Bruce METZGER, Literary Forgeries and Canonical Pseudepigrapha, Journal of Biblical Literature 91 (1972) p. 19.

33) See for instance Ronald SYME, Fraud and Imposture, in: Pseudepigraphia, 1. Pseudopythagoria – Lettres de Platon – Littérature pseudépigraphique juive (Entretiens sur l'Antiquité classique 18, 1972) p. 3–17, esp. 13 (rp. in: Pseudepigraphie, ed. BROX, p. 295–310).

34) Salvian, Ep. VIII 16, ed. F. PAULY (CSEL 8, 1883) p. 221–222, tr. Jeremiah F. O'SULLIVAN (Fathers of the Church 3, 1947) p. 262.

35) Peter Abelard, Sic et non, prol., ed. Blanche BOYER and Richard MCKEON (1976–77) p. 91.

36) Reinhold MERKELBACH, in: Griechische Papyri der Hamburger Staats- und Universitäts-Bibliothek (Veröffentlichungen aus der Hamburger Staats- und Universitäts-Bibliothek 4, 1954) p. 52–55. PETER, Brief (as note 2) p. 172, considered the so-called letters of Trebellius Pollo and Vespicius to be forgeries because they promoted falsehoods as well as serving as rhetorical displays.

plucking the false plumage from these and other so-called letters of Antiquity[37].

Apocryphal epistles presented a special problem for early Christians[38]. They included the epistles of the Apostles (or Testament of Our Lord in Galilee) and to the Laodiceans and the letter from Christ to King Abgar of Edessa, which probably originated in the third century and was widely accepted as authentic in the East (where it still has some defenders), though it was rejected at an early date in the West[39]. The correspondence between Paul and Seneca dates from the fourth century. Owing to its acceptance by Jerome and Augustine, it greatly enhanced Seneca's prestige as a philosopher and moralist, though the legend of his conversion to Christianity originated much later, in the fourteenth century. These letters were probably not a school exercise, as has been said, but a piece of pseudepigraphical propaganda, perhaps by more than one writer, whose purpose was to spread the values of educated Christians in the fourth century and to stress the need to read Paul's letters and to have a rhetorical education[40].

Caesarius of Arles referred to homilies as 'letters sent to us from our homeland' in heaven[41], and throughout the Middle Ages letters from divine

---

37) Alessandro RONCONI, Introduzione alla letteratura pseudoepigrafa (1955), rp. in his Filologia e linguistica (1968) p. 246–249. On the relative rarity of Latin as contrasted with Greek pseudepigraphy, see Gino FUNAIOLI, Studi di letteratura antica (1946–48) 1 p. 165–168; see also CUGUSI, Evoluzione (as note 12) p. 133–135, on forged Latin letters.

38) Montague Rhodes JAMES, The Apocryphal New Testament ([2]1955) p. 476–503, who suggested (p. 476) that epistles were less often forged than narratives and apocalypses because they were harder to forge and easier to detect.

39) A brief account of and bibliography on each of these can be found in The Oxford Dictionary of the Christian Church, ed. F. L. CROSS, ([2]1977) p. 5, 799, and 1353. In the late fourth century the pilgrim Egeria saw the letters from Christ to Abgar and from Abgar to Christ at Edessa: Itinerarium Egeriae, XVII 1 and XIX 8–19, CC 175, p. 58 and 60–62.

40) Epistolae Senecae ad Paulum et Pauli ad Senecam «quae vocantur», ed. Claude BARLOWE (Papers and Monographs of the American Academy in Rome 10, 1938) p. 69 and 80 and (on Alcuin's edition of the correspondence) 94–104; and Laura BOCCIOLINI PALAGI, Il carteggio apocrifo di Seneca e San Paolo (Accademia toscana di scienze e lettere "La Columbaria", Studi 46, 1978) p. 11–16, see also p. 35–54, relating these letters to other pseudepigraphical writings of the fourth century.

41) Germain MORIN, Un nouveau recueil inédit d'homélies de S. Césaire d'Arles, Revue bénédictine 16 (1899) p. 243. On epistolary sermons in the thirteenth century, see Monika ASZTALOS, Les lettres de direction et les sermons épistolaires de Pierre de Da-

figures, adapted to various needs, appeared from time to time and were read from pulpits. The best-known and most persistent was the letter from Christ concerning the observance of Sunday, which first appeared in Spain in the sixth century and was incorporated into the homiliary of Toledo and of which versions cropped up all over the Christian world until the sixteenth century[42]. The preacher Eustace of Flay used it in the early thirteenth century in his campaign to suppress commercial activity on Sunday in England, according to Roger of Hoveden, who also cited 'the epistle of Toledo' prophecying the eventual victory of the Christians over the Moslems and Jews[43]. The annals of Worcester and Tewkesbury both recorded under the year 1206 that a letter was brought to the king by a cleric on behalf of the Virgin Mary[44]. Letters from the Devil also appeared in the thirteenth century. A long letter addressed by the Devil to all prelates and clerics circulated in the fourteenth century[45], and the

---

cie, in: The Editing of Theological and Philosophical Texts from the Middle Ages, ed. Monika ASZTALOS (Acta Universitatis Stockholmiensis: Studia latina Stockholmiensia 30, 1986) p. 161 – 184, esp. 161 and 166. Geoffrey of Auxerre incorporated three treatises in epistolary form into his commentary on the Song of Songs, V, prol., ed. Ferruccio GASTALDELLI (Temi e testi 19 – 20, 1974) 2 p. 361, see intro. 1 p. xii and xxxviii – xlvii.

42) Hippolyte DELEHAYE, Note sur la légende de la lettre du Christ tombée du ciel (1899) rp. in his Mélanges d'hagiographie grecque et latine (Subsidia hagiographica 42, 1966) p. 150 – 178; Robert PRIEBSCH, Letter from Heaven on the Observance of the Lord's Day (1936), with an edition of the text on p. 35 – 37; Clovis BRUNEL, Versions espagnole, provençale et française de la lettre du Christ tombée du ciel, Analecta Bollandiana 68 (1950 = Mélanges Paul Peeters 2) p. 383 – 396; and Étienne DELARUELLE, La lettre tombée du ciel sur l'autel de Saint-Baudile à Nîmes, in: Carcassonne et sa région. Actes des XLIe et XXIVe congrès d'études régionales tenus par la Fédération historique du Languedoc méditerranéen et du Roussillon et par la Fédération des Sociétés académiques et savantes de Languedoc-Pyrénées-Gascogne. Carcassonne 17 – 19 Mai 1968 (1970) p. 47 – 55, with an edition of another version of the text on p. 55.

43) Roger of Hoveden, Chronica, ed. William STUBBS (Rolls Series 51, 1868 – 71) 4 p. 167 – 172, with an edition of the text on p. 167 – 169. See William R. JONES, The Heavenly Letter in Medieval England, Medievalia et Humanistica 6 (1975) p. 166 – 172.

44) Annales monasticae, ed. Henry LUARD (Rolls Series 36, 1864 – 1869) 1 p. 58, and 4 p. 393 – 394. See JONES, Heavenly Letter p. 178 n. 48.

45) Wilhelm WATTENBACH, Über erfundene Briefe in Handschriften des Mittelalters, besonders Teufelsbriefe (SB Berlin 1892.9) p. 91 – 123; JONES, Heavenly Letter (as note 43) p. 174. I have not seen the unpublished Ph. D. dissertation (Northwestern University) of Helen C. FENG, Devil's Letters: Their History and Significance in Church and Society: 1100 – 1500. According to Professor Robert Lerner, to whom I am indebted for bringing this work to my attention, Devil's letters appeared in the thirteenth century and spread in anti-papal circles in the fourteenth century.

letter from Lentulus, which gave a physical description of Christ, drawn in part from earlier materials, continued to be cited even after Valla declared it a forgery[46]. John of Landsberg's Letter from Jesus Christ to the Premonstratensian nuns of Hensberch, which was in essence a moral treatise on the Christian life, was translated into Spanish, French, and English in the sixteenth and seventeenth centuries[47]. Less exalted causes were also promoted by apocryphal letters. The letters written by Ademar of Chabannes to prove the apostolicity of St. Martial were immediately recognized as forgeries[48], but scholars are still disagreed over the precise date and purpose of the alleged letter of Alexius Comnenus to Robert of Flanders. It seems to have been put together between 1090 and 1105 on the basis of the sermons of Urban II, a catalogue of relics in Constantinople, and information available in Flanders, but its substantial authenticity still has at least one defender[49]. Even more puzzling is the letter of Prester John to Manuel Comnenus, which first appeared in the West in the 1160s and of which at least five interpolated versions, in addition to the original, survive in over a hundred manuscripts[50]. It has been seen as an encouragement for crusaders, a criticism

---

46) See JAMES, Apocryphal New Testament (as note 38) p. 477–478, who dated it not before the thirteenth century, and Cora E. LUTZ, The Letter of Lentulus Describing Christ, The Yale University Library Gazette 50 (1975) p. 91–97, who dated it early fourteenth century and mentioned 75 manuscripts.

47) John of Landsberg, A Letter from Jesus Christ, tr. John GRIFFITHS (1981).

48) Epistola de apostolatu sancti Martialis and the apocryphal letter of Pope John XIX in MIGNE PL 141 col. 87–112 and 1149–50. See Louis SALTET, Une prétendue lettre de Jean XIX sur saint Martial, Bulletin de la littérature ecclésiastique 26 (1925) p. 117–139; Robert Lee WOLFF, How the News was brought from Byzantium to Angoulême; or, The Pursuit of a Hare in an Oxcart, in: Essays Presented to Sir Steven Runciman (Byzantine and Modern Greek Studies 4, 1978) p. 163–175; and Richard LANDES, A Libellus from St. Martial of Limoges Written in the Time of Ademar of Chabannes (989–1034), Scriptorium 37 (1983) p. 178–204 (esp. 189), with a new edition of the papal letter (p. 200–201).

49) Alexius Comnenus, Ad Robertum I Flandriae comitem epistola spuria, ed. Paul RIANT (1879). See Paul RIANT, Inventaire critique des lettres historiques des croisades, Archives de l'Orient latin 1 (1881) p. 71–89, no. 31, and, for recent views concerning this letter, Hans Eberhard MAYER, Geschichte der Kreuzzüge (⁶1985) p. 255.

50) Friedrich ZARNCKE, Der Priester Johannes (Abh. Leipzig 7.8 and 8.1, 1876–79) p. 872–908 (= 46–82 of independent publication). See Bernard HAMILTON, Prester John and the Three Kings of Cologne, in: Studies in Medieval History presented to R. H. C. Davis, ed. Henry MAYR-HARTING and Robert I. MOORE (1985) p. 179–191, who cited the unpublished work of A. A. VASILIEV, Prester John, Legend and History,

of contemporary western society, an anti-Byzantine diatribe, a contribution to the dossier of the Three Kings at Cologne, and a piece of propaganda in support of Frederick Barbarossa against Alexander III, whose reply, written in 1177, may have been a counterblast, when his position was secure, rather than a serious effort to get in touch with Prester John[51].

The degree of confidence with which these letters are labelled forgeries depends on a knowledge, which is often lacking, of why they were written and how they were seen by contemporaries. If Alexander really believed that he was writing to a great monarch in the East named Prester John, his letter is authentic, even if it circulated in the West. If both he and his readers knew that Prester John did not exist, then the letter is a literary fiction, but perhaps not fraudulent. The same can be said of the three letters attributed to Frederick Barbarossa, Archbishop Hillin of Trier, and Pope Hadrian IV, of which the content varies but the consistent style betrays their single authorship[52]. Some letters, based on the works of other writers, may be called mosaic-forgeries, like the letters in the Salzburg formulary, which include so many fragments from other works (in this case Jerome) that their real character is in doubt[53], and others are imitation-forgeries, inspired by literary convention or genuine admiration. Jaeger has suggested that at least the prologue to the Historia calamitatum may have been written in imitation of Abelard[54]. The final verdict on the letters attributed to Abelard and Heloise is still not in, and may never be. Silvestre has recently marshalled the arguments against their authen-

---

and other relevant literature, to which can be added Karl HELLEINER, Prester John's Letter: A Mediaeval Utopia, The Phoenix 13 (1959) p. 47 – 57, supporting the view (also held by Vasiliev) that the letter 'was first composed in Greek' (p. 56).

51) ZARNCKE, Priester Johannes p. 941 – 944 (= 115 – 118), which is accepted as authentic in JL no. 12942, but on which see HAMILTON, Prester John p. 189 – 190.

52) Norbert HÖING, Die "Trierer Stilübungen." Ein Denkmal der Frühzeit Kaiser Friedrich Barbarossas, AfD 1 (1955) p. 257 – 329, who maintained that these letters were written as school exercises. This and other examples are cited by C. Stephen JAEGER, The Prologue to the Historia calamitatum and the "Authenticity Question", Euphorion 74 (1980) p. 11 n. 39.

53) Bernhard BISCHOFF, Salzburger Formelbücher und Briefe aus Tassilonischer und Karolingischer Zeit (SB München 1973.4) p. 55 – 56, on which see Bengt LÖFSTEDT und Carol LANHAM, Zu den neugefundenen Salzburger Formelbüchern und Briefen, Eranos 63 (1975) p. 96 – 97.

54) JAEGER, Prologue (as note 52) esp. p. 14, though in his conclusion he defended its authenticity.

ticity, a position formerly held by Benton, who in the paper presented at this congress maintains that they were all written by Abelard[55].

Even if the letters are genuine in the sense that they were written by Abelard and Heloise, and sent between them, they were revised into a literary work which was intended to be read in its entirety as a retrospective narrative. The Alexander letters formed part of the Alexander romance[56], and the paired letters in Ovid's Heroides 'clearly contain the potentiality for the kind of dramatic development that can be seen in the best epistolary novels'[57]. Sequences of letters which amount to novelle can be found in rhetorical collections of the thirteenth century, like that of Boncompagno of Siena, where Benson drew attention to a set of seven clearly fictional letters, of a somewhat suggestive nature, between a community of nuns and their abbess-elect, on one side, and a bishop and his chamberlain, on the other[58]. They point the way both towards Boccaccio and towards the type of epistolary novel that enjoyed a great vogue in the eighteenth and nineteenth centuries and is still occasionally written today. Such works can consist of either an exchange of letters (which critics call a 'Briefwechselroman'), as in Boncompagno, or of the letters of a single writer[59]. Richardson's Pamela, of which the first two volumes appeared in 1740, was the first full-scale epistolary novel. This form, according to Iser, 'offered itself as a means whereby Richardson could capture the introspection he sought to portray ... The letter form facilitates this self-examination insofar as it externalizes inner emotions'[60]. Richardson himself remarked on 'this lively present-tense manner' in Clarissa Harlow, and critics have drawn attention

---

55) Hubert SILVESTRE, L'idylle d'Abélard et Héloise: la part du roman, Acad. Belgique 5 S. 71 (1985.5) p. 157–200. For a German version of this article see below, p. 121–165.

56) MERKELBACH, Griechische Papyri (as note 36) p. 52–54.

57) Duncan KENNEDY, The Epistolary Mode and the First of Ovid's Heroides, The Classical Quarterly 34 (1984) p. 414.

58) Robert BENSON, Protohumanism and Narrative Technique in Early Thirteenth-Century "Ars Dictaminis", in: Boccaccio: Secoli di vita. Atti del Congresso Internazionale: Boccaccio 1975. Università di California, Los Angeles, 17–19 ottobre, 1975, ed. Marga COTTINO-JONES and Edward F. TUTTLE (1977) p. 42–50. On Boncompagno and his views of the art of letter-writing, including the need to lie, see Ronald G. WITT, Boncompagno and the Defense of Rhetoric, Journal of Medieval and Renaissance Studies 16 (1986) p. 1–31.

59) Bertie ROMBERG, Studies in the Narrative Technique of the First-Person Novel (1962) p. 46–55.

60) Wolfgang ISER, The Implied Reader: Patterns of Communication in Prose Fiction from Bunyan to Beckett (1974) p. 61.

to the immediacy, verisimilitude, sense of personal involvement, and potential for drama in a series or exchange of letters[61]. Such considerations were not lost on the writers of letters in the Middle Ages, and many of their epistolary fictions, including the letters of Christ and Prester John – and possibly also those of Abelard and Heloise –, should be seen not as conscious deceptions and exploitations of credulity but in the same light as the works of Richardson, Rousseau, Goethe, and other writers whose works belong in the realm of literary imagination more than that of historical truth.

III

It is time to return from fiction to fact, however, and to the concerns of Cyprian and John of Rouen for the veracity of their letters. The greatest practical dangers of fraud or forgery of medieval letters lay not in the false contents or attributions of fictional letters but in the composition, writing, delivery, revision, and preservation of letters, to which I now turn[62].

Most letters in Antiquity and the Middle Ages were dictated to a secretary, scribe, or notary who took them down on tablets, either word for word or in shorthand, and later wrote them on sheets of papyrus or parchment, or occasionally on tablets of wood or of ivory or wood covered with wax[63]. Some

---

61) Godfrey Frank SINGER, The Epistolary Novel (1933) p. 47 and 55; Frank Gees BLACK, The Epistolary Novel in the Late Eighteenth Century (University of Oregon Monographs: Studies in Literature and Philology 2, 1940) p. 51; ROMBERG, Studies (as note 59) p. 206 (and 218 for the quotation from Richardson); and KENNEDY, Epistolary Mode (as note 57) p. 413.

62) Among other works cited in CONSTABLE, Letters (as note 10) p. 42–62, see especially Wilhelm WATTENBACH, Das Schriftwesen im Mittelalter (^{3}1896); Eligius DEKKERS, Les autographes des Pères latins, in: Colligere Fragmenta. Festschrift Alban Dold (Texte und Arbeiten herausgegeben durch die Erzabtei Beuron I 2, 1952) p. 127 n. 3, who said that he knew no certain use in patristic Latin of dictare in the sense of 'compose'; Hartmut HOFFMANN, Zur mittelalterlichen Brieftechnik, in: Spiegel der Geschichte. Festgabe für Max Braubach (1964) p. 141–170; and Bernard GUENÉE, L'historien par les mots, in: Le métier d'historien au moyen âge. Études sur l'historiographie médiévale, ed. Bernard GUENÉE (Publications de la Sorbonne. Études 13, 1977) p. 8–10.

63) The letters described by Alan K. BOWMAN, The Roman Writing Tablets from Vindolanda (1983) p. 18–22, were on thin slices of wood (not covered with wax), written in two columns, with the name of the sender and addressee in the first line and (if the letter was written by a scribe) with the final line of greeting in the hand of the sender.

authors dictated in full, but others gave their secretaries only a draft or sketch or simply verbal instructions, which left many openings for both misunderstandings and distortions. The meaning of the term *dictare* seems to have changed from 'dictate' in Antiquity to 'compose' in the Middle Ages, and it was increasingly used in contrast to *scribere*, which referred to the physical act of writing[64]. The art of dictamen, or letter writing, governed the composing rather than the writing of letters, and the role of the dictator and that of the scribe or notary were distinct, even when they were performed (as they sometimes were) by the same person. Bernard of Clairvaux distinguished four steps in preparing a letter when he wrote that, 'The mind (*ingenium*) should stop from composing, the lips from speaking, the fingers from writing, [and] the messengers from running'[65].

The role of secretaries and dictatores in writing letters is one of the most disputed points in medieval epistolography. Many letters were composed by secretaries in the early Middle Ages[66], and an ever-increasing number as the rules and forms of letter-writing were defined and established in the twelfth and thirteenth centuries. Bernhard Schmeidler, who was one of the greatest though most controversial students of medieval epistolography, held that any unified letter-collection, even when ostensibly written by several authors,

---

64) See A. ERNOUT, Dictare "Dicter", allem. Dichter, Revue des études latines 29 (1951) p. 155 – 161, and other references in CONSTABLE, Letters (as note 10) p. 42 – 44, to which can be added Jean LECLERCQ, Saint Bernard et ses secrétaires (1951) rp. in his Recueil d'études sur saint Bernard et ses écrits (Storia e letteratura 92, 104, 114, 1962 – 69) 1 p. 3 – 11 and 23 – 25; and LECLERCQ, Saint Pierre Damien ermite et homme d'église (Uomini e dottrini 8, 1960) p. 155.

65) Bernard, Ep. 90.1, ed. LECLERCQ (as note 28) 7 p. 237. See Christopher R. CHENEY, Gervase, Abbot of Prémontré: A Medieval Letter-Writer, Bulletin of the John Rylands Library 33 (1950 – 1) p. 29, where Hugh of Prémontré referred to 'some letters composed (*dictatas*) by him [Gervase] and written by me', and Caesarius of Heisterbach, Dialogus miraculorum IV 94, ed. Josef STRANGE (1851) 1 p. 261, referring to a letter both composed and written by a nun. Alan of Lille, Anticlaudianus V 273 – 277, ed. R. BOSSUAT (Textes philosophiques du moyen âge 1, 1955) p. 131, distinguished the pen (*calamus*, which he described as *reticens scriptoris carta*) from the scribe (*scriba*) and from the author (*actor*). See WATTENBACH, Schriftwesen (as note 62) p. 459.

66) Dag NORBERG, Qui a composé les lettres de Saint Grégoire le Grand?, Studi medievali 3a ser. 21 (1980) p. 1 – 17, esp. 12 – 13. The letters composed by Gregory the Great himself can be distinguished from those written in his chancery on the basis of the stricter use of regular *clausulae* by the chancery than by the pope.

depended upon the activities of a single dictator[67]. Dictatores who were responsible for composing and collecting as well as writing letters could easily forge or falsify them. The archbishop of Ravenna wrote to Pope Eugene III that he had imprisoned a former papal scribe 'who when he had the position of dictator (*locum dictandi*) in your court presumed with proud audacity to compose (*componere*) many false letters'[68]. Some writers developed and took pride in their imitative skills, without necessarily any evil intent. Hugh of Prémontré in the early thirteenth century both wrote and collected the letters of his abbot Gervase, who was well-known 'for his style of speaking and of composing (*dictandi*)', and he prayed to imitate Gervase 'both in way of life and in the knowledge of composing (*dictandi scientia*)'[69].

An ambition of this sort may have inspired the best-known epistolary forger of the twelfth century, Nicholas of Montiéramey, who was accused by Bernard of Clairvaux in 1151 of sending 'many false letters under our false seal (*multae litterae falsatae sub falsato sigillo nostro*)' and later of having three seals in his possession: 'one his own, the other the prior's, and the third ours, and that not the old one but the new one, which I was recently forced to change owing to his deceits and secret frauds'[70].

Bernard went on to say that 'no one more richly deserves perpetual punishment', but the real nature of Nicholas' fault seems to have been not that he forged the seals but that he misused them and thus betrayed the trust put in him by those for whom he wrote letters. His falseness probably lay in authenticating letters which misrepresented the meaning and intentions of Bernard, for whom the seal was a symbol of integrity. In an interesting passage in his

---

67) Bernhard SCHMEIDLER, Kaiser Heinrich IV. und seine Helfer im Investiturstreit (1927) p. 344, and ID., Die Briefsammlung Froumunds von Tegernsee, HJb 62–69 (1949) p. 200–201.

68) Hermann KALBFUSS, Eine Bologneser Ars dictandi des XII. Jahrhunderts, QFIAB 16.2 (1914) p. 19. This letter may be a rhetorical exercise, but there is no reason to doubt its evidence about the position of the *dictator*.

69) CHENEY, Gervase (as note 65) p. 29.

70) Bernard, Epp. 284 and 298, ed. LECLERCQ (as note 28) 8 p. 199 und 214. Nicholas as a monk of Clairvaux would not have had a seal of his own, and the first seal may be Bernard's old seal, which Bernard had given him. On Nicholas, see The Letters of Peter the Venerable, ed. Giles CONSTABLE (Harvard Historical Studies 78, 1967) 2 p. 326–329, and John BENTON, in: Dictionnaire de Spiritualité 11 (1982) p. 255–259, who said that the most charitable interpretation was that Bernard considered Nicholas to have betrayed his confidence.

second sermon on the Nativity, Bernard compared man's loss of his likeness to God to the breaking of a seal by a falsifier (*falsarius*), who destroyed the truth, unity, and justice for which the seal stood[71]. A letter of Arnulf of Lisieux written to Nicholas in about 1170 shows that he was involved in another suspected case of forgery, this time by a young canon of Troyes who was accused of obtaining money 'by the falseness of a letter in the name of the count' of Champagne, that is, by forging or making false use of the count's seal. Arnulf also said that he himself had received 'from him' (apparently the canon but perhaps the count) a second letter of the count which he recognized from the style to be the work of Nicholas[72], whose talents remained in demand even after his falling-out with Bernard of Clairvaux. He was evidently a brilliant adapter and imitator[73]. Some of his sermons and letters are still hard to distinguish from authentic works by the writers in whose names he wrote[74].

Most of Bernard's letters were written by his secretaries, according to the pioneering study of Bernard's chancery by Rassow, who argued that they were based on directions given by Bernard rather than texts dictated in full[75]. He was unable to see all his letters even after they were written, and he wrote to Peter the Venerable, apologizing for a sharply-worded letter, that his scribes sometimes forgot his meaning (*sensum*) and sharpened their style beyond measure[76]. Busy men have at all times relied on assistants to draft and sometimes to compose their letters, and some of these inevitably fail to express

---

71) Bernard, In nativitate sermo II 3, ed. LECLERCQ (as note 28) 4 p. 253.

72) Arnulf of Lisieux, Ep. 66, ed. Frank BARLOW (Camden Society 3 S. 61, 1939) p. 116–118. The outcome of this case is unknown.

73) According to JAEGER, Prologue (as note 52) pp. 12–13, Nicholas's borrowings 'fall under the heading of literary imitation'.

74) At least two of Bernard's sermons (De diversis 19 and 93) were composed by Nicholas: see his letter to Peter of Celle, Ep. 1.50, in MIGNE PL 202 col. 474–475 A, where Nicholas said *Furtum enim feceram propter vos, nunc furatus sum me mihi pro vobis* and deplored his work as a writer, which was incompatible with his vocation as a monk, and Geoffrey of Auxerre, Expositio III, ed. GASTALDELLI (as note 41) 1 p. 191: *Scriptus est sermo, quem super hoc ipse dixit, etsi non ipse dictauit* (see intro. 1 p. liii–liv).

75) Peter RASSOW, Die Kanzlei St. Bernhards von Clairvaux [1], StMGBO 34 (1913) p. 67–84, esp. 75. See also Jean LECLERCQ, Recherches sur les sermons sur les Cantiques de Saint Bernard, III. Les sermons sur les Cantiques ont-ils été prononcés? (1955) rp. in his Recueil (as note 64) 1, p. 193–212, and ID., Recherches sur la collection des épîtres de saint Bernard, Cahiers de civilisation médiévale 14 (1971) p. 205–219, esp. 207–210 on the role of secretaries.

76) Bernard, Ep. 387, ed. LECLERCQ (as note 28) 8 p. 355.

the intention of the sender, and may in a real sense be described as false, but not necessarily as forged.

Perhaps in part to avoid these dangers, letters from the eleventh century on were increasingly written in accord with the rules laid down in the manuals of letter-writing known as *artes dictaminis*, which were often accompanied by collections of letters designed both to illustrate the points made in the manuals and to serve as models for letter-writing. The precise distinction between collections of literary and model letters, formularies, letter-books, and registers is unclear, and it is not known just how such collections were compiled and used. I have seen a work published in 1983 entitled the Director's and Officer's Complete Letter Book, which contains, according to the introduction, '133 ready-to-use model letters and 988 alternate phrases and sentences' which can be adapted 'with hardly any effort' to meet specific situations[77]. The letters are described as 'proven' and 'field-tested', and many of them are written on the stationary of well-known companies, but it is hard to be sure that they were actually sent or, even harder, to know what to call a letter derived from one of these models, even with alternate phrases and sentences. Paradoxically, the copy may, because it is sent, be a more genuine letter than the model on which it is based.

Medieval letter-collections present many similar puzzles. Some scholars believe that a coherent collection found in manuscripts going back close to the time of composition can be relied upon as evidence of the authenticity of individual letters, but spurious letters are found in some of the oldest and best-known collections, including those of Jerome, who inserted fictional letters that were never sent into his own collection, Fulbert of Chartres, and Hildegard of Bingen[78]. Gilbert Foliot included in his collection the drafts of

---

77) Director's and Officer's Complete Letter Book, ed. J. A. VAN DUYN ([2]1983) p. 7.
78) On Jerome: D. DE BRUYNE, Notes sur les lettres de saint Augustin, RHE 23 (1927) p. 528; Giorgio PASQUALI, Storia della tradizione e critica del testo ([2]1952) p. 456; and ARNS, Technique du livre (as note 28) p. 102–103; on Fulbert: Frederick BEHRENDS, Two Spurious Letters in the Fulbert Collection, Revue bénédictine 80 (1970) p. 253–275; on Hildegard: Bernhard SCHMEIDLER, Bemerkungen zum Corpus der Briefe der hl. Hildegard von Bingen, in: Corona Quernea. Festgabe Karl Strecker (Schriften des Reichsinstituts für ältere deutsche Geschichtskunde [MGH] 6, 1941) p. 364–365, and Marianna SCHRADER and Adelgundis FÜHRKÖTTER, Die Echtheit des Schrifttums der heiligen Hildegard von Bingen (1956) esp. p. 26–103 on the letters, defending the authenticity of the works attributed to her. Joseph DE GHELLINCK, Patristique et moyen âge. Études d'histoire littéraire et doctrinale (Museum Lessianum

letters which were never sent, and Petrarch revised some of his letters so fully that it is hard to say whether they are fabricated or real[79]. The forger of the letters of St. Nilus was described as 'a rather unintelligent late admirer of Nilus whose purpose was merely to produce an edition of the great man's correspondence'[80]. Serious questions have been raised about the letters transmitted by Widukind, and the letters of Gasperino Barzizza, which were accepted as authentic even by so stern a critic as Bertalot, are now considered fictional[81]. Inclusion in a collection is no guarantee, therefore, of either authenticity or authorship.

The same is true of formularies and even of registers, into which forgeries − or documents issued contrary to the intentions of the issuer − were occasionally inserted[82]. Langlois wrote that 'Many formularies were made up in total or in part of genuine letters (lettres véritables) which the dictator who compiled them simply expurgated of excessively detailed particulars', and the Liber epistolaris of Richard of Bury, according to Denholm-Young, contained 'real letters, usually with the dates omitted and the names reduced to initials'[83]. But

---

6−7 and 9, 1946−48) 2 p. 205, said that pseudo-materials were often inserted into collections, especially those not compiled by the writers.

79) Adrian MOREY and C. N. L. BROOKE, Gilbert Foliot and His Letters (Cambridge Studies in Medieval Life and Thought N. S. 11, 1965) p. 24−30; Hans BARON, From Petrarch to Leonardo Bruni (1968) p. 15−17; and WITT, Medieval "Ars Dictaminis" (as note 23) p. 30−31.

80) Alan CAMERON, The Authenticity of the Letters of St. Nilus of Ancyra, Greek, Roman, and Byzantine Studies 17 (1976) p. 194.

81) Anna NÜRNBERGER, Die Glaubwürdigkeit der bei Widukind überlieferten Briefe (Quellenstudien aus dem historischen Seminar der Universität Innsbruck 5.2, 1913) p. 73; Ludwig BERTALOT, Studien zum italienischen und deutschen Humanismus, ed. Paul O. KRISTELLER (Storia e letteratura 129−130, 1975) 2 p. 31−102; and Cecil H. CLOUGH, The Cult of Antiquity: Letters and Letter Collections, in: Cultural Aspects of the Italian Renaissance. Essays in Honour of Paul Oskar Kristeller, ed. Cecil CLOUGH (1976) p. 37 and 40. On the forged correspondence between Virgil and Maecenas published by Pier Candido Decembrio in 1426, see Remigio SABBADINI, Le scoperte dei codici latini e greci ne' secoli XIV e XV, ed. Eugenio GARIN (Biblioteca storica del Rinascimento 4, ²1967) p. 176.

82) Michael T. CLANCHY, From Memory to Written Record: England, 1066−1307 (1979) p. 140.

83) C. V. LANGLOIS, Lettres missives, suppliques, pétitions, doléances, in: Histoire littéraire de la France 36.2 (1927) p. 539; The Liber Epistolaris of Richard de Bury, ed. N. DENHOLM-YOUNG (1950) p. xi, who defined the Liber Epistolaris as 'an unofficial formulary of Latin letters' (p. xxv).

Richard himself was apparently taken in by two letters of Henry of Winchester and Brian Fitz-Count, which are still cited as authentic in biographies of King Stephen but were probably exercises in Latin composition on set themes drawn from genuine earlier letters[84]. It is also hard to accept without
* hesitation the 'secret' letter of Siboto of Falkenstein in 1180/90 ordering the murder of an enemy, even though it is found in the Codex Falkensteinensis[85]. Some formularies may have consisted entirely of invented letters[86], and many were mixed bags made up of material, real and fictional, that came to the hand of the compiler[87]. A letter-writer who made use of a formulary might therefore be copying an authentic earlier letter or one that had been invented by the dictator. Since almost no work has been done on how formularies were used, however, and there are no examples of genuine letters certainly based on formulary models, there are still many unanswered questions about this aspect of the composition of letters.

---

84) N. DENHOLM-YOUNG, Richard de Bury (1287–1345) and the Liber Epistolaris (1937), revised rp. in his Collected Papers (1969) p. 22–24, and John TAYLOR, Letters and Letter Collections in England, 1300–1420, Nottingham Medieval Studies 24 (1980) p. 60–61 (mentioning this and another collection including real and fictional letters). The letters were published from a seventeenth-century transcript by H. W. C. DAVIS in the English Historical Review 25 (1910) p. 297–303, and were cited as authentic in R. H. C. DAVIS, King Stephen, 1135–1154 (1967) p. 67; H. A. CRONNE, The Reign of Stephen 1135–1154: Anarchy in England (1970) p. 120; and Ralph V. TURNER, The Miles Literatus in Twelfth- and Thirteenth-Century England: How Rare a Phenomenon?, American Historical Review 83 (1978) p. 936. If they are later rhetorical exercises, they show a remarkable sense of history, as does the form fund-raising letter ascribed to Abbot Geoffrey of Crowland (1109–c. 1124) in the continuation (attributed to Peter of Blois) of the forged Historia Croylandensis of Ingulf, in Rerum anglicarum scriptores veteres, ed. William FULMAN (1684) p. 113, on which see W. G. SEARLE, Ingulf and the Historia Croylandensis (Cambridge Antiquarian Society: Octavo Publications 27, 1894) p. 2 and 49–50. The forger, working in the mid-fourteenth or early fifteenth century, may have made use of an authentic letter.

85) Codex Falkensteinensis. Die Rechtsaufzeichnungen der Grafen von Falkenstein, ed. Elisabeth NOICHL (Quellen und Erörterungen zur bayerischen Geschichte N. F. 29, 1978), p. 163–164, no. 183 (with a full bibliography). The verb deponere in this context clearly means 'dispose of', and carrina means a payment for murder. It is amazing that such a document, if authentic, found its way into the Codex.

86) BENSON, Protohumanism (as note 58) p. 36, argued that the number of invented letters in formularies increased after 1200.

87) Paul JOACHIMSOHN, Aus der Vorgeschichte des "Formulare und deutsch Rhetorica", ZfdA 37 (1893) p. 33, and TAYLOR, Letters (as note 84) p. 59.

How letters were authenticated after they were written also poses problems, since the methods of authentication were fewer and less secure than those for charters and official documents. In Antiquity it usually took the form of a line of greeting or subscription in the sender's own hand, which was presumably known to the recipient[88]. Cyprian specifically asked the clergy of Rome to examine the writing and subscription of the letter he returned. As time went on, increasing use was made of seals[89], but they were subject to misuse as well as fraudulent imitation, as the cases of Nicholas of Montiéramey and the young canon of Troyes show. Since Lanfranc had no doubt that the seal on the letter brought by Robert 'the colt' was genuine, the point at issue was whether Robert had used it improperly. Most letters, unlike charters, were closed by the seal, which had to be broken before the letter could be read[90]. The bishop of Soissons was suspicious of an open letter from Bernard of Clairvaux, who sent in its place a closed letter, explaining that 'In the other one I only thought that a letter addressed to several people is not customarily closed with wax'[91].

The style of writing was another recognized, but more dangerous, criterion of authenticity. Bernard in two well-known passages in letters to the king of France and the bishop of Noyon-Tournai said that 'My seal was not to hand, but whoever reads this will recognize the style, since I composed it myself' and that 'Let the manner of speech be in place of a seal, since it was not to hand'[92]. Style could also be misleading, however, as the work of Nicholas of Montiéramey shows. It was in the nature of epistolary style to be flexible and imitative and to reflect the styles not only of the author, dictator, or an admired

---

88) Among the works cited note 62 above, see especially DEKKERS, Autographes p. 128, and HOFFMANN, Brieftechnik p. 154–156.

89) Peter Damiani, Ep. I 11, in MIGNE PL 144 col. 214, wrote to Pope Alexander II that since he did not have his seal to hand he had told his nephew to see to it that the letter acquired 'the certitude of a seal'.

90) Carl ERDMANN, Untersuchungen zu den Briefen Heinrichs IV., AUF 16 (1939) p. 184–195 and 233.

91) Bernard, Ep. 223, ed. LECLERCQ (as note 28) 8 p. 90.

92) Bernard, Epp. 304 und 402, ed. LECLERCQ (as note 28) 8 p. 221 und 382. See HOFFMANN, Brieftechnik (as note 62) p. 163–164, on the meaning of stilum and dictavi in Ep. 304 and LECLERCQ, Épîtres (as note 75) p. 209 n. 31, on maneries in Ep. 402. Bernard's precise meaning in these letters is puzzling, since he can hardly have expected the king and the bishop to recognize his writing style in two letters of 10 and 5 lines respectively. See Materials for the History of Thomas Becket, ed. James C. ROBERTSON (Rolls Series 67, 1875–85) 6 p. 16, referring to the bishops' letter in 5 p. 408–413, of which the style and wording were recognizably those of Gilbert Foliot.

model, but sometimes also of the recipient. 'I have composed this [letter] to you', Petrarch wrote to his brother Gerard, who was a monk, 'not in my own but in a foreign and almost monastic style, [since I was] thinking of you rather than of myself'[93].

The surest safeguard of epistolary authenticity was the bearer, who was supposed to carry the letter from the hand of the sender to that of the recipient and often, in addition, to deliver an oral message[94]. In Antiquity, two copies (or even two versions) of the same letter were sometimes sent by different messengers for the sake of security[95]. Bearers were not always reliable, especially when they were unknown to the correspondents, and they occasionally falsified letters themselves, as Cyprian may have suspected of Crementius and Lanfranc, of Robert. It is probable that many letters were delivered orally by the bearer, who read the letter to the recipient[96]. Peter the Venerable wanted a letter he wrote to Bernard in 1149 to be delivered through (per) Nicholas of Montiéramey: 'Read it to him intently and carefully and urge him as strongly as you can to give effect to what I have written purely out of love'[97]. Letters to laypeople who knew no Latin were presumably delivered in the vernacular, and the few words in German which are found in the letter of Siboto of Falkenstein were included presumably to prevent any misunderstanding of the nature of the reward promised to the murderer of his enemy[98].

Finally, the conditions of preserving letters presented many opportunities for revising and falsifying the texts. The major question, on which there is no clear agreement among students of medieval epistolography, is whether the surviving versions of letters, nearly all of which are found in collections, derive

---

93) Petrarch, Fam. X 3, ed. Vittorio Rossi and Umberto Bosco (Edizione nazionale delle opere di Francesco Petrarca 10–13, 1933–42) 2 p. 300.

94) Constable, Letters (as note 10) p. 52–55. Owing to the apparent vapidity of medieval letters, it is sometimes said that they were essentially credentials for the bearer, who carried the real message orally. This may have been true, but written messages, even without information, were important as marks of friendship.

95) Habicht and Kussmaul, Neues Fragment (as note 4) p. 143–144.

96) See Ruth Crosby, Oral Delivery in the Middle Ages, Speculum 11 (1936) p. 88–110, and Donald E. Queller, Thirteenth-Century Diplomatic Envoys: Nuncii and Procuratores, Speculum 35 (1960) p. 196–213, citing the opinion of Azo that 'A nuncius is he who takes the place of a letter' and the equivalency in the Digest of a nuncius and epistola. The earliest letters like the earliest charters were probably all oral: Clanchy, Memory to Written Record (as note 82) p. 202–203.

97) Peter the Venerable, Ep. 151, ed. Constable (as note 70) 1 p. 372.

98) Codex Falkensteinensis, no. 183, ed. Noichl (as note 85) p. 164.

from the writers ('Autorenüberlieferung'), and if so whether from drafts or from final versions, or from the recipients ('Empfängerüberlieferung'), who were often asked to keep or return the letters they had received[99]. These questions are of concern here only to emphasize that letters were not always preserved in the form in which they were sent, received, and delivered.

Revisions were made not only to improve the style and clarify the wording, but also to change and occasionally to pervert the meaning[100]. It is a matter of opinion whether writers can forge their own letters by revision or excision, but some of the changes in letters by other writers are clearly fraudulent, as when the Cistercians suppressed a passage in Alexander III's bull Inter innumeras threatening to withdraw their privileges if they failed to live in accordance with their early economic ideals[101]. William of Malmesbury extensively altered the letters of Alcuin in order to make the style more uniform, clear, and classical[102]. Some of the humanist writers and collectors of letters created classical letters by adding a salutation and subscription to passages from prose works, as when a passage from Suetonius' Life of Horace was made into an imperial letter by putting *Caesar Augustus Horatio Flacco poetae optimo s. d.* at the beginning and *Vale* at the end[103].

It is hard to say whether a letter like this falls into the class of a literary fiction or of a forgery without knowing more about both the intentions of the creator and the perceptions of the reader, who may or may not have been aware of the deception. Similarly, the use of model letters, formulas, and topoi, like stylistic imitation and the use of fragments, is less of a sign of insincerity, let alone of

---

99) See CONSTABLE, Letters (as note 10) p. 57–60, with references to the works of SCHMEIDLER, ERDMANN, and others.

100) Owing to the conditions of preservation and transmission, letters were perhaps more likely to be revised than any other type of medieval text: see PASQUALI, Storia (as note 78) p. 449–465, and CONSTABLE, Letters p. 51–52, with further references. On the reworking of letters by humanists, see Vito GIUSTINIANI, La communication érudite: Les lettres des humanistes et l'article moderne de revue, in: La correspondance d'Erasme et l'epistolographie humaniste. Colloque international tenu en novembre 1983 (Université libre de Bruxelles: Travaux de l'Institut interuniversitaire pour l'étude de la Renaissance et de l'Humanisme 8, 1985) p. 109.

101) Jean LECLERCQ, Passage supprimé dans une épître d'Alexandre III, Revue bénédictine 62 (1952) p. 149–151.

102) Rodney THOMSON, William of Malmesbury and the Letters of Alcuin, Medievalia et Humanistica 8 (1977) p. 147–161.

103) SABBADINI, Scoperte (as note 81) p. 175, citing this and other examples; see also RONCONI, Introduzione (as note 37) p. 245.

dishonesty, than of the gap between the medieval and modern concepts of originality and authenticity. Borrowings of this sort are often harder to detect than outright fabrications, both because they contain an element of authenticity and because their purpose is unclear; but they show that historians must be extremely cautious in accepting the unsupported testimony of letters, even when they show no obvious signs of falsification, and that contemporaries like Cyprian and Lanfranc were justified in worrying about the veracity of their correspondence.

The rising tide of concern about forgery in the twelfth century related primarily to charters but also covered letters, and especially papal letters. John of Salisbury, writing in the name of Archbishop Theobald of Canterbury, said that falsifying the pope's seal put the entire church in danger because 'the mouths of all the pontiffs may be opened and closed by the marks of a single impression', and Stephen of Tournai, who referred to many forgeries in his letters to the pope and the archbishop of Reims, announced in one of them that the abbot of Anchin had absolved the abbot of St. Martin of Tournai for some false letters of which 'an adolescent boy could recognize the falsity'[104]. In 1157 the Cistercian chapter-general decreed that 'The forgers (falsarii) of charters and seals when they are discovered should, if they are clerics, minister only at private masses, and if they are laymen, should be last in order for a year and fast on bread and water every Friday; and no one should use their documents'[105].

The twelfth century has been called 'the golden age of medieval forgery'[106], and the extent and inventiveness of forgery at that time was never quite matched by the development of more sophisticated techniques to discover forgery and sterner measures to suppress it[107]. Forged letters were among the hardest types of forgery to detect because they had little bearing on the practical conduct of life, and they were hard to suppress, owing to the difficulty in

---

104) John of Salisbury, Ep. 67, ed. W. J. Millor, H. E. Butler, and C. N. L. Brooke (Nelson's [later Oxford] Medieval Texts, 1955–1979) 1 p. 109, see Epp. 57, 73, and 86 ibid. p. 98, 117, and 134; Stephen of Tournai, Ep. 297, ed. Jules Desilve (1893) p. 373, see Epp. 218, 227, 263, and 269, ibid. p. 271, 283, 328, and 337. See also the case of the papal dictator accused of forgery (cited note 68 above) and Constable, Forgery (as note 5) p. 18–19.

105) Statuta capitulorum generalium ordinis Cisterciensis, 1157.61, ed. J.-M. Canivez (Bibliothèque de la Revue d'histoire ecclésiastique 9–14 B, 1933–41) 1 p. 67.

106) Brooke, in: Letters of John of Salisbury (as note 104) 1 p. 98 n. 5 (see also Gilbert Foliot [as note 79] p. 127), and Speyer, Literarische Fälschung (as note 32) p. 317.

107) Constable, Forgery (as note 5) p. 13.

establishing a basis for distinguishing innocent fictions from deceitful frauds. Henry of Huntingdon's three letters in his History of the English were clearly a legitimate literary device, and the letters of Nicholas of Montiéramey, in spite of Bernard's fulminations, continued to be in demand. Contemporaries may have been no less puzzled than later scholars by the letters of Abelard and Heloise, if they were known, and by those of Alexius Comnenus and Prester John. Whether or not letters like these should be considered forgeries, although they clearly pretend to be something they are not, presents a continuing problem for students of medieval epistolography, and for the participants in this congress.

Dictators and Diplomats in the Eleventh and Twelfth Centuries: Medieval Epistolography and the Birth of Modern Bureaucracy

The efflorescence of letter writing and letter collecting in the eleventh and twelfth centuries was a response not only to literary, intellectual, and emotional developments, such as the desire for self-expression, but also to the political and administrative needs created by the growth of government and the emergence of national states.

One of the conspicuous features of the late twelfth century was the growing importance of carefully drafted letters in the conduct of business—not the brief and trenchant writs which are the clearest manifestation of the first age of effective government, but the elaborate unfolding of complicated matters which now occupied the chanceries of Europe.[1]

Persuasion and consultation were central to effective rule in the Middle Ages, and as the world expanded letters were the principal means of influencing actions and opinions and of communicating with people at a distance.[2] Letters bridged

the gap not only between individuals but also between people and institutions and between official documents and works of literature cast in epistolary form. Together with law, the art of writing letters (*ars dictandi* or *dictaminis*) paralleled the arts of public speaking (*ars arengandi*) and preaching (*ars praedicandi*) as subjects of study for those preparing for careers in ecclesiastical or secular government.

In this article I shall be concerned less with the writers of official and business documents, which were drawn up in chanceries and of which the purpose is usually clear, than with the writers of missive letters (*missiles litterae*), which are harder to classify because (as the so-called Saxon *summa* on letter writing, which was written in the second quarter of the thirteenth century, put it) they conferred no authority, had no legal force, and created no necessity: "They express and declare only the intention of the sender and of the recipient."[3] Alberic of Monte Cassino, the author of the earliest known treatise on letter writing, defined a letter as "a suitable arrangement of discourses (*sermones*) established to express the intention of the sender" or as "an oration suitably and clearly put together out of its parts fully expressing the mind of the sender."[4] The terms *epistola*, *carta*, and *opus-*

This article is a revised version of a paper presented at the Sixth International Penn-Paris-Dumbarton Oaks Colloquium held at the Villa Serbelloni in Bellagio from 27 November to 1 December 1989. It benefited from the comments of Alexander Kazhdan and other participants, especially Robert Benson and Ronald Witt, and later of John Baldwin and Kenneth Wolf. Fuller documentation on some points will be found in my other works on medieval epistolography, especially the introduction to *The Letters of Peter the Venerable*, 2 vols., Harvard Historical Studies 78 (Cambridge, Mass., 1967); *Letters and Letter-Collections*, Typologie des sources du Moyen Age occidental 17 (Turnhout, 1976); and "Forged Letters in the Middle Ages," in *Fälschungen im Mittelalter*, 5 vols., MGH, *Schriften* 33 (Hannover, 1988), V, 11–37.

[1] R. W. Southern, "Peter of Blois: A Twelfth-Century Humanist?," (1963), repr. in his *Medieval Humanism and Other Studies* (Oxford, 1970), 110. See also W. Patt, "The Early 'Ars dictaminis' as Response to a Changing Society," *Viator* 9 (1978), 133–55, esp. 148, and R. I. Moore, *The Formation of a Persecuting Society: Power and Deviance in Western Europe 950–1250* (Oxford, 1987), 136, who remarked on how literate clerks replaced warriors "as the agents of government and the confidants of princes" and on the "specialization or professionalization of government."

[2] See my article "Papal, Imperial, and Monastic Propaganda in the Eleventh and Twelfth Centuries," in *Prédication et propa-*

gande au Moyen Age. Islam, Byzance, Occident, Penn-Paris-Dumbarton Oaks Colloquia 3 (Paris, 1983), 179–99. According to R. Lane Fox, *Pagans and Christians* (San Francisco, 1988), 635, Constantine used letters in addition to buildings, inscriptions, and edicts as a medium of deliberate publicity.

[3] L. Rockinger, *Briefsteller und Formelbücher des eilften bis vierzehnten Jahrhunderts*, 2 vols. paginated consecutively, Quellen und Erörterungen zur bayerischen und deutschen Geschichte 9.1–2 (Munich, 1863–64), 260.

[4] Ibid., 10. A similar definition is found in the *Summa dictaminis* of Orléans (ibid., 103), which called a letter "a suitable oration, well put together out of its parts fully expressing the state of mind" and went on that "I said 'suitable oration' to exclude those which are not orations . . . [and] 'fully expressing

culum were equated by Onulf of Speyer in the eleventh century, and were used interchangeably not only with *littera* and *schedula* but also with *oratio* and *sermo*.[5] Bernard of Clairvaux wrote at the end of his treatise *On precept and dispensation*, which was written in the form of a letter, that he had exceeded the epistolary mode (*modum epistolarem*) and that the reader could call his discourse (*sermo*) either a book (*librum*) or a letter (*epistolam*).[6]

The writers of such letters were more than simply monastic or chancery scribes and often combined their letter writing activities with broader advisory and administrative functions. They are found at various times in late Antiquity and the early Middle Ages, but they took on a new importance in the eleventh and twelfth centuries, when they formed a distinct group of recognizable personalities whose activities extended beyond the scriptorium. Both the style and content of their letters were influenced by the revival of interest in classical literature and epistolography, which went back at least to the tenth century. The classical interests of Gerbert of Rheims, the future Pope Sylvester II and a notable letter writer, were continued by Heriman, among whose students was Meinhard of Bamberg, whose letters were marked by a "conscious classicism" and "Ciceronian style".[7] Alberic of Monte Cassino cited Cyprian, Paul, and Sallust to illustrate the *verba scematica* used for praise and blame in letters, and Hugh of Bologna cited Cicero and Sallust as examples of (unmetrical) prose *dictamen* as distinct from the (metrical) prose and letter (*prosa et epistola*) of St. Paul.[8] The

Ars poetica of Horace, of which more than a hundred and fifty complete or partial manuscripts survive, was a model of poetic epistles in which an older poet guided a younger writer. Seneca was popular for both his own letters and his apocryphal correspondence with St. Paul, which was known to Abelard and Peter the Venerable in the twelfth century and of which there are some three hundred late medieval manuscripts.[9]

Pride of place among ancient letter writers belonged to Cicero, who influenced medieval epistolography directly through his own letters and his treatise *De amicitia*, and indirectly through his philosophical and rhetorical works.[10] Medievalists no longer accept the view that Petrarch's "discovery" of Cicero's letters heralded the shift from medieval to humanist epistolography and the emergence of the literary *epistolarium*. Gerbert cited Cicero repeatedly and in a letter written in 984/5 said that he wanted, like Cicero, to combine the honest and the useful and hoped that "these most honest and sacred friendships" would be useful to both sides.[11] The letter collections of Meinhard of Bamberg and other writers during the reign of Henry IV are full of references to Cicero. The influence of Cicero on John of Salisbury and Peter of Blois is well known.[12] Monastic letter writers like Peter the Venerable and Aelred of Rievaulx also cited Ci-

---

the state of mind' because the sender should open his heart to the recipient." Hugh of Bologna (ibid., 55) said that prose (as distinct from poetic) *dictamen* was "an oration freed from the law of meter." See R. Witt, "Medieval 'Ars dictaminis' and the Beginnings of Humanism: A New Construction of the Problem," *Renaissance Quarterly* 35 (1982), 9: "Alberico reflects well the tendency to assimilate the letter to a speech when he characterizes the task of the *exordium* as rendering the reader 'attentive, kindly disposed and docile' and illustrates his whole discussion of the structure of the letter by giving examples from speeches found in Sallust." On Alberic see F. J. Worstbrock, "Die Anfänge der mittelalterlichen Ars dictandi," *Frühmittelalterliche Studien* 23 (1989), 1–42, with references to previous literature.

[5] W. Wattenbach, "Magister Onulf von Speier," *SBBerl, Phil.-hist. Kl.* (1894), 380.

[6] Bernard of Clairvaux, *De praecepto et dispensatione*, XX (61), ed. J. Leclercq et al., *Sancti Bernardi opera*, 8 vols. in 9 (Rome, 1957–77), III, 294.

[7] Meinhard's letters are edited in *Briefsammlungen der Zeit Heinrichs IV.*, ed. C. Erdmann and N. Fickermann, MGH, *Briefe* 5 (Weimar, 1950). On their classicism, see J. R. Williams, "The Cathedral School of Rheims in the Eleventh Century," *Speculum* 29 (1954), 665.

[8] Rockinger, *Briefsteller*, 33 and 55 (see note 3 above).

[9] B. Munk Olsen, *L'étude des auteurs classiques latins aux XIe et XIIe siècles*, 3 vols. (Paris, 1982–87), I, 426 (on Horace) and II, 373–77 (on Seneca). See L. D. Reynolds, *The Medieval Tradition of Seneca's Letters* (Oxford, 1965), esp. 104–11, and on the apocryphal correspondence between Seneca and Paul, *Epistolae Senecae ad Paulum et Pauli ad Senecam <quae vocantur>*, ed. C. W. Barlowe, PAAR 10 (Rome, 1938), 8–70, and L. Bocciolini Palagi, *Il carteggio apocrifo di Seneca e San Paolo*, Accademia toscana di scienze e lettere "La Columbaria," Studi 46 (Florence, 1978).

[10] N. Valois, *De arte scribendi epistolas apud Gallicos medii aevi scriptores rhetoresve* (Paris, 1880), 23. See M. Manitius, "Handschriften antiker Autoren in mittelalterlichen Bibliothekskatalogen," *Zentralblatt für Bibliothekswesen* 67 (Leipzig, 1935), 20–39; Olsen, *Étude*, I, 119; and K. Fredborg, "The Scholastic Teaching of Rhetoric in the Middle Ages," *Cahiers de l'Institut du Moyen-Âge grec et latin* [Copenhagen] 55 (1987), 85–105, esp. 88 on the 12th century.

[11] Gerbert, *Ep.* 44, ed. J. Havet, *Lettres de Gerbert (983–997)*, Collection de textes pour servir à l'étude et à l'enseignement de l'histoire 6 (Paris, 1889), 42, and ed. F. Weigle, *Die Briefsammlung Gerberts von Reims*, MGH, *Briefe* 2 (Weimar, 1966), 72–73. See K. Pivec, "Die Briefsammlung Gerberts von Aurillac," *MittÖIG* 49 (1935), 68, who called Gerbert's collection "an autobiography in documents" and "the forerunner of later memoir-literature," and B. P. McGuire, *Friendship and Community: The Monastic Experience, 350–1250*, Cistercian Studies Series 95 (Kalamazoo, 1988), 148.

[12] *The Letters of John of Salisbury*, ed. W. J. Millor, H. E. Butler, and C. N. L. Brooke, 2 vols., [Nelson's and] Oxford Medieval Texts (London-Oxford, 1955–79), II, xxxii; B. Munk Olsen, "L'humanisme de Jean de Salisbury, un Cicéronien au 12e siècle," *Entretiens sur la renaissance du 12e siècle*, ed. M. de Gandillac

cero. Richard of Poitiers said that Peter resembled Cicero in his epistolary style and Tertullian in his scriptural commentaries, and Aelred may have had Cicero's letters in mind when he criticized monks who meditated on Virgil with the Gospels, Horace with the prophets, and Cicero with St. Paul.[13]

An important aspect of the charm—and the power—of letters was that they were addressed at the same time to an individual and to a larger audience and were thus both private and public. A letter was "the eye of the heart," the face of the inner man, "the mirror of the soul," and "the soul impressed on letters." Letter collections have been called documentary autobiographies. It is no accident that the golden age of medieval letter writing coincided with the revival of autobiography for the first time since Augustine, the popularity of dialogue form in literature, and the cult of friendship fostered by Cicero's De amicitia.[14] Bernard of Clairvaux wrote:

> It is human and necessary to feel for those who are dear, either pleasantly when they are present or sadly when they are absent. Social intercourse is not idle, especially among friends, and the dread of separation and reciprocal sadness in those who are separated show what mutual love feels for each other in those who are together.[15]

For Peter the Venerable, friendship was "the silver cord" which bridged the distance between friends:

"From distant I become close, from remote contiguous, from divided joined, from separated connected."[16] And Peter of Blois cited Cicero that "Neither water nor fire nor air are more useful to us than a friend," adding on his own that "Friendship is a ladder (gradus) which carries men to God. With love as intermediary, man draws close to God when he is made a friend of God out of a friend of man."[17] Absence created what scholars have called the epistolary situation (Briefsituation), which was filled by letters. The ancient descriptions of letters as sermo absentium quasi inter presentes and as acsi ore ad os et presens were often cited in the Middle Ages, in both East and West. St. Ambrose said that he was never less alone than in his letters, and Boccaccio at one point remarked that he had read some letters from friends "as though I had been in their presence and had conversed with them face to face."[18]

Friendship was more than a matter of personal feelings, however. It often involved political considerations and had a public as well as a private face. Many letters dealt with matters of concern to more than one person, and versions of the same letter were sometimes sent to several people.[19] Some writers were at pains to publicize their friendships. Anselm wrote, probably in the mid-1070s, to a monk named Maurice:

> It is a long time since we visited each other by our letters (nostris . . . litteris . . . visitavimus), because we are in no doubt about the solidity of our mutual love and have greeted each other when there was an opportunity by the words of messengers (nuntiorum sermonibus). Lest someone should for any reason think that [our] love has cooled, however, I think it suitable that it should sometimes be seen to burn in writings (schedulis) like sparks flying out from each [of us].[20]

and E. Jeauneau, Décades du Centre culturel international de Cérisy-la-Salle, n.s. 9 (The Hague, 1968), 53–69, esp. 54; and C. J. Nederman, "Aristotelian Ethics and John of Salisbury's Letters," Viator 18 (1987), 161–73. On Peter of Blois, see notes 16–17 and 61 below.

[13] E. Berger, Notice sur divers manuscrits de la Bibliothèque vaticane. Richard le Poitevin, moine de Cluny, historien et poète, BEFAR 6 (Paris, 1879), 121–22, cf. 75, and Aelred of Rievaulx, Speculum caritatis, II, 24, in PL 195, col. 573 BC. In his De spirituali amicitia, I, ibid., col. 664c, Aelred equated "the one heart and one soul" of Acts with Cicero's definition of true friendship. See also Walter Daniel, The Life of Aelred of Rievaulx, ed. F. M. Powicke, [Nelson's] Medieval Classics (London, 1950), lviii note 1.

[14] According to C. Morris, The Discovery of the Individual 1050–1200, Church History Outlines 5 (London, 1972), 79, "Autobiography was . . . not an isolated phenomenon, but part of [a] general tendency to examine, and publish, one's personal experience." P. von Moos, "Literatur- und bildungsgeschichtliche Aspekte der Dialogform im lateinischen Mittelalter," in Tradition und Wertung. Festschrift für Franz Brunhölzl zum 65. Geburtstag, ed. G. Bernt, F. Rädle, and G. Silagi (Sigmaringen, 1989), commented not only on the "new culture" of the dialogue but also (203–4) on the monastic confabulatio/collocutio fraterna. On friendship, see J. Leclercq, "L'amitié dans les lettres au moyen âge. Autour d'un manuscrit de la bibliothèque de Pétrarque," Revue du moyen âge latin 1 (1945), 391–410, esp. 400; the articles of A. Fiske gathered in her Friends and Friendship in the Monastic Tradition, CIDOC Quaderno 51 (Cuernavaca, 1970); and McGuire, Friendship.

[15] Bernard, Super Cantica 26, VI (10), ed. Leclercq, I, 178.

[16] Peter the Venerable, Epp. 6 and 54, ed. Constable, I, 12–13 and 174. In Ep. 81 to his friend Bishop Hato of Troyes (ed. Constable, I, 218, and II, 39), Peter cited a passage from Cicero's De amicitia which was also used by Aelred of Rievaulx and Peter of Blois in their treatises on friendship.

[17] Peter of Blois, De amicitia christiana, I, 3, ed. M.-M. Davy, Un traité de l'amour du XIIe siècle. Pierre de Blois (Paris, 1932), 118–20. Peter Lombard identified the Holy Spirit with both the love of God and the love of other men: Sententiae, I, 17.1.2, Spicilegium Bonaventurianum 4–5 (Grottaferrata, 1971–81), I.2, 142.

[18] Ambrose, Ep. 49.1, in PL 16, col. 1203c, cf. Ep. 47.6, ibid., 1200c (on Ambrose, see McGuire, Friendship, 45–46); and Boccaccio, Ep. 11, in Opere latine minori (Bari, 1928), 144.

[19] Peter Damiani sent Ep. 49 to at least four recipients: Die Briefe des Petrus Damiani, 2 vols., ed. K. Reindel, MGH, Briefe 4 (Munich, 1983–88), II, 62 (note). James of Vitry also sent out various versions of the same letter: Lettres de Jacques de Vitry (1160/70–1240), ed. R. B. C. Huygens (Leiden, 1960), 47.

[20] Anselm, Ep. 69, ed. F. S. Schmitt, S. Anselmi . . . opera omnia, 6 vols. (Edinburgh, 1946–61), III, 189.

For Anselm the words of a messenger were private, like the knowledge of mutual love, but a letter was expected to be seen or heard by others. The distinction between writing and speaking was less sharp in the Middle Ages than it is today. Letters were called *sermones* and *orationes* because they were spoken in the course of preparation and were often delivered orally, as speeches, even to recipients who knew Latin and how to read. *Legere* and *audire* were used as synonyms, and "read and hear" was a commonplace in medieval works of both prose and poetry at least until the fourteenth century.[21] Many letters were in effect either letters of introduction or diplomatic instructions, and the real message was delivered orally. Peter the Venerable described a letter to Bernard of Clairvaux as "tongueless (*elingues*) because it is entrusted to the tongue of the bearer," and he asked Nicholas of Montiéramey to present a letter to Bernard by word of mouth: "Read it to him intently and carefully and exhort him as strongly as you can to carry out what I have written solely out of love."[22] The art of speaking was closely related to the art of composition, and the effectiveness of a letter depended as much on how it was presented as on how it was written.[23] Eloquence was a valuable asset in the conduct of practical affairs. Lambert of Ardres said that Sifrid the Dane won the favor of the count of Flanders and his followers by addressing them *satis eleganter et urbane*,[24] and members of the family of Hauteville, according to Geoffrey of Malaterra, were so adept in the arts of flattery and eloquence "that you attend even to the boys as if they were rhetoricians."[25]

Almost all letter writers in the eleventh and twelfth centuries made use of scribes and messengers to write and deliver their letters. Peter Damiani had a *juvenculus* named Sylvester who "not only wrote this while I dictated but transferred onto parchment what was written on tablets." Peter was the *dictator* or composer of the letter. The actual work of taking down his words on wax tablets and of writing the letter (*schedule*) was done by *scriptores* and *notarii*, who presumably reconstructed the words of the dictator as best they could.[26] Bernard of Clairvaux, in a letter written in 1124, distinguished the functions in writing a letter respectively of invention (*ingenium*) in composing (*dictando*), lips in dictating (*confabulando*), fingers in writing (*scribendo*), and messengers in carrying (*discurrendo*) a letter.[27] These activities might be combined, but they were usually separated. Many letters were carried by bearers or chance travelers whose sole responsibility was to give them to the addressees. Others were given to messengers or *nuntii*, who either presented them as a speech—if necessary in translation—or supplemented them with a message. "A *nuncius* is he who takes the place of a letter," according to Azo, "he is just like a magpie and the voice of the principal sending him, . . . and he recites the words of the principal."[28]

Scholars have on the whole paid more attention to the form and content of medieval letters than to their writers, in the sense not of the men and women whose names appear in the salutations but of the actual drafters and writers. Very little is known about the activities of individual scribes except in Italy, where notaries were secularized and professionalized, and began to keep registers, at an earlier date than elsewhere in medieval Europe.[29] The work of a few scribes can be traced through groups of original charters, when they survive.[30] A scribe named G. was archivist and li-

[21] See especially R. Crosby, "Oral Delivery in the Middle Ages," *Speculum* 11 (1936), 88, and Witt, "Medieval 'Ars dictaminis'," 5–6: "Letter composition was oriented toward oral presentation of the message within a formal setting. Official communications, particularly important letters, were often read aloud by the recipient or in the recipient's presence and thus at the moment of communication took on the appearance of an oration."

[22] Peter the Venerable, *Epp.* 73 and 151, ed. Constable, I, 206 and 372; see also *Ep.* 2, ibid., 5. Bernard of Clairvaux wrote to Bishop Henry of Winchester in 1133 that "You can safely entrust to Abbot Ogerius, through (*per*) whom you have received this [letter] from us, whatever you may wish to write or instruct by word:" *Ep.* 93, ed. Leclercq, VII, 242.

[23] See P. O. Kristeller, *Eight Philosophers of the Italian Renaissance* (Stanford, 1964), 160, and Witt, "Medieval 'Ars dictaminis'," 20, who remarked on the "close link between *dictamen* and oratory."

[24] Lambert of Ardres, *Historia comitum Ghisnensium*, 11, in MGH, *Scriptores* in fol., XXIV, 567. Lambert was writing ca. 1200, though the event he described here occurred in the tenth century.

[25] Geoffrey Malaterra, *De rebus gestis Rogerii*, I, 3, ed. E. Pontieri, RISS V. 1 (Bologna, 1928), 8.

[26] Peter Damiani, *Op.* XIII, 14, in PL 145, col. 311D. See *Ep.* 1, 15, in PL 144, col. 229B, and *Op.* XIX, 9, in PL 145, col. 438D. See K. Reindel, "Studien zur Überlieferung der Werke des Petrus Damiani [I]," *DA* 15 (1959), 50–67, and J. Leclercq, *Saint Pierre Damien ermite et homme d'église*, Uomini e dottrine 8 (Rome, 1960), 155.

[27] Bernard of Clairvaux, *Ep.* 90, 1, ed. Leclercq, VII, 237.

[28] D. Queller, "Thirteenth-Century Diplomatic Envoys: *Nuncii* and *Procuratores*," *Speculum* 35 (1960), 199.

[29] Ronald Witt suggested that this may have been a factor in the relative dispersal of cultural life in Italy, in contrast to the concentration of clerical scribes in courts and monasteries north of the Alps, which contributed to the formation of literary and cultural circles there.

[30] See M.-C. Garand, "Copistes de Cluny au temps de saint Maieul (948–994)," *BEC* 136 (1978), 5–36; idem, " 'Giraldus

brarian at the abbey of St. Victor in the 1160s; an anonymous monk of Trois-Fontaines wrote forty-three charters between 1169 and 1196; and more than a hundred surviving documents were written by the notary known only as M A, who was active at Metz from 1185 until 1221.[31] Though these men clearly played an important part in running the institutions with which they were associated, they were still essentially scribes, and are known from the documents and books they copied.[32] They all worked for more than one master, however. Albert *Teutonicus* of Cluny wrote charters for at least eight people in eight different places. The scribe of Trois-Fontaines wrote in twelve and M A in almost forty names. They copied books as well as documents. Albert was an artist, and G. a librarian. Though none of them stepped far outside the scriptorium, they played a larger role than simply that of anonymous scribes, and they pointed the way toward the emergence of a class of identifiable writers occupied with the written business of society.

The growing importance of letters in medieval society created a demand for a new type of scribe who had, according to Southern, "a smattering of law" and "a taste for polemic" in addition to "a command of the ornate diction of correct epistolary style."[33] These writers, in order to write convincing letters, needed a knowledge of the world and society, and of human character, as well as of

grammar and letters. This need promoted the compilation of treatises on letter writing, accompanied by collections of form letters, and the emergence of centers for the study of letter writing, as at Bologna and Orléans, where letters were a battlefield for rivalries between scholarly factions.[34] Owing to its practical value, the study of letter writing came to dominate other branches of rhetoric.[35] The term *ars dictandi* or *dictamen* derived from *dictare* and was related to *dicere* and the German *Dichter*. It originally meant to declare or dictate (and by extension to prescribe or order, hence the modern use of dictator for a ruler), but already in late Antiquity it took on the meaning of compose as distinct from speak or write. "To dictate," according to the *dictator* Henry *Francigena*, "is to express the concept of the soul by a proper construction of reasons," and Bernard of Meung, who lived in the second half of the twelfth century, wrote that "*Dictamen* is a written presentation distinguished by the beauty of its words [and] adorned, or ordained, by the lustres of its sentiments."[36] In practice the *ars dictandi* in the Middle Ages was the art of composing elegant and effective letters.

The rules laid down in the treatises on *dictamen* dealt with every aspect of a letter from the opening protocol and salutation to the conclusion, including the selection and arrangement of words. The importance of tactful and correct wording of letters was brought out in the account given in the Life of John of Gorze of the correspondence between Otto I and Abd ar-Rahman III of Cordova in the middle of the tenth century.[37] In 1082 Abbot Desiderius of Monte Cassino (the home of Alberic, the early writer on *dictamen*) sent no reply to a letter from Henry IV "because he did not know with what sort of salutation he should write to him." He eventually settled on "the obedience of due fidelity (*debitae fidelitatis obsequium*)," which was ambiguous and left open the question of what, if any, fidelity

Levita', copiste de chartes et de livres à Cluny sous l'abbatiat de saint Odilon (+ 1049)," in *Calames et cahiers. Mélanges . . . Léon Gilissen* (Brussels, 1985), 41–48; and M. Hillebrandt, "Albertus *Teutonicus*, copiste de chartes et de livres à Cluny," *Mémoires de la Société pour l'histoire du droit et des institutions des anciens pays bourguignons, comtois et romands* 45 (1988), 215–32.

[31] F. Gasparri, "Le 'scribe G', archiviste et bibliothécaire de l'abbaye de Saint-Victor de Paris au XIIe siècle," *Scriptorium* 37 (1983), 92–98; M. Parisse, "Un scribe champenois du XIIe siècle et l'évolution de son écriture," *Archiv für Diplomatik* 29 (1983), 229–41; and P. Acht, *Die Cancellaria in Metz. Eine Kanzlei- und Schreibschule um die Wende des 12. Jahrhunderts*, Schriften des wissenschaftlichen Instituts des Elsass-Lothringer im Reich an der Universität Frankfurt, N.F. 25 (Frankfurt-am-Main, 1940), 34–40 and 85–92.

[32] Gasparri, " 'Scribe G'," 95: "Le XIIe siècle n'est pas celui des fonctionnaires et la mise en place progressive des rouages administratifs, qui se produit alors, n'a pas encore engendré cette classe de notaires professionnels et besogneux qui formeront, au siècle suivant, le personnel spécialisé et presque exclusif des chancelleries."

[33] Southern, "Peter of Blois," 111. On the association of the study of *dictamen* with law, see Patt, "Early 'Ars dictaminis'," 151–52, and C. Vulliez, "L'évêque au miroir de l'*Ars dictaminis*. L'exemple de la *Maior compilatio* de Bernard de Meung," *Revue d'histoire de l'Eglise de France* 70 (1984), 277–304, esp. 302–3, where he referred to "l'imprégnation par le droit canonique du temps de la *maior compilatio* de Bernard de Meung."

[34] B. Roy and H. Shooner, "Querelles de maîtres au XIIe siècle: Arnoul d'Orléans et son milieu," *Sandalion* 8–9 (1985–86), 315–41.

[35] E. R. Curtius, *Europäische Literatur und lateinisches Mittelalter* (Bern, 1948), 83. See also Witt, "Medieval 'Ars dictaminis'," 25, on the tendency in the 12th century to define rhetoric as *dictamen*.

[36] Cited respectively in A. Bütow, *Die Entwicklung der mittelalterlichen Briefsteller bis zur Mitte des 12. Jahrhunderts*, (Greifswald, 1908), 48, and Vulliez, "L'évêque au miroir de l'*Ars dictaminis*," 277.

[37] *Vita Iohannis Gorziensis*, cc. 115–29, in MGH, *Scriptores in fol.*, IV, 370–75. See R. Collins, *Early Medieval Spain: Unity and Diversity, 400–1000* (London, 1983), 201.

he owed to the emperor.[38] A trained letter writer knew the suitable terms of salutation and the correct order of names, which reflected the respective social and political positions of the writer and addressee.[39] Frederick Barbarossa told his notary to put the pope's name after the emperor's and to address him in the singular.

Although this way of writing was common in antiquity, it was considered changed by modern men owing to a certain honor and reverence for persons. The emperor said that either the pope ought to preserve the custom of his predecessors in writing to the person of the emperor or that he himself ought to observe the custom of ancient princes in his letters.[40]

The risks of an incautious (or perhaps calculated) choice of words in high matters of state is illustrated by Pope Hadrian IV's letter to Frederick Barbarossa at Besançon, where the word *beneficium* almost became a *casus belli* between the emperor and the pope. The terms of address used in the text of a letter, which are often lost in translation, were designed to appeal to particular qualities of the addressee. A request to redress a grievance, for instance, was addressed to Your Justice, for revenge to Your Honor, and for money to Your Generosity. Gregory VII in a letter to Lanfranc in 1072 invoked his will, person, prudence, religion, and weariness, and Lanfranc, depending on his purpose, addressed himself to his correspondents' beatitude, benignity, excellency, fraternity, greatness, love, majesty, paternity, prudence, religion, and other qualities.[41] Bishop Arnulf of Lisieux in a single letter to Nicholas of Montiéramey cited his discretion, religion, skill, sanctity, goodness, compassion, generosity, benevolence, and magnificence, each selected to flatter Nicholas in a particular way.[42]

The choice and arrangement of the words in

many letters and documents was controlled by the rules for rhythmical prose of the papal chancery, known as the *cursus curiae Romanae*, or of some other metrical system, which regulated the length of syllables especially at the beginnings and ends of sentences and phrases. Biblical and other quotations, which resonated in ways now lost, had to be used appositely, and the correct person and number, as Frederick Barbarossa stressed, chosen with regard to the sensibilities of both the sender and the addressee. Gilbert Foliot changed his style in the middle of a letter to Abbot Froger of St Florent at Saumur. He began by congratulating Froger on his election as abbot in somewhat formal and conventional terms that gave little or no hint that Froger was an old friend. He then quite suddenly wrote that "We turn to that style (*stilum*) which the present need of writing imposes upon us" and went on to present three requests, including one concerning a monk named Robert who wanted to return to St Florent from England. Gilbert's tone in this section was more personal and intimate precisely because he was asking a favor. "We invade the camp of a friend with confidence," he wrote, "although asking many things which we believe may offend you." It is not surprising that in this passage he appealed to Froger as Your Kindness and Your Grace.[43]

Some letter writers resisted and even rejected these rules. Peter the Venerable complained that "The manner of writing letters (*modus epistolarum*), especially of modern letters, so restricts the pen wishing to pour forth that it cannot write even about essential matters."[44] Peter's use of *moderni* here shows that he had in mind recent developments. It would be a mistake, however, to overemphasize either the novelty of these epistolary rules and practices, many of which predated the earliest treatises on *dictamen*,[45] or their rigidity. They seem restrictive to us, as they did to some contempora-

[38] *Chronica monasterii Casinensis*, 3, 50, in MGH, *Scriptores* in fol., XXXIV, 431. See H. E. J. Cowdrey, *The Age of Abbot Desiderius* (Oxford, 1983), 156–57.
[39] See my article on "The Structure of Society according to the *Dictatores* of the Twelfth Century," in *Law, Church, and Society: Essays in Honor of Stephan Kuttner*, ed. K. Pennington and R. Somerville (Philadelphia, 1977), 253–67.
[40] Rahewin, *Gesta Friderici imperatoris*, IV, 21, 3rd ed. G. Waitz and B. von Simson, MGH, *Scriptores . . . in usum scholarum* (Hannover-Leipzig, 1912), 260–61. See W. von Giesebrecht, *Geschichte der deutschen Kaiserzeit*, VI, ed. B. von Simson (Leipzig, 1895), 382–83.
[41] Lanfranc, *Ep.* 6, ed. H. Clover and M. Gibson, *The Letters of Lanfranc Archbishop of Canterbury*, Oxford Medieval Texts (Oxford, 1979), 58–59. See my review in *Speculum* 56 (1981), 159–60.
[42] Arnulf of Lisieux, *Ep.* 66, ed. F. Barlow, *The Letters of Arnulf of Lisieux*, Camden Third Series 61 (London, 1939), 116–18.

[43] Gilbert Foliot, *Ep.* 152, ed. Z. N. Brooke, A. Morey, and C. N. L. Brooke, *The Letters and Charters of Gilbert Foliot* (Cambridge, 1967), 199. See A. Morey and C. N. L. Brooke, *Gilbert Foliot and His Letters*, Cambridge Studies in Medieval Life and Thought, n.s. 11 (Cambridge, 1965), 15–19. John of Salisbury remarked on Gilbert Foliot's style in a letter to Thomas Becket in *Materials for the History of Thomas Becket*, ed. J. Robertson and J. B. Sheppard, 7 vols., Rolls Series 67 (London, 1875–85), VI, 16, *Ep.* 231.
[44] Peter the Venerable, *Ep.* 40, ed. Constable, I, 134. See *Ep.* 24 (ibid., 44–45) and II, 35–36, for some parallel passages.
[45] P. O. Kristeller, *Renaissance Philosophy and the Mediaeval Tradition*, Wimmer Lecture 15 (Latrobe, 1966), 89 note 19, stressed that "The practice of [systematic] letter writing preceded . . . the theory of the *Dictamen*." See also Patt, "Early 'Ars dictaminis'," 139.

ries, but they came easily to trained letter writers and did little to hinder the writing of long and elaborate letters. A scribe learned the *cursus curiae Romanae* or other system of metrical prose during his apprenticeship until it became almost a second nature, like meter and rhythm to a modern poet. Letter writing in the eleventh and twelfth centuries was marked by a happy balance of old and new elements, and many of the great letter writers were men of affairs as well as men of letters. The eventual triumph of the *dictatores* tended to restrict the writing of letters to professionals and marked the end of the great age of medieval letter writing.[46]

Much work remains to be done on the individual scribes and secretaries who moved out of the scriptorium into the world of larger affairs. It was the nature of such men to hide behind the more prominent figures for whom they worked. An examination of the *cursus* in various letters might show which were dictated verbatim and which were drawn up by scribes, but not their names or personalities.[47] A comparative study of the senders and recipients of the letters in several contemporary collections might reveal the existence of overlapping circles of correspondents, including some *dictatores* writing under their own names, but no such study, so far as I know, has been made, and the contents of most collections vary greatly.[48] Bernhard Schmeidler argued that all unified collections of medieval letters went back to the "single writer personality (*Verfasserpersönlichkeit*)" of the *dictator* who drew them up, often in the names of many senders, and who preserved copies or drafts of his letters in a letter book, which in its original form constituted a chronological picture of the writer's life.[49] This view has not been widely accepted because many letter collections are grouped around an issue or episode rather than a single writer, are manifestly not the work of an individual *dictator*, and are not in chronological or-

der.[50] It is almost impossible to generalize about the writing or collecting of letters in the Middle Ages. Some collections may go back to a single *dictator*, but others are more haphazard and problematical. Schmeidler's work concentrated attention, however, on the notaries who by the twelfth century were found in almost every monastery and episcopal court and who were responsible for a range of practical affairs in addition to drafting and writing letters.[51]

The old type of scribe who copied books and letters and the new bureaucrat who acted as his master and exercised influence himself were combined in Nicholas of Montiéramey, whose career illustrates both the opportunities and the ambiguities, not to say risks, of the emerging civil service.[52] He combined literary and diplomatic skills with an ingratiating personality. "From my earliest youth I have pleased the mighty and greatest princes of the world," he wrote toward the end of his life to Count Henry of Champagne.[53] He first appeared in the 1130s in the household of Bishop Hato of Troyes, whom he served as an envoy to Rome and to Cluny, where he met Peter the Venerable.[54] He was on familiar terms with at least three popes; Henry of France (the brother of Louis VII and future bishop of Beauvais and archbishop of Rheims); Abbot Peter of Celle, who later became bishop of Chartres; and many other prominent figures to whom he tried to make himself useful. About half the letters in his collection were written in the names of other people, including an unsavory letter, perhaps written for Bishop Hugh of Auxerre, accusing his canons of treachery and loose living.[55] Nicholas was at Clairvaux probably

---

[46] On the changes in *dictamen* in Italy ca. 1200, see R. Benson, "Protohumanism and Narrative Technique in Early Thirteenth-Century Italian 'Ars Dictaminis'," in *Boccaccio: Secoli di vita. Atti del Congresso internazionale: Boccaccio 1975, Università di California, Los Angeles 17–19 ottobre 1975*, ed. M. Cottino-Jones and E. F. Tuttle (Ravenna, 1977), 31–50.

[47] See, for instance, D. Norberg, "Qui a composé les lettres de saint Grégoire le Grand?," *StMed*, 3rd series, 21 (1980), 1–17, esp. 12–13.

[48] *Varietas* both of recipients and of types of material was an important feature of many letter collections.

[49] See especially B. Schmeidler, "Die Briefsammlung Froumunds von Tegernsee," *HJ* 62–69 (1949), 220–38, and the evaluation by C. Erdmann in his article on "Die Briefe Meinhards von Bamberg," *NA* 49 (1930–32), 332–431, esp. 335–40 and 384–87.

[50] P. Classen, "Aus der Werkstatt Gerhochs von Reichersberg. Studien zur Entstehung und Überlieferung von Briefen, Briefsammlungen und Widmungen," *DA* 23 (1967), 31–92, and Huygens, *Jacques de Vitry* (note 19 above), 37–49. On the question of chronological order, see O. Meyer, "Feuchtwangen, Augsburger Eigen-, Tegernseer Filialkloster," *ZSav* 58, *Kanonistische Abt.* 27 (1938), 630–31.

[51] C. R. Cheney, *English Bishops' Chanceries 1100–1250*, Publications of the Faculty of Arts of the University of Manchester 3 (Manchester, 1950), 120–21, and S. J. Heathcote, "The Letter Collection Attributed to Master Transmundus, Papal Notary and Monk of Clairvaux in the Late Twelfth Century," *Analecta Cisterciensia* 21 (1965), 35–111 and 167–238, esp. 57–58.

[52] On Nicholas, see *Peter the Venerable*, II, 316–30, and J. F. Benton in the *DSp*, XI (1982), 255–59, with further references.

[53] Nicholas, *Ep.* 56, in PL 196, col. 1652A.

[54] Hato referred to this mission in a letter to Peter the Venerable in 1141 ("Negotia nostra quae magister Nicholaus amicus uester Romam portauit, melius quam sperabamus tractata sunt."): *Peter the Venerable*, I, 222, *Ep.* 85. The use of *magister* suggests Nicholas had some formal academic training.

[55] J. F. Benton, "An Abusive Letter of Nicholas of Clairvaux for a Bishop of Auxerre, Possibly Blessed Hugh of Mâcon,"

from the early 1140s to 1152 and assisted Bernard with his sermons as well as his letters,[56] but he continued to visit Cluny and to serve Peter the Venerable, one of whose letters, we have seen, he presented to Bernard orally.

Bernard sometimes gave only instructions to his secretaries, who then wrote his letters. "The mass of my work is to blame," he wrote to Peter the Venerable in apology for some bitter words to which Nicholas had drawn his attention, "since when my writers (*scriptores*) do not properly remember the meaning (*sensum*), they sharpen their style beyond measure, and I am not able to see what I ordered to be written."[57] Late in 1151 Bernard wrote to the pope (citing 2 Cor. 11:26) that he was in danger from false brethren and that many false letters had been sent under his false seal.[58] Bernard had Nicholas in mind, since a few months later he wrote again to the pope, denouncing Nicholas as a thief, forger, and traitor. "Who can say to how many people he has written in my name whatever he wanted without my knowledge?"[59] Exactly what Nicholas had done is unknown, but Bernard was outraged at this breach of confidence. His indignation and the strength of his language were doubtless sharpened by a sense of betrayal and perhaps also by an awareness of his failure to supervise Nicholas more closely.

Nicholas left Clairvaux immediately, but he went on to serve other important men, including the count of Champagne. In about 1170 Bishop Arnulf of Lisieux wrote to Nicholas about a canon of Troyes who had apparently obtained money by writing a false letter in the name of the count and

using his seal.[60] Arnulf wrote that a second letter from the count, "which a most tender affection seemed to have composed (*dictare*)," appeared to have been written by Nicholas, since it "exuded the style of your skill (*stilum uestre peritie*), and the characteristics (*apices*) of that [letter] which I recently received from Your Sanctity fully expressed to me by sure signs the identity of the hand." The facts of the case are unclear, but the canon had apparently copied Nicholas's style, which is ironic because Nicholas was himself an accomplished imitator of the style of others. Such gifts could be abused, but they were also useful in a world that depended on the services of trained writers and diplomatists who could be relied upon to write and speak for their masters.

Some of the best-known letter writers of the twelfth century were churchmen and writers, like John of Salisbury, Peter of Blois, and Stephen of Tournai, who were not themselves in positions of power, though they usually held ecclesiastical offices, but who served in the courts of the great and performed a variety of functions in the increasingly literate and bureaucratic world of the time. John and Peter were students of both friendship and the classics—Peter's treatise *De amicitia christiana* was influenced by Cicero[61]—and also of law, since the study of law and *dictamen* were often associated. John of Salisbury had no formal legal training, but he had a good knowledge of law, and Peter of Blois, who studied law at Bologna in the 1150s, was competent in both canon and civil law.[62] Stephen studied at Bologna and at Chartres and was considered an authority on canon law. He served several popes and many bishops and acted as adviser and envoy of the king of France, for whom he composed various letters.[63]

John of Salisbury was in effect the executive assistant to Archbishop Theobald of Canterbury and

---

[56] *MedSt* 33 (1971), 365–70. His exact role in writing letters for other people is not known, but he was clearly in demand as a letter writer.

[56] PL 202, col. 475A, and Geoffrey of Auxerre, *Expositio in Cantica Canticorum*, ed. F. Gastaldelli, 2 vols., Temi e Testi 19 (Rome, 1974), I, 191, see intro., liii-liv. See also J. Leclercq, "Les collections de sermons de Nicholas de Clairvaux" (1956), repr. in his *Recueil d'études sur saint Bernard et ses écrits*, I, Storia e letteratura 92 (Rome, 1962), 50.

[57] Bernard, *Ep.* 387, ed. Leclercq, VIII, 355–56. See J. Leclercq, "Saint Bernard et ses secrétaires" (1951), repr. in his *Recueil*, I, 6–7, where he suggested (7 note 1) that *stylus* means "pen" rather than "style."

[58] Bernard, *Ep.* 284, ed. Leclercq, VIII, 199. Following Paul's reference to false brethren, Bernard used the term *falsatus* three times in this sentence. It clearly means "deceptive" rather than "forged" in the modern sense, as some scholars have assumed.

[59] Bernard, *Ep.* 298, ed. Leclercq, VIII, 214. "No man more richly deserves perpetual imprisonment," he wrote to the pope, "nothing is more fitting for him than perpetual silence."

[60] Arnulf of Lisieux, *Ep.* 66, ed. Barlow, 117. Arnulf was a shrewd and experienced administrator and apparently thought he knew the characteristics of Nicholas' style.

[61] Davy, *Traité de l'amour* (note 17 above), 31.

[62] C. N. L. Brooke, "John of Salisbury and his World," in *The World of John of Salisbury*, ed M. Wilks, Studies in Church History, Subsidia 3 (Oxford, 1984), 7; S. Kuttner and E. Rathbone, "Anglo-Norman Canonists of the Twelfth Century," *Traditio* 7 (1949–51), 285–86; and Southern, "Peter of Blois," 107–8.

[63] J. W. Baldwin, *The Government of Philip Augustus: Foundations of French Royal Power in the Middle Ages* (Berkeley-Los Angeles-London, 1986), 32, 53, and 69, and C. Vulliez, "Etudes sur la correspondance et la carrière d'Etienne d'Orléans dit de Tournai (+ 1203)," in *L'abbaye parisienne de Saint-Victor au Moyen Age*, ed. J. Longère, Bibliotheca Victorina 1 (Paris-Turnhout, 1991), 195–231, esp. 211, 210–17, and 228–9.

gave an interesting account of his epistolary responsibilities in a letter written in 1160 to Henry II's chancellor, Thomas Becket, whom the aged archbishop wanted to recall to his service:[64] "In accordance with the command of Your Love, I had drawn up (*conceperam*) a letter from my lord to the lord king and to you with such severity that the pressing need of [your] return might be indicated to you." Before this letter was sent, however, one from the king arrived, stressing his need for Becket "with flatteries and promises," and Theobald instructed John to temper the severity of this letter "and to make some allowance for public need (*necessitati publicae*)." He therefore discarded the former letter (*litteras conceptas*) and after some hesitation sent Henry and Becket a letter "which was as pressing as I could but gave way a bit to the king's desire." This letter included a request for the promotion of Archdeacon Bartholomew of Exeter, which John hoped the king would receive favorably "if you will endeavor to promote it." John then went on to other matters, but this passage shows the importance and delicacy of his position, caught between the archbishop of Canterbury, the king of England, and Thomas Becket, who served both the archbishop and the king.

Wibald of Stavelot was more of a statesman and less of a secretary, since in addition to serving as abbot of Stavelot and Corvey (and for a time also of Monte Cassino) he was an adviser of Conrad III and, until his death in 1158, of Frederick Barbarossa. His letter collection is an important source for the history of the empire in the middle of the twelfth century and includes letters written both by himself and by or for others.[65] In 1149 Wibald wrote to the canon and schoolmaster Manegold of Paderborn, after discussing his own training in the liberal arts, theology, and sacred writings, that without a knowledge and love of God it was of little or no use

to write correctly, read clearly, speak aptly, know the qualities and bases of arguments, persuade by speech, understand the power and nature of numbers, distin-

guish harmony and intervals, excel on the abacus, gnomon, and astrolabe, [and] judge the interrelations and connections of degrees.

These accomplishments corresponded to the liberal arts, and the first five to the Trivium, one to writing and the other four to reading, speaking, and debating. Later in the letter Wibald specifically stressed the importance of eloquence: "It is a matter of no little time or brief study or moderate effort to know the power and nature of souls, to rouse those who are behind and to check and rein in, as it were, those who are ahead." He then described the use and misuse of oratory and eloquence in the courts, both secular and ecclesiastical, and in the pulpit; and he urged Manegold, if he wished to achieve "the glories of speaking (*gloria dicendi*)," to copy a speaker whose eloquence pleased his own spirit. "It is the unanimous opinion of the greatest orators that one can speak more elegantly and fully by copying those who are eloquent than by following the rules of the art."[66]

Wibald was referring here to the *ars arengandi* rather than the *ars dictandi*, but he linked writing, reading, speaking, arguing, and persuading as useful accomplishments. Statesmen, and those who spoke for them and wrote their letters, had to know "the power and nature of souls" and to be able by the power of their words to rouse and restrain their readers and hearers. The letter writers of the twelfth century made themselves indispensable in the conduct of government and brought their intellectual concerns to bear on the conduct of practical affairs. In this, as in their activities and other interests, they resembled the later humanists who served the rulers of late medieval and Renaissance Europe.[67] The abilities to persuade in writing and speech joined in the art later known as

---

[64]John of Salisbury, *Ep.* 128, ed. Millor, I, 221–22. See Brooke, "John of Salisbury," 16.

[65]H. Zatschek, "Wibald von Stablo. Studien zur Geschichte der Reichskanzlei und Reichspolitik unter den älteren Staufern," *MittÖIG*, Erg.-Bd. 10 (1928), 237–495, esp. 273–312; cf. B. Schmeidler, "Bamberg, der *Codex Udalrici* und die deutsche Reichsverwaltung im 11. und 12. Jahrhundert," *Zeitschrift für bayerische Landesgeschichte* 2 (1929), 231, who maintained that Wibald's collection was "ein ganz normales Brief- und Geschäftsbuch von einer einheitgebenden Person."

[66]Wibald of Corvey, *Ep.* 167, ed. P. Jaffé, *Monumenta Corbeiensia*, Bibliotheca rerum germanicarum 1 (Berlin, 1864), 282, 284, and 286. Sections of this letter are translated, with a commentary, by G. Ellspermann in *Readings in Medieval Rhetoric*, ed. J. Miller, M. Prosser, and T. Benson (Bloomington-London, 1973), 209–14 (esp. 210 note 3, on the correspondence between the list of talents and the liberal arts) and Fredborg, "Scholastic Teaching of Rhetoric" (note 10 above), 89–91, with references to the classical sources.

[67]See Kristeller, *Eight Philosophers* (note 23 above); idem, "The Humanist Movement," in his *Renaissance Thought and Its Sources*, ed. M. Mooney (New York, 1979), 24–25; Witt, "Medieval 'Ars dictaminis'," 1; and other references in J. F. Tinkler, "Renaissance Humanism and the *genera eloquentiae*," *Rhetorica* 5 (1987), 279. Nederman in his article on John of Salisbury (note 12 above) said (173) that "The attempt to impart to current affairs a distinctly philosophical cast intrigued John as much as it would his successors in the Renaissance."

diplomacy, which derived from diploma or document. The diplomat or diplomatist knew how to write and present documents. The history of letters, and of those who wrote them, thus merges into the history of bureaucracy and diplomacy and forms an important chapter in the development of government and administration in the Middle Ages.

IV

PAST AND PRESENT IN THE ELEVENTH AND TWELFTH CENTURIES. PERCEPTIONS OF TIME AND CHANGE

I

This paper is concerned with the awareness of the past, and especially of the present in relation to the past and future, in the eleventh and twelfth centuries. I shall look in particular at the sense of time and at the attitude towards change. And a third section, which for lack of time forms a separate paper, looks at the ways in which a sense of the past was shaped by visual experiences, behavioral patterns, and other non-verbal materials. It is my belief that, while there was no decisive change in any single way of approaching the past in the eleventh and twelfth centuries, various aspects of historical thinking at that time came together in a way which marked a significant departure from the early Middle Ages [1].

These are questions which would have been asked in a different way, if at all, a hundred or even only fifty years ago. The traditional approach

---

[1] B. GUENÉE, *Les premiers pas de l'histoire de l'historiographie en occident au XIIe siècle*, « Académie des Inscriptions et Belles-Lettres: Comptes rendus», 1983, pp. 136-152, stresses the self-consciousness of twelfth-century historians, and their recognition of the autonomy of history (p. 148). There are bibliographies of works on medieval historiography in *Geschichtsdenken und Geschichtsbild im Mittelalter*, ed. W. LAMMERS (Wege der Forschung, 21), Darmstadt 1965, pp. 460-475, and in B. GUENÉE, *Histoire et culture historique dans l'occident médiéval*, Paris 1980, pp. 371-409. See also B. SMALLEY, *Historians in the Middle Ages*, London 1974, and R.D. RAY, *Medieval Historiography through the Twelfth Century: Problems and Progress of Research*, « Viator », V (1974), 33-59. The two articles of G. SIMON, *Untersuchungen zur Topik der Widmungsbriefe mittelalterlicher Geschichtsschreiber bis zum Ende des 12. Jahrhunderts*, « Archiv für Diplomatik », IV (1958), 52-119, and V-VI (1959-60), 73-153, will be cited here as SIMON, *Untersuchungen 1* and 2, and the series of articles by R.W. SOUTHERN, *Aspects of the European Tradition of Historical Writing*, « Transactions of the Royal Historical Society », 5th S., XX (1970), pp. 173-196 (1. *The Classical Tradition from Einhard to Geoffrey of Monmouth*), XXI (1971), pp. 159-179 (2. *Hugh of St Victor and the Idea of Historical Development*), XXII (1972), pp. 159-180 (3. *History as Prophecy*), and XXIII (1973), pp. 243-263 (4. *The Sense of the Past*), will be cited as SOUTHERN, *Aspects 1, 2, 3*, and *4*. I have not seen F.J. SCHMALE, *Funktion und Formen mittelalterlicher Geschichtsschreiber. Eine Einführung*, Darmstadt 1985.

towards medieval historiography, typified in the national repertories of Wattenbach, Gross, and Molinier, and still found in the more recent works of Thompson, Gransden, and Smalley, was to study the writings of individual historians in order to establish when they were written and on what sources they were based. Of the twenty contributions to the Spoleto volumes on early medieval historiography, seventeen were devoted to individual writers and regions, and none to general premises[2]. For these scholars the most important question about an historical work is the trustworthiness of the information it contains, not the point of view from which it was written, and the first responsibility of an historian is to factual accuracy and objective truth.

Historians in the Middle Ages also laid great emphasis on truth and honesty in writing history, and on their responsibility to gather, and not to invent, material[3]. History was defined as « the narration of what has been done » by Isidore of Seville, who derived the word from the Greek term for seeing or knowing and distinguished history from argument and fable in its concern for truth:

> For history deals with true things that have been done; argument with those things that could have been done, though they were not; and fable with those things which, because they are against nature, neither were done nor could be done[4].

Sulpicius Severus wrote in his *Life* of Martin that he would prefer « to be silent than to say something false », and Bede in the preface to the *Ecclesiastical history of the English people* denied responsibility for any departure from the truth, saying that he followed « the true law of history (*vera lex historiae*) » in writing down for the instruction of posterity « what I have gathered from common report »[5]. Many writers expres-

---

[2] *La storiografia altomedievale*, 2 vols. paginated consecutively (Settimane di studio del Centro italiano di Studi sull'alto medioevo, 17), Spoleto 1970. The other three are concerned with Late Antiquity, images, and hagiography. See also *The Inheritance of Historiography, 350-900*, ed. C. HOLDSWORTH - T.P. WISEMAN, Exeter 1986, which contains essays on nine early medieval writers, of which I have seen an offprint of one.

[3] P. ROUSSET, *La conception de l'histoire à l'époque féodale*, in *Mélanges d'histoire du Moyen Age dédiés à la mémoire de Louis Halphen*, Paris 1951, pp. 623-624; SIMON, *Untersuchungen*, 2, pp. 81-82 and 92; L. BOEHM, *Der wissenschaftstheoretische Ort der historia im früheren Mittelalter*, in *Speculum historiale* (Festschrift Johannes Spörl), ed. C. BAUER - L. BOEHM - M. MÜLLER, Freiburg-Munich 1965, pp. 672-675; GUENÉE, *Histoire...*, pp. 18-19, and *L'historien par les mots*, in *Le métier d'historien au moyen âge. Études sur l'historiographie médiévale*, ed. B. GUENÉE (Publications de la Sorbonne: Études, 13), Paris 1977, p. 12, where he said that Stowe's charge that Grafton took from other writers marked the end of medieval history.

[4] ISIDORE OF SEVILLE, *Etymologiae*, I, 41 and 44, ed. W.M. LINDSAY, 2 vols., Oxford 1911, n.p.

[5] SULPICIUS SEVERUS, *Vita s. Martini*, I, 9, ed. J. FONTAINE, 3 vols. (Sources Chrétiennes, 133-135: Textes monastiques d'occident, 22-24), Paris 1967-69, I, 254; BEDE, *Historia ecclesiastica gentis Anglorum*, praef., ed. B. COLGRAVE - R.A.B. MYNORS (Oxford Medieval Texts), Oxford 1969, p. 6, which is cited,

sed a concern for truth in historical works. « I follow truthful history », wrote the author of book IX of the *Miracles of St Benedict*, « and I put in no fallacy, knowing that it is written: "A false witness will not be unpunished" », and according to the chronicle of St Trond,

> The historiographer's duty is not to leave the path of truth either for assent, love, hate, or fear; I therefore write, with God as my witness, exactly what I have learned from many people and what I have been able to discover more truthfully from the brothers who were with us at that time and who later told me these things coming through the ear to the mouth[6].

These high-flown sentiments, though well-meant, were something of a topos, and scholars have become increasingly aware that *historia* in the Middle Ages involved the method of selecting and presenting facts as well as the facts themselves[7]. In « the style of history » it was shameful to tell lies and dangerous to tell the truth, said Sidonius Apollinaris, who was reluctant to turn from his letters to historical writing because « it begins with envy, continues with toil, and ends in hate »[8]. Bede believed that history had an ultimately moral and religious purpose, and his *vera lex historiae* (which derives from Jerome) was intended, according to Jones, not as « a plea for literal truth but... to achieve an image in which the literal statement is itself incongruous »[9]. Adalbold of Utrecht, writing in the early eleventh century, said in his *Life* of Henry II that the two things to look for in describing events were « that the writer adheres to

among others, in the preface of JOHN OF MARMOUTIER to the *Gesta consulum Andegavorum*, in *Chroniques des comtes d'Anjou et des seigneurs d'Amboise*, ed. L. HALPHEN-R. POUPARDIN (Collection de textes pour servir à l'étude et à l'enseignement de l'histoire, 48), Paris 1913, p. 163.

  [6] *Les miracles de saint Benoît*, IX, prol., ed. E. DE CERTAIN (Société de l'histoire de France), Paris 1858, p. 357, and *Chronique de l'abbaye de Saint-Trond*, IV, 11, ed. C. DE BORMAN, 2 vols., Liège 1877, I, 62.

  [7] J.M.A. BEER, *Narrative Conventions of Truth in the Middle Ages* (Études de philologie et d'histoire, 38), Geneva 1981, stressed the conventionality of assertions of truth, comparing them to the brevity formulas (p. 10) and saying that « Truth in the *Gesta Guillelmi* [of William of Poitiers] was a complex combination of eulogy and didacticism, eye-witness detail and omission, contemporary documentation and classical illustration, Norman politics and universal truth, "meager prose" and rhetorical embellishment » (p. 22); and G. SPIEGEL, *Forging the Past: The Language of Historical Truth in the Middle Ages*, « The History Teacher », XVII (1984), pp. 267-283, who cited various examples of « truth-claims », especially in vernacular works of the early thirteenth century and said that « those instances in which truth-claims for history are most boldly asserted are precisely those in which ideological partisanship is most actively at play ». On history in a rhetorical sense as *sermo verus* in contrast to *fabula* as *integumentum*, see F. OHLY, *Bemerkungen eines Philologen zur Memoria*, in *Memoria. Der geschichtliche Zeugniswert des liturgischen Gedenkens im Mittelalter*, ed. K. SCHMID - J. WOLLASCH (Münstersche Mittelalter-Schriften, 48) Munich 1984, p. 46.

  [8] SIDONIUS APOLLINARIS, *Ep.* IV, 22, 1 and 5, ed. and tr. W.B. ANDERSON, 2 vols. (Loeb Classical Library), Cambridge (Mass.) 1936-65, II, 144 and 148.

  [9] C.W. JONES, *Saints' Lives and Chronicles in Early England*, Ithaca 1947, rp. 1968, p. 83. See also J.M. WALLACE-HADRILL, *Bede and Plummer*, in *Famulus Christi*, ed. G. BONNER, London 1976, p. 375.

the truth in his presentation and the reader acquires profit from the reading » [10]. Grosseteste in the thirteenth century said that « The truth of things is their essence as they ought to be, and their rectitude and conformity to the Word by which they are eternally spoken » [11]. All historical works involve a « perception de phénomène » or « Geschichtsbild ». The number of recent works concerned with the « viewpoint », « thought-world », and « world-view » of writers of history shows the shift of scholarly interest away from the dates and sources of historians to their ideas and attitudes, the traditions out of which they came, and the purposes and audiences for which they wrote [12]. Some reputations have suffered as a result. Guibert of Nogent's scepticism with regard to relics, which was once highly praised by scholars, is now seen as a characteristic expression of the sentiments of his age [13]. Even William of Malmesbury, who was long ranked high on the scale of historical honesty and impartiality, has been declared deceitful and unworthy to be called an historian because the facts in his Historia novella were twisted to serve the needs of Robert of Gloucester, to whom it is dedicated [14], and similar political or religious bias could

---

[10] ADALBOLD OF UTRECHT, Vita Henrici II imperatoris, proem., c.1, in PL, CXL, 89A. I have not seen the edition of this work by H. VAN RIJ cited by N. LETTINCK, L'intérêt de l'analyse de termes pour l'étude de l'historiographie médiévale, in Actes du « workshop ». Terminologie de la vie intellectuelle au moyen âge, Leyde/La Haye 20-21 septembre 1985, The Hague 1986, p. 33. On the style of this passage, see E.T. SILK, Pseudo-Johannes Scottus, Adalbold of Utrecht, and the Early Commentaries on Boethius, « Mediaeval and Renaissance Studies », III (1954), 4.

[11] GROSSETESTE, De veritate, in Die philosophischen Werke des Robert Grossetestes, ed. L. BAUR (Beiträge zur Geschichte der Philosophie des Mittelalters, 9), Münster 1912, p. 135. See also p. 137, where he said, « The truth of something is its conformity with its reason in the eternal Word ».

[12] ROUSSET, La conception de l'histoire..., p. 632: « L'histoire ainsi conçue est à la fois notation de l'événement et perception du phénomène »; M.-D. CHENU, Conscience de l'histoire et théologie (1954), rp. in his La théologie au douzième siècle (Études de philosophie médiévale, 45), Paris 1957, p. 65 (tr. J. TAYLOR - L.K. LITTLE, Nature, Man, and Society in the Twelfth Century, Chicago 1968); LAMMERS, in Geschichtsdenken..., p. XIV: « Geschichte schreiben ist nur möglich mit und in einem Geschichtsbild »; and N. LETTINCK, Geschiedbeschouwing en beleving van de eigen tijd in de eerste helft van de twaalfde eeuw, Amsterdam 1983, of which a resumé of chap. 4 appeared as Comment les historiens de la première moitié du XIIe siècle jugeaient-ils leur temps?, « Journal des savants » (1984), 51-77.

[13] J. CHAURAND, La conception de l'histoire de Guibert de Nogent (1053-1124), « Cahiers de civilisation médiévale », VIII (1965), 381-395; BOEHM, Der wissenschaftstheoretische Ort..., pp. 688-690: K. SCHREINER, « Discrimen veri ac falsi »: Ansätze und Formen der Kritik in der Heiligen-und Reliquienverehrung des Mittelalters, « Archiv für Kulturgeschichte », XLVIII (1966), 31-33; Zum Wahrheitsverständnis im Heiligen-und Reliquienwesen des Mittelalters,« Saeculum », XVII (1966), 148-149; C. MORRIS, A Critique of Popular Religion: Guibert of Nogent on « The Relics of the Saints », «Studies in Church History », VIII (1972), 55-60; RAY, Medieval Historiography..., pp. 46-47; and R.I. MOORE, Guibert of Nogent and his World, in Studies in Medieval History, presented to R.H.C. Davis , ed. H. MAYR-HARTING - R.I. MOORE, London 1985, pp. 107-117.

[14] R. PATTERSON, William of Malmesbury's Robert of Gloucester: A Re-evaluation of the « Historia novella », « American Historical Review », LXX (1965), 983-997, who said (p. 996) that « The work smacks of a conscious effort to deceive ». See also GUÉNÉE, Histoire..., pp. 287-288, and P. CLASSEN, « Res

doubtless be found in other historical works. This is not to say that they lacked any critical sense. As time went on, indeed, there was a growth, fostered by the influence of practical affairs, in the skills of testing evidence, and in the late twelfth century William of Newburgh and Gerald of Wales showed a new scholarly sensitivity in questioning the reliability of Geoffrey of Monmouth [15]. These areas of doubt, however, are themselves evidence of the attitudes and expectations of historians.

I shall not discuss here the philosophical or anthropological views of time and change, except in so far as they have influenced the interpretation of medieval historiography. The role of history in different societies has been analyzed in terms of Bergson's distinction between time (*temps*) as an external and quantitative concept and duration (*durée*) as an internal experience [16]. Husserl distinguished outer time from inner, remembered, or displaced time, in which (as in myths) experiences and processes are not temporally differentiated [17]. Traditional societies tend to live in « a continual present », Eliade said, and to see history not as a linear progression of irreversible and unforeseeable events but as a perpetually regenerated rotation [18], while Lévi-Strauss contrasted « cold » societies, in which history is subordinated to system, and « hot » societies where the process of historical evolution is accepted and internalized [19]. The Middle Ages inherited both « cold » and « hot » elements from its pagan, classical, and Christian past, and the balance between them changed as they moved from a predominantly oral to a written society [20]. The presence of cyclical and historical attitudes derived from

gestae », *Universal History, Apocalypse: Visions of Past and Future*, in *Renaissance and Renewal in the Twelfth Century*, ed. R.L. BENSON - G. CONSTABLE, Cambridge (Mass.) 1982, p. 392. On William as an historian and scholar, see R. THOMSON, *William of Malmesbury and Some Other Western Writers on Islam*, « Medievalia et Humanistica », N.S. VI (1975), 179-187, and J. CAMPBELL, *Some Twelfth-Century Views of the Anglo-Saxon Past*, « Peritia », III (1984), 136, who said that William was « perhaps the greatest, and [...] certainly the most admired, of the Anglo-Norman historians ».

[15] GUENÉE, *Histoire...*, p. 141, and N.F. PARTNER, *Serious Entertainments: The Writing of History in Twelfth-Century England*, Chicago-London 1977, pp. 52 and 62-65. See G. CONSTABLE, *Forgery and Plagiarism in the Middle Ages*, « Archiv für Diplomatik », XXIX (1983), esp. 13-14, on the development of critical techniques to detect forgeries in the twelfth and thirteenth centuries.

[16] R. GLASSER, *Time in French Life and Thought*, tr. C.G. PEARSON, Manchester 1972, pp. 2-6. This valuable work is ostensibly a translation of the German edition of 1936, but it has been revised and updated in places.

[17] See R. SOKOLOWSKI, *Timing*, « Review of Metaphysics », XXXV (1982), 687-714 on this (pp. 700, 704, and 711) and other philosophical views of time.

[18] M. ELIADE, *The Myth of the Eternal Return or, Cosmos and History*, tr. W. TRASK (Bollingen Series, 46), Princeton 1954, corrected rp. 1965, p. 86: A.J. GUREVICH, *Categories of Medieval Culture*, tr. G.L. CAMPBELL, London-Boston-Melbourne-Henley 1985, p. 95.

[19] C. LÉVI-STRAUSS, *The Savage Mind*, Chicago 1966, pp. 232-234.

[20] See, in particular, among recent works, M.T. CLANCHY, *From Memory to Written Record: England, 1066-1307*, Cambridge (Mass.) 1979, and B. STOCK, *The Implications of Literacy*, Princeton 1983.

the Germanic settlers may help to explain the persistent attitude of mythomania, which drew the present towards the past, as Marc Bloch said, and blended the colors of the two[21]. This approach has concentrated the attention of scholars on the social function of historical writings, and on how and why the past was presented in the Middle Ages. One result has been to include within the scope of historiography a wider range of works than the histories, chronicles, annals, and biographies which are normally considered « historical » and many more types of writers than those who are usually counted as historians. Poets, canonists, civil lawyers, writers of letters and treatises all helped to shape the view of the past. Above all, theologians like Rupert of Deutz, Honorius of Augsburg, Hugh of St Victor, Anselm of Havelberg, Gerhoh of Reichersberg, and Joachim of Fiore are now considered to have contributed more to the development of historical thought in the twelfth century than even the greatest annalists and chroniclers. Just as chronicles and annals formed the link between history and theology, cartularies were the point of contact between history and law, and their compilers should be considered historians[22]. The emergence of new types of historical works and the use of new types of sources is one of the most striking aspects of historical writing in the eleventh and twelfth centuries. The author of the history of St Martin at Tournai made use of charters, saints' lives, and confraternity-lists[23]. The cartulary-chronicles and foundation-histories of houses like Abingdon, Ely, Muri, Petershausen, and Zwiefalten point the way towards institutional histories[24], while the chronicle of Caffaro for Genoa and the *Liber Maiorichinus* of Pisa show an awareness of the importance of the development of communes[25]. Smalley devoted a chapter in her book on medieval historians to « civil service history », in which she included

---

[21]   See M. BLOCH, *Feudal Society*, tr. L.A. MANYON, Chicago 1961, pp. 91-92.

[22]   D. WALKER, *The Organization of Material in Medieval Cartularies*, in *The Study of Medieval Records: Essays in Honour of Kathleen Major*, ed. D.A. BULLOUGH - R.L. STOREY, Oxford 1971, pp. 132-150, and J.-P. GENET, *Cartulaires, registres et histoire: l'exemple anglais*, in *Le métier d'historien...*, pp. 95-138.

[23]   HERMAN OF TOURNAI, *Liber de restauratione monasterii sancti Martini Tornacensis*, cc. 45-47, in *Monumenta Germaniae Historica* [= *MGH*], *Scriptores* in fol., XIV, 295.

[24]   J. KASTNER, *Historiae fundationum monasteriorum. Frühformen monastischer Institutionsgeschichtsschreibung im Mittelalter* (Münchener Beiträge zur Mediävistik und Renaissance-Forschung, 18), Munich 1974, esp. Part A. Sometimes the narrative has crystalized around a particular document or documents; sometimes, as in MS Auxerre, Bibl. mun., 227, a history, annals, and cartulary are found together and (though often published separately) form part of a larger whole: see *Monumenta Vizeliacensia*, ed. R.B.C. HUYGENS (Corpus Christianorum: Continuatio mediaevalis [= CC:CM], 42), Turnhout 1976.

[25]   See C.B. FISHER, *The Pisan Clergy and an Awakening of Historical Interest in a Medieval Commune*, « Studies in Medieval and Renaissance History », III (1966), 143-219, and CLASSEN, « Res gestae »..., p. 388.

Galbert of Bruges and John of Salisbury's *Papal history*. Among more personal types of historical writings are letters — « the mirror of the soul » — and the autobiographical writings of Otloh of St Emmeram, Guibert of Nogent, Rupert of Deutz, Abelard, and Herman the Convert, which show a degree of conscious self-disclosure unknown since the *Confessions* of Augustine [26]. Works like these not only represented new genres of historical writing but also filled the needs of the individual in medieval society and of the emerging national states. The passion for revival and renewal in the eleventh and twelfth centuries affected national life as well as the church, and stimulated pride and interest in the achievements of the past. Historical self-consciousness increasingly took the form of patriotism [27]. Landulf in the prologue to his *History of Milan* said that he was « led by love of my fatherland and city » [28], and William of Malmesbury cited his affection for his fatherland and the authority of those who encouraged him as reasons for attempting to fill the gap in English history between the works of Bede and Eadmer. Later he also expressed his discontent with previous writers and desire to throw light on hidden events [29]. Saxo the Grammarian was asked to write his *History of the Danes* « because other nations commonly take pride in the accounts of their affairs and get pleasure from the memory of their great men » [30].

Great and visible historical changes had both to be justified and to be explained and understood, and much historical writing was inspired by major events like the Norman Conquest and the crusades [31]. Around the year 1100 the monks of Canterbury gathered and reorganized the records of the Anglo-Saxon past in an apparent effort to fit them into the broader framework of history of which England was increasingly a part [32]. For

---

[26] G. MISCH, *Geschichte der Autobiographie*, 3 vols. (3rd ed. of 1), Frankfurt a. M., 1949-62, has sections on Ratherius, Otloh, Guibert, Suger, Abelard and Heloise, Gerald of Wales, and other autobiographical writers of the eleventh and twelfth centuries. See also C. MORRIS, *The Discovery of the Individual, 1050-1200* (Church History Outlines, 5), London 1972, p. 79: « Autobiography [...] was not an isolated phenomenon, but part of [a] general tendency to examine, and publish, one's personal experience ».

[27] SIMON, *Untersuchungen*, 1, pp. 58-77, who mentioned most of the examples cited here.

[28] LANDULF, *Historia Mediolanensis*, I, prol. in *MGH, Scriptores* in fol., VIII, 36.

[29] WILLIAM OF MALMESBURY, *Gesta regum*, I, prol. and II, prol., ed. W. STUBBS, 2 vols. (Rolls Series, 90), London 1887-89, I, 2 and 103-104. On this prologue, see B. GUENÉE, *L'histoire entre l'éloquence et la science. Quelques remarques sur le prologue de Guillaume de Malmesbury à ses « Gesta regum Anglorum »*, « Académie des Inscriptions et Belles-Lettres: Comptes rendus », 1982, pp. 357-370.

[30] SAXO THE GRAMMARIAN, *Gesta Danorum*, prol., ed. J. OLRIK-H. RAEDER-F. BLATT, 2 vols., Copenhagen 1931-57, I, 3.

[31] SOUTHERN, *Aspects, 4*, p. 246, remarked on the stimulus given to the writing of history by « a crisis in national affairs, which seemed to alienate men from their past ». This can be extended to any perceived historical crisis.

[32] D. DUMVILLE, *Some Aspects of Annalistic Writing at Canterbury in the Eleventh and Early Twelfth Centuries*, « Peritia », II (1983), 23-57, esp. 38-39, 48, and 54.

contemporaries, probably the single most exciting historical work of the first half of the twelfth century was Geoffrey of Monmouth's *History of the Kings of Britain*, which today is hardly considered history at all but which formed the basis of early English history until at least the seventeenth century. The enthusiasm at the discovery of Geoffrey's *History* (which was expressed both by Henry of Huntingdon, who saw it at Bec in 1139, and later by Robert of Torigny, who claimed to have given it to Henry[33]) has been attributed to a « background of antiquarian expectancy and... sentimentality » in a « waiting public » in early twelfth century England[34]. It was certainly a key work in the flowering of Anglo-Norman historiography after the Conquest, which included Ordericus Vitalis, William of Malmesbury, Henry of Huntingdon, and others who attempted to come to terms with the historical issues presented by the failure of the Anglo-Saxon kingdom and the establishment of the Normans in England[35]. William especially, but also later writers like Simeon of Durham and Gervase of Canterbury, show a concern for historical continuity that was at least in part a reaction to the upheavals of the previous century[36]. A similar crisis was presented by the initial success and subsequent problems of the crusades, which occupied the attention of some of the most eminent historians of the twelfth century. Guibert of Nogent in his *Deeds done by God through the Franks* saw the First Crusade as fulfilling God's plan for the triumph of Christianity and as offering a new means of salvation to mankind; Otto of Freising and John of Salisbury tried to explain the failure of the Second Crusade[37]; while

[33] HENRY OF HUNTINGDON, *Historia Anglorum*, VIII, ed. TH. ARNOLD (Rolls Series, 74), London 1879, p. XXI, and ROBERT OF TORIGNY, *Chronicle*, prol., in *Chronicles of the Reigns of Stephen, Henry II., and Richard I.*, ed. R. HOWLETT, 4 vols. (Rolls Series, 82), London 1884-89, IV, 65.

[34] T.D. KENDRICK, *British Antiquity*, London 1950, rp. 1970, p. 11. On Geoffrey, see, in addition to the works cited in note 35, C.N.L. BROOKE, *Geoffrey of Monmouth as a Historian*, in *Church and Government in the Middle Ages: Essays presented to C.R. Cheney*, ed. C.N.L. BROOKE - D.E. LUSCOMBE - G.H. MARTIN - D. OWEN, Cambridge 1976, pp. 77-91, who ranked him « among the most ingenious historians of the age » and called him « perhaps the most popular of all medieval historical writers »; V.I.J. FLINT, *The « Historia regum Britanniae » of Geoffrey of Monmouth: Parody and Its Purpose. A Suggestion*, « Speculum », LIV (1979), 447-468; and CAMPBELL, *Some Twelfth-Century Views...*, p. 144, who called Geoffrey's *History* part of « a rising tide of nonsense ».

[35] See R. HANNING, *The Vision of History in Early Britain from Gildas to Geoffrey of Monmouth*, New York-London 1966, p. 173. See also C.N.L. BROOKE, *Historical Writing in England between 850 and 1150*, in *Storiografia altomedievale*, esp. pp. 238-239; R.W. LECKIE, *The Passage of Dominion: Geoffrey of Monmouth and the Periodization of Insular History in the Twelfth Century*, Toronto 1981, and, for the later twelfth century, PARTNER, *Serious Entertainments...* According to CAMPBELL, *Some Twelfth-Century Views...*, p. 131, « The greatest advances in the study and understanding of Anglo-Saxon history made before the nineteenth century were those of the twelfth ».

[36] A. GRANDSEN, *Realistic Observation in Twelfth-Century England*, « Speculum », XLVII (1972), 33-40.

[37] G. CONSTABLE, *The Second Crusade as Seen by Contemporaries*, « Traditio », IX (1953), 213-279, esp. 266-276.

William of Tyre looked at the Third Crusade from the point of view of an insider who was already established in the East [38]. The views of these writers on the nature of history and the interpretation of great events were in many respects derived from classical sources [39]. The roles of *historicus* and *poeta* came together for medieval writers in the rhetoric of Virgil and Lucan, who was admired for his *verisimilitas* as well as his *veritas* [40]. The concern for individuation and for topography found in twelfth-century English historical writings has been attributed to the influence of Suetonius and other classical historians; the view of Pisa as a « chosen people » in the *Liber Maiorichinus* may have come from Virgil; and the appeal of Sallust's distinctive blend of history, ethics, and rhetoric was so great, Smalley suggested, that medieval historians were closer to the facts the further they were from Sallust [41].

The language used by historians has also been used, especially by Guenée and Lettinck, to throw light on their views both of the past and of the present [42]. « The fortunes of words are among the least well charted areas of the past », according to Southern [43], and more research needs to be done on the meaning of words like *historia, veritas, aevum, aeternitas, processus, progressus, novus, antiquus, modernus, vetus*, and the many terms for reformation, restoration, renewal, and rebirth [44]. Hugh of St Victor, for instance, defined *historia* in the *Didascalicon* as « the truth of what has been done » and in the introduction to his *Chronicle* as « the narrative of what has been done expressed by the first sense of the letter », distinguishing it from allegory and tropology. In his treatise *On the Scrip-*

---

[38] ROUSSET, *La conception de l'histoire...*, pp. 625 and 627, and CLASSEN, « Res gestae »..., p. 388, commented on the influence of the crusades on the writing of history.

[39] SOUTHERN, *Aspects, 1*, pp. 178-179, studied in particular the influence of Sallust, Suetonius, Virgil, and Lucan.

[40] P. VON MOOS, « *Poeta* » *und* « *Historicus* » *im Mittelalter. Zum Mimesis-Problem am Beispiel einiger Urteile über Lucan*, « Beiträge zur Geschichte der deutschen Sprache und Literatur », XCVIII (1976), 93-130, who drew a parallel with OTTO OF FREISING'S double role as a poet and historian in the *Gesta Friderici* (p. 123). See also J. ADAMS, *The Influence of Lucan on the Political Attitudes of Suger of Saint-Denis*, in *Proceedings of the Annual Meeting of the Western Society for French History*, XII (1984), pp. 1-11.

[41] GRANDSEN, *Realistic Observation...*, pp. 40-47; FISHER, *The Pisan Clergy...*, pp. 193 and 217; and B. SMALLEY, *Sallust in the Middle Ages*, in *Classical Influences on European Culture A.D. 500-1500*, ed. R.R. BOLGAR, Cambridge 1971, pp. 165-175. See also J. SCHNEIDER, *Die Vita Heinrici IV. und Sallust. Studien zu Stil und Imitatio in der mittellateinischen Prosa* (Deutsche Akademie der Wissenschaften zu Berlin. Schriften der Sektion für Altertumswissenschaft, 49), Berlin 1965, who also mentioned the influence of Suetonius and Livy (pp. 14-33).

[42] See especially GUENÉE, *L'historien...*, and the two articles by LETTINCK, *Comment les historiens...*, and *L'intérêt de l'analyse....*

[43] R.W. SOUTHERN, *The Historical Experience* (Rede Lecture, 1974), « Times Literary Supplement », 24 June 1977, 771.

[44] See G. CONSTABLE, *Renewal and Reform in Religious Life*, in *Renaissance and Renewal...*, esp. p. 39.

tures and sacred writers he said that the term history derived from the Greek word for seeing and narrating and that in Antiquity historians described only events seen by themselves. « History is accurately and strictly named according to this [definition], but it is customarily taken more broadly, so that the sense which is given to something in the first place from the meaning of the words is named history »[45]. Chenu commented on Hugh's use of *mundus* and *saeculum* in *On the moral ark of Noah*, saying that

> This conjunction denotes, precisely in these words, the very significant perception of the coherence of cosmic time and historical time and of geography and history. The very economy of salvation involves this double dimension: « In works of restoration, the order should be considered in three ways: according to place, according to time, [and] according to dignity [...] The order of place and the order of time, however, seem to run together in almost all things according to the series of events »[46].

In this passage Hugh meant near or far by « place » and earlier or later by « time », and when he said that they run together in the *series rerum gestarum* — an important historical term for Hugh, like *series narrationis* and *series temporum* — he may have had in mind the concept of *translatio* which postulated the gradual movement of political power and learning from the East to the West[47].

II

Tempus is one of the most complicated words in the historical vocabulary of the eleventh and twelfth centuries. It is easy to translate, because

---

[45] HUGH OF ST VICTOR, *Didascalicon*, IV, 3, ed. C.H. BUTTIMER (Catholic University of America: Studies in Medieval and Renaissance Latin, 10), Washington (D.C.) 1939, pp. 113-114 (= *PL*, CLXXVI, 799BC), where he went on to say that history involved studying what was done (the business), when (the time), where (the place), and by whom (the person); W.M. GREEN, *Hugo of St Victor « De tribus maximis circumstantiis gestorum »*, « Speculum », XVIII (1943), 488-492, where he specified persons, places, and times; and *De scripturis et scriptoribus sacris*, c. 3, in *PL*, CLXXV, 12A. See J. EHLERS, « *Historia, allegoria, tropologia* » - *Exegetische Grundlagen der Geschichtskonzeption Hugos von St. Viktor*, « Mittellateinisches Jahrbuch », VII (1972), 155-158, on the primacy of history in interpreting biblical texts; G.A. ZINN JR., *Hugh of Saint Victor and the Art of Memory*, « Viator », V (1974), 227-228; and G. EVANS, *Hugh of St Victor on History and the Meaning of Things*, « Studia monastica », XXV (1983), 223-234, esp. 227-228 on history, allegory, and tropology.

[46] CHENU, *La théologie...*, p. 67, nn. 2 and 5 (tr. TAYLOR and LITTLE, p. 171), citing HUGH OF ST VICTOR, *De arca Noe*, IV, 9, in *PL*, CLXXVI, 677BD, of which the two passages quoted here are cited separately by Chenu, who glossed *dignitas* as « religious diversity ». Hugh defined it as in terms of more or less humility or other qualities. GLASSER, *Time in French Life...*, pp. 31-32, interpreted *saeculum* as both a spatial and a temporal concept.

[47] Among the many works on the concepts of *translatio imperii* and *translatio studii*, of special relevance here are B. SMALLEY, *English Friars and Antiquity in the Early Fourteenth Century*, Oxford 1960, pp. 70-71: E. GÖSSMANN, *Antiqui und Moderni in Mittelalter. Eine geschichtliche Standortbestimmung* (Veröffentlichungen des Grabmann-Institutes zur Erforschung der mittelalterlichen Theologie und Philosophie, N.F. 23), Munich-Paderborn-Wien 1974, pp. 47-50; and CLASSEN, « Res gestae»..., p. 402.

« time » in English (and the equivalent words in most European languages) retains the ambiguity it had in the Middle Ages. But behind it lie not
only the difference between external, measurable time and internal,
experienced duration, which I have already mentioned, but also a mixture of cyclical, linear, and folkloristic concepts inherited from antiquity,
the Bible, early Christianity, and the Germanic tribes, each of which had
its own prehistory [48]. Views of time can be classified not only according
to computistical systems but also according to differing occupations and
social needs; and more than one view can be found together even in the
same person, depending on the circumstances [49]. The writers of works on
chronology, philosophy, theology, and history in the Middle Ages used
varying concepts of time, according to their needs and interests, as did
parish priests, merchants, and agricultural laborers — and as people still
do today. « Agrarian time, family time (or, genealogical, dynastic time),
biblical (or liturgical) time, cyclic time, and finally historical time are not
identical and are, indeed, often contradictory », wrote Gurevich, who
elsewhere distinguished the time scale of pagan myth, with its rites,
seasons, and generations, from that of Christianity, which united sacral
and secular time into a single category of historical time, the history of
salvation [50]. The cosmic or natural time of the solar, seasonal, and gene-
rational rotations is often distinguished from the linear view found in the
Bible, where time flows under God's direction from the beginning of the
world to the end, with (for Christians) the Incarnation somewhere in the
middle [51]; but the two views are found together in some societies and can

---

[48]   There is a large literature on time in Antiquity and the Middle Ages. In addition to the works of ✶
GLASSER and GUREVICH cited above, see generally the two collective volumes Aiôn. Le temps chez les
Romains, ed. R. CHEVALLIER (Caesarodunum, X bis), Paris 1976, and Le temps chrétien de la fin de
l'antiquité au moyen âge, IIIe-XIIIe siècles (Colloques internationaux du Centre national de la recherche
scientifique, 604), Paris 1984; on Late Antiquity: the texts translated with an introduction in S.
SAMBURSKY - S. PINES, The Concept of Time in Late Neoplatonism, Jerusalem 1971; and on the Middle Ages:
J.F. CALLAHAN, Four Views of Time in Ancient Philosophy, revised ed., Westwood (Conn.) 1979; the
articles by J. LE GOFF, Au moyen âge: Temps de l'Église et temps du marchand, « Annales », XV (1960), 417-
433, and Le temps du travail dans la « crise » du XIVe siècle: du temps médiéval au temps moderne, « Moyen
Age », LXIX (1963), 597-613, and by J. LECLERCQ, Experience and Interpretation of Time in the Early Middle
Ages, « Studies in Medieval Culture », V (1975), 9-19.
[49]   GLASSER, Time in French Life..., pp. 99-106, and LE GOFF, Au moyen âge..., p. 428, discuss different
types of time suited to various activities and attitudes.
[50]   GUREVICH, Categories..., pp. 110 (« Historical time is subordinate to sacral time, but is not dissol-
ved in it. ») and 141.
[51]   TH. MOMMSEN, St. Augustine and the Christian Idea of Progress: The Background of « The City of God »
(1951), rp. in his Medieval and Renaissance Studies, ed. E. RICE JR., Ithaca 1959, p. 276, associated the
linear view of time with Jewish thought and the cyclical view with the Greeks, and G. QUISPEL, Zeit und
Geschichte im antiken Christentum, « Eranos-Jahrbuch », XX (1951), 115-140, tr. in Man and Time: Papers
from the Eranos Yearbooks (Bollingen Series, 30.3), Princeton 1957, pp. 85-107, esp. 88 on the development
in early Christianity of the « idea of rectilinear history and its unrepeatable uniqueness ». Y.-M. DUVAL,

be combined in spirals, or developing cycles [52]. Greeks and Christians were exposed to both. Plato's view of time as the image of eternity was embodied in the *Consolation of philosophy* of Boethius, who said that time derived from eternity [53]. Isidoros of Alexandria in the fifth century compared time to a wheel [54], and the endless cycles of liturgical ceremonies created a distinct category of clerical or religious time for men and women in the Middle Ages.

Time was considered to be common property, or the property of God, and the view that it was a commodity, which could be bought and sold like other commodities, emerged only towards the end of the Middle Ages. Thomas of Chobham, writing about 1216, accused the usurer of selling « not what is his, but only time, which is God's », and in an *exemplum* of the late thirteenth century usurers were said to break the universal law « because they sell time, which is the common property (*commune*) of all creatures » [55]. Quinones contrasted the medieval disregard for the value of time with the concern for « temporal management [...] diligence, constant application, and long effort » in the Renaissance, when time became « an agent of conversion [...] from aesthetic awareness to ethical action » and when « a state of war was declared between man and time » [56]. Time is still often seen as an enemy, or at least a threat, and as an ally of human weakness [57]. I shall cite later some medieval expressions of the dangers of losing or wasting time. Some scholars have dated the emergence of what may be called a professional, urban, or mercantile sense of time in the late thirteenth and fourteenth centuries and have associated it both with the development of towns and trade and

Temps antique et temps chrétien, in *Aiôn...*, pp. 253-259, questioned the distinction between «Greek» cyclical time and « Christian » linear time, saying that there was also a linear view of time among the Greeks.

[52] See A. MILLER, *Maya Rulers of Time*, Philadelphia 1986, on the political implications of cyclical and linear times in Maya society.

[53] BOETHIUS, *Consolatio philosophiae*, III, m. 9, ed. W. WEINBERGER (CSEL, 67), Wien-Leipzig 1934, p. 63, and ed. L. BIELER (CC, 94.1), Turnhout 1957, p. 51. On later commentaries, see notes 78-79 and 96.

[54] ISIDOROS, *Ep.* II, 158, in *PG*, LXXVIII, 614A.

[55] THOMAS OF CHOBHAM, *Summa confessorum*, D. VI, q. XI (De usura), c. 1, ed. F. BROOMFIELD (Analecta mediaevalia Namurcensia, 25), Louvain-Paris 1968, p. 505 (see p. LXII on the date), and *La « Tabula exemplorum secundum ordinem alphabeti ». Recueil d'exempla compilé en France à la fin du XIIIe siècle*, ed. J. TH. WELTER (Thesaurus exemplorum, 3), Paris-Toulouse 1926, p. 82, n. 304, who cited on p. 139 a parallel from the fourteenth-century collection in MS Paris, Bibl. nat., Lat. 13472, f. 3ᵛB: « Preterea usuarii sunt latrones quia uendunt tempus quod non est suum et uendere alienum, inuito domino, furtum est ». See J. LE GOFF, *La bourse et la vie. Économie et religion au moyen âge*, Paris 1986, pp. 42-44, citing these examples.

[56] R.J. QUINONES, *The Renaissance Discovery of Time* (Harvard Studies in Comparative Literature, 31), Cambridge (Mass.) 1972, pp. 494-497.

[57] G. RAVERAT, *Period Piece*, London 1952, p. 184, cited the example of William Darwin, who before retiring each night said, « Let me see; how goes the Enemy? ».

with the growing use of mechanical clocks. « For the merchant », wrote Le Goff, « the technological milieu placed a new measurable time, directed and foreseeable, on top of the time ... of the natural milieu » [58]. The history of clocks, and of their influence on the concept of time and on social history generally, is debated by scholars. Some say that they were first used in religious houses, and later spread to towns, and others that people in the Middle Ages had adequate ways of telling time without clocks, of which the real importance lay in the modern period [59]. Even today, when time is often seen as « the single valid measuring stick in a rational and objective world », the view that time is relative has not disappeared and has been reasserted by scientists who have shown that the number of days per year is slowly decreasing and that the life-spans of short- and long-lived animals are comparable in terms of their life expectancies [60]. The concept of piece-work stresses the product itself rather than the time taken to make it, and the length of prison sentences and examination questions reflects social values and show that time still has a symbolic role in society [61]. Clocks did not therefore drive out other ways of looking at time, but their precise measurement promoted a linear, externalized view of time, « proceeding from the past to the future through a point called the present », as Gurevich put it, and ordering the relations between both individuals and groups in society [62].

In the Middle Ages, the precise measurement of time by clocks was perhaps less important than the introduction of hours of equal length

[58] LE GOFF, Au moyen âge..., p. 425. See also S. STELLING-MICHAUD, Quelques aspects du problème du temps au moyen âge, « Schweizer Beiträge zur allgemeinen Geschichte », XVII (1959), 7-30; C. CIPOLLA, Clocks and Culture 1300-1700, London 1967; and D. LANDES, Revolution in Time: Clocks and the Making of the Modern World, Cambridge (Mass.)-London 1983, esp. pp. 67-84.
[59] O. SPENGLER, The Decline of the West, tr. C.F. ATKINSON, New York 1927, p. 15, n. 1, speaking of the invention of clocks (which he dated 1000-1200), wrote: « Observe the significant association of time measurement with the edifices of religion » (cf. GLASSER, Time in French Life..., p. 54, who has « the structure of religious worship » in place of « the edifices of religion »). LE GOFF, Les temps du travail..., p. 607, said that monastic life was « the great master of the use of time ». See also A. D'HAENENS on the clock at Villars in his article in the present volume. C.M. RADDING, A World Made by Men: Cognition and Society, 400-1200, Chapel Hill-London 1985, pp. 17-18, considered the idea of merchants' time an example of the difficulty of correlating trends in intellectual and technological history. For G. Flaubert in 1850, buying a watch was a « definitive step » as his friend Ernest Chevalier became solemn, respectable, and « gave up imagination »: The Letters of Gustave Flaubert, ed. and tr. F. STEEGMULLER, Cambridge (Mass.) 1980-82, I, 133.
[60] S.J. GOULD, The Panda's Thumb, New York-London 1980, pp. 302 and 322-323. What is « middle-aged » today was « old » in the Middle Ages, just as the present age of retirement in the United States was the average life-expectancy in the Bible.
[61] See GLASSER, Time in French Life..., p. 67.
[62] GUREVICH, Categories..., p. 52, and GLASSER, Time in French Life..., p. 87.

(and, later, the division of the day into two sets of hours)[63], which introduced into the concept of time a type of abstraction which has been compared to the shift from orality to scribality and which fostered a more abstract and less personal and relative way of looking at the world[64]. Gent in his book on *The Problem of Time* attributed « the beginning of real historical consciousness » to the invention of the wheeled clock, which he dated to about 1000, and Glasser wrote,

> It is indeed probable that the clock, thanks to the enhanced awareness of time and of temporal relations which it engendered, did prepare the ground for the growth of a new faculty of historical vision[65].

Clocks by their nature associated time with motion, as had Aristotle, and (when the clock had a dial) with circular motion[66], and thus fostered a cyclical or spiral view, in which time consisted of a succession of identical, or similar, cycles. For Dante the clock which summoned the faithful to prayer and filled them with love by its very motion and sound was a symbol of the heavenly movements and music, and its precision paralleled the dances and songs he saw and heard in paradise[67]. Without more knowledge of the development and use of clocks, it is impossible to say to what extent these views influenced the traditional concepts of time in the eleventh and twelfth centuries. Time in the Bible, though linear from a human point of view, is comprehended less by its quantity or extent than by its quality and immediacy[68]. God preceded the creation and will endure beyond it, and His timelessness is expressed in the verse from the Psalms that « a thousand years in Thy sight are as yesterday, which is past » and in Christ's reply to the Jews who said He had not seen Abraham: « Before Abraham was made, I

[63] See PH. WOLFF, *Le temps et sa mesure au moyen âge*, « Annales », XVII (1962), 1141-1145. An amusing passage on the popular reaction to the introduction of equal hours at Parma is given by G. CASANOVA, *History of My Life*, tr. W.R. TRASK, 6 vols., New York 1966-71, III, 48-49.

[64] According to STOCK, *The Implications of Literacy*, p. 84, « Time was externalized, offering a parallel to the abstract, depersonalized, and apparently objective world of the text ». See also the article by D'HAENENS in this volume.

[65] W. GENT, *Das Problem der Zeit. Eine historische und systematische Untersuchung*, Frankfurt a.M. 1934, p. 155, and GLASSER, *Time in French Life...*, p. 55.

[66] SOKOLOWSKI, *Timing...*, pp. 690 and 692, distinguished two motions in clock (as apart from calendar) time: the motion clocked and the act of clocking, to which he added the motion of the clocker who observed the two motions and held them together. There is an important difference in this respect between dial clocks and digital clocks.

[67] DANTE, *Par.*, X, 139-144, and XXIV, 12-14. See P. DRONKE, *Dante and Medieval Latin Traditions*, Cambridge 1986, pp. 101-102.

[68] J. MUILENBERG, *The Biblical View of Time*, « Harvard Theological Review », LIV (1961), 238 and 249-250.

am »[69]. For Plato, time was the image or shadow of eternity; for Aristotle, it was the number or measure of the movement of material bodies; for Plotinus, it existed in and with the soul, while the later Neoplatonists saw it as an intelligible static, like a river at rest[70]. The Stoics also seem to have had a static view of time, in which all time is present, against which Tatian argued in his *Oration to the Greeks*: « Why do you divide up time, saying that part of it is past, part present, and part future? How can the future become past, if the present exists? »[71]. Seneca wrote in Letter 49 that « Whatever time has passed is in the same place », and in Letter 88,

> See how many questions are asked concerning time alone: first, whether it is anything in itself; second, whether anything exists before time or without time; and [third, whether] time began with the world or whether even before the world, because something existed, time also existed[72].

The idea that man lives in an eternal present is found in both pagan and Christian works of late Antiquity. Julian in his *Letter to the Athenians* said that human wisdom « looks only to the present moment » and should be thankful to avoid mistakes even for a brief time[73]. According to Gregory of Nyssa, the example of Moses showed that men should live in the present, and the permanence of an historical event (like the crossing of the Red Sea) was spiritually transposed into the living moment[74]. Augustine in the *City of God* contrasted God's comprehension of temporal events « in a stable and eternal present » with man's division of time into past, present, and future[75]; and in a famous passage in the *Confessions*, after saying that for God, who was before time and changeless, there was no time, Augustine asked:

---

[69] Ps. 89. 4 (cf. II Peter 3.8) and John 8.58.

[70] On these views, see (in addition to SAMBURSKY - PINES, *The Concept of Time...*, and CALLAHAN, *Four Views of Time...*) V.N. BARAN, *L'expression du temps et de la durée en Latin*, in *Aiôn...*, p. 2.

[71] TATIAN, *Oratio ad Graecos*, c. 26, ed. and tr. M. WHITTAKER (Oxford Early Christian Texts), Oxford 1982, p. 49. He went on to say that the Age stood still while the observers moved, like a ship sailing past a mountain. See SAMBURSKY - PINES, *The Concept of Time...*, pp. 10-11 and 102-103.

[72] SENECA, *Epp.* 49 and 88.33, tr. R.M. GUMMERE, 3 vols. (Loeb Library), London 1917-25, I, 322, and II, 368-370. On Seneca's view of time, see J.N. SEVENSTER, *Paul and Seneca* (Supplements to Novum Testamentum, 4), Leiden 1961, pp. 30-32.

[73] JULIAN THE APOSTATE, *Works*, tr. W. C. WRIGHT, 3 vols. (Loeb Library), London 1913, II, 261-263. He gave this as the reason that people give no heed to « things that are to happen thirty years hence, or things that are already past, for the one is superfluous, the other impossible ». See M. MESLIN, *Temps initiatique et progrès spirituels dans la nouvelle religiosité*, in *Le temps chrétien...*, p. 53.

[74] M.A. BARDELLE, *La vie de Moïse de Grégoire de Nysse ou le temps spirituel vécu à travers l'imaginaire d'un modèle historique*, in *Le temps chrétien...*, p. 259.

[75] AUGUSTINE, *De civitate Dei*, XI, 21, in *CC*, XLVIII, 339-340.

What then is time? If no one asks me, I know; if I want to explain it to a questioner, I do not know. But at any rate this much I dare affirm I know, that if nothing passed away, there would be no past time; if nothing were coming, there would be no future time; and if nothing were existing, there would be no present time.

Later he concluded:

What is now evident and clear is that future and past things do not exist and that it is inaccurate to say that there are three times: past, present, and future; but it would perhaps be accurate to say that there are three times: a present concerning past things, a present concerning present things, and a present concerning future things. For these three are in the spirit (*anima*), and I do not see them elsewhere: the present concerning past things is memory; the present concerning present things is perception (*contuitus*); the present concerning future things is expectation[76].

Augustine thus saw, rather than three times, three ways of seeing the present in relation respectively to present, past, and future events; and ultimately, like Plotinus, he located it in the soul, which has the power « to recall the past and anticipate the future »[77].

Echoes of these views were heard throughout the Middle Ages. The distinction between eternity and time, and the equation of God with eternity and the created world with temporality, found a *locus classicus* in the *Consolation of philosophy*, III, m. 9, where Boethius, drawing on Plato, described God « who orders time to go from eternity (*qui tempus ab evo ire iubes*) »[78]. According to an anonymous commentary, once attributed to John the Scot but possibly later, « Whatever is or was or will be is either eternal or perpetual or has time »; and it went on to say that eternity has no beginning or end, perpetuity has a beginning and no end, and temporal things are all subject to change, and that time was like a circle moving around the unmoving and indivisible center of eternity[79].

---

[76] AUGUSTINE, *Confessiones*, XI, 14 (17) and 20 (26), in *CC*, XXVII, 202-203 and 206-207. The translations are my own, but they have been compared with those of W. SHEED and V. BOURKE, who in the second passage respectively translated *anima* and *contuitus* as « mind » and « sight » and as « soul » and « immediate vision ». On the parallels between the first passage and SENECA'S *De brevitate vitae* (cited n. 111 below), see M. CRISTIANI, *L'évocation de l'enfance dans le 1er livre des « Confessions »: Problèmes culturels et anthropologiques*, in *Le temps chrétien...*, pp. 400-401, and on Augustine's concept of memory, OHLY, *Bemerkungen...*, pp. 34-36.

[77] CALLAHAN, *Four Views of Time...*, pp. 157, 169, and 181. See SAMBURSKY - PINES, *The Concept of Time...*, pp. 11-12 on Plotinus (and 18, on the view of Proclus that time is prior to the soul), and QUISPEL, in *Man and Time...*, pp. 95-107, esp. 100, on Augustine's transposition of time into the human soul.

[78] See n. 53 above. On early medieval commentators on Boethius, see R.B.C. HUYGENS, *Mittelalterliche Kommentare zum « O qui perpetua... »*, « Sacris Erudiri », VI (1954), 373-427, and SILK, *Pseudo-Johannes Scottus...*

[79] *Saeculi noni auctoris in Boetii « Consolationem philosophiae » commentarius*, ed. E.T. SILK (Papers and Monographs of the American Academy in Rome, 9), Rome 1935, pp. 157-158 and 175-176.

Bovo of Corvey, writing in the late ninth or early tenth century, also stressed motion and mutability, equating *motatio* with *mutatio*: « Every created thing, from wherever it begins to be, embarks on a journey of time », which for incorporeal creatures is only in time and for bodily creatures, in both time and space [80]. Adalbold of Utrecht in the early eleventh century took from the commentary attributed to John the Scot (though the dependency may be the other way around) the view of eternity as a center around which the circle of time moved [81]. His definition of time as « the image of eternity » came from Plato, while the equation of time with motion was Aristotelian. John the Scot cited Maximus Confessor to support his concept of the spatio-temporal unity of the Creator, of Whom space and time were aspects, and Ermenrich of Ellwangen wrote in the mid-ninth century that « In the deity there are no measures of position and no times, and it has no more and no less, which is the same thing » [82]. Later Honorius of Augsburg also cited Maximus on the inseparability of time and place, saying that « The essence of all existing things is local and temporal » [83].

Peter Damiani in his letter on divine omnipotence said that for God

There was no yesterday or tomorrow but an eternal today. Within the bosom of His wisdom He encloses, fastens, and fixes forever all times, that is, the past, the present, and the future, so that He suffers nothing new to approach Him nor anything by passing by to leave Him [84].

In his commentary on Genesis 2.2 Damiani said that the verse « Abide in me, and I in you » (John 15.4) meant that for mankind God is

an untemporal time and an unplaceable place. Unplaceable, that is, because He is not circumscribed by place; untemporal, because He will never finish. God is therefore

---

[80]   *PL*, LXIV, 1240BC = HUYGENS, *Mittelalterliche Kommentare...*, p. 385; cf. SILK, *Pseudo-Johannes Scottus...*, p. 3.

[81]   HUYGENS, *Mittelalterliche Kommentare...*, pp. 410-411, and SILK, *Pseudo-Johannes Scottus...*, p. 26.

[82]   M. CRISTIANI, *Lo spazio e il tempo nell'opera dell'Eriugena*, « Studi medievali », 3 S., XIV.1 (1973), 39-136, esp. 92-102, and ERMENRICH OF ELLWANGEN, *Epistola ad Grimaldum abbatem*, c. 32. in *MGH*, *Epistolae*, V, 572. On the spatial extension of primary time in the work of Damascius, see SAMBURSKY - PINES, *The Concept of Time...*, p. 19.

[83]   HONORIUS OF AUGSBURG, *Clavis physicae*, c. 46, ed. P. LUCENTINI (Temi e testi, 21), Rome 1974, p. 28.

[84]   PETER DAMIANI, *De divina omnipotentia*, cc. 10 and 17, in *PL*, CXLV, 607A and 618D, ed. and tr. A. CANTIN (Sources Chrétiennes, 191: Textes monastiques d'Occident, 11), Paris 1972, pp. 425 and 472. G. BÖWERING in a lecture on *Borrowing in Sūfī Qur'ān Commentary* discussed the Sufi mystic Daylami, who defined time as an eternal present, into which past and present were compressed. On Eckhart's concept of « a present now » or « now time », see L. VAUGHAN, *Time in a Meister Eckhart Sermon: « Impletum est temus Elizabeth »*, « Germanic Notes », XVII (1986), 20-21.

time for us, when He said in the gospel of John, « Are there not twelve hours of the day?» [85].

Anselm of Canterbury, drawing his definitions of eternity and time from the *City of God*, attributed to free will the fact that time unlike eternity changed. In eternity there is no « was » or « will be » but only « is » and « now », an eternal present, « in which all times are contained. Since just as the present time contains all place and whatever is in any place, so all time and whatever is at any time is enclosed together in an eternal present » [86]. Peter Lombard said in his discussion of the omniscience and prescience of God that He « knows always whatever He knows at any time ». He knew both that He would create the world and, after He created it, that it was created, just as for a person speaking at different times the same day may be yesterday, today, and tomorrow. The ancients who knew that Christ would be born and die and we who know that He was born and died believe the same thing, « "For times are varied", as Augustine said, and therefore words "not faith" are changed » [87].

For these writers the principal characteristic of time was mutability. The very word time was said to derive from temperament in the early medieval computistical texts, from which it passed into the works both of Isidore of Seville, who associated *tempora* with the four seasons tempered by wet, dry, hot, and cold, and of Bede, who further distinguished three ways of reckoning time by nature (solar and lunar years), custom (months of thirty days), and authority, both divine (such as the seventh day or year), and human (such as indictions) [88]. In the ninth century Rabanus Maurus, following Bede, said that « Time runs from the beginning of the world (*mundus*) up until the end of the age (*seculum*) [...] It

[85] PETER DAMIANI, *Expositio libri Geneseos*, c. 7, in *PL*, CXLV, 843D-844A; cf. *De divina omnipotentia*, 8, *ibi*, 605B (ed. CANTIN, p. 420): « Est enim, ut ita dixerim, locus inlocalis qui sic in se continet omnia loca ut non moveatur ipse per loca ».

[86] ANSELM OF CANTERBURY, *De concordia*, I, 5, in *S. Anselmi opera omnia*, ed. F.S. SCHMITT, 6 vols., Edinburgh 1946-61, II, 254.

[87] PETER LOMBARD, *Sententiae*, I.41.7, in *PL*, CXCVI, 635 = 1.41.3 (183). 3-4 in 3rd ed., I.2 (Spicilegium Bonaventurianum, 4), Grottaferrata 1971, p. 293, cf. 1.44.4 in *PL*, CXCVI, 641 = 1.44.2 (189). 3, in 3rd ed., pp. 305-306. The citation is to AUGUSTINE, *In Ioan.*, XLV.9, in *PL*, XXXV, 1722, and *CC*, XXXVI, 392 (see n. 153 below). See CHENU, *La théologie...*, p. 93.

[88] ISIDORE OF SEVILLE, *Etymologiae*, V, 35 (see n. 4 above) and BEDE, *De temporum ratione*, c. 2, ed. C.W. JONES (Mediaeval Academy of America, Publ. 41), Cambridge (Mass.) 1943, p. 182. According to JONES (p. 331), « The distinction of three kinds of time is Bede's own, not to be found in any of his sources »; see also A. CORDOLIANI, *À propos du chapitre premier du « De temporum ratione »*, de Bède, « Moyen Age », LIV (1948), 209-224, who dated the work 725 and said it drew on various earlier computistical texts.

means the fit distribution of divine will»[89]. John the Scot in the *Periphyseon* defined time as «the sure and rational dimension in the duration and movement of changeable things», and he distinguished the *tempora aeterna* of Romans 16.25, which were equivalent to divinity, from the *tempora saecularia* of II Timothy 1.9, which came into existence with the world and presented a realization of multiplicity[90]. For Haimo of Auxerre, «The difference between time and eternity is that eternity is stable but time is changeable»[91]. Honorius of Augsburg in the early twelfth century described time in Platonic terms as «the shadow of eternity» and compared it to a rope, going from East to West and stretching backwards, which is rolled up every day and will eventually be used up. «Time is named for temperament and is nothing other than the vicissitude of things», he said in his treatise on *The image of the world*, and he defined it in his *Key to nature*, like John the Scot, as «the sure and rational dimension in the duration and movement of changeable things»[92].

William of Conches used the same words — *dimensio more et motus mutabilium rerum* — to describe time in his commentaries on the *Consolation of philosophy* and the *Timaeus*, and in the unpublished glosses on Macrobius and Priscian, where they were attributed to Augustine. Commenting on Boethius's reference to God «who orders time to go from eternity», William gave two descriptions of time as distinct from eternity (which he called «the present state of all things which are and which have been and which are in the future»): first, «that space which began to be with the world and will cease with the world, if the time and the

[89] RABANUS MAURUS, *De universo*, X, 1, in *PL*, CXI, 285A; cf. VI, 1, *ibi*, 146D-147A. See LECLERCQ, *Experience and Interpretation...*, p. 15.

[90] JOHN THE SCOT, *Periphyseon (De divisione naturae)*, I, 63, ed. I.P. SHELDON-WILLIAMS (Scriptores Latini Hiberniae, 7), Dublin 1978, p. 184 (= *PL*, CXXII, 507AB): «Est enim tempus mutabilium rerum morae motusque certa rationabilisque dimensio». These words are an addition, probably in John's handwriting, in MS Rheims, 875, and may be a citation from an unidentified earlier work: see WILLIAM OF CONCHES, *Glosae super Platonem*, ed. E. JEAUNEAU (Textes philosophiques du moyen âge, 13), Paris 1965, p. 176, n.b. On the difference between *tempora aeterna* and *tempora saecularia*, see CRISTIANI, *Lo spazio e il tempo...*, p. 117.

[91] HAIMO OF AUXERRE, *Explanatio in Ep. ad Titum*, in *PL*, CXVII, 812C. On the authorship, see B. SMALLEY, *The Study of the Bible in the Middle Ages*, 2nd ed., Oxford 1952, p. 39, n. 3.

[92] HONORIUS OF AUGSBURG, *De imagine mundi*, II, 1-3, in *PL*, CLXXII, 145D-147A, and *Clavis physicae*, c. 66, ed. LUCENTINI, p. 46. See GUREVICH, *Categories...*, p. 119, and M.L. ARDUINI, «*Rerum mutabilitas* »: *Welt, Zeit, Menschenbild und «Corpus Ecclesiae-Christianitatis» bei Honorius von Regensburg (Augustodunensis)*, «Recherches de théologie ancienne et médiévale», LII (1985), 78-108, esp. 93-94 on Honorius's view of time, and the shortened version, in Italian, in *L'homme et son univers au moyen âge. Actes de septième congrès international de philosophie médiévale (30 août-4 septembre 1982)*, ed. C. WENIN, 2 vols. (Philosophes médiévaux, 26), Louvain-la-Neuve 1986, I, 365-373, citing Honorius's views on *mutabilitas* in his *Elucidarium*, III, 78, in Y. LEFÈVRE, *L'Elucidarium et les lucidaires* (Bibliothèque des Écoles françaises d'Athènes et de Rome, 180), Paris 1954, pp. 462-463.

world will ever have an end », and, second, « the dimension in the duration and movement of changeable things. This time descends from eternity, because God provided all things from eternity and disposed by temporal successions » [93]. In his commentary on the *Timaeus*, after giving a similar definition of eternity, « whence the archetype of the world, which is divine wisdom, is rightly called the eternal world », William distinguished time as general, total, and partial. General time was « the dimension in the duration and movement of changeable things », within which he specified time « according to the delay of a changeable thing in [its] place » and time « according to the movement from place to place». Total time, like the first type described in the commentary on Boethius, was the space from the beginning to the end of the world. Partial time he defined, following Cicero's *On invention* I, 26, 39 as « a certain part of eternity », like a day, night, or month, which is established « by a certain quantity and a certain name » [94].

These texts show both the interest in the concept of time in the eleventh and twelfth centuries and the variety of overlapping views inherited from the past and adjusted to the present and future [95]. Gilbert of Poitiers in his commentary on Boethius's *On the Trinity* stressed the diversity of views of time, which expressed both being and movement. « For according to the number of things, which they last in times, is also the number of times of these things, by which they last » [96]. The precise

---

[93]   J.M. PARENT, *La doctrine de la création dans l'école de Chartres* (Publications de l'Institut d'études médiévales d'Ottawa, 8), Paris-Ottawa 1938, pp. 125-126, who also printed the second redaction of William's commentary on this passage, saying that it referred to the separation of temporal, changeable, things from unchanging eternity and to their similitude to (owing to their origin) and their dissimilitude from (owing to their change) eternity. « For time is nothing other than the changing of changeable things (*nil aliud est quam mutatio rerum mutabilium*) », resembles HONORIUS, *De imagine*, II, 3 (*PL*, CLXXII, 147A): « nihil aliud est quam vicissitudo rerum ».

[94]   WILLIAM OF CONCHES, *Glosae super Platonem*, c. 94, ed. JEAUNEAU, p. 176, and, with a few differences in the text, in T. GREGORY, *Anima mundi. La filosofia di Guglielmo di Conches e la scuola di Chartres* (Pubblicazioni dell'Istituto di filosofia dell'Università di Roma, 3), Firenze 1955, p. 57. William said the general definition fitted both the whole and any part, the total definition fitted the whole and no part, and the partial definition fitted a part but not the whole. « When therefore we say time, it is attributed to the sensible world and can be received according to both the general and the total definition ».

[95]   A similar situation seems to have prevailed in the East. Abu'l-Barakāt (a Jewish convert to Islam who died probably after 1164-65) apparently held that there were various measures of time depending on the wish of the observer and the correspondance between him and the number of movements: see S. PINES, *Studies in Abu'l-Barakāt al-Baghdādī Physics and Metaphysics* (The Collected Works of Shlomo Pines, 1), Jerusalem-Leiden 1979, p. 127, n. 2, esp. pp. 109-131 on his view of time, which he located in the soul (pp. 114-115).

[96]   GILBERT OF POITIERS, *Expositio in Boecii librum primum de Trinitate*, I, 4, 60 and 68, in *The Commentaries on Boethius by Gilbert of Poitiers*, ed. N. HÄRING (Pontifical Institute of Mediaeval Studies, Studies and Texts, 13), Toronto 1966, pp. 127-128. Gilbert said that there was no « absolute or simple understanding » of expressions of time, which must be understood as « a collation and collection of diverse times ».

measurement of time was fostered not only by clocks but also by the astrolabe, which by making possible precise observations of the skies promoted a new attitude towards astronomy and astrology and the revival of a view of history in which the sky was the master of time [97]. Such a view was directed towards the future more than the past. It was individualistic but fatalistic, and one of the concerns of Honorius of Augsburg in his *Image of the world* was to defend divine providence and human free will against fatalism. « It may be that more Christian writers than we have so far suspected turned to history with both the attraction and the threats of magic and astrology very much in mind » [98].

Astronomical observations also gave new life to various cyclical views of time, which had never died out in the early Middle Ages [99]. Time was a moving circle around the unmoving center of eternity in the ninth-century commentary on Boethius and for Adalbold of Utrecht; and Hugo Eterianus in the twelfth century cited Aristotle to support the view of time as the measure of motion and of man in time, which defines and measures all the years of his life [100]. « The day was regarded not as a unit of time but as a unit of experience », wrote Glasser, and « The concept of time was coterminous with that of life » in early French, where the terms *durer* and *tens* both referred to the length of a lifetime [101]. There was a revival of interest in the cyclical rise and fall of nations in the works concerned with the Norman conquest of Anglo-Saxon England, especially in Geoffrey of Monmouth's *History of the Kings of Britain* [102]. And a tradition of practical concern with historical cycles was kept alive by the dating of documents according to indictions, regnal years, and

---

[97] See T. GREGORY, *Temps astrologique et temps chrétien*, in *Le temps chrétien...*, pp. 557-573, esp. 559-560, and. R.W. SOUTHERN, *Robert Grosseteste: The Growth of an English Mind in Medieval Europe*, Oxford 1986, pp. 103-104, who commented on the increasing use of astrology, and rapid change of attitude towards it, in the middle of the twelfth century.

[98] V. FLINT, *World History in the Early Twelfth Century: The « Imago Mundi » of Honorius « Augustodunensis »*, in *The Writing of History in the Middle Ages: Essays Presented to Richard William Southern*, ed. R.H.C. DAVIS - J.M. WALLACE-HADRILL, Oxford 1981, p. 235, who also stressed (p. 225) the increased knowledge of astronomy, astrology, and divination in the late eleventh and early twelfth centuries.

[99] According to GLASSER, *Time in French Life...*, p. 58, « The natural elements of time, such as the year and human life, were raised to an intellectual and symbolic status ». See also GUREVICH, *Categories...*, p. 111.

[100] HUGH Eterianus, *De haeresibus*, III, 18, in *PL*, CCII, 382D-383A. On Hugh, see A. DONDAINE, *Hugues Éthérien et Léon Toscan*, « Archives d'histoire doctrinale et littéraire du Moyen Age », XXVII (1952), 67-125 (114-116 on *De haeresibus*).

[101] GLASSER, *Time in French Life...*, pp. 18 and 46. The phrase « perde son tans » in *Aliscans*, l. 216, ed. F. GUESSARD - A. DE MONTAIGLON (Les anciens poètes de la France, 10), Paris 1870, p. 7, means « lost their lives »; cf. another version cited by GLASSER, *Time in French Life...*, p. 132, n. 115.

[102] HANNING, *The Vision of History...*, pp. 126, 136-144, and 171: « In the *Historia*, the regulation of history by repetitive patterns of personal behavior and national progress has replaced the Christian system of movement toward a final happiness or reward ».

other arbitrary and astronomical periods, such as the golden number, epact, dominical letter, and concurrent, which were only gradually replaced by the year of grace as the exclusive style of dating [103].

There was even greater persistence of mythological and folkloristic views of time, in which (as in inner or remembered time) the now and then, the before and after, and the past, present, and future were lost in a single experience which is recreated by the proper ritual or behavior [104]. The concern for regularity and punctuality in all aspects of medieval life corresponded to the stress on verbal precision in legal and other social proceedings [105]. Dominic *Loricatus* showed an almost superstitious regard for temporal precision when Peter Damiani asked him why he always added « about » in answer to questions about the time, saying that he feared to tell a lie: « For whether the hour has passed or is approaching, one is close, that is, not far from the moment at which we are speaking » [106]. Countless medieval folk-tales underlined the need to do things at a certain time, or after a specified period, or not to do them at some other time [107]. The episodes in medieval romances where events took place at the right time or after the right interval are paralleled by tales of temporal formalism in religious life, like the story in the *Dialogue of miracles* by Caesarius of Heisterbach about a monk who recovered the learning he had lost after being bled when he was bled again a year later « on the same day and at the same hour » [108]. This attitude helps to explain the anachronisms in medieval art and literature, when a past

---

[103] Some people still date letters only by the day of the week or the month, which is useless for future historians.

[104] See ELIADE, *The Myth...*, pp. 73-92, on the regeneration of time through ritual, and SOKOLOWSKI, *Timing...*, pp. 700-706. For the Nuer, according to Evans-Pritchard, « Beyond the annual cycle, time-reckoning is a conceptualization of the social structure, and the points of reference are a projection into the past of actual relationships between persons [...] Time is not a continuum, but is a constant structural relationship between two points, the first and last persons in a line of agnatic descent »: cit. by M. DOUGLAS, *Edward Evans-Pritchard*, Harmondsworth 1981, pp. 87-88.

[105] P. WEIMAR, *Der Punkt der Pünktlichkeit*, in À propos Artemis, Zürich 1982, pp. 155-158, argued that the *puncta* in the word punctuality referred to the obligation of teachers of law in the twelfth century to explicate certain « points ».

[106] PETER DAMIANI, *Vita ss. Rodulphi et Dominici Loricati*, XII, in *PL*, CXLIV, 1022BC. See LECLERCQ, *Experience and Interpretation...*, pp. 16-17.

[107] See S. THOMPSON, *Motif-Index of Folk-Literature*, 2nd ed., 6 vols., Bloomington-London 1975, I, 508 (C230), 515 (C402), 528 (C630), 530 (C666), 534 (C750) on time taboos and II, 91 (D791.1) and III, 76 (F377) on supernatural periods and lapses of time. On the time of folklore, as distinct from the times of history and the church, see J.-C. SCHMITT, *Temps, folklore et politique au XIIe siècle. À propos de deux récits de Walter Map*, « De nugis curialium » *I 9 et IV 13*, in *Le temps chrétien...*, pp. 489-515 and MILLER, *Maya Rulers...*, p. 18 who remarked on the importance of doing things at the right time in pre-Columbian Mexico.

[108] CAESARIUS OF HEISTERBACH, *Dialogus miraculorum*, X, 4, ed. J. STRANGE, 2 vols., Cologne-Bonn-Brussels 1851, II, 220. See GLASSER, *Time in French Life...*, pp. 62-63.

event was often depicted or described as if it were in the present, since the mythological view of time, like many rites and ceremonies, brought the past into the present and endowed it with an immediate relevance and meaning [109]. Finally, there was a new concern with the moral value of time as the Middle Ages progressed. Its call to ethical action was not heard only in the Renaissance, and its wise and careful use was urged by various medieval writers who found parallel ideas in both ancient and patristic works [110]. Seneca in particular, whose works were widely read in the Middle Ages and whose prestige as a moralist was unrivalled among ancient writers, said in his treatise *On the shortness of life* that time was « the most precious of all things » and expressed amazement that people should ask for or give time as if it were free. They should consider not time itself, he said, but how it is used, and they would value it more highly if they knew how long they had to live. Men have enough time, but they lose much of it [111]. The Cappadocian fathers knew the dangers of wasting and losing time; Isidoros of Alexandria stressed its value and transitory nature; and Dorotheos of Alexandria cited the saying in the *Apophthegmata* that lost time, unlike gold and silver, can never be recovered [112]. Time was not seen here as a commodity, to be bought and sold, but as an opportunity given by God to man. The stress in saying that time was short or valuable was on the verb rather than the adjective [113]. Since time passes quickly and never returns, it must be used carefully.

Similar ideas are found in the twelfth century. Bernard of Clairvaux

---

[109] This point will be discussed in the article, mentioned above, on *A Living Past: The Historical Environment of the Middle Ages*, to appear in the acts of the conference held at Morigny on 4-7 November 1986. *

[110] See BARAN, *L'expression du temps...*, pp. 10-11.

[111] SENECA, *De brevitate vitae*, VIII, 1, tr. J.W. BASORE, 3 vols. (Loeb Library), London-New York 1928-35, II, 310; see also *Consolatio ad Marciam*, 1 and 4, *ibi*, pp. 72-74. See on Seneca's view of time, BARAN, *L'expression du temps...*, p. 14, and CRISTIANI, *L'evocation de l'enfance...*, pp. 400-401 and 412, n. 10, and, on his later influence, K.D. NOTHDURFT, *Studien zum Einfluss Senecas auf die Philosophie und Theologie des zwölften Jahrhunderts* (Studien und Texte zur Geistesgeschichte des Mittelalters, 7), Leiden-Cologne 1963; L.D. REYNOLDS, *The Medieval Tradition of Seneca's Letters*, Oxford 1965, esp. pp. 104-124 on the twelfth century, when the popularity of Seneca's letters was at its peak; and, on Petrarch, n. 121 below.

[112] ISIDOROS OF ALEXANDRIA, *Ep.* III, 173, and V, 266 and 399, in *PG*, LXXVIII, 863D-866A, 1491B, and 1566B; and DOROTHEUS, *Doct.*, XI, 114, citing *Apophthegmata* 265 (see *Verba seniorum*, XI, 40, in *PL*, LXXIII, 939A), ed. L. REGNAULT - J. DE PRÉVILLE (Sources chrétiennes, 92), Paris 1963, pp. 358-359; see also *Doct.*, X, 104, ed. REGNAULT, pp. 336-337. On the Cappadocians, see M. HARL, *Les modèles d'un temps idéal dans quelques récits de vie: Pères Cappadociens*, in *Le temps chrétien...*, pp. 220-241, esp. 225-226 on asceticism, of which the central aim was the careful use of time in preparation for the real « moment » of death.

[113] LECLERCQ, *Experience and Interpretation...*, pp. 16-17.

divided time into the past, present, and future, saying that « Whoever performs penance rightly loses none of these »[114]. In his sermon on St Malachy he praised Malachy's use of time, « For although he had time free from the necessities of the people, [it was] however not a rest from holy meditations, from the zeal in prayer, from the leisure of contemplation »[115]. Among the themes gathered from Bernard's sermons by Godfrey was one that « Nothing is more precious than time but nothing, alas, is esteemed more cheaply today », and another that « Brief are the days of man until his conscience is roused by the stimulus of penance and conversion either internally, by the spirit, or externally »[116]. The author of the *Life* of Count Louis of Arnstein, who died in 1185, wrote that among the many necessities of human life, « Nothing is more precious than time, which cannot be recovered by silver or gold or any effort when it has once elapsed by any process or order »[117]. Here as in the *Apophthegmata* the value of time was compared with that of gold and silver, though the meaning is moral. The phrase « perdroie mon tans » in Chrétien de Troyes's *Cligès* also probably means devoting oneself to something worthless or useless[118]. The fifth chapter of Edmund of Abingdon's *Mirror of the church*, written in the first half of the thirteenth century, was entitled « How a man ought to expend his time », where the terms *expendere* and *suum* suggest an economic and proprietary parallel, though the content was moral[119]. This attitude became increasingly common in the fourteenth and fifteenth centuries[120]. Petrarch frequently referred to the need to use time wisely and his own determination not to

[114] BERNARD OF CLAIRVAUX, *De diversis*, 106.1, in *Sancti Bernardi opera*, ed. J. LECLERCQ a.o., 8 vols. in 9, Rome 1957-1977, VI.1, 378.

[115] BERNARD OF CLAIRVAUX, *Sermones varii*, 5: *De sancto Malachia* (= *In transitu sancti Malachiae*, II), c. 4, ed. LECLERCQ, VI.1, 53.

[116] GODFREY, *Declamationes ex S. Bernardi sermones*, 53 and 54, in *PL*, CLXXXIV, 465C. See also GUERRIC OF IGNY, *Sermo quintus in purificatione*, 3, in *PL*, CLXXXV, 90A, and ed. J. MORSON - H. COSTELLO, 2 vols. (Sources chrétiennes, 166 and 202: Textes monastiques d'Occident, 31 and 43), Paris 1970-73, I, 374: « Quotiens dormitat "anima mea prae taedio" [Ps, 118. 28], diemque fere totum, ac si tempus revocabile esset, in inertia consumo? » See LE GOFF, *Le temps du travail...*, p. 611.

[117] S. WIDMANN (ed.), *Die Lebensbeschreibung des Grafen Ludwig III. von Arnstein »*, « Annalen des Vereins für Nassauische Altertumskunde und Geschichtsforschung », XVII (1882), 245.

[118] CHRÉTIEN DE TROYES, *Cligès*, V. 2738-2740, ed. W. FOERSTER, 3rd ed. (Romanische Bibliothek, 1), Halle a. S. 1910, p. 75: « Car se mil ans avoire a vivre, / Et chascun jor doblast mes sans, / Si perdroie je tot mon tans ». See GLASSER, *Time in French Life...*, pp. 122-123, who said that *tans* here was the same as life and meant « committing one's life to something worthless and useless », not just « wasting time ».

[119] EDMUND OF ABINGDON, *Speculum ecclesiae*, V, in *Bibliotheca maxima veterum patrum*, 27 vols., Lyons 1677, XXV, 318A; see W. WALLACE, *Life of St. Edmund of Canterbury*, London 1893, pp. 352-362.

[120] For late medieval proverbs relating to the loss and bad use of time, see J. WERNER, *Lateinische Sprichwörter und Sinnsprüche des Mittelalters*, 2nd ed. P. FLURY, Heidelberg 1966, pp. 20 (A37) and 29 (C51).

waste it [121]. Ficino in his letters stressed the need to use time « cautiously and wisely », and not to lose it, and Thomas à Kempis in the *Imitation of Christ* urged the reader « Always remember your end, and that lost time never returns » [122].

III

A heightened sense of the changing nature of the created world, and of its relative autonomy, and a growing recognition of the value of time, in both a spiritual and a secular sense, were important aspects of historical thought in the twelfth century, and among its influential legacies to later medieval attitudes towards the past. They were associated with a linear view of time and history as a series of unique events upon which the salvation of mankind, both collectively and individually, depended. More subtly, they fostered human effort and a positive attitude towards historical development and change.

One of the most familiar aspects of medieval thought is the sense of inferiority towards the past and the feeling that, as the world grew old and approached its end, it was decaying and any change was for the worse [123]. The Middle Ages inherited from Antiquity a backwards-looking attitude towards the golden age and good old days and a fear of *res novae*, which was associated with tyranny and revolution, and later with heresy. Misoneism is the technical term used for unreasoning dislike of innovation, which was acceptable for many people in the Middle Ages only when it was seen as a return to the past. A change or new development was therefore often masked by the prefix *re-* and presented as a reform, renewal, rebirth, or restoration, especially in the eleventh and twelfth centuries [124]. The ambiguity of this attitude towards the past was

---

[121] FRANCESCO PETRARCA, *Fam.* XXXI, 12, ed. V. ROSSI - U. BOSCO, 4 vols. (Edizione nazionale delle opere di Francesco Petrarca, 10-13), Firenze 1933-42, IV, 85; see index IV, 424, for other references to time, and also *Il « De otio religioso » di Francesco Petrarca*, ed. G. ROTONDI (Studi e testi, 195), Città del Vaticano 1958, p. 72. QUINONES, *The Renaissance Discovery of Time*, pp. 106-171, discussed Petrarch's sense of time as an antagonist (p. 107) and its flight and value (p. 146), which he attributed to the influence of Seneca (p. 109).

[122] *The Letters of Marsilio Ficino*, I, London 1975, pp. 75-76, 130-131, and 136, nn. 35, 82, and 86, and THOMAS À KEMPIS, *Imitatio Christi*, I, 25, tr. L. SHERLEY-PRICE, Harmondsworth 1952, p. 66.

[123] On the concept of the aging world in the eleventh and twelfth centuries, see H. GRUNDMANN, *Studien über Joachim von Floris* (Beiträge zur Kulturgeschichte des Mittelalters und der Renaissance, 32), Leipzig-Berlin 1927, p. 81; J. SPÖRL, *Das Alte und das Neue im Mittelalter*, « Historisches Jahrbuch », L (1930), 316-317; CHENU, *La théologie...*, pp. 76-77; and G. MICCOLI, *Chiesa gregoriana. Ricerche sulla riforma del secolo XI* (Storici antichi e moderni, N.S. 17), Firenze 1966, pp. 301-303.

[124] CONSTABLE, *Renewal...*, pp. 37-66.

epitomized in the famous *dictum* of Bernard of Chartres that « We are like dwarfs sitting on the shoulders of giants » and in the saying « the more youthful, the more perspicacious », which emphasized that the moderns see further than the ancients only because they depend upon them and need to look more carefully than they did [125].

« New » and « unaccustomed » were widely used as terms of abuse in the eleventh and twelfth centuries. Smalley in her study of the attitude of the church towards novelty contrasted the hostility of Manegold of Lautenbach and Guibert of Nogent in about 1100 with the acceptance of Thomas of Celano and Robert Grosseteste in the mid-thirteenth century, saying that « An emotional change has come about in some hundred and fifty years. *New* has ceased to be a dirty word » [126]. The change was less categorical than this implies, however. « New » was used in a favorable as well as unfavorable sense throughout the Middle Ages, and it continued to be a term of abuse, down to modern times, especially for unpopular political changes and religious opinions. Heretics were often accused of innovations. There are many instances of both a favorable and unfavorable use of new in the same work, depending on the point of view of the writer and the nature of the change. Ralph Glaber welcomed the innovations of churches in the early eleventh century, for instance, and Marbod of Rennes wrote in his *Life* of Robert of La Chaise-Dieu that « This new saint overturned for us the old order of sanctity » [127].

Guibert of Nogent thoroughly disliked the « new and evil name » of the commune at Laon [128], but he was full of enthusiasm for the deeds of God accomplished by the Franks on the First Crusade:

It is well known that some people customarily condemn the deeds of modern men, not always wrongly, and exalt earlier ages. It is indeed proper to praise the modest happiness and restrained liveliness of the ancients, but their prosperity should not in any

---

[125] JOHN OF SALISBURY, *Metalogicon*, III, 4, ed. C.C.J. WEBB, Oxford 1929, p. 136. See E. JEAUNEAU, « *Nani gigantum humeris insidentes* ». *Essai d'interprétation de Bernard de Chartres*, « Vivarium », V (1967), 79-99; H. SILVESTRE, « *Quanto iuniores, tanto perspicaciores* ». *Antécédents à la querelle des anciens et modernes*, in *Recueil commémoratif du Xe anniversaire de la Faculté de Philosophie et Lettres* (Publications de l'Université Lovanium de Kinshasa, 22), Louvain-Paris 1968, pp. 231-255; and B. STOCK, *Antiqui and Moderni as « Giants » and « Dwarfs »: A Reflection of Popular Culture*, « The Journal of Modern Philology », LXXVI (1979), 370-374.

[126] B. SMALLEY, *Ecclesiastical Attitudes to Novelty, c. 1100-c. 1250*, « Studies in Church History », XII (1975), 113-131. See also M.-D. CHENU, *L'éveil de la conscience dans la civilisation médiévale* (Conférence Albert-le-Grand, 1968), Montréal-Paris 1969, pp. 14-15.

[127] R. GLABER, *Historiae*, III, 4 (13), ed. M. PROU (Collection de textes pour servir à l'étude et à l'enseignement de l'histoire, 1), Paris 1886, p. 62; MARBOD OF RENNES, *Miracula b. Roberti Abbatis Casae-Dei*, in *PL*, CLXXI, 1517B.

[128] GUIBERT OF NOGENT, *De vita sua*, III, 7, ed. G. BOURGIN (Collection de textes pour servir à l'étude et à l'enseignement de l'histoire, 40), Paris 1907, p. 156. On Guibert, see the works cited in n. 13 above.

way be preferred to any of our types of virtue. For although virtue shone among the ancients, the gift of nature has not vanished among ourselves, in spite of the coming end of the ages. In previous times deeds were justly praised owing to the newness of men, but the deeds performed by untried men while the world is sliding into old age are much more justly proclaimed [129].

Guibert especially praised the crusade as « a new way of winning salvation (novum [...] salutis promerendae genus) » and called the crusading army the nova militia Dei [130]. Later in the twelfth century the novelty of the military orders was praised in similar terms by Bernard of Clairvaux, Anselm of Havelberg, and Otto of Freising [131]. There was a long tradition of approval of novelty in Christian thought and teaching [132]. Jesus was the new man, and Christians, like Him, became new men through baptism. « Put on the new man », wrote Paul in Ephesians 4.24, and he told the readers of Colossians 3.10 to strip themselves of the old man and to put on « Him who is renewed into knowledge, according to the image of Him that created Him ». This terminology was embedded in theology and liturgy, especially the ceremonies of baptism and entry to monastic life. The Mandatum novum of Christ (John 13.34) gave its name to the ceremony of foot-washing, and ultimately to Maundy Thursday. « This is a new man, a new creature », Rupert of Deutz said of Christ [133], and conversions, both from paganism to Christianity and from one type of life to another, were all considered to involve a change to a new and better condition [134]. The description by Eusebius, as translated by Rufinus, of man's preparation by law and philosophy for the coming of Christ, was reworked by Otto of Freising in the prologue to book III of his History of the two cities:

---

[129]   GUIBERT OF NOGENT, Gesta Dei per Francos, I, 1, in Recueil des historiens des croisades: Historiens occidentaux, IV, Paris 1879, p. 123. The translation here simplifies the text in places.

[130]   Ibi, I, 1, and VII, 21, ed. cit., pp. 124 and 238. For these and other favorable references to novelty by Guibert, see LETTINCK, Comment les historiens..., pp. 62-65 and 75-77.

[131]   BERNARD OF CLAIRVAUX, De laude novae militiae, ed. LECLERCQ, III, pp. 213-239; ANSELM OF HAVELBERG, Dialogi, I, 10, ed. and tr. G. SALET (Sources chrétiennes, 118: Textes monastiques d'Occident, 18), Paris 1966, p. 98 (« nova religionis institutio »); and OTTO OF FREISING, Chronica sive historia de duobus civitatibus, VII, 9, ed. A. HOFMEISTER, 2nd ed. (MGH, Scriptores... in usum scholarum; Hannover-Leipzig 1912), p. 320.

[132]   J. MOLTMANN, Die Kategorie « Novum » in der christlichen Theologie, in Ernst Bloch zu Ehren, ed. S. UNSELD, Frankfurt a.M. 1965, pp. 243-263.

[133]   RUPERT OF DEUTZ, De sancta Trinitate, I, 2, in CC:CM, XXIV, 1824.

[134]   G.R. EVANS, A Change of Mind in Some Scholars of the Eleventh and Early Twelfth Centuries, * « Studies in Church History », XV (1978), 27-38, discussed various conversion-experiences described by Guibert of Nogent, Anselm, Otloh of St Emmeram, and Herman the Convert. On the term conversio, see G.B. LADNER, The Idea of Reform: Its Impact on Christian Thought and Action in the Age of the Fathers, Cambridge (Mass.) 1959, p. 366, and R. JAVELET, Image et ressemblance au douzième siècle: De saint Anselme à Alain de Lille, 2 vols., Strasbourg 1967, II, 239, n. 370.

Then as wisdom, mediated by the teaching of philosophers, slowly grew and advanced both by the community of men living together and by their combining to establish laws, when, as I said, the whole world had submitted to the strength of the Romans and been instructed by the wisdom of the philosophers, and the natures of men were ready to commit themselves to the higher precepts of life, then it was fitting for the Savior of all to appear in the flesh and to establish new laws for the world [135].

Otto's use of *crescente ac proficiente, altiora vitae praecepta*, and *novas leges* show that he not only accepted but welcomed historical change and innovation.

The favorable use of *novus* (*novitas*) and *modernus* (*modernitas*) in the works of Guibert of Nogent, Hugh of Fleury, Ordericus Vitalis, and William of Malmesbury has been studied by Lettinck [136], whose researches need to be extended to other eleventh- and twelfth-century writers. Many religious reformers, in spite of the charges of novelty brought against them by their enemies [137] and of their own claims to follow ancient origins or models, which they sought to restore or renew, were not reluctant to proclaim their newness. The Cistercians of the *Novum monasterium* rejoiced, in the words of Paul, to have put off the old man and put on the new, and they were described by Nicholas of Montiéramey, writing from his cell at Clairvaux, as new men in a newness of life [138]. This was true of nuns as well as monks, and in a charter of 1138 concerning the foundation of Godstowe, Bishop Alexander of Lincoln praised « the new growth » of the church, « the new light of holy religion » which illuminated it, and the foundation of « new churches » in his time [139]. The Premonstratensian Adam Scot, writing in the 1170s, stressed that new regular canons must visibly display in their way of life « the novelty of holiness [...] so that it may be clear to all who see you that you have converted to a new rectitude from your old twistedness » [140]. Gerald of Wales showed his admiration for novelty when he criticized theological works which were put together out of other works

---

[135] OTTO, *Cronica*, III, prol., ed. HOFMEISTER, p. 133, cf. EUSEBIUS-RUFINUS, *Historia ecclesiastica*, I, 2, 23, ed. E. SCHWARTZ - TH. MOMMSEN, 2 vols. (Die griechischen christlichen Schriftsteller der ersten drei Jahrhunderts, 9.1-2), Leipzig 1903-08, I, 25.

[136] LETTINCK, *Comment les historiens...*, pp. 51-77, showed that these writers (like Guibert) were not uniformly critical of their own age, even when they disliked particular aspects of it.

[137] See G. LUNARDI, *L'ideale monastico nelle polemiche del secolo XII sulla vita religiosa*, Noci 1970, pp. 80-83; SMALLEY, *Ecclesiastical Attitudes...*, pp. 121-122.

[138] *Exordium parvum*, 15, in *Les plus anciens textes de Cîteaux*, ed. J. DE LA CROIX BOUTON - J.B. VAN DAMME (Cîteaux: Studia et documenta, 2), Aachel 1974, p. 77; NICHOLAS OF MONTIÉRAMEY, *Ep.* 35, in *PL*, CXCVI, 1627A.

[139] WILLIAM DUGDALE, *Monasticon anglicanum*, ed. J. CALEY - H. ELLIS - B. BANDINEL, 6 vols. in 8, London 1846, IV, 362.

[140] ADAM SCOT, *Liber de ordine*, VI, 2, in *PL*, CXCVIII, 489D, see also 490CD.

« as if they were made *de novo*, but in truth artificially innovated »[141]. *Novus* is used five times, always favorably, in a short passage from a twelfth- or early thirteenth-century dialogue *Against religious hypocrites*, stressing the need for « those new commentators of a new religion who carry a new cross » to find « the new Christ who promises a new rest »[142]. The foolishness of rejecting novelty and praising antiquity for its own sake was stressed in the *Life* of the Emperor Henry II by Adalbold of Utrecht, whose views of history and of time were mentioned above. All old things were new at one time, he said, and « Novelty came first so that antiquity might follow ». He thus turned the tables on the critics of novelty, saying

> It is therefore foolish to spurn what comes first and to receive what follows and comes from that which comes first. For a thirsty person rarely seeks a river when the spring is at hand. We say this in order not that antiquity should be spurned but that novelty may be received[143].

William of Malmesbury defended his *Life* of Wulfstan of Worcester on the grounds that in moral instruction example is more effective than exhortation. A reader may revere an old saint, he said, but will be moved by the life of a recent saint « in which they are seen as in a mirror, as if it were a living simulacrum of religion ». Novelty (*novitas*) enhances the account because « No one despairs of being able by God's grace to do himself what he hears was recently done by another »[144]. Rupert of Deutz expressed the same view in a different context in the prologue to his commentary on the Apocalypse, written in 1119-21, where he refuted those who said that it was rash and improper to add to the existing commentaries. He cited Genesis 26.18-22, where Isaac dug successive wells, to justify his own efforts to study Scripture and to dig more wells, as it were, « by the plowshare of his own talent »[145].

---

[141] GERALD OF WALES, *Speculum duorum, or A Mirror of Two Men*, ed. Y. LEFÈVRE - R.B.C. HUYGENS (Board of Celtic Studies, University of Wales: History and Law Series, 27), Cardiff 1974, p. 172.

[142] *Contra religionis simulatores*, c. 65, in *Analecta Dublinensia*, ed. M.L. COLKER (Mediaeval Academy of America, Publ. 82), Cambridge (Mass.) 1975, p. 45.

[143] ADALBOLD OF UTRECHT, *Vita Henrici II imperatoris*, proem., c. 3, in *PL*, CXL, 89D-90A. See SIMON, *Untersuchungen*, 1, p. 97, who suggested a parallel with TACITUS, *De oratoribus*, cc. 16-26 (though this work was hardly known in the Middle Ages), and LETTINCK, *L'intérêt de l'analyse...*, p. 33.

[144] WILLIAM OF MALMESBURY, *Vita Wulfstani*, prol., ed. R.R. DARLINGTON (Camden Society, 3rd S., 40), London 1928, pp. 2-3.

[145] RUPERT OF DEUTZ, *Commentarium in Apocalypsim*, prol., in *PL*, CLXIX, 825A-826A. See J. VAN ENGEN, *Rupert of Deutz* (Publications of the UCLA Center for Medieval and Renaissance Studies, 18), Berkeley-Los Angeles-London 1983, p. 276.

There was a growing sense at this time of the present as distinct from the past. The terms *modernus* and *modernitas*, which comes from *modo* or « now », referred to a writer's own times, stretching back, as Guenée has shown, some sixty or seventy years [146]. Suger contrasted « the modernity of our times » with « the antiquity of many times » in his *Life* of Louis VI; and Walter Map in his *Courtiers' trifles* defined modernity as the period of a hundred years during which notable events are clear in the memory [147]. Peter the Venerable in the prologue to the second book of his *On miracles* deplored the fact that events of 500 or 1000 years ago were better known than those of the past forty or fifty years, « so great appears the distance of our times and those of former men » [148]. Gilbert of Poitiers in the prologue to his commentaries on Boethius suggested a tripartite division of history, distinguishing *antiqui* and *posteri* from men of his own time (*nos*), and Ralph of Diceto divided events into very ancient, ancient, and modern, which covered from 1148 to the time he was writing [149]. The term modernity was as a rule neutral, but occasionally it was used with approval, as when Otto of Freising in a letter to the pope written about 1147 referred to the failure of royal abbeys to observe « the modern institutions and constitutions of monks » and described the resistance at Tegernsee to changing « the ancient statutes of the monastery » [150].

The feeling of historians in the twelfth century for « the autonomy of modern times » [151], formed part of a broader tendency to see the past,

---

[146] B. GUENÉE, *Temps de l'histoire et temps de la mémoire au moyen âge*, « Bulletin de la Société de l'Histoire de France », 487 (1976-77) pp. 34-35; see also B. STOCK, *Myth and Science in the Twelfth Century: A Study of Bernard Silvester*, Princeton 1972, p. 228 and note 81; GÖSSMANN, *Antiqui und Moderni...*, pp. 35-39; and J.-P. DELUMEAU, *La mémoire des gens d'Arezzo et de Sienne à travers des dépositions de témoins (VIIIe-XIIe s.)*, in *Temps, Mémoire, Tradition au moyen âge. Actes du XIIIe Congrès de la Société des historiens médiévistes de l'enseignement supérieur public, Aix-en-Provence, 4-5 juin 1982*, Aix-en-Provence 1983, pp. 49, who estimated on the basis of an inquiry at Arezzo in 1177 that memory went back not beyond the early twelfth century.

[147] SUGER, *Vita Ludovici Grossi*, c. 28, ed. H. WAQUET (Classiques de l'histoire de France au Moyen Age, 11), Paris 1929, p. 230; WALTER MAP, *De nugis curialium*, I, 30, ed. and tr. M. R. JAMES, rev. C.N.L. BROOKE - R.A.B. MYNORS (Oxford Medieval Texts), Oxford 1983, p. 122. See CHENU, *La théologie...*, p. 81.

[148] PETER THE VENERABLE, *De miraculis*, II, prol., in *Bibliotheca Cluniacensis*, ed. M. MARRIER - A. DUCHESNE, Paris 1614, col. 1298AB and ed. D. BOUTHILLIER, in *CC: CM*, LXXXIII, 94.

[149] GILBERT OF POITIERS, *Commentaries on Boethius*, pp. 53-54; *The Historical Works of Master Ralph of Diceto*, ed. W. STUBBS, 2 vols. (Rolls Series, 68), London 1876, I, 18-20. It is unclear whether Ralph equated these three ages with those before the law, under the law, and under grace, which he mentioned at the beginning of his history (p. 3). See CHENU, *La théologie...*, p. 81.

[150] K. MEICHELBECK, *Historia Frisingensis*, 2 vols., Augsburg-Graz 1724-29, I, 331.

[151] GUENÉE, *Temps de l'histoire...*, p. 28. See W. FREUND, *Modernus und andere Zeitbegriffe des Mittelalters* (Neue Münstersche Beiträge zur Geschichtsforschung, 4), Cologne-Graz 1957, p. 66, and STOCK, *The Implications of Literacy...*, p. 456. On *modernus* as a category of learned organization, see GÖSSMANN, *Antiqui und Moderni...*, pp. 64-67.

distant as well as near, not in terms of arbitrary chronological and dynastic blocks but as distinct periods marked by coherent characteristics and what may be called a collective mentality[152]. « Times are varied, not faith », wrote Augustine; Bede gave the *ratio temporum* as the reason why the sacraments differed while faith remained unchanged; and Peter Lombard cited Augustine to explain the single faith of those who knew of Christ both before and after His birth and death[153]. Changes were rung in the twelfth century on the theme *O tempora, o mores*[154]. The saying *nunc aliud tempus, alii pro tempore mores* was used by Hildebert of Le Mans, who elsewhere attributed Cornelius's lack of belief to the « quality of the times (*qualitas temporum*) », and especially by Gerald of Wales, who cited it at least five times, twice with attributions to Peter Comestor and Walter Map[155]. The Cistercian Burchard of Bellevaux, explaining some of the differences between his own and the apostolic age, said that « changes of times demand changes of customs (*mutationes temporum mutationes morum exposcunt*) », implying that the present, like each former period of time, had its own character[156]. Although, therefore, the twelfth century on the whole, as Funkenstein emphasized, tended to look for historical coherence on a symbolic rather than a human basis and to attribute it to the workings of God rather than man, « its fondness for new and richer periodizations [...] reflected the urge to interpret the complexity of recent history and to express the sense of new achievements in the light of historical retrospection ». The *processus saeculi* or

---

[152] A. FUNKENSTEIN, *Periodization and Self-Understanding in the Middle Ages and Early Modern Times*, « Medievalia et Humanistica », N.S., V (1974), 3-23. The fourteenth-century historian, RALPH HIGDEN *Polychronicon*, I, 4, ed. C. BABINGTON - J. R. LUMBY, 9 vols. (Rolls Series, 41), London 1865-66, I, 30-36, defined eight criteria for distinguishing ages: places, things, times, kingdoms, rites, ages, actions, and methods of reckoning.

[153] Augustine, commenting on John 10.8 (« and the sheep heard them not »), said that the same faith in Christ inspired those who at different times believed in Him, even before His coming (see note 87 above); BEDE, *Expositio super acta apostolorum*, IV, in PL, XCII, 953A.

[154] A. OTTO, *Die Sprichwörter und sprichwörtlichen Redensarten der Römer*, Leipzig 1890, rp. 1965, p. 343; BARAN, *L'expression du temps...*, pp. 16-17; and, on the Middle Ages, S. SINGER, *Sprichwörter des Mittelalters*, 3 vols., Bern 1944-47, I, 166-167 (« Adduxere novos semper nova sæcula ritus »), and *Proverbia sententiaeque Latinitatis medii aevi*, ed. H. WALTHER, 8 vols. to date (Carmina medii aevi posterioris latina, 2), Göttingen 1963f, III, 546 (no. 19586a); cf. V, 285, for other proverbs concerning how people change with the times.

[155] HILDEBERT OF LE MANS, *Carmina minora*, 17, ed. A. B. SCOTT (Bibliotheca... Teubneriana), Leipzig 1964, p. 6, and ID., *Tractatus theologicus*, c. 2, in PL, CLXXI, 1073A. GERALD OF WALES, *De invectionibus*, VI, 27; *Gemma ecclesiastica*, II, 6 and 38; and *Speculum ecclesiae*, III, 14, and IV, 39, in *Giraldi Cambrensis opera*, ed. J.S. BREWER - J.F. DIMOCK - G.F. WARNER, 8 vols. (Rolls Series, 21), London 1861-91, I, 192; II, 187 and 360; and IV, 223 and 350. See *Proverbia*, III, 504 (no. 19331) and B. SMALLEY, *Peter Comestor on the Gospels and his Sources*, « Recherches de théologie ancienne et médiévale », LXVI (1979), 128.

[156] BURCHARD OF BELLEVAUX, *Apologia de barbis*, II, 11, ed. R.B.C. HUYGENS, in CC: CM, LXII, 170.

series temporum thus came to be seen in a more hopeful light and in terms of new and less pessimistic systems of periodization [157]. Since changeability was the rule of the created world, and of time as contrasted with eternity, medieval thinkers tended to look backward in order to find a pattern of change to project into the future [158]. Gerhoh of Reichersberg in his commentary on Psalm 67.9 (« The earth was moved, and the heavens dropped at the presence of the God of Sina ») said that « In these words, past history is commemorated in such a way that future grace is announced at the same time » [159]. Most of the schemes of successive historical ages emphasized degeneration and the coming end of the world. The ancient Greek succession of ages of gold, silver, bronze, and iron survived in the references of William of Hirsau to « this age of iron » in a letter to the anti-king Hermann in 1082-83 and the statement a century later by Alan of Lille that « the poverty of iron clothes the world » [160]. The biblical systems based on the days of creation, the dream of Daniel, and the vision of the Apocalypse were all given specific interpretations presenting a gloomy picture of the present and of the immediate future [161]. More optimistic signs could be found, however, in the basic Christian patterns of two ages, before and after Christ, who brought the hope of salvation into the world, and three ages before the law, under the law, and under grace [162].

These three ages were equated with shadow and figure, figure and truth, and truth alone by Bruno of Segni, with the generations not seeking

---

[157] FUNKENSTEIN, *Periodization...*, p. 11, and CHENU, *La théologie...*, pp. 66-67.

[158] M. E. REEVES, *History and Prophecy in Medieval Thought*, « Medievalia et Humanistica », N.S., V (1974), 51-53, stressed the need of historians « to interpret the moving moments of time against an unchanging eternal pattern of reality »; see also M.L. ARDUINI, *Per una interpretazione storiografica della « Christianitas » medioevale (secoli XI e XII). Le categorie del profetico e del simbolico*, « Bullettino dell'Istituto storico italiano per il Medio Evo », XCI (1984), 1-113.

[159] GERHOH OF REICHERSBERG, *In psalmos*, VII, in *PL*, CXCIV, 174B; see EVANS, *Hugh of St Victor...*, pp. 230-231.

[160] *Hildesheimer Briefe*, 18, in *Briefsammlungen der Zeit Heinrichs IV.*, ed. C. ERDMANN - N. FICKER-MANN (*MGH*, Briefe der deutschen Kaiserzeit, 5), Weimar 1950, p. 42, and ALAN OF LILLE, *De planctu naturæ*, XI, ed. N. HÄRING, « Studi Medievali », 3d. S., XIX (1978), 851. See I. ROBINSON, *Authority and Resistance in the Investiture Contest: The Polemical Literature of the Late Eleventh Century*, Manchester 1978, p. 13, n. 27, and on the ages of metals in Antiquity, A. MOMIGLIANO, *The Origins of Universal History* (1982), rp. in *Settimo contributo alla storia degli studi classici e del mondo antico* (Storia e letteratura, 161), Rome 1984, pp. 78-79.

[161] GRUNDMANN, *Studien...*, pp. 88-95, and R. SCHMIDT, *Aetates mundi. Die Weltalter als Gliederungsprinzip der Geschichte*, « Zeitschrift für Kirchengeschichte », LXVII (1955-1956), 288-317.

[162] On the sense of improvement following the Incarnation in the works of Melito, Tertullian, Origen, and Arnobius, see MOMMSEN, *St. Augustine...*, pp. 279-280. On the patterns of two and three ages in the work of Joachim of Fiore, see M. REEVES - B. HIRSCH-REICH, *The Seven Seals in the Writings of Joachim of Fiore*, « Recherches de théologie ancienne et médiévale », XXI (1954), 223, who consider the pattern of two pessimistic and that of three, optimistic.

the Lord, sought by Him, and seeking Him by Bernard of Clairvaux, and with the synagogue, the church, and the sky [163]. Rupert of Deutz was perhaps the first to associate them with the Father, Son, and Holy Spirit, whose special work was the sanctification of created beings. Rupert's *On the victory of the word of God* has been called « an early and remarkable product of the new twelfth-century fascination with salvation history » [164]. His most important follower in this respect was Joachim of Fiore, whose contribution was to see the present as the age of the Son, under the law, and the future as the age of the Spirit, under grace, which would come, in time, before the end of the world [165].

Hugh of St Victor, Anselm of Havelberg, Gerhoh of Reichersberg, and Philip of Harvengt, who all came between Rupert and Joachim, still saw the present age as the last but used overlapping patterns of three and of six (or seven) ages with varying degrees of optimism [166]. Hugh postulated two conditions (*status*), three ages (of Nature, Scripture, and Grace), and six periods, of which the first five, before Christ, covered the four successions of patriarchs, lawgivers, kings, and priests and all six corresponded to the ages of man (infancy, boyhood, adolescence, youth, manhood, and old age). He gave a central place to development in his *On sacraments*, where he put forward what Southern called « a dynamic view of history » [167]. Anselm addressed himself particularly to the problem of « novelties » in the first book of his *Dialogues*, written probably in 1149, and defended the monks and canons who lived « according to their own desire » and assumed « for themselves whatever they wish », wearing « an unaccustomed habit » and following, according to their critics, « a new order of living », « a new way of psalmody », and « a new mode of abstinence ». Anselm justified these changes as part of a progressive evolution of historical institutions and as part of God's plan to renew and

---

[163]   R. GRÉGOIRE, *Bruno de Segni* (Centro italiano di studi sull'alto medioevo, 3), Spoleto 1965, pp. 153 and 339-340; BERNARD OF CLAIRVAUX, *Sermo in labore messis*,III (previously *De diversis*, XXXVII) 2 and 9, ed. LECLERCQ, V, 223 and 227-228.

[164]   VAN ENGEN, *Rupert of Deutz*, pp. 287, also 340-341. See GRUNDMANN, *Studien...*, p. 91; CHENU, *La théologie...*, pp. 81-82; CLASSEN, «Res gestae»..., pp. 404-405; ARDUINI, *Per una interpretazione...*, pp. 54-85: « La storia e la lettura profetica della storia sono il nucleo costitutivo dell'esegesi rupertiana » (p. 74); and, on trinitarian systems of history, REEVES, *History and Prophecy...*, pp. 54-55.

[165]   Among the many works on Joachim, those of Grundmann and Reeves are preeminent; see also SOUTHERN, *Aspects, 3*, pp. 175-176, and CLASSEN, « Res gestae »..., pp. 411-414.

[166]   On these writers, see in addition to works cited in other notes, CLASSEN, « Res gestae »..., pp. 406-414.

[167]   See EHLERS, *Historia...*, p. 159, and SOUTHERN, *Aspects, 2*, pp. 168 and 172-174, on Hugh's unpublished chronicle. See in addition to the works cited in note 45 above, G. ZINN, *The Influence of Hugh of St Victor's « Chronicon » on the « Abbreviationes chronicorum » by Ralph of Diceto*, « Speculum », LII (1977), 38-61, and GUENÉE, *Les premiers pas...*, pp. 138-140.

strengthen the monastic order. As a prophet of progress rather than of doubt, Southern said, Anselm of Havelberg « spoke for his whole generation » [168].

> No one therefore should object or be surprised that the church of God before the law, under the law, and under grace is divided by changing laws and observances of the unchanging God, since it is fitting for the signs of the spiritual graces, which increasingly declare that very truth, to grow according to the procession of the times (*processus temporum*), and for the knowledge of truth to grow from time to time with the effectiveness of salvation, and thus good things are proposed at first, then better things, and finally the best things [169].

The term *processus temporum* here does not mean progress in the modern sense, and even when Otto of Freising referred to the *progressus* of the City of God described by Augustine, he probably had in mind temporal progression rather than improvement [170], but he and other historians of the eleventh and twelfth centuries had an optimistic sense of historical growth. Already in the first half of the eleventh century, Guido of Arezzo was aware of the advance of music, and Beaujouan said that in science « it is indisputable that the idea of progress was not totally foreign to twelfth-century thought » [171]. The stress on evolution and accomodation, which allowed for adjustments in the working out of God's plans, implied a « relative autonomy of human history » [172]. Augustine's comparison in *The City of God* of an individual's process of learning to that of the human race rising from visible and earthly things to invisible and eternal things « through the joints of the times as it were of ages » was cited both by Hugh of Fleury, who said he would show how the Old Testament prefigured the New « just as a youthful age customarily precedes a manly age » [173], and by Hugh of St

---

[168] SOUTHERN, *Aspects, 3*, p. 165.

[169] ANSELM OF HAVELBERG, *Dialogi*, I, 7, ed. SALET, pp. 96-106. On Anselm's view of history and defense of diversity and progress, see W. BERGES, *Anselm von Havelberg in der Geistesgeschichte des 12. Jahrhunderts*, « Jahrbuch für die Geschichte Mittel- und Ostdeutschlands », V (1956), 47-54; K. FINA, *Anselm von Havelberg* [V], « Analecta Praemonstratensia », XXXIV (1958), 33-38; CHENU, *La théologie...*, pp. 70 and 77; A. FUNKENSTEIN, *Heilsplan und natürliche Entwicklung. Formen der Gegenwartsbestimmung im Geschichtsdenken des hohen Mittelalters*, Munich 1965, pp. 60-67; SOUTHERN, *Aspects, 3*, pp. 165-166; and SMALLEY, *Ecclesiastical Attitudes...*, pp. 124-125.

[170] OTTO, *Chronica*, I, prol., ed. HOFMEISTER, p. 9; see CLASSEN, « Res gestae »..., p. 400, n. 63.

[171] G. BEAUJOUAN, *The Transformation of the Quadrivium*, in *Renaissance and Renewal...*, p. 485.

[172] FUNKENSTEIN, *Periodization...*, pp. 10-13, see also *Heilsplan...*, pp. 115-116.

[173] HUGH OF FLEURY, *Historia ecclesiastica*, II, 2, prol., in *MGH, Scriptores* in fol., IX, 354, citing AUGUSTINE, *De civitate Dei*, X, 14 (*CC*, XLVII, 288) adding « of faith » after « learning » and « grades » to « joints ». On the sense of improvement and progress in the works of Eusebius and Augustine, see MOMMSEN, *St. Augustine...*, pp. 284-285 and 297-298.

Victor, who applied it to secular as well as spiritual affairs in order to show the « role of physical necessity in prompting man's ascent », and the « upward movement in every department of life »[174]. Peter Comestor, though he had no theory of historical development like Rupert, Hugh, or Anselm, was not always looking over his shoulder at the *ecclesia primitiva*, like some of this contemporaries, and had « an implicit theory of historical change »[175]; and even a lawyer like Gratian, whose professional orientation was towards the past rather than the future, recognized that the law of the church had developed and that some of the changes introduced « at the counsel of perfection [...] after the apostolic institutions » should not be rejected simply because they did not appear among the gospel and apostolic precepts [176].

These and other works reflected a willingness (and occasionally a desire) to understand God's conduct towards man and the internal laws of earthly life more through events than by abstract definitions, as Chenu put it: « Historical causalities became perceptible in terms of social awareness »[177]. The « medieval evolutionary models defied the apocalyptical insistence on the utter passivity of man in history », according to Funkenstein, and allowed for « the partial autonomy of man's evolution »[178]. This attitude can be seen perhaps most clearly in man's relation to nature, and the effort to improve it. Sigebert of Gembloux in his poem *In praise of the town of Metz* said that human strength and skill supplied what nature failed to provide: « Art sent the waters which you, Nature, denied »[179]. William of Malmesbury showed his appreciation of his own age, and its achievements in engineering, even more strikingly when he contrasted the period when Ely was inaccessible by land with « our more capable age » which « has conquered nature, put roads over the swamps, furnished a path by land, and made the island accessible by foot »[180]. There is no reference here to God, and

[174] SOUTHERN, *Aspects*, 2, pp. 169-172, who said that Hugh was « a prophet of a new age » and that his attitude showed the receptivity of western European culture to technological change.

[175] SMALLEY, *Peter Comestor*, pp. 127-128.

[176] GRATIAN, *Decretum*, dictum post C. XXXV, q. 1, c. un., in *Corpus iuris canonici*, ed. E. FRIEDBERG, 2 vols., Leipzig 1879, I, 1263, on which see G. OLSEN, *The Idea of the « Ecclesia primitiva » in the Writings of the Twelfth-Century Canonists*, « Traditio », XXV (1969), 79-80.

[177] CHENU, *La théologie...*, pp. 71-72.

[178] FUNKENSTEIN, *Periodization...*, p. 14. See also HANNING, *The Vision...*, pp. 126 and 176, and STOCK, *The Implications of Literacy...*, p. 87: « Man [...] was not the passive receptacle of natural or divine judgments; he could understand and therefore alter the everyday world in which he lived; the weight of decision-making was partly shifted to his own shoulders ».

[179] SIGEBERT, *Vita Deoderici I*, c. 17, in *MGH, Scriptores* in fol., IV, 478.

[180] WILLIAM OF MALMESBURY, *De gestis pontificum Anglorum*, IV, 184, ed. N.E.S.A. HAMILTON (Rolls Series, 52), London 1870, p. 325: « Sed nostra aetas sollertior vicit naturam, aggeribusque in paludem

though William surely believed that the roads were part of God's plan, he presented them as the result of human efforts. *Nostra aetas* was not only distinct from the time before the roads were built, but it was also *sollertior*. Casual references like these were not based on a formulated theory, but they showed the way in which historical thought was moving. The past was divided into successive periods in which mankind exercised increasing control over its own affairs. No aspect of this attitude was entirely new in the twelfth century, but they came together in the historical writings of that time in a way which pointed towards a new vision of history in the future.

jactis, tramitem terrestrem praebuit, et insulam pedibus accessibilem fecit ». The first version (A) reads: « Sed nostra aetas sollertior pontem commenta aggeribus in paludem jactis, tramitem terrestrem et insulam pedibus accessibilem fecit ». See his remarks on Thorney, *ibi*, IV, 186, p. 326, and LETTINCK, *Comment les historiens...*, p. 73.

V

A Living Past:
The Historical Environment of the Middle Ages

This paper looks at some questions that arose in the course of preparing an article on the attitude towards time and the past in the twelfth century.[1] I particularly noticed that the environment created by art, architecture, and ceremony fostered a closeness, and at times an identity, with history. People lived the past in a very real sense, and the past, living in them, was constantly recreated in a way that made it part of everyday life. Scholars tend to rely so heavily on verbal sources that they underestimate the influence of the senses in developing an awareness of history. Sight, smell, hearing, and touch were all enlisted in the task of reconstructing the past. Even speech was a dramatic performance, and the actions that accompanied many rites and ceremonies helped to bring past people and events into the present, giving meaning to history and linking it to the future. The bridges between "was," "is," and "will be" were thus stronger in the Middle Ages than at other times in European history, and they enabled people to move easily between periods and to experience them without losing a sense of their integrity and reality.

This point distinguishes the attitude studied in this paper from other medieval attitudes towards history. I shall not study here either the sense of continuity, identity, and changelessness, which is sometimes called traditionalism, nor the various techniques by which one thing was taken for another, such as allegory, metaphor, symbolism, exemplarism, and impersonation.[2] The historical bridges were between related but different periods and invited observers to participate in both. I shall be concerned less with the questions of artistic production and patronage—how and for whom works of art were created[3]—than with the effect they had on the people

A version of this paper was originally presented at the fifth Penn-Paris-Dumbarton Oaks Colloquium held in Morigny, 4-7 November 1986, and will be printed, without illustrations, in its proceedings. The following abbreviations will be used: CC for Corpus Christianorum and CM for the Continuatio mediaevalis), MGH for Monumenta Germaniae historica, and PL for Patrologia latina. I am indebted for help in revising this paper, after the initial presentation, to various people who heard or read it, especially Elizabeth Beatson and Madeline Caviness.

[1] "Past and Present in the Eleventh and Twelfth Centuries: Perceptions of Time and Change," in L'Europa dei secoli XI e XII. Fra novità e tradizione: Sviluppi di una cultura. Atti della decima Settimana internazionale di studio. Mendola, 25-29 agosto 1986, Pubblicazioni dell'Università cattolica del Sacro Cuore: Miscellanea del Centro di Studi medioevali, 12 (Milan, 1989), pp. 135-170. See also my article on "The Ceremonies and Symbolism of Entering Religious Life and Taking the Monastic Habit, from the Fourth to the Twelfth Century," in Segni e riti nella Chiesa altomedievale occidentale, Settimane di studio del Centro italiano di studi sull'alto medioevo, 33 (Spoleto, 1987), II, 771-834. See Herbert L. Kessler, "On the State of Medieval Art

History," Art Bulletin, 70 (1988), 166-187, esp. 177: "The work of medieval art was more agent than object. It did not so much attract the beholder's eye to itself as mediate vision toward something beyond." On the concept of conformatio (= modern personification) in medieval art, see Karl-August Wirth, "In the Margins of a Twelfth-Century Psalter," Journal of the Warburg and Courtauld Institutes, 33 (1970), 22-23.

[3] Among recent works on these questions, see the papers presented at the Rennes conference on Artistes, artisans et production artistique au moyen âge: Rapports provisoires, 2 vols. (Rennes, 1983), of which the three volumes of the final publication have been published as Artistes, artisans et production artistique au moyen âge: Colloque international, I: Les Hommes, II: Commande et travail, and III: Fabrication et consommation de l'oeuvre, ed. Xavier Barral i Altet (Paris, 1986-90); Francis Salet, "Mécénat royal et princier au moyen âge," Académie des Inscriptions et Belles-Lettres: Comptes rendus, 1985, pp. 620-629; and Art and Patronage in the English Romanesque, ed. Sarah Macready and F. H. Thompson, Society of Antiquaries: Occasional Papers, n.s. 8 (London, 1986), which includes papers on patronage at Hereford and St Albans and by Thomas Becket and Henry of Blois.

who saw them, lived and worked in the buildings, and participated in the rites and ceremonies. The nature of the reaction naturally differed with the type of bridge, and the context in which it was presented. A manuscript illumination made a different impression than a building, and a fresco in the nave of a church than a painting in a chapter-house. But they had in common that they created in observers a tendency to enter into the past and experience it in their own lives.

The question of the reaction to works of art has tended to interest aestheticians more than historians, and to be approached from a personal rather than a collective point of view. For Walter Pater, "the salt of all aesthetic study" was not a painting itself but, "What, precisely what, is this to *me*?," and Oscar Wilde in *The Critic as Artist* said that Pater treated a work of art "simply as a starting point for a new creation."[4] More work has been done on the effect of works of art on individuals than on groups in society.[5] Otto Pächt in his *Rise of Pictorial Narrative in Twelfth-Century England* examined "the evolution and specific character of the visual imagination peculiar to the medieval mind" and the "special technique," as he called it, that developed in the Middle Ages "for finding pictorial equivalents for verbal utterances, whether spoken or written."[6] "The records of public response to painting" in fifteenth-century Italy were called "distressingly thin" by Baxandall, who asked, "What sort of painting would the religious public for pictures have found lucid, vividly memorable, and emotionally moving?"[7] Belting in his book on *The Image and its Public in the Middle Ages* showed that the form, function, and content of representations of the Passion were interrelated and appealed to different groups and individuals in different ways. Art is not a language, he said, but it has a language, and he referred to "image-language" (*Bildsprache*) and to works of art as "speaking."[8] More generally, Miles explained in *Image as Insight* that, since vision in the Middle Ages was regarded as a two-way process between the viewer and the object seen, messages received from works of art were no less important than those that were given, especially in the context of public worship and devotion.[9] The very use in these works of terms like speech, language, and message show the difficulty of describing non-verbal responses outside a framework that implies the use of words.

Horace in his *Ars poetica* gave a classic expression to the medieval view that the human mind is more moved by what is seen than by what is heard.[10] St. Augustine in his commentary on John wrote, " . . . a picture is seen in one way, and letters are seen in another way. When you see a picture, the whole thing is to have seen and praised; when you see letters, this is not the whole thing, since you also consider to read."[11] Leo the Great in effect equated vision, touch, and words in his sixty-ninth sermon, telling his listeners to receive the Gospel story of the Passion

[4] Michael Levey, *The Case of Walter Pater* (London, 1978), pp. 183 and 196.
[5] See, for instance, Millard Meiss, *Painting in Florence and Siena after the Black Death* (1951; rpt. Harper Torchbooks, New York, 1964), p. 106, who studied the effect of art on "the imagination, the will, and the actions of individuals," citing the examples of John Gualbert, Francis of Assisi, and especially Catherine of Siena, whose stigmatization was described in terms derived from visual rather than written sources; and also Chiara Frugoni, "Le mistiche, le visioni, e l'iconografia: Rapporti ed influssi," in *Atti del Convegno su 'La mistica femminile del Trecento'* (Todi, 1982), pp. 5–45, on the influence on late medieval visions of representations of the life of Christ, especially the Pietà.
[6] Otto Pächt, *The Rise of Pictorial Narrative in Twelfth-Century England* (Oxford, 1962), pp. vi and 55.
[7] Michael Baxandall, *Painting and Experience in Fifteenth-Century Italy* (London, Oxford, New York, 1972), pp. 24 and

43–45, described the experience of a painting as "a marriage between the painting and the beholder's previous visualizing activity on the same matter."
[8] Hans Belting, *Das Bild und sein Publikum im Mittelalter: Form und Funktion früher Bildtafeln der Passion* (Berlin, 1981), *passim* (esp. pp. 20, 30, 105, 126, 129, 223); see also his "Langage et réalité dans la peinture monumentale publique en Italie au Trecento," in *Artistes* (note 3), (provisional) I, 731–750, esp. 734, and (final) III, 491–511, esp. 494.
[9] Margaret Miles, *Image as Insight: Visual Understanding in Western Christianity and Secular Culture* (Boston, 1985), esp. pp. 7–9 and 28.
[10] Horace, *Ars Poetica*, 180–181. This passage was cited in the early thirteenth century in the *Liber sancti Gileberti*, ed. Raymonde Foreville and Gillian Keir, Oxford Medieval Texts (Oxford, 1987), p. 7.
[11] Augustine, *In Ioannis Evangelium*, 24.2, in *CC*, XXXVI, 245.

"without a shadow of hesitation" and "as manifest as if you encountered them all with bodily sight and touch." Elsewhere he said that the Passion should inhere so firmly in his listeners' hearts that their reading became a kind of seeing and that "the Gospel speech (*sermo*) told [the story] so openly and clearly that to hear what is read is the same for devout and pious hearts as to see what was done." In another sermon he said that the Passion "should not be remembered as something past but honored as something present" both by the daily sacraments and the truth of the Gospel.[12] Similar words were found nine centuries later in the *Vita Christi* of Ludolf of Saxony, who said in the introduction that

> although many of these things are narrated as if they were in the past (*in praeterito*) you should meditate on all of them as if they were done in the present (*in praesentia*), since you will without doubt taste a greater sweetness from this. Read, therefore, what has been done as if it were being done; place before your eyes deeds of the past as if they were present, and you will thus feel them as more tasty and agreeable.[13]

This stress on experience and on bringing the past into the present is found in many writers of late Antiquity and the Middle Ages, when there was a tendency for symbols to merge with what they represented.[14] Images, like texts, were no longer purely narrative and descriptive, and allowed the viewer to encounter the event or person portrayed directly. They synthesized an historical moment and bore witness to an historical truth.[15] This attitude may have influenced the interpretation of Gregory the Great's celebrated dictum that a picture "takes the place of reading" for the unlettered, who can "read by seeing on the walls what they are unable to read in books."[16] Giordano da Rivalto in a sermon given at Florence in 1305 said that pictures were "the book of laymen and also of all people" and that the paintings by saints like Luke and Nicodemus were important evidence and of great authority. Luke painted the Virgin from life, and Nicodemus, who had been present at the crucifixion, showed the form and manner (*il modo e la figura*) of Christ on the cross. "Whoever sees the painting, fully sees almost the entire event (*fatto*)."[17]

² Leo the Great, *Tractatus*, 52.1, 69.3, and 70.1, in *CC*, CXXXVIIIA, 307, 421, and 426; see William Loerke, " 'Real Presence' in Early Christian Art," in *Monasticism and the Arts*, ed. Timothy Verdon and John Dally (Syracuse, 1984), pp. 38–41; and *Tractatus*, 64.1 in *CC*, CXXXVIIIA, 389. On the eucharist as a link between the past and present, see Gilles Quispel, "Zeit und Geschichte im antiken Christentum," *Eranos-Jahrbuch*, 20 (1951), pp. 115–140, tr. in *Man and Time: Papers from the Eranos Yearbooks*, Bollingen Series, 30.3 (Princeton, 1957), p. 91.

³ Ludolf of Saxony, *Vita Jesu Christi*, Proem, I, 7, cited in Charles A. Conway, Jr., *The Vita Christi of Ludolf of Saxony and Late Medieval Devotion Centred on the Incarnation*, Analecta Carthusiana, 34 (Salzburg, 1976), p. 124.

⁴ Michel Meslin, "Temps initiatique et progrès spirituel dans la nouvelle religiosité" (on Julian) and M. A. Bardolle, "La vie de Moïse de Grégoire de Nysse ou le temps spirituel vécu à travers l'imaginaire d'un modèle historique" (on Gregory of Nyssa) in *Le temps chrétien de la fin d'Antiquité au moyen âge: IIIe-XIIIe siècles*, Colloques internationaux de Centre national de la recherche scientifique, 604 (Paris, 1984), pp. 53 and 259. John Matthews discussed what he called the theatrical mode of reality in the fourth century in a lecture at Princeton on 14 November 1986.

⁵ Michelangelo Cagiano de Azevedo, "Storiografia per immagini," in *La storiografia altomedioevale*, Settimane di studio del Centro italiano di studi sull'alto medioevo, 17 (Spoleto, 1970), I, 119; see also Loerke, " 'Real presence' " (note 12), pp. 30–32, who stressed how the viewer of early medieval art passed "through the text to the event itself," and Kessler, "Medieval Art History" (note 2), p. 184:

"Art's testimonial power assured pictorial narrative a special place in medieval culture."

¹⁶ Gregory the Great, *Registrum epistolarum*, IX, 208 and XI, 10, ed. Paul Ewald and Ludo M. Hartmann, 2 vols, MGH, Epistolae, 1–2 (Berlin, 1887–94), II, 195 and 270 = IX, 209, and XI, 10 in the edition by Dag Norberg in *CC*, CXLA, 768 and 874. These texts were cited or alluded to by countless writers in the Middle Ages, and later, to show the parallel of seeing by the illiterate with reading by the literate and, by implication, the superiority of words over pictures, though this may not have been Gregory's intention. See the recent contributions on this subject by Michael Camille, "Seeing and Reading: Some Visual Implications of Medieval Literacy and Illiteracy," *Art History*, 8 (1985), 26–49; Herbert Kessler, "Pictorial Narrative and Church Mission in Sixth-Century Gaul," *Studies in the History of Art*, 16 (1985), 75–91; and especially the paper of Lawrence Duggan, "Was Art Really the 'Book of the Illiterate'?" to which I owe the citations from Theodulf and Strabo and which I read in typescript and has been published in *Word and Image*, 5 (1989), 227–251.

¹⁷ *Prediche inedite del B. Giordano da Rivalto . . . recitate in Firenze dal 1302 al 1305*, ed. Enrico Narducci, Collezione di opere inedite o rare dei primi tre secoli della lingua (Bologna, 1867), pp. 170–171. Elizabeth Beatson kindly supplied this reference and one to the "Breve dell'arte de' pittori senesi" of 1355, who described themselves as "manifestatori agli uomini grossi che non sanno lectera, de le cose miraculose operate per virtù et in virtù de la santa fede": *Documenti per la storia dell'arte senese*, ed. Gaetano Milanesi, 3 vols. (Siena, 1854–56), I, 1.

The question of how images were seen was central in the battle over the veneration of icons that disturbed the Greek church in the eighth and ninth centuries. The acts of the Second Council of Nicea in 787 cited the description of the icon of the passion of St Euphemia by Asterius, who stressed the realism of the scenes of suffering and their emotional effect upon him, until he broke down in tears and was unable to speak.[18] The emperors Michael and Theophilus in their letter to Louis the Pious in 824 referred to pictures placed in high places "in order that the picture itself might be taken for scripture (*pro scriptura*)."[19] John of Damascus in his *Exposition of the Orthodox Faith*[20] stressed the importance of images for those without "a knowledge of letters nor time for reading," saying that "the honour rendered to the image passes over to the prototype," and he used the philosophical view of sight in his three orations *Against the Calumniators of Images*.[21] The high value attributed to pictures in the Greek church was in part attributable to this view of the superiority of sight to hearing and, consequently, of pictures to written words.[22] Photius in a homily delivered at the unveiling of the image of the Virgin and Child in Hagia Sophia said that

> Just as speech is transmitted by hearing, so a form is imprinted by the faculty of sight upon the tablets of the soul, giving to those whose apprehension is not soiled by wicked doctrines a representation of knowledge concordant with piety. Martyrs have fought for the love of God, and have shown with their blood the dearest of their zeal, and their memory is contained in books. These things are seen enacted in pictures, also, which make the martyrdom of these blessed men more vivid to learn than from the written word. . . . These things are conveyed by speech and by pictures, but it is the spectators rather than the hearers who are drawn to imitation.[23]

Meanwhile, in the West, Theodulf of Orleans wrote in the *Libri Carolini*, after arguing for a middle course between worshipping and destroying images, that "painters can to some degree recall to memory the history of what is past," though he went on to say that writers, rather than painters, could understand "those things which are perceived by the senses only and expressed by words."[24] A generation later Walafrid Strabo cited Constantine, who in his vision had recognized the apostles from their portraits, as an example of someone "who learned the history of the ancients from pictures," and said,

> We sometimes see simple and unlettered people, whom words can scarcely bring to believe in what is past, so moved by a picture of the Lord's Passion or some other marvel that they show by their tears how the outer and visible forms are impressed like letters on their hearts.[25]

The phrase *exteriores figuras cordi suo lituris impressas* shows the parallel of pictures and words and underlines the importance of the concept of *figura*, which was also

[18] Asterius of Amasea, *Hom.* XI on the martyrdom of St Euphemia, *Patrologia graeca*, XL, 336A-337C. See Daniel J. Sahas, *Icon and Logos* (Toronto, 1986), pp. 130-131.
[19] *Concilia aevi Karolini*, ed Albert Werminghoff, *MGH*, Leges, 3: Concilia, 2 (Hanover-Leipzig, 1906-08), p. 475. See Judith Herrin, *Formation of Christendom* (Princeton, 1987), p. 469, n. 79.
[20] John of Damascus, *Expositio fidei*, IV, 16, ed. Bonifatius Kotter, *Die Schriften des Johannes von Damaskos*, vol. 2 (Berlin, New York, 1973), pp. 207-208.
[21] John of Damascus, *Contra imaginum calumniatores orationes tres*, I, 17, ed. Bonifatius Kotter, *Die Schriften des Johannes von Damaskos*, vol 3 (Berlin, New York, 1975), p. 93.
[22] Ibid., p. 19, n. 40. See Kessler, "Medieval Art History" (note 2), p. 183.

[23] Francis Dvornik, "The Patriarch Photius and Iconoclasm," *Dumbarton Oaks Papers*, 7 (1953), 91.
[24] *Libri Carolini*, III, 23, ed. Hubert Bastgen, *MGH*, Leges, 3: Concilia, 2 suppl. (Hanover-Leipzig, 1924), p. 153. I am indebted to Paul Meyvaert for verifying the text of this passage.
[25] Walafrid Strabo, *De exordiis et incrementis rerum ecclesiasticarum*, 8, in *Capitularia regum Francorum*, ed. Alfred Boretius and Victor Krause, 2 vols., *MGH*, Leges, 2: Capitularia, 1-2 (Hanover, 1883-97), II, 484. The reading *lituris* is either a variant or perhaps a misprint for *litteris*, or, according to Du Cange, for *liniaturis*.

used by Giordano da Rivalto. According to Auerbach, "*figura* is clearly distinguished from most of the allegorical forms known to us from other contexts, by the historical reality of both what signifies and what is signified."[26] A *figura* (which may be a person or an event) is real, not a substitute for something else, and it therefore mediates between the realities of the past and of the present.

The clearest examples of *figurae* of this sort are found in Biblical typology. Abel, Melchizedec, Abraham, and Christ were almost interchangeable figures in making their respective offerings and sacrifices; and each was identified with the priest who celebrated the eucharist, as the prayer following the consecration in the liturgy of the mass shows. Leo presumably had this in mind when he said that the Passion was "not past but present" in the sacraments and the pages of Scripture, and Walafrid when he referred to "the external figures" of the Passion and other marvellous events which moved the hearts of observers. The figures of Cato, Virgil, and Beatrice in the *Divine Comedy* "can 'mean more' than themselves precisely because Dante conceives of them as fully alive and real, and *not* as allegories."[27] It is impossible to judge the precise impression made by such figures and scenes. Some Biblical cycles are divided into historical and typological, which suggests that they were seen as either stories (their "real" meaning) or allegories (their "other" meaning); but others have mixed scenes, without any obvious correspondence between them. Strohm said of the twelfth-century carved stone medallions in the south porch of Malmesbury Abbey that "the effect of so many popular types on an audience accustomed to typology must have been to bind the Old Testament subjects to the New with a series of veiled promises of Christ's victory over Satan."[28]

Scenes of historical events often conveyed a figurative rather than literal reality.[29] Lifelike details were sometimes added, as in the painting described by Paul the Deacon, showing the deeds of the Lombards in the palace at Monza, in which "it is clearly shown how the Lombards at that time cut their hair and what was their clothing and costume."[30] Liutprand of Cremona said that Otto I had a painting of his victory over the Magyars in 933 painted at Merseburg "so that you may see the true thing rather than the likeness of truth."[31] This distinction between *veri similis*—likeness of truth — and *vera res* — the true thing—probably came from the pseudo-Ciceronian *Ad Herennium*, which said that a narrative is made more similar to truth if it is in accord with custom, common opinion, and nature, and that these should be observed whether or not the subject matter is true, "for truth is often unconvincing if these are not preserved."[32] Paul the Deacon and Liutprand were

Erich Auerbach, "Figura," in his *Gesammelte Aufsätze zur romanischen Philologie* (Berne-Munich, 1967), pp. 55-92, esp. 77, as translated in Peter Dronke, *Dante and Medieval Latin Traditions* (Cambridge, 1986), p. 7. See also Horst Günther, *Freiheit, Herrschaft und Geschichte: Semantik der historisch-politischen Welt* (Frankfurt, 1979), pp. 29-33, who stressed the specific chronological connections (*Zeitvorstellung*) associated with *figurae*, which link the past, present and future, and Belting, in *Artistes* (note 3), (provisional) I, 739, and (final) III, 499, who suggested that the two aspects are linked by likeness or *similitudo*, where the resemblance is at the same time literal and allegorical. Dronke, *Dante* (note 26), p. 7.
Paul Strohm, "The Malmesbury Medallions and Twelfth Century Typology," *Mediaeval Studies*, 33 (1971), 180-187 (quotation on 186). See Piotr Skubiszewski, "Die Bildprogramme der romanischen Kelche und Patenen," in *Metalkunst von der Spätantike bis zum ausgehenden Mittelalter*, ed. Arne Effenberger, Staatliche Museen zu Berlin: Schriften der frühchristlich-byzantinischen Sammlung, 1

(Berlin, 1982), p. 220, and generally on the iconographical programs in Romanesque chalices and patens, "The Iconography of a Romanesque Chalice from Trzemeszno," *Journal of the Warburg and Courtauld Institutes*, 34 (1971), 40-64, and "Bildprogramme," pp. 199-206 and 215.
[29] Cagiano de Azevedo, "Storiografia" (note 15), pp. 128-130.
[30] Paul the Deacon, *Historia Langobardorum*, IV, 22, in *MGH, Scriptores rerum langobardorum et italicarum saec. VI-IX* (Hanover, 1878), p. 124.
[31] Liutprand of Cremona, *Antapodosis*, II, 31, ed. Joseph Becker, *MGH, Scriptores rerum germanicarum in usum scholarum* (Hanover-Leipzig, 1915), p. 52: "adeo ut rem ueram potius quam ueri similem videas."
[32] Ps-Cicero, *Ad Herennium*, I, IX, 16, ed. and tr. Harry Caplan, Loeb Library (Cambridge, Mass., 1954), p. 28: "Veri similis narratio erit si ut mos, ut opinio, ut natura postulat dicemus. . . . Si uera res erit nihilominus haec omnia narrando conservanda sunt, nam saepe veritas, nisi haec servata sint, fidem non potest facere; sin erunt ficta, eo magis erunt conservanda."

describing the visual equivalent of the technique of raconteurs who add fictitious details to their stories in order to make them more vivid and lifelike. Other representations embodied historical truth without attempting to reproduce an actual event, like the mosaics of Justinian and Theodora at Ravenna, and others were frankly propagandistic in character, like the twelfth-century frescoes in the Lateran palace showing the triumph of the reformed popes of the eleventh and twelfth centuries, where the hierarchical presentation made no effort to be factually accurate but embodied the deeper truth of the historical events.[33]

Abstract shapes and forms also conveyed meanings that could not always be put into words. Roundness, for instance, and the associated concepts of smoothness and evenness, conveyed a sense of perfection and completeness that went back to Antiquity and is not entirely lost today, as in the description of a "well-rounded" person.[34] Plato regarded the round or sphere as "the most perfect and the most self-similar of all shapes," which, for Marcus Aurelius, "irradiates a light whereby it sees the reality of all things and the reality that is in itself." Horace's description of a man as "strong [and] self-contained, smooth and rounded" was cited by many medieval writers. Ausonius added "in the manner of the world, too smooth for any blemish from without to settle upon him,"[35] where the words *instar mundi* show the parallel between the microcosm of man and the macrocosm of the world. The medieval depictions of a man with outstretched arms and legs enclosed within a circle illustrated perfection and harmony, like other homocentric diagrams in the twelfth century.[36] A town depicted within a circuit of walls, with order inside and chaos outside, was a sign of security and protection.[37] The toleration of open vistas in Antiquity contrasted with "the strong sense of enclosure" in the Middle Ages, when the theme of the man-made garden reflected "both medieval idealism and medieval 'inwardness' ", looking backward to an ideal of paradisaical perfection (Figure 1).[38]

[33] In addition to the works mentioned in my article on "Papal, Imperial and Monastic Propaganda in the Eleventh and Twelfth Centuries," in *Prédication et propagande au Moyen Age: Islam, Byzance, Occident.* Penn, Paris, Dumbarton Oaks *Colloquia, 3: Session des 20-25 octobre 1980* (Paris, 1983), pp. 185-186, see Christopher Walter, "Papal Political Imagery in the Medieval Lateran Palace," *Cahiers archéologiques,* 20 (1970), 155-176, and 21 (1971), 109-136; and Ernst Kitzinger, "The Gregorian Reform and the Visual Arts: A Problem of Method," *Transactions of the Royal Historical Society,* 5th ser., 22 (1972), 99-100; and "The Arts as Aspects of a Renaissance: Rome and Italy," in *Renaissance and Renewal in the Twelfth Century,* ed. Robert Benson and Giles Constable (Cambridge, Mass., 1982), pp. 643-644 and 648 (with further references).

[34] I am indebted to Professor John Callahan of Georgetown University for several references on this subject, which is discussed (with some of the references cited below) by Jean Leclercq, "Aux sources des sermons sur les Cantiques" (1959) and "Saint Bernard écrivain" (1960), in his *Recueil d'études sur saint Bernard et ses écrits,* 3 vols., Storia e letteratura, 92, 104, and 114 (Rome, 1960-69), I, 292, 333, and 351, n. 4, and in his introd. to Bernard of Clairvaux, *On the Song of Songs,* IV, Cistercian Fathers Series, 40 (Kalamazoo, 1980), pp. xxi-xxii. Bernard substituted *perfecte* for *rotunde* in his description of the unity of the Father and Son in his sermon 71 on the Song of Songs: *Serm. super Cantica,* 71.6, in *Opera omnia,* ed. Jean Leclercq a. o., 8 vols. in 9 (Rome, 1957-77), II, 218. Leclercq, in his introd. to the translation of this sermon, attributed this change to Bernard's pastoral sense, since *perfecte* was more abstract and familiar than *rotunde,* with its antique,

poetic, and visual associations. On the expression of divine order in the abstract patterns of Cistercian grisaille glass, see Meredith Lillich, "Monastic Stained Glass; Patronage and Style," in *Monasticism and the Arts* (note 12), pp. 218-222.

[35] Plato, *Timaeus,* 33 B (cf. 34 B); Marcus Aurelius, *Meditationes,* XI, 12 (cf. VIII, 42, and XII, 3); Horace, *Sat.,* II, vii, 86; Ausonius, *Ecloga,* III, 1. 5; Augustine, *De quantitate animae,* XVI, 27; Paschasius Radbertus, *Vita s. Adalhardi,* 15 (*PL,* CXX, 1516C); Peter Damiani, *Liber qui dicitur Dominus vobiscum,* 19, and *De institutis ordinis eremitorum,* 27 (*PL,* CXLV, 249C and 360A); Honorius, *Gemma animae,* I, 195 (*PL,* CLXXII, 603 BC); and Sicard of Cremona, *Mitrale,* II, 1 (*PL,* CCXIII, 59B).

[36] Madeline Caviness, "Images of Divine Order and the Third Mode of Seeing," *Gesta,* 22 (1983), 109, wrote that "the human figure itself . . . reflects the order of the universe in its perfect symmetry, calm contour, and evocation of rhomboid, rectilinear, spherical, and elliptical forms." On the macrocosm/microcosm in the twelfth century, see also Marian Kurdzialek, "Der Mensch als Abbild des Kosmos," in *Der Begriff der Repraesentatio im Mittelalter,* ed. Albert Zimmermann, Miscellanea Mediaevalia, 8 (Berlin, New York, 1971), pp. 35-75, esp. 47-57.

[37] Chiara Frugoni, *Una lontana città. Sentimenti e immagini nel medioevo,* Saggi, 651 (Turin, 1983), pp. 10-11 and 124, cites among other sources the poem in honor of the city of Metz by Sigebert of Gembloux, who praised its walls "non facilis solvi, non expugnabilis hosti," in *MGH, Scriptores* in fol., IV, 477.

[38] Derek Pearsall and Elizabeth Salter, *Landscapes and Seasons of the Medieval World* (London, 1973), p. 54.

Figure 1. Hortus conclusus *(round walled garden with locked door and sealed well-head), ca. 1350. Darmstadt, Hessischer Landes- und Hochschulbibliothek,* Speculum humanae salvationis, *Ms. 2505, f. 7r (detail).*

With regard to architecture, Cassiodorus wrote in his *Variae* that old buildings should be maintained in their pristine splendor and new ones built "in the likeness of antiquity . . . so that only the newness of the materials differs from the work of the ancients."[39] The design of Charlemagne's church at Aachen reflected the proportions of Solomon's temple as described in the Old Testament. Other churches built during the Carolingian Renaissance and, most impressively, in Italy in the late eleventh and early twelfth centuries were modelled on the Christian basilicas of the Constantinian and post-Constantinian age.[40] "All or nearly all the twelfth-century

---

[39] Cassiodorus, *Variae*, VII, 5, in *MGH, Auctores antiquissimi*, 15 vols. (Berlin, 1877-1919), XII, 204-205, cf. VII, 15 (ibid., p. 211) where he said that ancient buildings should be renewed, "excluding the defects," and new buildings clothed with the glory of antiquity. See Beat Brenk, "Spolia from Constantine to Charlemagne: Aesthetics versus Ideology," *Dumbarton Oaks Papers*, 41 (1987), 109. In the *Institutiones*, I, 15, 15, ed. R. A. B. Mynors (Oxford, 1937), 50, Cassiodorus wrote that in a textual emendation letters should be formed "so that they may be thought to have been written by the ancients."

[40] See Richard Krautheimer, "The Carolingian Revival of Early Christian Architecture," *Art Bulletin*, 24 (1942), 30, who wrote, "The aim of the Carolingian Renaissance was not so much a revival of Antiquity in general as a revival of Rome, and specifically of one facet of the Roman past:

the Golden Age of Christianity in that city." See also, especially on the role of Monte Cassino, Émile Bertaux, *L'art dans l'Italie méridionale de la fin de l'Empire Romain à la conquête de Charles d'Anjou* (Paris, 1903; rpt. 1968), p. 190; Kitzinger, "Gregorian Reform" (note 33), p. 95, and "A Virgin's Face: Antiquarianism in Twelfth-Century Art," *Art Bulletin*, 62 (1980), 19; Richard Krautheimer, *Rome: Profile of a City, 312-1308* (Princeton, 1980), pp. 178-181; and Herbert Bloch, "The New Fascination with Ancient Rome," in *Renaissance and Renewal* (note 33), pp. 615-621, esp. 619. On contrasting architectural developments in the Greek East, where churches in the eleventh and twelfth centuries became more intimate, diverse, and irregular, see Alexander Kazhdan and Ann Wharton Epstein, *Change in Byzantine Culture in the Eleventh and Twelfth Centuries* (Berkeley, Los Angeles, London, 1985), pp. 144 and 194.

V

Figure 2. S. Giovanni a Porta Latina, *Rome, 1191. The simple plan conforms to Roman basilicas of the fourth century. Columns, plinths, and some capitals are spolia.*

standard plans in Rome go back to early Christian local prototypes" (Figure 2).[41] This can be seen as a manifestation of the movement of revival and renewal that is collectively referred to as the Renaissance of the Twelfth Century and also, more specifically, as part of a campaign on the part of the papacy to win support for the reform movement.[42] The plans and decoration of some twelfth-century churches outside Rome, as in the Valdinievole and lower valley of the Arno, may also have been designed to show their subordination to Rome and connection with the ancient traditions of the papacy.[43] It would be unwise to push this point too far, however, since the enemies of the papacy also appealed to ancient tradition, and Roman architectural forms and motifs were used in many parts of Europe.[44] These reminis-

[41] Krautheimer, *Rome* (note 40), p. 176 (pp. 161-202 generally). See also Hélène Toubert, "Le renouveau paléochrétien à Rome au début du XIIe siècle," *Cahiers archéologiques,* 20 (1970), 99-154, rpt. in *Un art dirigé. Réforme grégorienne et iconographie* (Paris, 1990), 239-310, and the articles by Bloch and Kitzinger in *Renaissance and Renewal* (notes 33 and 40).

[42] Krautheimer, *Rome* (note 40), p. 179. Kitzinger, "Gregorian Reform" (note 33), p. 97 (also p. 101), in particular argued that the Gregorian reformers consciously went back to the buildings and mosaics of the fourth and fifth centuries, rather than the first and second, in order "to resume a tradition associated with the first golden age of the papacy."

[43] This point was made by Romano Silva in a talk on "Le pieve romaniche della Valdinievole" at the conference on St Allucio at Pescia on 19 April 1985.

[44] See Willibald Sauerländer, "Architecture and the Figurative Arts: The North," in *Renaissance and Renewal* (note 33), p. 677 (with references) and, generally, Piotr Skubiszewski, "*Ecclesia, Christianitas, Regnum,* et *Sacerdotium* dans l'art des Xe-XIe s. Idées et structures des images," *Cahiers de civilisation médiévale,* 28 (1985), 133-179, esp. 144 and 179; and, on secular visual propaganda, E. Baldwin Smith, *Architectural Symbolism of Imperial Rome and the Middle Ages,* Princeton Monographs on Art and Archeology, 30 (Princeton, 1956), esp. pp. 89-94, 100-103, and 156-157 on the eleventh and twelfth centuries, and Chiara Frugoni, "L'ideologia del potere imperiale nella 'Cattedra di S. Pietro,' " *Bullettino dell'Istituto Storico Italiano per il Medio Evo,* 86 (1976-77), 67-181, esp. 88-96.

ences of antiquity may have impressed modern scholars more than they did people at the time, who were used to seeing a mixture of old and new in buildings. Many aspects of twelfth-century art and architecture seem to show a desire to recreate (or at least to establish an association with) the ambiance of antiquity, and especially of the primitive church. At Rome, "the classicizing taste of the period found some of its fullest and freest expression" in the furnishings of the new churches; and the decorations in the nave of Sta Maria in Cosmedin, the crypt of San Nicola in Carcere, and the apse of San Clemente, all of which date from about 1120, were based both in details and in overall composition on antique and especially early Christian models.[45] The statues of the *lupa* and of Marcus Aurelius, and even the collection of ancient sculpture at the Lateran Palace, carried a political message, as had the wolf and equestrian statue of Theodoric taken by Charlemagne to Aachen.[46] The later paintings of the *navicella* in old St Peter's, and probably also those in churches north of the Alps, stood at once for Christ's rescue of Peter and His support of the church.[47] The frescoes in the chapter-house of the abbey of the Trinity at Vendôme, which show the feast of Emmaus, the miraculous catch of fishes, the investiture of St Peter, the mission of apostles, and the ascension of Christ, have been associated with the visit of Pope Urban II in 1096 and with his program of ecclesiastical reform and centralization.[48] More generally, the many representations of the apostles in Romanesque sculpture reflected the new stress in the twelfth century on the *vita apostolica* and invited the viewers to participate in apostolic activities (Figure 3).[49]

The desire to draw together old and new may explain the medieval practice of reusing ancient works of art and fragments, known as *spolia*, and of adapting old objects to new uses.[50] Modern taste, which favors stylistic consistency and purity, often finds such mixtures displeasing, aside from the high standard of workmanship.[51] They were appreciated in the Middle Ages, however, probably because they embodied the sense of renewal and continuity that Heckscher called the *principium unitatis*: "What the medieval mind chiefly sought in the remains of the past was— in contradistinction to modern romanticism—the permanent form, the opposite of the ruin."[52] Brenk in an article on "*Spolia* from Constantine to Charlemagne" stressed

Kitzinger, "Arts" (note 33), pp. 639-640, and Toubert, "Renouveau" (note 41), esp. 101-112.

Karl der Grosse: Lebenswerk und Nachleben, ed. Wolfgang Braunfels (Dusseldorf, 1965), III (*Karolingische Kunst*), pp. 169, 307, 439, 451, and 572, and Krautheimer, *Rome* (note 40), p. 193.

Belting, in *Artistes* (note 3), (provisional) I, 736, and (final) III, 496.

Hélène Toubert, "Les fresques de la Trinité de Vendôme, un témoignage sur l'art de la réforme grégorienne," *Cahiers de civilisation médiévale*, 26 (1983), 297-326; cf. *Un art dirigé* (note 41), 365-402.

Ilene Forsyth, "The *Vita Apostolica* and Romanesque Sculpture: Some Preliminary Observations," *Gesta*, 25 (1986), 75-82, esp. 79-80.

A session at the meeting of the College Art Association in Boston (12-14 February 1987) was devoted to "The Perception of Antiquity in the Middle Ages: Ancient Spoils and Medieval Art," where Dale Kinney pointed out that the term *spolia* now used for such borrowings is of recent origin and groups together types of objects that were particularized in the Middle Ages. Ilene Forsyth in the abstract of her paper on "The Role of Spolia in the Cumulative Work of Art," said that such works of art conveyed "a special sense of cumulative historical tradition." See also William S. Heckscher, "Relics of Pagan Antiquity in Mediaeval Settings," *Journal of the Warburg Insti-*

tute, 1 (1937), 204-220, rpt. in his *Art and Literature: Studies in Relationship*, ed. Egon Verheyen, Saecula Spiritalia, 17 (Baden-Baden, 1985), pp. 31-51, who is primarily concerned with gems but makes many remarks of wider concern, and the references to works on *spolia* given in *Renaissance and Renewal* (note 33), pp. 617, n. 4, 619, n. 17, and 639, n. 7.

[51] Sauerländer, "Architecture" (note 44), pp. 675-676, was impressed by the fact "that this juxtaposition of classical and barbaric forms was not felt to be disturbing," and attributed the efforts of scholars to explain the "apparently senseless mustering of antique forms" on the façade of St. Gilles to "an inadequate understanding of what one might describe as the fragmentizing, spoliating manner of borrowing from Antiquity which occurred here just as it did in Burgundy." Thomas Lyman in the abstract of his paper on "*Composito* vs. *Venustas*: Constrasting Use of Spolia in Romanesque Architecture" at the College Art Association (note 50) said that scholars customarily attribute the use of *spolia* "to limitations in resources if not simply in taste and judgement."

[52] Heckscher, "Relics" (note 50), p. 205 ("It is in the light of this 'principium unitatis' that we must understand the mediaeval attempts to restore Antiquity which go under the name of renovatio," and p. 210 (rpt., pp. 32 and 37). Lyman in the paper cited above (note 51) related the use of *spolia* to medieval concepts of order.

V

58

Figure 3. The Way to Emmaus, cloister relief, twelfth century, Silos, S. Domingo. Christ is dressed as a medieval pilgrim, and his scrip is decorated with the shell of Compostella.

the aesthetic and ideological use of *spolia* to evoke the past and to establish connections with the traditions of the empire and early Christian Rome.[53] Abbot Suger of St Denis in particular wanted what he called "a combination and coherence of old and new work" in his buildings and works of art.[54] He had the famous eagle vase in the Louvre made, as he said, "by transferring it from an amphora into the form of an eagle," which preserved the ancient work while changing its form and use (Figure 4); and he had a fluted cup of sardonyx, possibly of Byzantine origin, made into the chalice which is now in the National Gallery in Washington.[55] It

[53] Brenk, "Spolia" (note 39), pp. 103-109.

[54] Suger of St Denis, *De consecratione ecclesiae sancti Dionysii*, 2, ed. A. Lecoy de la Marche, *Oeuvres complètes de Suger*, Société de l'histoire de France (Paris, 1867), p. 218, tr. Erwin Panofsky, *Abbot Suger, On the Abbey Church of St.-Denis and its Art Treasures* (Princeton, 1946), p. 90. See the article (of which the title was taken from this phrase by Suger) by Madeline Caviness, " 'De convenientia et cohaerentia antiqui et novi operis': Medieval Conservation, Restoration, Pastiche and Forgery," in *Intuition und*

Kunstwissenschaft: Festschrift für Hanns Swarzenski (Berlin, 1973), pp. 205-221.

[55] Suger, *De rebus in administratione sua gestis*, 34, ed. Lecoy de la Marche, p. 208, tr. Panofsky (note 54), p. 78. See the articles of Danielle Gaborit-Chopin, "Suger's Liturgical Vessels," and William D. Wixom, "Traditional Forms in Suger's Contributions to the Treasury of Saint-Denis," in *Abbot Suger and Saint-Denis: A Symposium*, ed. Paula Gerson (New York, 1986), pp. 285-289 and 295-297.

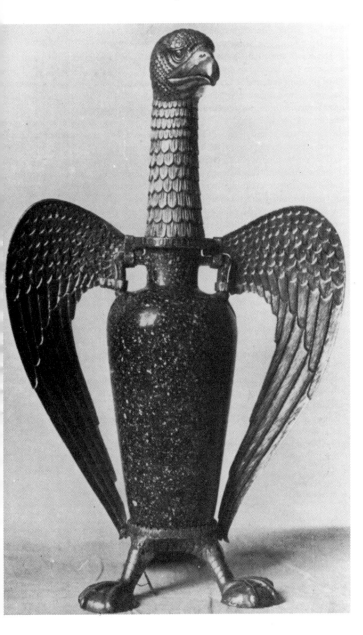

Figure 4. Eagle Vase, *Musée du Louvre, Paris. Antique porphyry vase, the gold and silver mount added by Abbot Suger (1081-1151) of St. Denis.*

has a somewhat Greek form and may have been designed specifically for use in the Greek liturgy at St Denis.[56] The copies and pastiches made in the eleventh and twelfth centuries combined a concern for "iconographic content, truth, and tradition" with "a degree of personal freedom and artistic license," and were designed not to deceive but to bring past and present together by using old styles for new uses.[57] Some copies may have been forgeries in the modern sense, made in order to deceive, or for some other ulterior motive, like the so-called tomb of St Hilary, which was associated with the controversy over the relics of St Sernin. But even those that included conscious (and to us sometimes deceptive) imitations of earlier styles should not be considered forgeries. One side of the St Guilhem sarcophogus, for example, was made in the twelfth century, apparently to match the others, which date from the fourth; and in the cloister at Ripoll the three fourteenth-century sides reflect the style of the twelfth-century side (Figure 5).[58] There is no obvious motive for this other than the desire, as expressed by Suger, to combine old and new elements in a way that would embody the principles of unity, continuity, and authority. Giordano da Rivalto said that St Luke's portrait of the Virgin at Rome showed Her "exactly as She was."[59] The icons at Sta Maria Nuova and at San Sisto were both believed to be by St Luke. Each had its personality, and they greeted one another when they met in processions. They were often copied, and one of them served as the model for the image of the Virgin seated on the right hand of Christ in the twelfth-century mosaic in the apse of St Maria in Trastevere (Figure 6). The image of Christ there derived from the icon at the Lateran, and those of SS Peter and Paul from early Christian prototypes, so that the entire mosaic served to mediate between past and present.[60]

Perhaps the most puzzling aspect of the interweaving of old and new elements in medieval art and literature was the tendency to combine apparently incompatible and inconsistent elements and to separate form and theme, investing ancient forms with modern meanings and presenting ancient themes in modern form. Panofsky called this the principle of disjunction, which he described as "a basic inability to make what we would call 'historical' distinctions" and as "an irresistible urge to 'compartmentalize' such psychological experiences and cultural activities as were to coalesce or merge in the Renaissance."[61] According to Heckscher's principle of unity, a sense of historical continuity and renewal brought together

[56] This suggestion was made by Philippe Verdier at the conference on linguistic pluralism in Montreal on 3 May 1986. On the Greek liturgy at St-Denis, see Niels K. Rasmussen, "The Liturgy at Saint-Denis: A Preliminary Study," in *Suger and Saint-Denis* (note 55), p. 44.

[57] Hanns Swarzenski, "The Role of Copies in the Formation of the Styles of the Eleventh Century," in *Studies in Western Art: Acts of the Twentieth International Congress of the History of Art*, I: *Romanesque and Gothic Art* (Princeton, 1963), p. 9. Cf. the remarks by Meyer Schapiro in *Art News*, 54, no. 5 (Sept., 1955), 44 and 59-60; and Caviness, " 'De Convenientia' " (note 54). See also Margarete Bieber, *Ancient Copies: Contributions to the History of Greek and Roman Art* (New York, 1977), p. 174.

[58] On this and other examples cited here, see Caviness, " 'De convenientia' " (note 54), pp. 212-218, who remarked (p. 217) on "a conscious archaism" in the style, composition, and motifs of the St-Hilaire tomb.

[59] Giordano da Rivalto, *Prediche inedite* (note 17), p. 171.

[60] Cf. Kitzinger, "A Virgin's Face" (note 40), pp. 6-19, who argued that the representation derived from the Sta Maria Nuova icon and was a sort of visual citation, set off by

style rather than quotation marks, and Hans Belting, who said in a lecture at Princeton University on 10 March 1988 that it was modelled on the San Sisto icon and saw it as representing the marriage of Christ and the church and the union of the church and the people of Rome. See also Dale Kinney, "Spolia from the Baths of Caracalla in Sta Maria in Trastevere," *Art Bulletin*, 68 (1986), 379-397, who suggested (p. 394) that the heads of couples on the capitals paralleled the coupling of Christ and Mary in the mosaic and underlined the relation of the old and new images, and Kessler, "Medieval Art History" (note 2), p. 176.

[61] Erwin Panofsky, *Renaissance and Renascences in Western Art* (Stockholm, 1960; rpt. 1972), pp. 84 and 106. During the Middle Ages, according to Panofsky (pp. 110-111), "The classical world was not approached historically but pragmatically, as something far-off yet, in a sense, still alive and, therefore, potentially useful and potentially dangerous." On these views, see the article of Cormier cited below (note 64) and the introduction to *Renaissance and Renewal* (note 33), pp. xxiv-xxv.

Figure 5a. and b. Fragments of Relief Sculpture from the Tomb of St. Guilhem *(d. 812), Museum, St. Guilhem-le-Desert.*

a) Fragment of Miracle Scene, *from the front panel, fourth century.*

b) The Three Magi, *from the back panel, ca. 1138.*

V

62

Figure 6. S. Maria in Trastevere,
Rome, Apse mosaic, ca. 1130.

differing forms and contents that Panofsky said remained apart until the Renaissance, when a new sense of history distinguished the past from the present.

These divergences apply not only to temporal and spatial inconsistencies (anachronism and anatopism) but also to timelessness and spacelessness (uchronia and utopia), which look forward as well as backward.[62] It is an odd fact of linguistic usage that although the words utopia and anachronism—being in no place or in the wrong time-framework—are both familiar, the parallel terms uchronia and anatopism—being out of time or in the wrong place—are rarely used, though they are equally useful. Réau in his book on Christian iconography studied these inconsistencies under the headings of places (events depicted in "wrong" settings), people (portraits of later people in scenes of earlier events), and clothing (people dressed in historically "wrong" costumes). Anachronism can also take the form of simultaneity, where events that took place at different times are shown or described together (as in charters, where it has led to many mistaken charges of forgery); and anatopism appears as a lack of perspective, where events and objects seem to be in the wrong place or position in relation to each other. Towards the end of the

[62] See Louis Réau, "L'anachronisme dans l'art médiéval," which was originally published in the *Mélanges Souriau* in 1952 and republished as chap. 4 of vol. 1 of his *Iconographie de l'art chrétien*, 3 vols. in 6 (Paris, 1955-59), which is cited here. On the terms anachronism (uchro-nia) and anatopism (utopia), which are of comparatively recent origin, see ibid., pp. 280, n. 1, and 283, n. 1, and Aimé Petit, *L'anachronisme dans les romans antiques du XIIe siècle* (Lille, 1985), pp. 31-37. I am indebted to Professor Raymond Cormier for bringing this work to my attention.

Middle Ages painters increasingly used perspective and "authentic" detail to create spatial and chronological distance, so that objects and places receded into space and people and event into time. Mantegna, whose tone has been called cool and timeless, especially tried to depict the past "as it really was." Though anachronism never * disappeared, it was no longer the prevailing mode and was finally defeated in the sixteenth and seventeenth centuries by archaeology, which by providing an ever-increasing stream of factual details about the past tended to embalm historical events in a single moment of time.[63] Historical painters of the eighteenth and nineteenth centuries still adjusted the settings of the scenes to suit their needs, however, and some modern artists and producers have revived a sense of the values of anachronism and anatopism, which relate the past more directly to the viewer and give it a broader meaning than when it is presented in a strictly historical manner.

The mixtures of old and new and of far and near in the Middle Ages reflected a distinctive way of seeing and ordering the observable world and its past. In old French texts antique characters were sometimes presented as pagans and sometimes not, according to Cormier, who said that anachronisms were part of the medieval sense of relevance and renewal, functioning "as necessary mediators of past and present."[64] Gurevich called anachronism "an inseparable feature of medieval historiography" and said that seeing Old Testament kings and prophets side by side with New Testament figures and men from Antiquity on cathedral portals made people aware of "history in its fullness, its coherence and its unity, its immutability and the continuation of time past in time present."[65] Anachronism and anatopism thus kept events alive and inserted them into the contemporary current of life.

Scriptural scenes especially were given a direct relevance by showing the participants in contemporary settings and clothing, or simply in timeless flowing robes. The paintings of the Last Supper in refectories, of which the earliest known examples date from the twelfth century, often show the analogy between the painted and the observing eaters, and may also have had a eucharistic significance (Figures

Figure 7. Guido da Rimini?, Last Supper; Christ enthroned between St. Benedict, the Virgin, John the Baptist, and Abbot Guido of Pomposa; Abbot Guido (d. 1046) turning water into wine (1318). Pomposa Abbey, refectory.

[63] In addition to Réau, see Anthony Grafton, "Renaissance Readers and Ancient Texts: Comments on Some Commentaries," *Renaissance Quarterly*, 38 (1985), 629-630, and John Pope-Hennessey, in *Times Literary Supplement*, 21 November 1986, p. 1315.

[64] Raymond J. Cormier, "The Problem of Anachronism: Recent Scholarship in the French Medieval Romances of Antiquity," *Philological Quarterly*, 53 (1974), 145-157 (quotation on 157), who criticized Panofsky for overlooking

the nuances in the medieval attitude towards Antiquity. See also Petit, *Anachronisme* (note 62), who analyzed the various types of anachronism in twelfth-century romances of Antiquity and argued that through anachronism they became syntheses of an ideal world, embodying both ancient and medieval elements.

[65] Aron J. Gurevich, *Categories of Medieval Culture*, tr. G. L. Campbell (London, Boston, Melbourne, Henley, 1985), pp. 129-130.

Figure 8. Last Supper, *twelfth century (before 1123), St. Albans Psalter, f. 21r, Hildesheim, St. Godehard.*

7 and 8).[66] In the St Albans psalter the representation of Christ washing the feet of the apostles paralleled the monastic ceremony of the Mandatum, in which the abbot washed the feet of guests,[67] and the scene of the descent from the cross was used as an occasion for the display of grief by the mourners (Figures 9 and 10).

[66] Creighton Gilbert, "Last Suppers and their Refectories," in *The Pursuit of Holiness in Late Medieval and Renaissance Religion,* ed. Charles Trinkaus and Heiko Oberman, Studies in Medieval and Reformation Thought, 10 (Leiden, 1974), pp. 371–402, esp. 372, 375, and 385, and Peter Fergusson, "The Twelfth-Century Refectories at Rievaulx and Byland Abbeys," in *Cistercian Art and Architecture in the Brit-* ish Isles, ed. Christopher Norton and David Park (Cambridge, 1986), p. 175.

[67] *The St. Albans Psalter (Albani Psalter),* ed. Otto Pächt, C. R. Dodwell, and Francis Wormald, Studies of the Warburg Institute, 25 (London, 1960), pp. 88–89, citing Meyer Schapiro, who described the depiction as "a dramatic reenactment" of the contemporary rite.

Figure 9. Washing of Feet, twelfth century (before 1123), St. Albans Psalter, f. 19v, Hildesheim, St. Godehard.

Pächt called this "the first realization in Western art of the potentialities of this theme as a vehicle of religious sentiment," and he compared it with the *Deposition* by Roger van der Weyden in the Prado (Figure 11), calling it a kind of *tableau vivant* in which "the presence of the beholder for whom the scene is enacted is acutely felt." For Pächt, medieval pictorial narrative was like stagecraft and "a basically theatrical form."[68] It was not owing to ignorance or chance that in representations of the crucifixion the good thief is sometimes shown in contemporary dress. The scenes from the life of John the Baptist in his oratory at Urbino, painted in the early fifteenth century, show a crowd of well-dressed burghers listening to John preach, seeing

---

[68] Pächt, *Pictorial Narrative* (note 6), pp. 31-32.

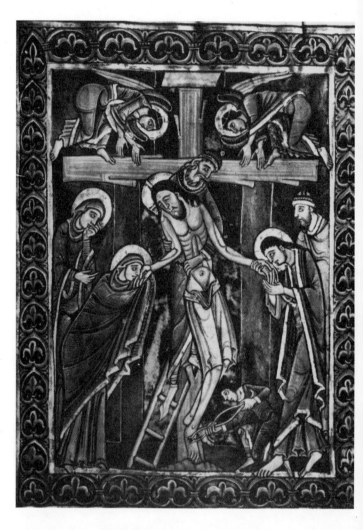

Figure 10. Deposition, *twelfth century (before 1123), St. Albans Psalter, f. 24r, Hildesheim, St. Godehard.*

him baptize Christ, and taking off their clothes to be baptized themselves (Figure 12). The immediacy and applicability of the scenes would have been lost if the onlookers had been depicted as Israelites of the first century.

People in the Middle Ages were thus encouraged and invited to participate in the life of the past, which was also the life of the present, both by their created surroundings and by their religious life and ceremonies. Christian history was confirmed and extended by religious paintings, like those described by Giordano da Rivalto, showing that the Magi were great lords "because they are painted with royal crowns on their heads."[69] For Peter Comestor, "The gospel lived on in the

⁶⁹ Giordano da Rivalto, *Prediche inedite* (note 17), p. 171.

sacred drama of divine service. . . . The liturgy in his view re-enacted, recalled and even offered evidence for the gospel story."[70] In paintings and sculptures of the central events of Christian history, the miscellaneous observers, like the later donors, were not anachronistic intruders but actual witnesses and participants. Liturgical drama in particular mediated between the events of Christian history and religious images and works of art. The Passion-ceremonies that developed in the East in the eleventh century, and later spread to the West, created new functions for icons, and the life-sized figures in sculptural deposition-scenes of the twelfth and thirteenth centuries probably represent Good Friday ceremonies in which the faithful participated (Figure 13).[71] These figures are not overtly allegorical or symbolic; and as naturalistic *figurae*, they represent at the same time the historical event of the deposition, its re-enactment in the Good Friday liturgy, and the participants in the ceremony.

For many Christians, the reality of the religious past lay in a direct experience without the intermediary of either art or the liturgy. They were literally in touch

Figure 11. Roger van der Weyden, Deposition, Prado, Madrid. The dress of the sorrowing participants is partly timeless and partly contemporary. Nicodemus, supporting Christ's legs, wears the rich brocaded mantle of a Flemish fifteenth-century merchant, and Mary Magdalen a jewelled belt.

[70] Beryl Smalley, "Peter Comestor on the Gospels and his Sources," *Recherches de théologie ancienne et médiévale*, 66 (1979), 116-127: "His account of the entry into Jerusalem, the Last Supper, the Crucifixion and Resurrection read like a commentary on the liturgy for Holy Week and Easter" (p.116), and "Relics threw another bridge to the past" (p. 121).

[71] Belting, *Bild* (note 8), pp. 160 and 225-234, and Neil Stratford, "Le mausolée de saint Lazare à Autun," in *Le tombeau de saint Lazare et la sculpture romane à Autun après Gislebertus* (Autun, 1985), p. 28 and n. 124, who on p. 16 described the mausoleum itself as "a living theatre" in stone.

V

Figure 12. Lorenzo and Giacomo of Sanseverino, Baptism of Christ (1416), S. Giovanni Battista, Urbino. The group of onlookers to the right are dressed as fifteenth-century citizens, in contrast to the Baptist and the kneeling apostles and disciples on the opposite bank.

with persons and events of Christian history through the saint, to whom honor and gifts were given and from whom favors and protection were expected as if they were present, and whose living reality was confirmed by miracles and by appearances in visions and dreams,[72] and above all through pilgrimages, which brought pious Christians from all over Europe to the *loca sancta* where the saints and martyrs had lived and died. Time was suspended for pilgrims, who by their presence were transformed from observers into witnesses and frequently into participants in the events that had occurred in the places they visited.[73] Paula in the fourth century adored the cross "as if she saw the Lord hanging [on it]"; she kissed the stone that the angel rolled from His tomb; and she licked the place where His body lay "as if thirsting by faith for the desired waters."[74] A few years later Egeria stressed the immediacy of her experiences when travelling in the Holy Land, and the realism of ceremonies like the Good Friday procession at Jerusalem, when "the bishop

[72] See Chiara Frugoni, " 'Domine, in conspectu tuo omne desiderium meum'; visioni e immagini in Chiara da Montefalco," in *S. Chiara da Montefalco e il suo tempo: Atti del quarto convegno ... organizzato dall'archidiocesi di Spoleto (Spoleto 28-30 dicembre 1981),* ed. Claudio Leonardi and Enrico Menestò, Quaderni del "Centro per il collegamento degli studi medievali e umanistici dell'Università di Perugia," 13 (Perugia, Florence, 1985), p. 175.

[73] See Loerke, " 'Real Presence' " (note 11), pp. 34-37, who said that the *loca sancta* stressed "the actuality and historicity of the event" and the "actual experience" of the pilgrim.
[74] Jerome, *Ep.* 108.9, ed. Isidore Hilberg, 3 vols., Corpus scriptorum ecclesiasticorum latinorum, 54-56 (Vienna-Leipzig, 1910-18), II, 314-316; see also *Ep.* 46.11, ibid. I, 340-341.

Figure 13. Deposition, *thirteenth century (slightly under life-size; cross, ladder, and footrests modern). Pescia, S. Antonio Abate.*

was accompanied in the very way that the Lord was accompanied."[75] Countless pilgrims and, later, crusaders were inspired by the desire of the psalmist to "adore in the place where his feet stood."[76] Replicas of the church of the Holy Sepulchre, and sometimes, as at Bologna, whole complexes based on the holy places in Jerusalem were built for those who were unable to go to the Holy Land.[77]

[75] *Itinerarium Egeriae,* XXXI, 3, in *CC,* CLXXV, 77, tr. John Wilkinson (London, 1971), p. 133; see E. D. Hunt, *Holy Land Pilgrimage in the Later Roman Empire AD 312-460* (Oxford, 1982), pp. 115-116. On parallel ceremonies at Rome, see A. Baumstark, *Liturgie comparée* (Chevetogne, n.d.), p. 153.

[76] Peter the Venerable cited this passage in a letter asking the patriarch of Jerusalem to serve in his stead, since he himself as a monk was forbidden physically to see, kiss,

and weep at the places of Christ's passion and his own redemption: *Ep.* 83, in *The Letters of Peter the Venerable,* ed. Giles Constable, 2 vols., Harvard Historical Studies, 78 (Cambridge, Mass., 1967), I, 220.

[77] Robert Ousterhout, "The Church of San Stefano: A 'Jerusalem' in Bologna," *Gesta,* 20 (1981), 311-322, who argued that the complex was more than a souvenir and was a real reconstruction used in the Easter liturgy.

Pilgrims, like penitents and holy men, were set off and associated with revered figures of the past by their distinctive clothing and appearance. Ailbert, the founder of Rolduc, was said to have worn a "moderate" habit "neither poor nor rich, but tighter and shorter than the modern usage, hardly touching the top of his feet, such as the clergy used in ancient times, when religion was still flourishing."[78] The author of the treatise *On the truly apostolic life* said that monks, because they shared the privileges of the apostles, should also wear their costume, which derived from the seamless robe of Christ. This poor clothing, reaching to their feet, showed their contempt for the world, whereas the large tonsures, deriving from the crown of thorns, showed that by carrying Christ's cross in this world they would inhabit His kingdom in the next.[79] Here the analysis left the realm of *figurae* and entered that of allegory and symbolism, where one thing stood for something else and where the links with the present were more in evidence than those with the past.

Such figures, dressed in archaic costumes modelled on those of Christ, the apostles, and the early monks, seem anomalous today, as they did to some contemporaries, but they were not out of place in the eleventh and twelfth centuries, when the spirit of rebirth and the desire to renew ancient ideals were in the air. They were living anachronisms, in place but out of time, just as the people who came to the churches built and decorated in the style of the fourth century were living anatopisms, in time but out of place. They were the counterparts of the medieval paintings showing distant events transplanted to familiar settings and surroundings, and more remotely, of the mixture of old and new found in buildings and works of art, and in the representations of biblical and classical figures.[80] People in the Middle Ages were not unaware of chronological or topographical distinctions, or of the differences between their own and other ages and lands; but they were profoundly alive to the continuity of history and constantly reinforced their links with the past, which at the same time pointed to the future. Through works of art, buildings, and religious ceremonies and experiences, they created a framework of historical consciousness that was lost and changed when a different sense of history, and of the relation of the present to the past, emerged in succeeding ages.

---

[78] *Annales Rodenses* (facsimile ed.), ed. P. C. Boeren and G. W. A. Panhuysen (Assen, 1968), p. 30 (f. 3r).
[79] *De vita vere apostolica*, V, 22, in *Veterum scriptorum et monumentorum . . . amplissima collectio*, ed. Edmond Martène and Ursin Durand, 9 vols. (Paris, 1724-33), IX, 1026AD.

[80] Heckscher, "Relics" (note 50), p. 220 (rpt. 417), suggested an analogy between Wibald's use of "Scito te ipsum" on the church at Corvey and the use of ancient architectural and decorative elements, and also the ancient works of art transformed by medieval settings.

VI

THE LANGUAGE OF PREACHING IN THE TWELFTH CENTURY

The questions of how medieval sermons were prepared, in what language they were delivered, when and where they were preached, and to whom they were addressed have been discussed by scholars for many years. Mabillon in one of the prefaces to his edition of the works of Bernard of Clairvaux concluded that the sermons were written down, either by Bernard himself or by his secretaries, in the form they were delivered and that those addressed to the monks of Clairvaux were in Latin and those addressed to the lay brothers, or to lay outsiders, were in the vernacular.[1] A parallel conclusion for Italy was reached in the mid-eighteenth century by Apostolo Zeno, who cited a charter published by Muratori showing that at the consecration of Santa Maria delle Carceri at Padua in 1189 "the patriarch [of Aquileia] wisely preached in a lettered fashion and Bishop Gerard of Padua explained his sermon in a maternal fashion," where *litteraliter* and *maternaliter* meant respectively "in Latin" and "in the mother, or vernacular, tongue."[2]

The famous manuscript of Bernard's sermons in French, which once belonged to the Feuillants and is now in the Bibliothèque nationale in Paris, was at the center of this dispute in the eighteenth and nineteenth centuries. Le Roux de Lincy in his edition of 1841 listed five scholars, including Mabillon, who thought Bernard wrote them in this form, four who considered them translations from Latin, and two who did not commit themselves.[3] There was a parallel controversy over the homilies of Maurice of

This article was originally written for the conference on "Linguistic Pluralism in Medieval Society" in Montreal in 1986 and has been presented as a lecture several times subsequently. It has been revised in places, though not in such a way as to take full account of all the relevant literature published since 1985. In particular, it has benefited from the criticism of, among others, Henrik Birnbaum (UCLA), Nicole Bériou (Paris), Anne Clark(University of Vermont), H. A. Kelly (UCLA), Erik Kooper (Utrecht), Florence Ridley (UCLA), and Nancy van Deusen (Claremont Graduate School). The works of Bernard of Clairvaux are cited in the editions of Jean Mabillon, in the Gaume reprint (Paris 1839), of which the first volume has four parts and the second two (which are sometimes cited as six volumes); and of Jean Leclercq (Rome 1957–1977) in eight volumes, of which volume six has two parts.

[1] Jean Mabillon, "Praefatio in tomum tertium" 8–15, in Bernard, ed. Mabillon, 1.2.1595–1602.

[2] L. A. Muratori, *Delle antichità estensi ed italiane* (Modena 1717) 1.356. See Apostolo Zeno, in his notes to Giusto Fontanini, *Biblioteca dell'eloquenza italiana* (Venice 1753) 425, cited by Lucia Lazzerini, " 'Per latinos grossos . . . ': Studio sui sermoni mescidati," *Studi di filologia italiana* 29 (1971) 219–220; O. Behaghel, "Lingua materna," *Behrens-Festschrift: Dietrich Behrens zum siebzigsten Geburtstag dargebracht*, suppl. of Zeitschrift für französische Sprache und Litteratur 12 (Jena 1929) 14; Leo Spitzer, "Muttersprache und Muttererziehung," in his *Essays in Historical Semantics* (New York 1948; repr. 1968) 15–16.

[3] Antoine Le Roux de Lincy, *Les quatre livres des rois traduits en français du XIIe siècle*, Collection de

Sully, the only twelfth-century preacher whose vernacular sermons survive in several manuscripts. Most older authorities, like Lebeuf and Daunau, held that they were translated from the Latin; others, including Paulin Paris, said the Latin versions were translations from the French; one modern editor was of the opinion that both versions evolved from a common nucleus and that Maurice himself wrote, and later expanded, the French homilies and probably also the Latin ones, while another argued in favor of the priority of the Latin version.[4]

The prevailing scholarly view was formulated in the second half of the nineteenth century by Lecoy de la Marche, who maintained, with Mabillon, that sermons addressed to clerics and monks were in Latin and those to the laity were in the vernacular, even if they were written down and preserved in Latin.[5] Both he and Bourgain rejected the proposal of Hauréau that some sermons in Latin may have been delivered to the laity, some in the vernacular to the clergy, and some in a mixed or "macaronic" language.[6] Linsenmayer, writing at the same time in Germany, likewise maintained that sermons in Latin were given only to clerics and that sermons to the laity, including lay brothers, were in the vernacular even if they were written down in Latin.[7] Most subsequent scholars have accepted the view that medieval sermons were given to two distinct audiences in two different languages, and that sermons preserved in Latin were presented to a lay audience in the vernacular and sermons delivered in the vernacular were written down in Latin.[8]

I shall look later at some of the evidence in favor of this position, which is supported

---

documents inédits sur l'histoire de France 73 (Paris 1841) cxxxiv–cxli; see also Michel Zink, *La prédication en langue romane avant 1300*, Nouvelle bibliothèque du Moyen Age 4 (Paris 1976) 69.

[4] C. A. Robson, *Maurice of Sully and the Medieval Vernacular Homily* (Oxford 1952) 24 and 45–46 (on their popularity) and 62–72 (on the manuscripts and printed editions); Jean Longère, *Les sermons latins de Maurice de Sully, évêque de Paris (d. 1196)*, Instrumenta patristica 16 (Steenbrugge 1988). See also Zink (n. 3 above) 33–36; Michel Zink, "La prédication en langues vernaculaires," in *Le moyen âge et la Bible*, ed. Pierre Riché and Guy Lobrichon, Bible de tous les temps 4 (Paris 1984) 496–498, 508–509; and Jean Longère, "La prédication en langue latine," ibid. 529–530.

[5] A. Lecoy de la Marche, *La chaire française au moyen âge, spécialement au XIIIe siècle*, ed. 2 (Paris 1886) 233–269.

[6] Barthélemy Hauréau, "Sermonnaires," in *Histoire littéraire de la France* 26 (Paris 1873) 388–389; L. Bourgain, *La chaire française au XIIe siècle* (Paris 1879) 169–196.

[7] Anton Linsenmayer, *Geschichte der Predigt in Deutschland* (Munich 1886; repr. 1969) 36–40.

[8] Elphège Vacandard, *Vie de saint Bernard* (Paris 1895) 1.455 ("Les auditeurs forment deux groupes bien distincts"); G. R. Owst, *Preaching in Medieval England* (Cambridge 1926) 223 ("The verdict for twelfth-century France remains equally good for our fourteenth-century England"); Joseph de Ghellinck, *L'essor de la littérature latine au XIIe siècle*, Museum Lessianum: Section historique 4–5 (Brussels 1946) 1.207–223; Etienne Delaruelle, "La culture religieuse des laïcs en France au XIe et XIIe siècles," in *I laici nella "Societas christiana" dei secoli XI e XII: Atti della terza settimana internazionale di studio, Mendola, 21–27 agosto 1965*, Pubblicazioni dell'Università cattolica del Sacro Cuore, Contributi ser. 3: Varia 5 (Milan 1968) 578–579; Phyllis Roberts, *Stephanus de Lingua-Tonante: Studies in the Sermons of Stephen Langton*, Pontifical Institute of Mediaeval Studies: Studies and Texts 16 (Toronto 1968) 52 ("The kind of audience addressed determined the language of preaching"); Robert J. Sullivan, "The Sermons of Geoffrey of St. Thierry," Ph.D. diss. (Harvard University 1973) 570 n. 225 ("The opinion of Mabillon, Lecoy de la Marche, and Bourgain stands. In the twelfth century sermons to lay people and lay brothers were preached in the vulgate"); Louis J. Bataillon, "Approaches to the Study of Medieval Sermons," *Leeds Studies in English* n.s. 11 (1980 [for 1979]) 22–23. The article by Jean Longère, "Le vocabulaire de la prédication," in *La lexicographie du latin médiéval et ses rapports avec les recherches actuelles sur la civilisation du moyen-âge: Paris 18–21 octobre 1978*, Colloques internationaux du Centre national de la recherche scientifique 589 (Paris 1981) 303–320, is concerned with terms to designate the act of preaching and its literary transcription.

both by common sense—"It seems obvious," wrote Roberts, "that preachers spoke to their congregations in the language they best understood"[9]—and by a natural dislike for incomprehensible or mixed languages, which seem better suited to parody and humor than serious discourse. This view also appealed to the prejudices of those who propounded it. Mabillon wanted Bernard to preach to the lay brothers and the laity in their own language, and Lecoy de la Marche, arguing against the view that sermons were preached in mixed languages, wrote that "The church was too concerned for the diffusion of its teaching to speak to our fathers in any other way than they themselves spoke," and he went on to say that it used not an amalgam but "the pure French of the thirteenth century, that rich, supple, logical French."[10] A parallel example of linguistic nationalism is found in *Literature and Pulpit in Medieval England* by G. R. Owst, who said that the English language, which was threatened by both Latin and French from the eleventh to the fourteenth centuries, was preserved by preaching: "A long thin line of homilies and kindred metrical paraphrases . . . holds the fort for our English tongue from the days of Aelfric and Wulfstan to those of Rolle and Mannyng, until a more brilliant relief arrives, and the siege is raised."[11]

The division of languages and audiences also fits the view that there was a growing distinction in the eleventh and twelfth centuries between the clergy and the laity— between an elite "Latin" and a popular "vernacular" culture—which were distinguished linguistically as well as socially and institutionally. The key issue is not whether sermons were preached in the vernacular as well as in Latin, which is undoubted, but the extent of vernacular preaching, especially in view of the relatively small number   ✳ of surviving vernacular sermons—fewer than seven hundred in French from before 1300, compared with thousands in Latin[12]—and above all the division of audiences according to language. The evidence of the well-known Carolingian decrees which required bishops to preach in a way everyone could understand "according to the quality of the language" and homilies to be translated into the Roman and German tongues, "in which everyone can understand more easily what is said," cuts, like all legislative evidence, both ways.[13] They may reflect the increasing definition of the vernacular languages, as Latin was standardized in the ninth century, and they certainly

[9]Roberts (n. 8 above) 54.
[10]Lecoy de la Marche (n. 5 above) 258.
[11]G. R. Owst, *Literature and Pulpit in Medieval England*, ed. 2 (Oxford 1961) 4.
[12]De Ghellinck (n. 8 above) 1.210; Zink (n. 3 above) 85. On sermons in German, see Hilarion Petzold, "Die altdeutsche Predigt als geschriebenes und gesprochenes Wort," *Theologie und Philosophie* 44 (1969) 196–232; Karin Morvay and Dagmar Grube, *Bibliographie der deutschen Predigt des Mittelalters* (Munich 1974); and, on collections, Johann B. Schneyer, *Geschichte der katholischen Predigt* (Freiburg 1969) 104–106.
[13]*Capitularia regum Francorum*, ed. Alfred Boretius and Victor Krause, 2 vols., MGH *Leges* 2.1–2 (Hanover 1883–1897) 1.174 no. 78 (813 provincial council 14) and 2.176 (847 Mainz 2); *Concilia aevi Karolini* 1, ed. Albert Werminghoff, MGH *Leges* 3.2 (Hanover 1906–1908) 255 (813 Reims 15), 268 (813 Mainz 25), and 288 (813 Tours 17). Pirmin was said to have preached to the people in both Roman and Frankish, "since he knew both languages very well"; *Vita Pirminii* 3, MGH *Scriptores* in fol. 15 (Hanover 1887–1888) 22. Willibald's well-known statement in his *Vita Bonifatii*, ed. Wilhelm Levison, MGH *Scriptores rerum germanicarum in usum scholarum* 57 (Hanover 1905) 50, that Boniface spoke to the Frisians "patria admonens voce" (which Linsenmayer [n. 7 above] 37 interpreted as *Landessprache*) may have meant "with a paternal voice," as the following reference to Tob. 5.13 suggests. Zink 87–88 stressed the connection in the development of vernacular preaching of the role of the lower clergy and the use of patristic sources; see also Michael Richter, "A quelle époque a-t-on cessé de parler Latin en Gaule? A propos d'une question mal posée," *Annales* 38 (1983) 441, and Zink and Longère (n. 4 above) 491–493 and 519.

represented an ideal rather than a reality. They show that not all preaching was comprehensible to lay audiences, and their occasional reissue suggests that the problem continued. The validity of the accepted view of a strict dichotomy of languages and audiences has been further called into question in recent years by research coming from three different directions.

The first of these is the way in which medieval sermons were prepared and transmitted, and the differences between how they were delivered and written down.[14] "Between the dictation by the author and the text which is transmitted to us," wrote De Ghellinck, "there are two stages to cross": first, from the ear to the hand of the tachygrapher and, second, from the eye to the hand of the scribe who transferred the shorthand to normal writing.[15] Some sermons were delivered in writing rather than orally, like the letter Hildebert of Lavardin sent to Adela of Blois *pro sermone*.[16] The texts of many sermons were reconstructed from notes or based on general instructions. Peter Rassow in his study of the chancery of Bernard of Clairvaux concluded that *dictare* in Bernard's letters meant "to dictate"—or better "to compose"—rather than "to write," as Mabillon maintained, and that many of Bernard's letters were written by his secretaries on the basis of instructions from Bernard himself. These conclusions were applied to his sermons by Jean Leclercq, who distinguished the four operations of *conferre*, *scribere*, *corrigere (recogitare)*, and *legendum praebere* in the preparation of a sermon. Aside from a few outlines dictated by Bernard or based on sermons he gave, most of the surviving texts are later compositions drawn up by either himself or his secretaries, and they bear little resemblance to what he actually preached, if they were ever delivered.[17] Leclercq revised Mabillon's interpretation of the passage at the beginning of Bernard's fifty-fourth sermon on the Song of Songs, where he said that the points made in his previous sermon "were written as they were spoken *(ut dicta sunt)* and taken down by pen, like the other sermons."[18] Since there are several authentic versions of this sermon in the manuscripts, Leclercq argued that *ut dicta sunt* did not mean either "in the same way," as Mabillon said, or "just as they were spoken," as he himself had previously held; nor could it mean "at the very moment," which would have been physically impossible.[19] It may have been, like other passages in Bernard's sermons suggesting that he was speaking directly to his monks, a literary for-

[14]See Linsenmayer (n. 7 above) 39–40; Roberts (n. 7 above) 57–59; Zink (n. 3 above) 199–301; and especially Richard H. Rouse and Mary A. Rouse, *Preachers, Florilegia, and Sermons: Studies on the "Manipulus florum" of Thomas of Ireland*, Pontifical Institute of Mediaeval Studies, Studies and Texts 47 (Toronto 1979).

[15]Joseph de Ghellinck, *Patristique et moyen âge: Etudes d'histoire littéraire et doctrinale*, Museum Lessianum: Section historique 6–7, 9 (Gembloux 1946–1948) 2.217. On the terms *dictare* and *scribere* in Antiquity and the Middle Ages, see Giles Constable, *Letters and Letter-Collections*, Typologie des sources du moyen âge occidental 17 (Turnhout 1976) 42–44.

[16]André Wilmart, "Les sermons d'Hildebert," *Revue bénédictine* 47 (1935) 35.

[17]Peter Rassow, "Die Kanzlei St. Bernhards von Clairvaux," *Studien und Mitteilungen zur Geschichte des Benediktinerordens und seiner Zweige* 34 (1913) 63–103 and 243–294, esp. 67–84; Jean Leclercq, "Saint Bernard et ses secrétaires" (1951), in his *Recueil d'études sur saint Bernard et ses écrits*, 4 vols., Storia e letteratura 92, 104, 114, 167 (Rome 1962–1987) 1.3–11 and 23–25.

[18]Bernard, ed. Leclercq, 2.102; see Mabillon, "Praefatio" 10, in Bernard, ed. Mabillon, 1.2.1599–1600.

[19]Leclercq (n. 17 above) 1.7; Jean Leclercq, "Recherches sur les sermons sur les Cantiques de saint Bernard 3: Les sermons sur les Cantiques ont-ils été prononcés?" (1955), in *Recueil* (n. 17 above) 1.204–205, which was translated as the introduction to Bernard of Clairvaux, *On the Song of Songs*, trans. Kilian Walsh, 2, Cistercian Fathers Series 7: The Works of Bernard of Clairvaux 3 (Kalamazoo 1976) xx–xxii.

mula, throwing no light on the form of the sermon or how it was delivered, but it may also underline (contrary to the way it has been taken by scholars) the difference between the spoken and written forms of a sermon.

As the techniques for preparing sermons were formalized in the twelfth century, it is increasingly hard to determine what an individual preacher actually said or wrote.[20] A large role in preparing Bernard's sermons seems to have been played by Nicholas of Montiéramey, who replied to a request for a copy of Bernard's works that he had been forced to write against his will and his profession as a monk:

> For who is more in the crowd than he who is involved in making literary compositions *(ille qui faciendis dictaminibus implicatur)*? . . . I have forced myself against myself, however, and send you two volumes of the sermons of the man of God, in one of which I composed *(dictavi)* that which begins: "The apostle Paul is accustomed."[21]

This is Bernard's sermon 19 *de diversis*, which would otherwise be considered as Bernard's own work. Geoffrey of Auxerre in his commentary on the Song of Songs cited Bernard's sermon 93 *de diversis* ("On the properties of teeth") saying that "The sermon which he spoke *(dixit)* concerning this was written *(scriptus est)*, although he did not himself compose *(dictavit)* it."[22] This suggests that Bernard delivered sermons which were then written down in a finished form by others.[23]

Many twelfth-century collections of sermons include texts by several preachers, of which the authorship is doubtful,[24] and when in the thirteenth century preaching took on a quasi-sacramental character, the precise attribution of sermons is almost impossible.[25] The transmission of the texts of sermons involved the successive steps, after a

---

[20]Preachers in the thirteenth and fourteenth centuries relied heavily on memory, which was considered a gift of the Holy Spirit: see Jacques Berlioz, "La mémoire du prédicateur: Recherches sur la mémorisation des récits exemplaires (XIIIe–XVe siècles)," in *Temps, Mémoire, Tradition au moyen âge: Actes du XIIIe congrès de la Société des historiens médiévistes de l'enseignement supérieur public, Aix-en-Provence, 4-5 juin 1982* (Aix-en-Provence 1983) 159–183.

[21]Peter of Celle, Ep. 1.50, PL 202.474D–475A; see, for the sermon, Bernard, ed. Leclercq, 6.1.161–165; Jean Leclercq, "Les collections de sermons de Nicolas de Clairvaux" (1956), in *Recueil* (n. 17 above) 1.75; Henri Rochais, "Remarques sur les sermons divers et les sentences de saint Bernard," *Analecta Cisterciensia* 21 (1965) 9. Nicholas of Montiéramey, on the other hand, wrote of a collection of sermons he sent to the count of Champagne that they were "conceived according to my idea [and] composed in my style, except for what in a few places I received from the ideas of others": *Bibliotheca patrum Cisterciensium*, ed. Bertrand Tissier (Bonne Fontaine 1660-1664) 3.193, and Leclercq 50: "meo sensu inuentos, meo stylo dictatos, nisi quod paucis in locis de sensibus alienis accepi."

[22]Geoffrey of Auxerre, *Expositio in Cantica Canticorum* 3, ed. Ferruccio Gastaldelli, Temi e testi 19 (Rome 1974) 1.191, see intro., liii–liv, and, for the sermon, Bernard, ed. Leclercq, 6.1.349-352, and Rochais (n. 21 above) 17.

[23] Jean Leclercq, "L'authenticité bernardine du sermon 'In celebratione Adventus' " (1960), in *Recueil* (n. 17 above) 2.289, who defended the attribution to Bernard (which Mabillon had questioned) of the sermon "On the celebration of Advent" precisely because it represented an intermediate stage of composition, saying that "Il y a plusieurs degrés ou, pour mieux dire, plusieurs formes d'authenticité."

[24]Wilmart (n. 16 above) 12–51 and Bataillon (n. 8 above) 25–28 stressed the difficulties of attributing and dating sermons. See also for the early twelfth century Sullivan's edition (n. 8 above) of the sermons of Geoffrey of St. Thierry, a century later, Roberts (n. 8 above) 57–58.

[25] Rouse and Rouse (n. 14 above) 61. On some of the changes in the techniques of preaching and of preserving sermons in the late twelfth and early thirteenth centuries, see Louis J. Bataillon, "Les problèmes de l'édition des sermons et des ouvrages pour prédicateurs au XIIIe siècle," in *The Editing of Theological and Philosophical Texts from the Middle Ages*, ed. Monika Asztalos, Acta Universitatis Stockholmiensis: Studia latina Stockholmiensia 30 (Stockholm 1986) 105–106.

sermon was delivered, of recording (and if necessary translating) it, collecting various texts, and then distinguishing the sermons of individual preachers.[26] Copies of sermons were incorporated into handbooks of preaching, of which the descendants are still in use today, and Gerald of Wales in his *Mirror of the Church* accused Bishop Cadogan of Bangor of preaching sermons "fabricated by others, but fixed and retained by him in his memory," just as a son mimics the words of his father.[27]

The second line of questioning arises from the researches especially of Schrijen, Mohrmann, and others into the type and degree of linguistic divergences in the Middle Ages, especially between Latin and the vernacular, which were less sharp than scholars whose training was in classical Latin once assumed. Augustine in *On Christian Doctrine* stressed that the Ciceronian low or unadorned style of speech *(sermo humilis)* should be used in teaching, and that eloquence should rouse rather than instruct the listener, contrasting a matter that is analyzed with care *(diligenter discutiatur)* from one that is presented with ardor *(ardenter pronuntietur)*.[28] Since the Christians had to express new ideas in old languages, the problem of the relation between linguistic form and content, or language and thought, was no less serious than that of regional linguistic diversity.[29] The character and earlier history of Christianity thus led to "the creation of a different standard of style, indeed, of a different language."[30] The *ministerium sermonis* paralleled the *ministerium altaris*; and the language of prayer, the liturgy, hymns, and sometimes also sermons, was as much a medium of expression as a means of communication.

Whether or not we accept the concept of a distinctive new language of Christianity (which in various periods and contexts is referred to as late, vulgar, Christian, liturgical, and medieval Latin), it was a living language which hovered between its classical ancestors and the new Roman (or Romance) tongues. The Roman stood in the same relation to Latin as a regional dialect or patois today stands to an established national language, and many people were at home in both. The very term Latin was used more broadly in the Middle Ages than it is today and was applied not only to various languages but to a simple narrative, as in Dante's *Paradiso* 10.120, and even to bird-songs and other means of communication.[31] It should be used in apposition, not in oppo-

---

[26]Roberts (n. 8 above) 59. On the thirteenth century, see Nicole Bériou, "La réportation des sermons parisiens à la fin du XIIIe siècle," *Medioevo e rinascimento* 3 (1989) 87–123.

[27]Gerald of Wales, *Speculum ecclesiae* 3.7, in *Giraldi Cambrensis opera*, ed. J. S. Brewer et al., Rolls Series 21 (London 1861–1891) 4.166.

[28]Augustine, *De doctrina christiana* 4.21, ed. and trans. M. Thérèse Sullivan, Catholic University of America Patristic Studies 23 (Washington 1930) 86.

[29]Gustave Bardy, *La question des langues dans l'église ancienne* (Paris 1948); Christine Mohrmann, "Linguistic Problems in the Early Christian Church" (1957), in her *Etudes sur le latin des chrétiens*, 4 vols., Storia e letteratura 65, 87, 103, 143 (Rome 1958–1977) 3.171–196, esp. 173 and 179–180, and "The Ever-Recurring Problem of Language in the Church" (1968), ibid. 4.143–159, esp. 150. On the parallel between the ministries of the altar and the word, see her essay "Praedicare—Tractare—Sermo" (1954), ibid. 2.63–72, esp. 71–72. Robin Lane Fox, *Pagans and Christians* (San Francisco 1988) 284–287, concluded that "the linguistic barrier thus merges into a wider one, the line between town and country."

[30]Ramsay MacMullen, "A Note on *Sermo Humilis*," *Journal of Theological Studies* n.s. 16 (1966) 111, commenting on Erich Auerbach's essay on "Sermo Humilis" in *Literary Language and Its Public in Late Latin Antiquity and in the Middle Ages*, trans. Ralph Manheim, Bollingen Series 74 (New York 1965) 27–66. See also Philippe Wolff, *Western Languages AD 100–1500* (New York 1971) 61.

[31] Daniel Devoto, "Latin," in *Mélanges offerts à René Crozet*, ed. Pierre Gallais and Yves-Jean Riou (Poitiers 1966) 1.47–58, and Peter Dronke, *Dante and Medieval Latin Traditions* (Cambridge 1986) 95. The

sition, to vernacular, which it frequently resembled. The pronunciation of Latin in the Middle Ages resembled that of the vernacular, "as if it were a part of the same language," and the evidence of charters shows that Latin was read aloud like the vernacular.[32] Lazzerini and Zink both spoke of the "perfect" or "perpetual" symbiosis between Latin on the one hand and Italian or French on the other—what Zink called a "demi-bilingualism functioning with a maternal and a nonmaternal but not foreign language."[33] Even in German-speaking areas, where the difference between Latin and the vernaculars was more marked than in Romance regions, there was a close interrelation between the written and spoken elements.

There was a constant exchange between the two languages not only in sermons but also in other types of literature. Throughout the Middle Ages Latin phrases and tags were used in vernacular works, as by Chaucer's Pardoner, and vernacular words appeared in Latin sermons.[34] The old view, which was rejected in the nineteenth century, that some sermons were actually delivered in two languages has therefore recently been revived.[35] The homily on following the cross in Cambrai Bibliothèque municipale (BM) MS 619, of the seventh century, is written in a mixture of Latin and Old Irish; and in the famous bilingual sermon on Jonah in the tenth-century Valenciennes BM MS 521, the preacher seems to have used Latin for biblical and patristic passages and French when he spoke *ex abundantia cordis*, that is, more spontaneously and emotionally.[36] Several of the sermons in the thirteenth-century Poitiers BM MS 97 (271) are written in both Latin and French, and it is hard to believe that they were not deliv-

---

term "ladino" conveys this awareness of linguistic and historical continuity between Latin and the Romance languages.

[32]H. A. Kelly, "Lawyers' Latin: *Loquenda ut vulgus,*" *Journal of Legal Education* 38 (1988) 201. The reformed classical pronunciation introduced in the nineteenth century tended to set Latin off from the vernacular languages to which it had previously been linked.

[33]Lazzerini (n. 2 above) 284; Zink (n. 3 above) 102 and 106.

[34]Ralph Ardens, who regularly preached *ad populum*, used various Romance words, such as *guerra* for *bellum*: Henk Hagoort, "Tussen Leken en Parijs . . . De prekenbundel van Radulphus Ardens (ca. 1190)," Ph.D. diss. (Utrecht 1988) 34–35. See also *The Oxford Poems of Hugh Primas and the Arundel Lyrics*, ed. C. J. McDonough, Toronto Medieval Latin Texts 15 (Toronto 1984) 52–60 no. 16, for a macaronic poem in Latin and Old French.

[35]Lazzerini (n. 2 above) 229, 250, 254, and 338, who argued that a tradition of linguistic hybridism went back to the *sermo humilis* of early Christianity and was related to the *sermo cotidianus* of university preaching. See also Zink (n. 3 above) 93–100 and Petzold (n. 12 above) 224, who stressed that through preaching the written (Latin) and spoken (German) word were combined in celebrating the Mass. There were several levels of macaronic bilingualism in Anglo-Saxon poetry. Klaus Grubmüller in a paper presented at the Montreal conference (of which he kindly sent me a copy) discussed the intermixture of Latin and German in fifteenth-century German writings, which show "manifold forms of linguistic contact and medleys of languages." On late medieval hymns in Latin and German, see W. Lipphardt, "Die liturgische Funktion deutscher Kirchenlieder in den Klöstern niedersächsischer Zisterzienserinnen des Mittelalters," *Zeitschrift für katholische Theologie* 94 (1972) 158–198, esp. 173.

[36]Whitley Stokes and John Strachan, *Thesaurus Palaeo-hibernicus* (Cambridge 1901–1903) 2.244–247, and Zink (n. 3 above) 21–23 and 103; cf. Lazzerini (n. 2 above) 221 and 226–227. The Bible was cited in Latin in the late medieval English sermons in London, British Library (BL) MS Royal 18 B. xxiii: *Middle English Sermons*, ed. Woodburn O. Ross, Early English Text Society 209 (London 1940). There is no reason to believe the preacher translated these passages when delivering the sermons. See also Peter C. Erb, "Vernacular Material for Preaching in MS Cambridge University Ii III.8," *Mediaeval Studies* 33 (1971) 63–84, who concluded (66) that there was "no evidence of translation" and that some of the sermons "may have been originally delivered in the bilingual form." Jan Rhodes sent me an example of a mid-sixteenth-century macaronic sermon in Latin and English in Cambridge University Library MS Mm I.25 fol. 27.

138

ered in both languages, like the famous sermon on *Bele Aelis*, which consists of a Latin commentary on an Old French dance song.[37] Passages in Latin were commonly translated or paraphrased in late medieval sermons, of which many were given largely in the vernacular.[38]

Even preachers who spoke in Latin tended to use the syntactical structures and sometimes also the vocabulary of the vernacular language.[39] The influence of the *lingua franca* on the Latin style of Bernard of Clairvaux was particularly stressed by Mohrmann, who called him ''a man of the spoken word'' and ''the first great French prosaist,'' though no work in French can be securely attributed to him.[40] The manuscripts of Bernard's sermons show that the Latin of the first redactions, and the short sermons, resembled the vernacular more than that of the revised versions and long sermons.[41] Bernard's spoken Latin ''was sometimes very close to the Romance tongue in its vocabulary and its grammar,'' Leclercq said, and the evidence of how the sermons were written down and preserved called for ''a more nuanced answer'' to the old question of their language. ''The question remains of knowing what sort of Latin Bernard habitually 'spoke.' ''[42] James of Vitry said that preachers should write

> in a simple and humble style for the instruction of children, not wrapping their meanings in the trappings of words or in ignorant talk [and] preferring to instruct the simple and the weak rather than to please the inquisitive. . . . Thus we stoop to simple and moderately lettered people.[43]

Who were these *simplices et mediocriter litterati*, and what languages did they speak and understand? This is the third question challenging the established view of the dichotomy of audiences and languages, since there seems to have been a higher degree

---

[37]A copy of this sermon from London, BL MS Arundel 292 fols. 38–39, was sent me by Robert Taylor of the University of Toronto, who remarked in an unpublished paper that the nature of the word-plays (especially on the name Aelis) show that the sermon was preached in Latin as well as French.

[38]See the two articles by Nicole Bériou, ''La prédication au béguinage de Paris pendant l'année liturgique 1272-1273,'' *Recherches augustiniennes* 13 (1978) 114 and n. 35, citing the example of Bonaventura, who apologized for his bad French, and ''Latin and the Vernacular: Some Remarks about Sermons Delivered on Good Friday during the Thirteenth Century,'' in *Die deutsche Predigt im Mittelalter: Internationales Symposium am Fachbereich Germanistik der Freien Universität Berlin 1989*, ed. Volker Mertens and Hans-Jocken Schiewer (Tübingen 1992) 268–284.

[39]Mohrmann, ''Medieval Latin and Western Civilization'' (1959), in *Etudes* (n. 29 above) 2.155–179, esp. 171 and 174; Zink (n. 3 above) 106–107; Longère, ''Prédication'' (n. 4 above) 533, who warned against exaggerating the distinction between the learned discourse and the popular exhortation.

[40]Mohrmann, ''Le style de saint Bernard'' (1953), in *Etudes* (n. 29 above) 2.347–367 (quotations on 351 and 363); see also ''Le latin médiéval'' (1958), ibid. 2.210–211, where she said that Bernard's style was a continuation and adaptation of early Christian Latin.

[41]Jean Leclercq and Henri Rochais, ''La tradition des sermons liturgiques de s. Bernard'' (1961), in *Recueil* (n. 17 above) 2.203–260, esp. 254.

[42]Jean Leclercq, *Etudes sur saint Bernard et le texte de ses écrits*, Analecta sacri ordinis Cisterciensis 9.1-2 (Rome 1953) 79, and (n. 19 above) 1.204–205; see also ''Sur le caractère littéraire des sermons de s. Bernard'' (1966), in *Recueil* (n. 17 above) 3.163–210, esp. 166, and on Bernard's speaking language, Jürg Zulliger, ''Bernhard von Clairvaux als Redner,'' *Medium aevum quotidianum* 27 (1992) 78–79.

[43]Paris, Bibliothèque nationale (BN) MS n.a.l. 1537 fol. Avb; see Léopold Delisle, *Bibliothèque nationale: Manuscrits latins et français ajoutés aux fonds des nouvelles acquisitions pendant les années 1875-91. Inventaire alphabétique* (Paris 1891) 609–611. The passage reads: ''simplici et humili stilo ad edificationem paruulorum scribentes, non uerborum phaleris nec sermonibus imperitis sententias inuoluentes, malentes instruere simplices et infirmos, quam delectare curiosos. . . . Nos autem ita simplicibus et mediocriter litteratis condescendimus.''

of functional bilingualism, and of understanding of Latin, than was once believed, especially by scholars who wanted to stress the growth of the vernacular languages. Einhard said that Charlemagne learned enough Latin "to pray equally in that and in the paternal language," and while he was clearly exceptional, some knowledge of Latin persisted, especially in the southern and western parts of the Carolingian domains.[44] In England in the twelfth century, according to Legge, "people who knew no Latin and little French were required to sit through sermons in those languages,"[45] but "the moderately lettered" in fact very likely knew some Latin. Although a preacher delivering a sermon which has survived in a macaronic form may have translated the Latin passages when speaking to a lay audience, it is also possible that his listeners, even if they were not lettered in the formal sense of the word, knew enough Latin to grasp his meaning or that they were at least (in Augustine's dichotomy) moved if not instructed by his words. Latin was the language not only of authority and orthodoxy, but also of mystery, sonority, and prestige. Adam Scot of Dryburgh, who died in 1212, referred to those "who although they have little or no understanding of Scripture entirely reject a sermon delivered to them unless it is all in Latin words and, which is more ridiculous, is presented with some pompous and unusual words."[46] The use of Old Church Slavonic similarly added a touch of mystery to sermons in the Slavic world, just as the inscriptions in churches, as in mosques, were sometimes written in illegible but nonetheless impressive scripts.

Preachers in the Middle Ages were not always as concerned as scholars think they should have been with how much Latin their listeners understood,[47] and they accepted that Latin was a medium of expression as well as a means of communication. Not all congregations were alike, and not all sermons had the same character and purpose. Some, perhaps including those the Carolingian legislators had in mind, were primarily catechetical and moral in purpose, and naturally had a content and approach different from those which were designed to create a sense of sin. Preaching in the eleventh and twelfth centuries took on an increasingly penitential character and it was designed to arouse large groups. The precise understanding of the words of these popular preachers, like evangelical preachers today, was less important than their power to move large congregations.

By the twelfth century many people, including some monks and clerics, did not know Latin. Milo Crispin in his *Life* of Lanfranc referred to a prior of Le Bec who was not literate, and Guibert of Nogent said in his memoirs, written in 1115, that some priests at a meeting with the pope at Langres in 1107 could not take part, owing to

---

[44]Einhard, *Vita Karoli Magni* 25, ed. G. H. Pertz and G. Waitz, ed. 6 O. Holder-Egger, MGH *Scriptores rerum germanicarum in usum scholarum* 25 (Hanover 1911) 30. See Michael Richter, "Die Sprachenpolitik Karls des Grossen," *Sprachwissenschaft* 7 (1982) 412–437, esp. 434, and (n. 13 above) 445.

[45]Mary Dominica Legge, *Anglo-Norman Literature and Its Background* (Oxford 1963) 313. She went on to say that "They were expected to enjoy plays in them." The text of the *Jeu d'Adam*, which dates from the mid-twelfth century, is in Anglo-Norman French and the stage directions in Latin.

[46]Adam (Scot) of Dryburgh, Serm. 15, PL 198.184C; see Bourgain (n. 6 above) 195.

[47]Theoderich of Amorbach, who died in 1027, complained that there were many bishops "qui non sunt contenti simplici sermone in doctrina catholica, sed ad semetipsos commendandos coeterisque preferendos yppotheticis atque cathegoricis utuntur syllogismis, quasi divinando infirmis auditoribus, nescientes, quod non sit regnum dei in sermone, sed in virtute": Ernst Dümmler, "Über Leben und Schriften des Mönches Theoderich (von Amorbach)," *Philosophische und historische Abhandlungen der Königlichen Akademie der Wissenschaften zu Berlin* (1894) 21 n. 2; see also 34.

VI

140

their ignorance of Latin, in a discussion "not in the mother speech but in lettered language." The Jewish convert Herman was said to have learned Latin within five years after becoming a canon.[48] Abbot Geoffrey of Vendôme wrote some time before 1118 to the bishop of Angers about a monk of Saint Nicholas of Angers "who because he is lay *(laicus)* replied not in Latin, which he has not learned, but in his mother tongue."[49] These references to *materna lingua* antedate the earliest instance of this term known to Behaghel and Spitzer, which was its use by Hesso Scholasticus in his account of the council of Reims in 1119. The bishop of Ostia first explained the order of business to the entire council in Latin, and then "the bishop of Châlons-sur-Marne at the order of the lord pope expounded this same to the clerics and laymen in the mother tongue."[50] This shows that there were clerics at the council who did not know enough Latin to understand the bishop of Ostia's speech.

It is often hard to tell just how much Latin an illiterate, or even a literate, person knew. According to a story in the *Fourth Life* of Bernard of Clairvaux, a lay brother named Humbert went for a walk with a monk who held a book of Bernard's miracles and expounded them "in the speech of the Roman tongue for his own and that man's edification."[51] Humbert presumably neither read nor understood Latin, but the monk's vernacular exposition of the text was for the benefit of both. A priest who told Pope Innocent III that "I do not know how to speak in Latin" went on to speak "rather timidly and rather incorrectly *(satis timide satisque corrupte)*" but well enough to convince the pope of the justice of his case.[52] In the late twelfth century Adam of Perseigne wrote to the countess of Chartres that "I would have written to you in the lay language had I not known that you have acquired some knowledge of Latin speech," and a few years later he wrote to Countess Blanche of Champagne, the daughter of Sancho the Wise of Navarre, praising her request for a copy of his sermons *(sermunculos)*, "if you can understand what is said in Latin or if they can be spoken in such a way that you may be edified by them." "Spoken" here means translated or expounded, since he went on to say, "You should know, my daughter, that as when a liquor which is trans-

[48]Milo Crispin, *Vita Lanfranci* 2, in *Lanfranci . . . opera omnia*, ed. Luc d'Achéry (Paris 1648) 1.3D; Guibert of Nogent, *De vita sua* 3.4, ed. Georges Bourgin, Collection de textes pour servir à l'étude et à l'enseignement de l'histoire 40 (Paris 1907) 141; Herman, *Opusculum de conversione sua* 20, ed. Gerlinde Niemeyer, MGH *Quellen zur Geistesgeschichte des Mittelalters* 4 (Weimar 1963) 122. Avrom Saltman, "Hermann's Opusculum de conversione sua: Truth or Fiction?" *Revue des études juives* 147 (1988) 31–56 argued that this work was written at the end (rather than the beginning, as was previously believed) of the twelfth century.

[49]Geoffrey of Vendôme, Ep. 3.8, PL 157.110B; see L. Compain, *Etude sur Geoffroi de Vendôme*, Bibliothèque de l'Ecole des hautes études 86 (Paris 1891) 77 and 195. The term *laicus* in this letter meant that the monk was illiterate and in no degree of holy orders, not that he was a layman or a lay brother, since he was a full monk and was called *domnus* in another letter. On Abbot Lambert of St. Nicholas of Angers (1096–1118), see *Gallia Christiana* 14 (Paris 1856) 672–675.

[50]Hesso Scholasticus, *Relatio de concilio Remensi*, in MGH *Scriptores* in fol. 12 (Hanover 1856) 425. On this work, which was more or less contemporary with the council, see Günther Hödl, "Die Admonter Briefsammlung 1158–1162," *Deutsches Archiv* 25 (1969) 423 and 26 (1970) 193. The other uses of the term mother-tongue or speech cited in this paper (by Guibert of Nogent, Geoffrey of Vendôme, Gaucher of Aureil, Norbert of Xanten, and Suger) show that the term was current in the first half of the twelfth century. Archbishop Alfanus of Salerno (d. 1085) referred to authors "whom mother Greece has educated" in his translation of Nemesios, *Premnon physicon*, *prol*. 9, ed. Karl Burkhard (Leipzig 1917) 2.

[51]*Vita quarta Bernardi* 2, ed. Mabillon 2.2.2486A. This passage was cited by Mabillon, "Praefatio" 9, ibid. 1.2.1597–1598, to show the distinction between literate monks and illiterate lay brothers.

[52]Caesarius of Heisterbach, *Dialogus miraculorum* 7.40, ed. Joseph Strange (Bonn 1851) 2.59.

ferred from a vessel is somewhat changed in color, flavor, or smell, so a spoken sentence which is translated from one tongue to another loses some of its flavor and composition in the foreign language."[53] Adam was apparently uncertain whether or not Blanche knew Latin and therefore warned her of the changes of a translation. Some lay people certainly knew Latin in the twelfth century, just as some monks and clerics did not, and as the century progressed the old equations of cleric with *litteratus* and lay with *illitteratus*, or *idiota*, broke down. Philip of Harvengt said that since many clerics were illiterate and many laymen literate, a literate soldier could legitimately be called a better cleric than an illiterate priest, and that a nun who could read and write was a *bonus clericus*.[54]

The most significant linguistic divisions in the twelfth century were not between clerics and laymen or men and women but between people living in different regions, and especially between the Germanic and Romance languages. The clergy in Eastern Europe and Wales were often ignorant of the local languages, and as late as the nineteenth century priests in France who wanted to be understood preached in the regional patois rather than in French.[55] In the early twelfth century the archbishop of Compostela wanted Pontius of Laraze (Léras) and his followers, who had come to Compostela as pilgrims, to remain in his diocese, but sent them home after he realized "that if they remained among men of another tongue they could accomplish little and would be considered barbarous by barbarians so long as they could not be understood when they spoke."[56] In this case a great distance was involved, but when Henry VI proposed Bishop John of Cambrai for the archbishopric of Cologne in 1193 the electors objected "that he did not know the speech of the country *(idioma terrae)*"; and Bernard of Clairvaux referred to a relatively short distance when he wrote to the monks of Saint-Germer-de-Flaix that their monastery was unknown to him "because we are separated from each other by great spaces of land, and diverse provinces, and different tongues."[57] Any religious house which attracted members from more than its own

---

[53] Adam of Perseigne, Epp. 22 and 23, PL 211.686D and 691D–692A, and in *Correspondance d'Adam, abbé de Perseigne (1188–1221)*, ed. and trans. J. Bouvet, Archives historiques du Maine 13 (Le Mans 1951–1962) 146 and 152, who dated these letters respectively after 1190 and ca. 1205/10. Hildebert also referred to his sermons as *sermunculos*: Wilmart (n. 16 above) 35.

[54] Philip of Harvengt, *De institutione clericorum* 4.90, PL 203.816BD. On this passage and lay literacy and knowledge of Latin generally in the twelfth century, see Artur Landgraf, "Zum Gebrauch des Wortes 'Clericus' im 12. Jahrhundert," *Collectanea franciscana* 22 (1952) 74–78; Herbert Grundmann, "Litteratus-illitteratus," *Archiv für Kulturgeschichte* 40 (1958) 1–65; Ralph V. Turner, "The *Miles literatus* in Twelfth- and Thirteenth-Century England: How Rare a Phenomenon?" *American Historical Review* 83 (1978) 925–945; Michael Clanchy, *From Memory to Written Record: England, 1066–1307* (Cambridge, Mass. 1979) 177–185.

[55] Robert Bartlett, *The Making of Europe: Conquest, Colonization and Cultural Change* (Princeton 1993) 222; Eugen Weber, *Peasants into Frenchmen* (Stanford 1976) 88–89. Bishop Otto of Bamberg in 1124 urged the pagans in his diocese to educate their children so that they could have clerics and priests "of their own language who know Latin": Herbord, *Dialogus de Ottone episcopo Bambergensi* 2.18, in *Monumenta Bambergensia*, ed. Philipp Jaffé, Bibliotheca rerum germanicarum 5 (Berlin 1869) 762.

[56] Hugh of Silvanès, *Tractatus de conversione Pontii de Larazio* 12, in *Miscellanea*, ed. Etienne Baluze, 3 (Paris 1680) 215–216, and ed. 2, 1 (Lucca 1761) 182. On Pontius's visit to Compostela, which took place about 1130, see *Cartulaire de l'abbaye de Silvanès*, ed. P.-A. Verlaguet, Archives historiques du Rouergue 1 (Rodez 1910) xv.

[57] Caesarius 6.29 (n. 52 above) 1.381, and Bernard, Ep. 67, ed. Leclercq 7.164. It was to Bernard's advantage in this case to stress his ignorance because he could not properly have received a monk from Flaix had it been known to him.

142

immediate surroundings must have experienced problems of communication both internally and with the outside world.

II.

The audiences of sermons in the twelfth century, even within religious communities, thus tended to be diversified, and some of the texts which have been used to show a linguistic separation of listeners are evidence of a variety in education and interests as well as of language. Among the men who were imbued with heavenly philosophy at Clairvaux, according to the seventh book of Bernard's *First Life*, were "not only many who were lettered and learned in the mysteries of the sacred law but also many laymen and illiterates."[58] Peter of Blois at the beginning of his sixty-fifth sermon wrote,

> You ask me, beloved brother, to communicate to you in writing my usual sermon to the people and to strive to put into Latin what I have crudely and roughly presented to laymen, according to their capacity. You clearly hope that the contents will become known owing not only to the renown of this manner of speech but also to the fluency of Latin discourse, because by the choice of this language a sentence gains great honor and efficacy from its words and a speech thus flows more suitably to its conclusion.[59]

According to James of Vitry,

> When we speak in the Latin idiom in a community or gathering of wise men, we can then say many things because it is unnecessary to descend to details. To laymen, however, it is necessary to demonstrate everything almost visibly and sensibly, so that the preacher's word may be open and clear "as a signet of an emerald in a work of gold" (Eccl. 32.7).

This passage is rubricated in the margin "That preaching should be in one way to clerics and in another way to laymen" and has been taken, on the basis of the phrase "in latino ydiomate," to mean that sermons to the clergy were in Latin and those to the laity in the vernacular. It probably refers to style rather than language, however, and belongs with the statement cited above, that preachers should write "in a simple and humble style for the instruction of children."[60]

Hugh of Saint Cher, writing in the first half of the thirteenth century, applied the three verses of Psalm 18.3-5 to preaching, which should, he said, be prudent ("Day to day uttereth speech: and night to night sheweth knowledge"), useful ("There are no speeches nor languages, where their voices are not heard"), and general ("Their sound hath gone forth into all the earth: and their words unto the ends of the world"). Concerning the utility of preaching, he wrote,

> Useful is when it is understood . . . since they [the speakers] should preach both in French and in Latin, in order to be understood according to the differences of the listeners, and more in the commoner language, which is the maternal. In this respect both preachers

---

[58]*Vita prima Bernardi* 7.23.39, ed. Mabillon 2.2.2361A. Mabillon cited the *Vita prima* 7.26.50-51, ibid. 2368AD, to show that Bernard preached to the lay brothers at Clairvaux. This story is also found in Herbert, *Liber miraculorum* 1.29, PL 185(2).1301A-1303A, and in the *Exordium magnum Cisterciense* 4.19, ed. Bruno Griesser, Series scriptorum s. ordinis Cisterciensis 2 (Rome 1961) 244-245.

[59]Peter of Blois, Serm. 65, PL 207.750D-751A. See also his Serm. 8, ibid. 21C-22A.

[60]Paris, BN MS n.a.l. 1537 fol. 1ra-rb. Lecoy de la Marche (n. 5 above) 265 printed this passage without the words "in a work of gold" and with the marginal rubrication included in the text.

and listeners are sometimes at fault, as when, in cloisters where there are many simple men, someone is willing to preach or someone is willing to listen only in Latin, although there are many who do not understand. For in 4 Kings 18 some men said "Speak to us in Syriac, for we understand." So say some pedants in the cloister and consider themselves disgraced if someone preaches in French in their monasteries, but the preaching they want is not useful, because it is not understood, as in 1 Corinthians 14: "If then I know not the power of the voice, I shall be to him to whom I speak a barbarian."[61]

This passage, like that by Adam of Dryburgh cited above, shows that a sermon in Latin had a snobbish appeal even when (or perhaps because) it was not understood by all the listeners. Other evidence confirms that many sermons were addressed to professionally and linguistically mixed audiences, or to clerics or laymen with a limited knowledge of Latin. Abbo of Saint Germain, writing in the early tenth century, intended his collection of sermons for simple clerics who were "moderately rich in loquacity but lacking in Latin" so that those "who do not understand the Gospels through the obscure commentaries of learned men and homilies may strive by reading or listening to this little book which is derived from them," and so that they could thus imbibe "the draught of preaching."[62] Guibert of Nogent showed in his *Book on the Way a Sermon Should Be Made* that he envisaged the preacher speaking to a mixed audience:

> While he preaches light and plain things to illiterate men he should try to mix in some loftier things which strike him as suitable for literate men, and while providing for these men what suits their capacity, he explains and expands, by grinding as it were with the tooth of circumlocution, and thus renders light and open what previously seemed obscure and difficult even to learned men, so that what is said can be clear to unlearned and simple men.[63]

Though the language of the sermon is not specified here, it was addressed to literate and illiterate listeners. The monk to whom Geoffrey of Vendôme referred presumably heard sermons in Latin, which he may have understood but apparently could not speak; and Bernard delivered his sermons on the Song of Songs not only to professed monks but also to novices and (if his words are taken literally) lay brothers, since in Sermon 63, after saying that the story of the little foxes in the vineyard applied to the present, he said, "You see those novices? They came recently, they are recently converted *(nuper conversi sunt)*. We cannot say of them that 'our vineyard hath flourished,' since it flourishes."[64] Even the indications *ad cleros* and *ad populum* occasionally found

---

[61]Hugh of St. Cher, *Postillae in Ps. 18.3-5* (Venice 1754) 2.40vb. The terms Hugh used were *discreta*, *utilis*, and *communis*. On Hugh, see Robert E. Lerner, "Poverty, Preaching, and Eschatology in the Revelation Commentaries of 'Hugh of St. Cher,' " in *The Bible in the Mediaeval World: Essays in Memory of Beryl Smalley*, ed. Katherine Walsh and Diana Wood, Studies in Church History: Subsidia 4 (Oxford 1985) 157–189, esp. 181–189 where he proposed (181) that " 'Hugh' was never really one author but always a consortium." Hugh's contemporary, Humbert of Romans, *De eruditione praedicatorum* 10, in *Opera de vita regulari*, ed. Joachim Joseph Berthier (Rome 1888–1889) 2.402, said that preachers should not be at a loss for words owing to a defect either of memory or of Latin or vernacular speech.

[62]Abbo of St. Germain in the *Argumentum* to his collection of sermons, PL 132.761-762.

[63]Guibert of Nogent, *Liber quo ordine sermo fieri debeat*, PL 132.25B; see Rouse and Rouse (n. 14 above) 49.

[64]Bernard, *Serm. super Cant.* 63.3.6, ed. Leclercq 2.164. Aelred of Rievaulx referred to both monks and lay brothers in his *Serm. de temp.* 7 (PL 195.249B), and he may have been speaking to both, according to Christopher Holdsworth, cited by C. N. L. Brooke, "St. Bernard, the Patrons and Monastic Planning," in

beside sermons in manuscripts are not decisive, since some sermons *ad populum* were certainly intended for clerics as well as laymen.[65]

Many sermons in the eleventh and twelfth centuries were addressed to mixed audiences.[66] The activities of popular preachers like Robert of Arbrissel, Bernard of Tiron, Vitalis of Savigny, and Gerald of Salles, and of heretics like Peter of Bruys, Henry of Lausanne, and Lambert le Bègue, are familiar,[67] and as the century progressed there were an increasing number of references to preaching by laymen, and also by lay-women.[68] As a rule more is known about the message of their preaching than about the techniques or language, but they sometimes spoke in the vernacular to clerics and even to monks. Ralph of Escures, who was abbot of Saint Martin at Séez and later arch-bishop of Canterbury, said in the late eleventh century that he had written down in Latin a sermon on the Virgin Mary which "I have more than once expounded in a con-gregation of monks, as best I could, in the vulgar tongue *(vulgariter)*";[69] and at the funeral of Geoffrey of Chalard in 1125 the hermit Gaucher of Auriel is said to have spoken "in the mother tongue" to a mixed audience of monks, clerics, and laymen, beginning "This good man is surely in port, brothers, while we are still at sea."[70] Robert of Arbrissel seems to have made no distinction between his listeners, since he is said to have given fully *(prolixe)* in the chapter of monks "the last sermon which he was about to give to the people." Even those who were present could not explain, according to the author of his *Other Life*,

---

Cistercian Art and Architecture in the British Isles, ed. Christopher Norton and David Park (Cambridge 1986) 17 n. 32.

[65]M.-M. Lebreton, "Recherches sur les principaux thèmes théologiques traités dans les sermons du XIIe siècle," *Recherches de théologie ancienne et médiévale* 23 (1956) 5; Roberts (n. 8 above) 47–48. Ralph Ardens customarily preached *ad populum* on Sundays and feast days but included in his sermons many references to *fratres mei* and *socii*: Hagoort (n. 34 above) 224.

[66]Abbot Dominic of Sora, who died in 1031, frequently spoke to the clergy and the people together: *Vita et miracula s. Dominici Sorani abbatis* 16 and 27, in *Analecta Bollandiana* 1 (1882) 288 and 294; Andrew of Vallombrosa (d. 1112), who founded Cormilly and Chézal-Benoît, urged "by preaching both rich and poor clerics and laymen" to enter the monastic life, in *Rouleaux des morts du IXe au XVe siècle*, ed. Léopold Delisle, Societé de l'histoire de France 11 (Paris 1866) 170; Bernard of Tiron preached to all people "according to their way of life and social status . . . and up to the capacity of their souls": Geoffrey *Grossus*, *Vita Bernardi Tironiensis* 5.39, PL 172.1391D; cf. 6.52 (1398A) where he was challenged by the archdeacon and priests of Coutances for preaching "publicly to the people."

[67]See Johannes von Walter, *Die ersten Wanderprediger Frankreichs* (Leipzig 1903–1906); Etienne Delaruelle, "Les ermites et la spiritualité populaire," in *L'eremitismo in Occidente nei secoli XI e XII: Atti della seconda settimana internazionale di studio, Mendola, 30 agosto–6 settembre 1962*, Pubblicazioni del-l'Università cattolica del Sacro Cuore, Contributi ser. 3: Varia 4 (Milan 1965) 215–219; Schneyer (n. 12 above) 109–130.

[68]The ancient decrees against the preaching of laymen and women are found in the *Decretum* of Gra-tian, *Dist.* XXXIII, 29, in *Corpus iuris canonici*, ed. Emil Friedberg (Leipzig 1879) 1.86, and Walter Map referred to the desire of "uneducated and illiterate" Waldensians to preach in *De nugis curialium* 1.31, ed. Montague R. James, rev. C. N. L. Brooke and R. A. B. Mynors (Oxford 1983) 124. See Schneyer (n. 12 above) 176–178; Rolf Zerfass, *Der Streit um die Laienpredigt*, Untersuchungen zur praktischen Theologie 2 (Freiburg 1974); Roberto Rusconi, *Predicazione e vita religiosa nella società italiana da Carlo Magno alla Controriforma* (Turin 1981) 64–111.

[69]André Wilmart, "Les homélies attribuées à s. Anselme," *Archives d'histoire doctrinale et littéraire du moyen âge* 2 (1927) 20–21; see Bataillon (n. 8 above) 23. Ralph gave the sermon, presumably in Nor-man French, in the chapters of Séez, Fécamp, and Troarn. There is an English version of about 1125–1130 in London, BL MS Cotton Vespasian D. XIV fols. 151–158.

[70]Gaucher, *Vita beati Gaufredi* 2.13, ed. A. Bosvieux, *Mémoires de la Société des sciences naturelles et archéologiques de la Creuse* 3 (1862) 116.

how sweetly, how piously, how mercifully, how devoutly, how prudently, how lovingly, how simply, how discreetly he taught his listeners by urging, imploring, and rebuking to leave evil and do good. . . . For the Lord gave him so great a grace of holy preaching that when he made a general sermon to the people, everyone received what was fitting for him.[71]

Obscure holy men and hermits, like Guy of Viconne's neighbor Hugh, who was described as "a *conversus* in habit and a priest in dignity," preached to the public, though in Hugh's case without success,[72] and by the end of the century popular preaching by monks, though still prohibited by canon law, was generally accepted in practice. Peter of Cornwall specifically expressed the hope that his *Pantheologus* would be ✶ useful "to monks who are accustomed to make sermons to both the clergy and the people."[73] While he may have intended different sermons to be delivered to the two audiences, there is no evidence for this in his treatise.

Bernard of Clairvaux was a great popular preacher. According to Geoffrey of Auxerre,

He spoke to rustic audiences as if he had been brought up in the country, and likewise to each other type of man as if he devoted his entire attention to studying their works. Lettered among the learned, simple among the simple, abounding in proofs of perfection and wisdom among spiritual men.

Geoffrey later said that Bernard rarely preached outside the neighborhood, "but when it was necessary he poured the [saving] waters over all men, publicly and privately announcing the word of God."[74] Otto of Freising said that Bernard was held "as a prophet and apostle" among the peoples of France and Germany; Odo of Deuil described him when he preached the Second Crusade at Vézelay as a "celestial organ," pouring forth "the dew of the divine word"; and Wibald of Corvey in a letter written in 1149 said that Bernard's power as a preacher depended as much on the way he spoke, and on his character and appearance, as on what he said: "The sight persuades before the hearing. . . . No wonder that by the great power of so many things he raises the sleeping, not to say the dead."[75] William of Saint Thierry wrote of Bernard that

The virtue of preaching began to shine so greatly in him that he softened even the hard hearts of his listeners and scarcely ever came home empty-handed. Since the net of God's word was effective in the hand of His fisher, by both the use of speech and the example

---

[71]*Vita altera Roberti* 23, PL 162.1068C–1069A, saying again that the sermon was delivered to monks. On Robert as a preacher, see Jacques Dalarun, *L'impossible sainteté: La vie retrouvée de Robert d'Arbrissel (v. 1045–1116) fondateur de Fontevraud* (Paris 1985) 182, 210, and 216.

[72]*Historia monasterii Viconiensis* 6, in MGH *Scriptores* in fol. 24 (Hanover 1879) 296.

[73]Richard W. Hunt, "English Learning in the Late Twelfth Century," *Transactions of the Royal Historical Society* ser. 4, 19 (1936) 40.

[74]*Vita prima Bernardi* 3.3.6 and 8, ed. Mabillon 2.2.2193CD and 2195C.

[75]Otto of Freising, *Gesta Friderici primi imperatoris* 1.35, ed. G. Waitz and B. von Simson, MGH *Scriptores rerum germanicarum in usum scholarum* 46 (Hanover 1912) 55; Odo of Deuil, *De profectione Ludovici VII in orientem*, ed. Virginia Berry, Columbia Records of Civilization 42 (New York 1948) 8; Wibald of Corvey, Ep. 167, in *Monumenta Corbeiensia*, ed. Philipp Jaffé, Bibliotheca rerum germanicarum 1 (Berlin 1864) 285. On Bernard's preaching of the Second Crusade see Vacandard (n. 8 above) 2.269–270; P. Alphandéry, "De quelques faits du prophétisme dans les sectes latines antérieures au Joachimisme," *Revue de l'histoire des religions* 52 (1905) 193–194; and Zulliger (n. 42 above) 58 and 78, who emphasized the dramatic element in Bernard's crusading sermons: "Nicht seine Worte, sondern sein Charisma, der *spiritus*, den er ausstrahlte, bewegte die Menschen."

of living, he began to catch such large crowds of rational fish that the ship of this house could be filled by each of his castings. Thus a feeble and dying man, who was scarcely strong enough to speak, brightened in deed and name a valley [Clairvaux] which had previously been dark, by a miracle which was greater than all the miracles he performed during his lifetime.[76]

These passages say nothing about Bernard's language, but they shed light on his preaching techniques, which put into practice the principles of Guibert of Nogent and James of Vitry. He was all things to all men: *litteratus* to the learned, *simplex* to the simple, and (most interestingly) *affluens documentis perfectionis et sapientiae* to spiritual men. These proofs or "documents of perfection and wisdom" were probably not just stories but emotional displays, such as weeping and breast-beating, and corresponded to the *exemplum conversationis* which William of Saint Thierry linked to *usus sermonis* in his description of Bernard's preaching.

Preachers in the twelfth century were frequently praised for the moving power of their words. Speaking and singing were closer in the Middle Ages than they are today, and the terms *dicitur*, *legitur*, and *canitur* were used interchangeably in manuscript rubrics.[77] Geoffrey Babion seems to have been unusual at that time in appealing to the intelligence of his listeners rather than trying to move them.[78] Gilbert of Sempringham was said to have weakened his eyes by the tears he shed "while he sowed his seeds." His preaching pierced the hearts of many hearers, producing "devotion from their hearts and tears from their eyes."[79] Joachim of Fiore, raising his voice in the course of his sermons, "not like a man but truly like an angel . . . impressed by a certain lively affection the word of God on the minds of those who heard him."[80]

* Some churchmen spoke two or even three languages. The new bishop John of Thérouanne in 1099 was learned in the Latin, Roman, and German languages; Suger of Saint Denis was said to have had "so great a grace of fluency in both tongues, maternal and Latin, that he seemed to read rather than speak whatever came from his mouth"; and Abbot Ivo II of Saint Denis, "being fluent in both speeches, vulgar and Latin, was not confused in the presence of kings and spoke with prudence and astonishing confidence on behalf of the church entrusted to him."[81] Innocent III in the prologue to his collected sermons said that "I have conceived and delivered some sermons

---

[76]*Vita prima Bernardi* 1.13.61, ed. Mabillon 2.2.2134CD. See Zulliger (n. 42 above) 81–85.

[77]Nancy van Deusen, "The Use and Significance of the Sequence," *Musica disciplina* 40 (1986) 11 n. 22.

[78]Jean-Paul Bonnes, "Un des plus grands prédicateurs du XIIe siècle: Geoffroy du Loroux dit Geoffroy Babion," *Revue bénédictine* 56 (1945–1946) 188.

[79]*Vita s. Gileberti* 26 and 43, in *The Book of St. Gilbert*, ed. Raymonde Foreville and Gillian Keir (Oxford 1987) 86 and 108.

[80]Luke of Cosenza, *Vita Joachimi*, ed. Herbert Grundmann, "Zur Biographie Joachims von Fiore und Rainers von Ponza" (1960), in his *Ausgewählte Aufsätze 2: Joachim von Fiore*, MGH *Schriften* 25.2 (Stuttgart 1977) 354. Luke went on to say that he never heard anyone complain that Joachim's sermons were too long.

[81]*Gesta abbatum s. Bertini Sithiensium* 2.56, in MGH *Scriptores* in fol. 13 (Berlin 1881) 647; William of St. Denis, *Vita Sugerii* 1, in *Oeuvres complètes de Suger*, ed. A. Lecoy de la Marche, Société de l'histoire de France 12 (Paris 1867) 382; *Rouleaux* (n. 66 above) 373. On John of Thérouanne, see Walter Simons, "Jean de Warneton et la réforme grégorienne," *Mémoires de la Société d'histoire de Comines-Warneton* 17 (1987) 35–54, esp. 46 on this passage. Abbot Matthew of Ninove at the end of the twelfth century was said to have had a wonderful grace of preaching "because he was very skilled in three languages": *Liber miraculorum Ninivensium sancti Cornelii papae* 39, ed. William Walker Rockwell (Göttingen 1925) 97; cf. Baldwin of Ninove, *Chronicon* s.a. 1195, in MGH *Scriptores* in fol. 25 (Hanover 1880) 536–537.

to the clergy and people, now in the lettered tongue/and now in the vernacular."[82] Abbot Samson of Bury Saint Edmunds knew English as well as French and Latin "and used to give sermons to the people in English, though in the language of Norfolk, where he was born and raised, and had a pulpit made in the church for both the convenience of the listeners and the adornment of the church."[83]

The ability to speak in several languages—the gift of tongues—was highly prized in the early church, and by no one more than Saint Paul, who wrote in his first letter to the Corinthians 14.19 that in order to instruct and help others he would prefer to speak five intelligible words ("with my understanding," in the King James and Douai versions) than ten thousand incomprehensible words.[84] Preachers who did not know the language of the people they were addressing made use of interpreters. The *Life* of Pachomius refers to "interpreter brothers who rendered his words into Greek for those foreigners and Alexandrians who did not understand the Egyptian tongue," and Egeria found on her travels that the bishop "always speaks in Greek, never in Syriac, and therefore has beside him a priest who translates the Greek into Syriac, so that everyone can understand what he means."[85] In the twelfth century the bishop of Châlons-sur-Marne served as an interpreter at the council of Reims, and the bishop of Padua at the dedication of Santa Maria delle Carceri.[86] Bernard of Clairvaux also used a translator when he preached outside Clairvaux and could not be understood "because he spoke in the Roman tongue."[87]

[82]PL 217.311–312. The terms *proposui* and *dictavi* may mean "published" and "dictated" rather than "conceived and delivered." See Bataillon (n. 8 above) 23–24, who cited a passage from Humbert of Romans showing that Innocent while he was preaching translated from Latin into the vernacular. Sermon 8 of Helinand of Froidmont, PL 212.544, of which the text is entirely in Latin, bears the annotation "Hic sermo totus Gallice pronuntiatus est, et ultimus fuit auctoris, ut habet autographum." This note is by Bertrand Tissier, the first editor, but it may reflect an early annotation.

[83]*The Chronicle of Jocelin of Brakelond*, ed. and trans. H. E. Butler (London 1949) 40.

[84]The apostles on the day of Pentecost "began to speak with diverse tongues, according as the Holy Ghost gave them to speak" (Acts 2.4). The statement by Irenaeus in *Against Heresies* 1, *praef.* 3 (see Bardy [n. 29 above] 74–75)—that since he lived among the Celts, and for the most part *(plerumque)* was without their language, he spoke "simply and truly and in an uneducated way *(idiotice)*" without any rhetorical art— was cited by Conyers Middleton, *A Free Inquiry into the Miraculous Powers* (London 1749) 119–122 (and from him by Gibbon in *The Decline and Fall of the Roman Empire* 15, ed. J. B. Bury [London 1898–1901] 2.28) who considered the gift of tongues to be one of the six principal types of early miracles and one which disappeared after apostolic times. When Ephraim Syrus visited Basil the Great, however, he was at first unable to understand him, and he simply applauded the Holy Spirit speaking through his mouth until at Basil's request God gave him the ability to speak Greek: in *Historia s. Ephraemi* 25, in *Sancti Ephraem Syri hymni et sermones*, ed. Thomas J. Lamy (Mechlin 1882–1886) 2.52–58, see 56 n. 1, and 1.xxxii–xxxiii on the debate between J. S. Assemani and the Bollandists over whether the gift was temporary or permanent.

[85]*Vita s. Pachomii bohairice scripta* 196, ed. and trans. Louis T. Lefort, Corpus scriptorum christianorum orientalium, 89 and 107 = Scriptores coptici 7 and 11 (Paris 1925–1936) 1.191 and 2.123; *Itinerarium Egeriae* 47.3–4, in Corpus christianorum 175 (Turnhout 1965) 89, and trans. John Wilkinson (London 1971) 146. Egeria went on to say that for those who knew Latin there were brothers and sisters familiar with Latin as well as Greek. See Bardy (n. 29 above) 140, and Ramsay MacMullen, "The Preacher's Audience (A.D. 350–400)," *Journal of Theological Studies* n.s. 40 (1989) 503–511, esp. 506 on language.

[86]See above at nn. 2 and 50.

[87]*Vita prima Bernardi* 6.4.16, ed. Mabillon 2.2.2290C. On the use of translators, see Zink (n. 3 above) 90–91, and, on the crusading sermon of the bishop of Porto in 1147, Ernst-Dieter Hehl, *Kirche und Krieg im 12. Jahrhundert: Studien zu kanonistischem Recht und politischer Wirklichkeit*, Monographien zur Geschichte des Mittelalters 19 (Stuttgart 1980) 259. See also Ebo, *Vita Ottonis episcopi Bambergensis* 2.3, in *Monumenta* (n. 55 above) 622.

There are many examples in medieval saints' lives and in folklore of a marvelous speed or miraculous ability in learning to read and write or to speak and understand foreign languages.[88] Several stories of this kind are found in the *Lives* of Bernard of Clairvaux, from which they passed into Herbert's *Book of Miracles* and into the *Great Beginning* of Cîteaux. A "simple and illiterate" lay brother named Humbert, who did not know the alphabet, was able to read two books brought to him by Bernard in a vision, and "with God illuminating his intellect and with the support of some of the monks, he was soon able not only to read but also to chant properly and agreeably enough."[89] A story found in the *Great Beginning* (and, in a shortened version, in Geoffrey of Auxerre's *Life and Miracles of St. Bernard* and Herbert's *Book of Miracles*) told of a lay brother at Clairvaux who was visited on his deathbed by the Holy Spirit.

> By a new and stupendous miracle his intellect was illuminated and his tongue was opened, and this rustic man, who had never learned his letters, began readily to use Latin eloquence, studying some marvelous scriptural sentences while proposing nothing that was not in accord with sound doctrine.

The story went on to stress again "the novelty of this occurrence" and the astonishment of the listeners at "the novelty of the miracle."[90]

Not all such stories were equally edifying. According to the *Life* of Norbert of Xanten, the devil, when he wished to show his learning, spoke through the mouth of a girl who knew only the Psalter, reciting the entire Song of Songs first in the Roman and then in the German language.[91] Heretics were sometimes said to learn languages with extraordinary speed. According to a text about heretics long attributed to a Cistercian monk in the mid-twelfth century, but now thought to date from the early eleventh century, "No one is so rustic that if he joins them he is not within eight days so wise that he can no longer be overcome either by words or by examples."[92] Gerald of Wales

[88]C. Grant Loomis, *White Magic: An Introduction to the Folklore of Christian Legend*, Mediaeval Academy of America Publ. 52 (Cambridge, Mass. 1948) 24, 72, and 114; Stith Thompson, *Motif-Index of Folk-Literature*, ed. 2 (Bloomington 1975) 2.334 (D 1819.4) and 3.196 (F 695.3).

[89]*Vita quarta Bernardi* 3, ed. Mabillon 2.2.2487BD; cf. Herbert, *Liber miraculorum* 1.32, PL 185(2). 1304BC, where the hero was Walter the *vestiarius*, of Clairvaux; *Exordium* 4.15 (n. 58 above) 240; and Caesarius 10.3 (n. 52 above) 2.219–220.

[90]*Exordium* 4.17 (n. 58 above) 242–243; cf. Herbert, *Liber miraculorum* 1.16, PL 185(2).1292AB; Robert Lechat, "Les fragmenta De vita et miraculis S. Bernardi par Geoffroy d'Auxerre," *Analecta Bollandiana* 50 (1932) 108 no. 36. Elisabeth of Schönau, who did not know how to compose in Latin, recited her visions in Latin; the angel who appeared to her spoke partly in German and partly in Latin; and her uncle addressed her "miscens verba latina teutonicis": *Die Visionen der hl. Elisabeth und die Schriften der Aebte Ekbert und Emecho von Schönau*, ed. F. W. E. Roth (Brünn 1884) 1 and 49, cited by Anne L. Clarke, *Elisabeth of Schönau: A Twelfth-Century Visionary* (Philadelphia 1992) 29 and 52.

[91]*Vita* [B] *s. Norberti* 8.22.45, PL 170.1288B.

[92]PL 181.1722A, and in *The Peace of God: Social Violence and Religious Response in France around the Year 1000*, ed. Thomas Head and Richard Landes (Ithaca 1992) 347–348. See Walter Wakefield and Austin Evans, *Heresies of the High Middle Ages*, Columbia Records of Civilization 81 (New York 1969) 138–139; R. I. Moore, "New Sects and Secret Meetings: Association and Authority in the Eleventh and Twelfth Centuries," in *Voluntary Religion*, ed. W. J. Sheils and Diana Wood (Oxford 1986) 50; Guy Lobrichon, "The Chiaroscuro of Heresy: Early Eleventh-Century Aquitaine as Seen from Auxerre," in *Peace of God* 80–103. Cf. Annals of Margam, s.a. 1163, in *Annales monastici*, ed. Henry R. Luard, Rolls Series 36 (London 1864–1869) 1.15: "si illiterati ad eos veniebant, infra viii. dies tam prudentes fiebant, ut nec literis nec exemplis superari possent."

described in the *Deeds Done by Himself* how a hermit of Locheis named Wecheleu (or Wedhelen, as he is called elsewhere) miraculously learned Latin one day at vespers but told Gerald that "My Lord who gave me the Latin tongue did not give it to me grammatically or by cases but only so much that I could understand others and be understood."[93] And when the hermit Wulfric of Hazelbury enabled a man who was dumb to speak both English and French, the priest Brihtric, who had served Wulfric for many years, was upset.

> For you have ministered the double office of the tongue to a foreigner for whom it would have sufficed to have enabled him to speak, and you have not given the use of French speech to me, who have to be almost silent when I come before the archbishop or archdeacon.[94]

These accounts were not concerned with preaching, though the lay brother at Clairvaux who used Latin eloquence in studying the scriptures may have preached, and Humbert and Wecheleu would presumably have understood a Latin sermon. There are also stories of the collective understanding by a congregation of a sermon in a foreign language. On one occasion, Vitalis of Savigny, who died in 1122, was preaching to a crowd in a church in England.

> But since many people were present who did not know the Roman tongue, God deigned to impart so great a grace of His generosity into the minds of his listeners that as long as the sermon lasted they all understood the Roman tongue which he used in speaking, although this grace of understanding did not persist in them when the sermon was over, that is, the power of understanding the words of the Holy Spirit which came from his mouth was with justice given for a time to his listeners but was prudently taken away later so that they could not use this same grace for idle chatter.[95]

A similar occurrence took place when Norbert of Xanten, who knew almost no French, preached in Valenciennes on the day after Palm Sunday 1118.

> He did not despair because [he knew that] if he gave honor to the word of God in his mother tongue, the Holy Spirit who once taught the diversity of a hundred and twenty tongues would make the barbarity of the German tongue or the difficulty of Latin eloquence easy for his listeners to understand.

And so it turned out that "by the grace of God he was received by everyone" and kept among them for some time.[96] The most celebrated occurrence of this type is described in the third book, by Geoffrey of Auxerre, of the *First Life* of Bernard, who was said to have spoken

> with marvelous effect even to the Germans, whose devotion was fostered more by his sermon, which as men of another tongue they could not understand, than by the speech

---

[93]Gerald of Wales, *De rebus a se gestis* 3.2 (n. 27 above) 1.91; cf. *De invectionibus* 6.20, ibid. 175, and Clanchy (n. 54 above) 153 and 191.

[94]John of Ford, *Vita Vulfrici* 14, ed. Maurice Bell, Somerset Record Society 47 (Frome 1933) 29. Among the "other miracles" of Gilbert of Sempringham was one (no. 10) about a deaf man who while sleeping heard Gilbert "preaching the counsels of salvation to the people," in Foreville and Keir (n. 79 above) 314.

[95]*Vitae bb. Vitalis et Gaufredi primi et secundi abbatum Saviniacensium* (*Vita Vitalis* 2.12), ed. E. Sauvage, *Analecta Bollandiana* 1 (1882) 26–27. On Vitalis as a preacher, see John M. Carter, " 'Fire and Brimstone' in Anglo-Norman Society: The Preaching Career of St. Vital of Mortain and Its Impact on the Abbey of Savigny," *American Benedictine Review* 34 (1983) 166–187 (181 on this miracle).

[96]*Vita* [B] *s. Norberti* 4.12.23, PL 170.1273C.

which they understood of the skillful interpreter who spoke after him. The clearest proof of this was their breast-beating and weeping.

Geoffrey went on to say that when Bernard spoke in church, God so filled him with the spirit of wisdom and understanding that (in the words of Job 28.11) "The depths also of rivers he hath searched, and hidden things he hath brought forth to light."[97] This story was incorporated, with one slight difference, into the *Second Life* by Alan of Auxerre,[98] and in a shortened form into the *Abbreviated Word* of Peter the Chanter, who, after relating how Bernard's listeners wept at his words, which they could not understand, and were unmoved by the translation, remarked, echoing Augustine's *On Christian Doctrine*, that "He who does not burn cannot kindle."[99]

Gerald of Wales repeated this story (probably from Peter the Chanter) in a letter to Bishop Geoffrey of Saint David's written in 1213/14. He first told of the visit to Wales of Archbishop Baldwin of Canterbury to preach the crusade.

> Although the Welsh did not understand his language, he continued to sow the words of salvation with his own mouth almost every day, and afterwards also had them carefully explained to those men by faithful interpreters. He thus instilled great devotion in them and persuaded a great multitude to take the cross, the purpose for which he came. I think that it is not beside the point also to cite here the example of Abbot Bernard, who preached to German laymen and moved them to tears and weeping, though they did not understand him. An excellent interpreter, a monk, translated his sermon after him, and after he spoke they were not moved. From this it is clear that a man who does not burn cannot kindle. For deeds *(res)* not words speak in the sacred scriptures, as the poet says: "Do deeds; you will be safe." In this matter deeds rather than words plead and persuade, for voices beat on the outside and do not penetrate, but it is the spirit which acts and works inside.[100]

Gerald repeated the story in his *Ecclesiastical Jewel*, saying that "This was done more by deeds than by words," and in his autobiography, where he added that it showed the power of the Holy Spirit "operating inwardly and wandering through hearts." From his own experience preaching the crusade in French and English, he said, "Innumerable common people who knew neither language nonetheless wept at his words and more than two hundred hastened to [take] the sign of the cross." Later, at Saint David's, many who were moved by Gerald's words to take the cross "withdrew from the vow they had received when they heard the interpreter's voice, which was not sufficiently methodical or gracious."[101]

The understanding of the audiences of Vitalis and Norbert was specifically attributed in their *Lives* to the intervention of God and the Holy Spirit; but these accounts,

[97]*Vita prima Bernardi* 3.3.7, ed. Mabillon 2.2.2194BC.

[98]*Vita secunda Bernardi* 14.42, ibid. 2435BC, which has "expert" for "skillful" in describing the translator.

[99]Peter the Chanter, *Verbum abbreviatum* 6, PL 205.37D; see John W. Baldwin, *Masters, Princes, and Merchants: The Social Views of Peter the Chanter and His Circle* (Princeton 1970) 1.107 and 2.75 n. 135, citing an unpublished longer version in which the translator was a black monk.

[100]Gerald of Wales, *Speculum duorum*, Ep. 8, ed. Yves Lefèvre and R. B. C. Huygens, trans. Brian Dawson, Board of Celtic Studies, University of Wales: History and Law Series 27 (Cardiff 1974) 280–281 (and xlix on the date). The poet is Ovid, *Remedia amoris* 144, who was also cited by Peter the Chanter.

[101]Gerald of Wales, *Gemma ecclesiastica* 1.51 (n. 27 above) 2.152, and *De rebus a se gestis* 2.18, ibid. 1.76.

although the events preceded Bernard's preaching, were written after his *Life*, and a spirit of emulation may have inspired the writers to emphasize their supernatural character. Since, according to Matthew 10.20, "It was not you that spoke, but the spirit of your Father that speaketh in you," the understanding of the listeners was evidence of the holiness of the speaker through whom the Spirit spoke. According to the *Second Life* of Robert of Arbrissel, for instance,

> His preaching was not without effect, but he transformed the hearts of his listeners so greatly that He Who was there was clearly understood. The Holy Spirit was certainly present, without whose aid the exterior sermon of a teacher labors in vain.[102]

Rational explanations can easily be found for these occurrences, and not all of them were regarded as miracles even by those who observed and recorded them. It is not extraordinary that a few Cistercian lay brothers learned Latin rapidly or seemingly instantaneously, especially with the help of some monks, as in the case of Humbert; that a hermit learned some ungrammatical Latin; or that Wulfric of Hazelbury enabled a dumb man (who may have already known some English and French) to speak. For Bernard's biographers the effect of his sermon on a German audience showed the sweetness of his eloquence (as in the Song of Songs 4.3) and his ability to vary his preaching so as to win souls for Christ, while for Peter the Chanter and Gerald of Wales it was an *exemplum* showing the need in preaching for emotion—the kindling fire— and devotional actions, which Geoffrey of Auxerre elsewhere called the evidence of perfection and wisdom and William of Saint Thierry the example of his life.

Events of this type, whether or not they are considered miracles, are found in other cultures at a time when a new religion is spreading into a linguistically diverse region. There is a striking parallel, for instance, in the Malay Annals, where two converts to Islam in the fourteenth and fifteenth centuries were granted the gift of reading the Koran.[103] These events corresponded to the need of converts to understand the religious message, as in the early church and again in the eleventh and twelfth centuries, when the role of speech in reaching lay audiences may have been as great as that of print four centuries later, and when a new wave of evangelical preachers addressed an ever-widening circle of men and women who knew little or no Latin and who spoke different languages in different parts of Europe. This sudden ability to speak or read a previously unknown language, or to understand a sermon in a foreign tongue, also throws some light on the questions raised at the beginning of this paper, since popular preachers like Vitalis, Norbert, and Bernard did not feel compelled to speak in a language known to their listeners.

Preaching in the twelfth century was a dramatic enterprise. As in an opera, the sound of the words was as important as their meaning, and, as in a play, the preacher sought to touch the hearts of his listeners by his actions as well as his words. Lupus of Ferrières in the early ninth century contrasted the *lenitas* and *sonoritas* of Latin with the roughness of German, and Peter of Blois in the twelfth praised the *dicendi celebritas* and *volubilitas* of Latin, which like a song could move the emotions even when

---

[102]*Vita altera Roberti* 23, PL 162.1069A, citing Matt. 10.20.

[103]*Sĕjarah Mĕlayu or Malay Annals* 72 and 83–84, trans. C. C. Brown (Kuala Lumpur 1970) 32–33 and 43; see R. Jones, "Ten Conversion Myths from Indonesia," in *Conversion to Islam*, ed. Nehemia Levtzion (New York 1979) 134. I am indebted to Peter Brown for this reference.

the words were not fully understood.[104] The German preachers Ulrich of Augsburg, Wolfgang of Regensburg, and Anno of Cologne in the tenth and eleventh centuries were said to have made frequent use of tears.[105] Bernard in his seventy-sixth sermon on the Song of Songs said that a good shepherd should feed his flock with good words and examples "and his own more than those of others." For if a preacher praises the mildness of Moses, the patience of Job, the mercy of Samuel, and the holiness of David while himself being harsh, hasty, merciless, and unholy, "the sermon becomes less attractive, and you receive it less eagerly."[106] After Adam and Eve were expelled from the Garden of Eden in the *Jeu d'Adam*, they were instructed to "strike their breasts and their thighs, manifesting their sorrows with their gestures,"[107] and in the sermon on *Bele Aelis* preaching was compared to part of a dance, in which the three necessary elements were

> a sonorous voice, a linking of arms, [and] the noise of feet. In order to dance for God, therefore, we have these three things in us: a sonorous voice, that is, holy preaching, pleasing to God and man; linking of arms, that is, the twin love of God and neighbor; and the noise of feet, that is, works to match our preaching, in imitation of Our Lord Jesus Christ, who first began to do good deeds and later to teach.[108]

These factors, in addition to the composition of the audiences and the pronunciation and construction of Latin, may help explain why so many sermons, including those clearly intended for unlearned audiences, are preserved in Latin, and why some were presented in a mixture of Latin and vernacular, and others in a vernacular unknown to the listeners. They widen the scope of this inquiry beyond simply the language of preaching to the broader problem, which is ultimately more difficult because it is outside the range of our own experience, of how listeners in the twelfth century were roused by preachers to a new sense of the individuality and urgency of the Christian message.

---

[104]Lupus of Ferrières, *Vita s. Wigberti, praef.*, PL 119.681B, and for Peter of Blois, n. 59 above.

[105]Petzold (n. 12 above) 223.

[106]Bernard, *Serm. super Cant.* 76.4.9, ed. Leclercq 2.260. Peter of Blois, ep. 219, PL 207.508CD, wrote to King Henry II in 1187, after the fall of Jerusalem, that the cardinals promised to preach the crusade "non solum verbo, sed opere et exemplo."

[107]David Bevington, *Medieval Drama* (Boston 1975) 103 (see 78 on the date), and Legge (n. 45 above) 42.

[108]"Vox sonora, nexus brachiorum, strepitus pedum. Ut ergo possimus Deo tripudiare, hec tria in nobis habeamus: vocem sonoram, id est predicacionem sanctam, gratam Deo et hominibus; nexus brachiorum, id est geminam caritatem, scilicet dilectionem Dei et proximi; strepitus pedum, id est opera concordancia nostre predicacioni, ad imitacionem Domini nostri Jhesu Christi, qui primo cepit bona facere et postea docere"; see n. 37 above. On the dramatic elements of preaching in the thirteenth century, especially by the mendicants, see Carla Casagrande and Silvana Vecchio, "Clercs et jongleurs dans la société médiévale (XIIe et XIIIe siècles)," *Annales* 34 (1979) 913–928, esp. 920–921 on Franciscan preachers, who were accused of behaving *ut histriones*.

THE CEREMONIES AND SYMBOLISM OF ENTERING RELIGIOUS LIFE AND TAKING THE MONASTIC HABIT, FROM THE FOURTH TO THE TWELFTH CENTURY

I*

There is a tendency today among Christians of all denominations to underestimate the importance of ritual in the medieval church and to misinterpret its significance.

(*) In addition the standard abbreviations (*AA. SS., C.C., C.C.:C.M., C.S.E.L., M.G.H., P.G., P.L.*), I shall use

C.C.C.	= Corpus Christi College
C.C.M.	= Corpus consuetudinum monasticarum
H.B.S.	= Henry Bradshaw Society
HERRGOTT, *Disciplina*	= MARQUARD HERRGOTT, *Vetus disciplina monastica*, Paris 1726
MARTÈNE, *De ritibus*	= EDMOND MARTÈNE, *De antiquis ecclesiae ritibus libri tres*, 3rd ed., Venice 1763-1764
R.B.	= *Regula Benedicti*, ed. PHILIBERT SCHMITZ, Maredsous 1955
R.M.	= *Regula Magistri*, in *La règle du Maître*, ed. ADALBERT DE VOGÜÉ, Paris 1964-1965 (Sources chrétiennes, 105-107: Textes monastiques, 14-16)

Pontificals and customaries will be cited, after the first reference, by the name of the places and persons with which they are associated, and the following commentaries on the *R.B.* will be cited by the name of the author alone, with a reference to the page or column of the edition cited:

DE VOGÜÉ	= *La règle de saint Benoît*, ed. and tr. ADALBERT DE VOGÜÉ and JEAN NEUFVILLE, VI: *Commentaire historique et critique (Parties VII-IX et Index)*, Paris 1971 (Sources chrétiennes, 186: Textes monastiques d'Occident, 39)
HILDEMAR	= *Expositio regulae ab Hildemaro tradita*, ed. R. MITTERMÜLLER, Regensburg-New York-Cincinnati 1880
MARTÈNE	= EDMOND MARTÈNE, *Commentarius in regulam S. P. Benedicti*, 2nd ed., Paris 1695, cited from rp. in *P.L.*,LXVI
SMARAGDUS	= *Expositio in regulam S. Benedicti*, ed. A. SPANNAGEL and P. ENGELBERT, Siegburg 1974 (*C.C.M.*, 8)
VAN HAEFTEN	= BENEDICTUS VAN HAEFTEN, *S. Benedictus illustratus sive disquisitionum monasticarum libri XII*, Antwerp 1644

772

« With every new century we become heirs to a longer and more vigorous anti-ritualist tradition, » wrote the anthropologist Mary Douglas. « This is right and good as far as our own religious life is concerned, but let us beware of importing uncritically a dread of dead formality in ourselves into our judgements of other religions. » Elsewhere she said:

> Ritual is more to society than words are to thought. ...Ritual focuses attention by framing; it enlivens the memory and links the present with the relevant past. ...By ritual and speech what has passed is restated so that what ought to have been prevails over what was, permanent good intention prevails over temporary aberration [1].

The very characteristics of ritual that now seem empty and meaningless are essential to this social function, as Victor Turner stressed:

> Always and everywhere ritual *ought to* have a pervasive archaic, repetitive, formal quality if it is to be a vehicle for values and experiences which transcend those of status-striving, money-grubbing, and self-serving. At the purely human level its archaisms and formalisms respond to deep collective needs [2].

Of all types of life in the Middle Ages, that of religious men and women living in enclosed communities was most governed by rules and ceremonies. From the moment when a child was brought to a monastery as an oblate or when a postulant came to the gate requesting admission,

---

(1) MARY DOUGLAS, *Purity and Danger*, Harmondsworth 1970 (Penguin Books), pp. 77-78 and 83; see also her *Natural Symbols: Explorations in Cosmology*, 2nd ed., London 1973, pp. 19-32.

(2) VICTOR TURNER, *Passages, Margins, and Poverty: Religious Symbols of Communitas*, « Worship », XLVI (1972), p. 392, see also p. 398, rp. in his *Dramas, Fields, and Metaphors: Symbolic Action in Human Society*, Ithaca-London 1974, pp. 231-271.

their behavior followed a customary routine or written code which varied in detail from community to community but always had the double purpose both of fostering unity and harmony among the members and of relating their lives to the broad spiritual ends of the life of religion. They communicated with God and man no less by their actions than by their tongues, and they kept watch not only over their words but also over their appearance, expression, and movements, each of which, according to Marcel Mauss, was a physio-psycho-sociological montage reflecting the social conditioning which dictated the performance of even the most routine and trivial actions [3]. Philip of Harvengt in his treatise *On the silence of clerics* said that signs were a form of speech and could be used, like words, to show « the secret of the will » and to give « information about hidden matters » [4]. He was probably referring here to the signs which were used in place of speech in many monasteries and were sometimes formulated into systems of sign-language [5], but he may also have had in mind a broader use of the term *signa*, covering all aspects of religious behavior. Adam of Dryburgh, addressing regular canons, said:

> You should show nothing bitter in your words, nothing shameful in your face, nothing disorderly in your gesture, nothing reprehensible in your habit, nothing light in your walk, finally you should as greatly as possible allow nothing to appear in any of your

(3) MARCEL MAUSS, *Les techniques du corps*, « Journal de psychologie normale et pathologique », XXXII (1955), p. 291.

(4) PHILIP OF HARVENGT, *De institutione clericorum*, VI: *De silentio clericorum*, 23, in *P.L.*, CCIII, col. 982AD. He gives examples of evil as well as good signs.

(5) See WALTER JARECKI, *Signa loquendi. Die cluniacensischen Signa-Listen*, Baden-Baden 1981 (Saecula Spiritalia, 5), with references to previous literature, and my review in *Mittellateinisches Jahrbuch*, XVIII (1983), pp. 331-334, citing some examples of the abuse of sign-language.

774

motions which might give offence or scandal to anyone who observed it [6].

In the early Middle Ages *signum* and *res* were identified not only in thoughts but also in actions, and any departure from the established pattern of behavior and appearance was regarded with suspicion as an indication of inner non-conformity. In deeply conservative institutions like monasteries, which find their models in the past and identify what has been with what should be, signs and ceremonies are of special importance in protecting conformity and continuity, both by bridging the gap between past and present, especially in periods of change, and by summing up and giving meaning to past experience. The timeless quality of monastic life is part of its essence, and rituals brought the people and events of the past into the present as if they were contemporary with the ceremonies in which they were commemorated [7]. This quality of timelessness, in which the real point of referral was the present rather than the past, endowed monastic ritual with a capacity to change, though often more slowly and imperceptibly, and sometimes more painfully, than in other areas of medieval life. There was a constant adjustment between the past and the present, and between the competing claims of conformity and individuality, of structure and community, and of hierarchy and equality. The original purpose and meaning of ceremonies might be forgotten, but new meanings were found, and some of the most creative energy of the Middle Ages went into shaping and interpreting the framework of religious life. The

---

(6) ADAM OF DRYBURGH, *De ordine, habitu et professione canonicorum ordinis Praemonstratensis*, Serm. VI, 3, in *P.L.*, CXCVII, col. 489D.

(7) See SABINE MAC CORMACK, *Christ and Empire, Time and Ceremonial in Sixth Century Byzantium and Beyond*, « Byzantion », LII (1982), p. 300.

danger of assuming that a given ceremony or text meant the same thing at all times, or of attributing to it from its origins a significance which it took on later, is increased by the frequency with which outmoded customaries and liturgical books were discarded. Those which survive often give a fragmentary and static impression of what was in reality a process of change and development. The eleventh and twelfth centuries in particular saw a widespread desire to shorten and in some ways rationalize the long and elaborate liturgy which formed one of the glories of monasticism in the previous period. *Signum* and *res* moved apart, and there was more emphasis on the ideal of inner than of outer conformity, though the two were still closely connected. Reformers wanted the form of the ceremony to match the meaning of the words, which should reflect the inner attitudes of the participants [8]. Some of the modern feelings about ritual began to emerge as it lost touch with its customary foundation and moved, as Brian Stock has emphasized, towards a textual basis [9].

Allowances were always made, furthermore, for human individuality, spontaneity, and above all weakness, of which the Devil took advantage when it was least expected. The defences were themselves ritualized, especially in blessings. « May they [the monks] be held in the embrace of fraternal love and being of one spirit be replenished in the precepts of continence » [10]. There were regular blessings for various parts of the monastery and for activities

(8) BERTILO DE BOER, *La soi-disant opposition de saint François d'Assise à saint Benoît*, « Etudes Franciscaines », N.S., VIII (1957), pp. 181-194, and IX (1958), pp. 57-65, and JOSEPH SZÖVÉRFFY, « *False* » *Use of* « *Unfitting* » *Hymns: Some Ideas Shared by Peter the Venerable, Peter Abelard, and Heloise*, « Revue Bénédictine », LXXXIX (1979), pp. 187-199.

(9) BRIAN STOCK, *The Implications of Literacy*, Princeton 1983, p. 529.

(10) EDMOND (EUGÈNE) MOELLER, *Corpus benedictionum pontificalium*, II, Turnhout 1971-1979 (*C.C.*, 162-162A-C), p. 458 (no. 1116), see also I, p. 42, and II, pp. 693 and 721-722 (nos. 96, 1692, and 1764).

776

with which danger was associated, such as shaving, hair-cutting, bathing, blood-letting, and writing, for which God was asked to

> Let the power of Your holy spirit descend on these books, O Lord, and by cleansing them may it purify and bless and sanctify and illuminate mercifully the hearts of all people and give true understanding and by fulfilling good works may it contribute to preserve and fulfill Your enlightened precepts according to Your will [11].

There were also supernatural interventions, such as miracles, to set things right when they went wrong and to provide additional protection against the attacks of the Devil. Most important was the cross, which sheltered the monastery and its inhabitants both symbolically and literally, as an omnipresent deterrent to the powers of evil. Abbot Richalm of Schönthal in his *Book of Revelations* recommended the sign of the cross as an almost universal antidote for the distractions and temptations of monks, especially when they were reading or studying. Of himself, Richalm said, « I think that I would already be a vagrant and fugitive on earth and dispersed to every wind, so that no part of me would adhere together, if the cross alone did not firmly bind me » [12].

Richalm's use of the terms *cohaerere* and *conglutinare*, albeit in a personal rather than an institutional sense, is of interest because it parallels the findings of anthropologists and social scientists about the importance of symbols and ceremonies as cohesive social forces. Ritual is a form of

(11) ADOLPH FRANZ, *Die kirchlichen Benediktionen im Mittelalter*, I, Freiburg B. 1909, p. 646 and, generally, 633-646.

(12) RICHALM OF SCHÖNTHAL, *Liber revelationum*, I, 5, in BERNARD PEZ, *Thesaurus anecdotorum novissimus,* I. 2, Augsburg-Graz 1721-1729, p. 391, see also pp. 392-393 and 423 (I, 7 and 46).

communication not only between past and present but also between individuals and various social groups and classes, since it promotes community and cooperation rather than hierarchy and conflict [13]. Rituals of sacrifice, in the course of which something is destroyed, are « a means of communication between the sacred and the profane worlds », according to Hubert and Mauss, and tie society together by giving a consciousness of the presence of collective forces; and even rituals which reverse the normal social order, as when fools or children rule for a day, reinforce its structure by releasing some of the tensions created by inequality [14]. Ritual is thus « an expression of a system of belief and its implementation in action », and it should be seen « in terms of the implicit cosmological and theological assumptions » on which it is based [15]. Rituals are not intrinsically irrational or superstitious, nor are they, as Clark put it, « surrogates for some more effective and more rational form of behavior » or signs of « the inadequacies of those who perform them ». They are practiced « in the context of intellectually coherent cosmological assumptions about agency and causation and in the expectation of a real not a spurious efficacy » [16].

Ritual played an especially important role in resolving conflict and transmitting the experience of the divine in

(13) See CLAUDE LÉVI-STRAUSS, *The Savage Mind*, Chicago 1966, p. 32; TURNER, *Social Dramas and Ritual Metaphors*, in *Dramas*, p. 56; DOUGLAS, *Natural Symbols*, p. 41: « Ritual is pre-eminently a form of communication ».

(14) HENRI HUBERT and MARCEL MAUSS, *Sacrifice: Its Nature and Function*, tr. W. D. HALLS, London 1964, p. 97, see also p. 102, and, on rituals of inversion, ERIC HOBSBAWN and GEORGE RUDÉ, *Captain Swing*, New York 1968, p. 60.

(15) G. M. CARSTAIRS, *Ritualization of Roles in Sickness and Healing*, in *A Discussion on Ritualization of Behaviour in Animals and Man*, ed. JULIAN HUXLEY, London 1966 (Philosophical Transactions of the Royal Society of London, B.251), pp. 307-308; see MEYER FORTES, *Religious Premises and Logical Technique in Divinatory Ritual*, ibid., pp. 410-411.

(16) STUART CLARK, *French Historians and Early Modern Popular Culture*, « Past and Present », C (1983), pp. 62-99 (quotations on pp. 74, 86, and 88).

778

Late Antiquity and the early Middle Ages, when Christian monastic life took institutional shape. Baptism and martyrdom, with both of which monasticism was compared, were rituals of reconciliation, according to MacDermot in *The Cult of the Seer in the Ancient Middle East*: baptism of conflict with the body and martyrdom of conflict with the previous society. The stories of the martyrs and the rituals surrounding their bodies were concerned with the relation of individuals to the human community, and holy men were marked by recognized physical signs like fire, light, beauty, and sweet smells [17]. « Even in his most personal and private acts of mortification...,» wrote Peter Brown, « the ascetic was seen as acting out a dramatic and readily intelligible ritual of social disengagement » [18].

In this paper I shall study particularly how entering religious life and taking the monastic habit developed over time and were related to the changing character of monasticism, especially in the West down to the beginning of the thirteenth century [19]. I shall be less concerned with the commitments made at the time of joining a community and their legal consequences, which have been studied by many writers, than with the ceremonies themselves and their symbolism, which have attracted relatively little scholarly attention, although they have long formed part of the dispute over the nature of religious life and the status of those who lead it [20]. Strong feelings

(17) VIOLET MACDERMOT, *The Cult of the Seer in the Ancient Middle East*, London 1971, pp. 179-233, esp. 211: « Collective ritual attributed divine powers to the martyr's body as it had to the mummy in ancient Egypt ».
(18) PETER BROWN, *The Making of Late Antiquity*, Cambridge (Mass.) 1978, pp. 87-88.
(19) On monastic profession in the East, which I shall mention only to the extent that it influenced developments in the West, see PIERRE RAFFIN, *Les rituels orientaux de la profession monastique*, Bellefontaine 1969 (Spiritualité orientale, 4).
(20) The most important works, all by monks, are MATTHÄUS ROTHENHÄUSLER, *Zur Aufnahmeordnung der Regula S. Benedicti*, in *Studien zur benediktinischen Profess*, Münster W. 1912 (Beiträge zur Geschichte des alten Mönchtums und des

were roused even in the Middle Ages by the relative importance of profession, benediction (or consecration), and wearing the habit, and modern scholars have debated the character of each step and the exact moment of legal entry to religious life [21]. A controversy has developed recently over the attitude of the early monks towards the liturgy and over the parallel which was often drawn between baptism and entry to religious life, which seems to some modern theologians to derogate from the uniqueness of baptism [22]. In the sixteenth and seventeenth centuries Bellarmine, Cajetan, and Suarez, while denying that profession was superior to baptism, defended the comparison

Benediktinerordens, 3); ILDEFONS HERWEGEN, *Geschichte der benediktinischen Professformel*, ibid.; PIERRE DE PUNIET, *Le pontifical romain*, II, Louvain-Paris 1931, pp. 63-95; HIERONYMUS FRANK, *Untersuchungen zur Geschichte der benediktinischen Professliturgie im frühen Mittelalter*, « Studien und Mitteilungen zur Geschichte der Benediktinerordens und seiner Zweige », LXIII (1951), pp. 93-139; PHILIPP HOFMEISTER, *Benediktinische Professriten*, ibid., LXXIV (1963), pp. 241-285; and RICHARD YEO, *The Structure and Content of Monastic Profession: A juridical study, with particular regard to the practice of the English Benedictine Congregation since the French Revolution*, Rome 1982 (Studia Anselmiana, 83). See also the article by JOACHIM WOLLASCH, *Das Mönchsgelübde als Opfer*, « Frühmittelalterliche Studien », XVIII (1984), pp. 529-545. I have not seen V. MUZZARELLI, *De professione religiosa a primordiis ad saec. XII*, Rome 1938, which YEO, *Profession*, pp. 50-53, cites with the comment that, « The usefulness of Muzzarelli's work is limited because he is looking for the seeds of modern doctrine ... » (p. 52). The same is true of Yeo's work, which is legal and structural rather than historical in approach, though it has useful sections on the views of various commentators on the elements of profession in *R.B.*, LVIII.

(21) Among the questions which have been discussed are the nature and relation of the promise and petition (especially whether they constituted a vow to God or a oath with Him as witness) and the differences between *conversio* and *conversatio*. See n. 51 below and YEO, *Profession*, ch. 9. and esp. pp. 250-260 on the views of Rothenhäusler, Zeiger (n. 36 below), and Capelle (n. 51 below). The canonical sources on these questions need further study.

(22) ELIGIUS DEKKERS, *Profession - Second Baptême. Qu'a voulu dire saint Jérôme ?* « Historisches Jahrbuch », LXXVII (1958), pp. 91-97; BURKHARD NEUNHEUSER, *Monastic Profession as Second Baptism and Present Day Theological Perspectives*, first pub. in « Liturgie und Mönchtum », XXXIII-XXXIV (1963-1964), pp. 63-69 (which I have not seen) and tr. in « Liturgy », XVIII (1984), pp. 3-12, with an editorial note concerning a meeting of monks and nuns who agreed to avoid both the term consecration and the idea of second baptism in connection with monastic profession, which should be seen, according to Neunheuser (pp. 11-12), as « the plenary fulfillment of one's baptism » and « a metaphor of a higher and more comprehensive significance ». See nn. 89-91 for further references.

780

against the criticism of the Protestant reformers [23]. The refounders of monasticism in the nineteenth century emphasized its liturgical and sacramental aspect and tended to look for a model to the elaborate liturgy and highly regulated life of the great monasteries of the tenth and eleventh centuries, in particular to Cluny [24]. They were followed by what may be called the spiritual or pneumatic school of monastic scholars, like Herwegen and Casel, for whom the purpose of monasticism was « to foster and confirm the pneumatic side of the church » and who therefore stressed the mystical and sacramental character of monastic life [25]. This view was challenged in the 1950s by Eligius Dekkers, who maintained that the early monks, most of whom were not ordained, were more concerned with the ideals of personal and ascetic perfection than they were with the liturgy or ecclesiastical ceremonies, and that they « never solemnized purely monastic events — entrance, clothing, etc. ...Only later do we meet the first signs of that ritualisation which was to become so luxuriant in the late Middle Ages » [26]. Armand Veilleux argued against this that one of the principal objects of the early Pachomian monks

(23) VAN HAEFTEN, pp. 440-441 (IV, 8, 2); see YEO, *Profession*, pp. 209-211 and n. 90 below.

(24) This is associated particularly with Solesmes, Beuron, and Maria Laach and with the names of Prosper Guéranger and Maur Wolter, on whom see *Théologie de la vie monastique d'après quelques grands moines des époques moderne et contemporaine*, Ligugé 1961 (Archives de la France monastique, 50 = *Revue Mabillon*, LI. 2-3), pp. 165-178 and 213-223, and (on Guéranger) YEO, *Profession*, pp. 233-234 and 343-346.

(25) On Ildefons Herwegen and Odo Casel (n. 28 below), see *Théologie*, pp. 249-255 and 257-263, and (on Casel) YEO, *Profession*, pp. 266-270. See also RAPHAEL MOLITOR, *Von der Mönchsweihe in der lateinishen Kirche*, « Theologie und Glaube », XVI (1924), pp. 584-612, on which see YEO, *Profession*, pp. 261-265.

(26) ELIGIUS DEKKERS, *Were the Early Monks Liturgical ?*, « Collectanea ordinis Cisterciensium reformatorum », XXII (1960), pp. 120-137 (quotation on p. 136). This influential article was first published in French in 1951 and has been republished and translated several times. Both here and in his article on *Moines et liturgie*, ibid., pp. 329-340, Dekkers showed his dislike for « that ritualistic mania which was so dear to certain monastic circles in the Middle Ages » (p. 137) and his liking for the « sober reaction » of the Cistercians against the ritualism of the Cluniacs (p. 336).

was liturgical prayer and worship both in solitude and in the monastic community [27].

Among the factors that have complicated these disputes has been the reluctance of some scholars, especially those who are themselves monks, to recognize that the character of monasticism varied regionally and changed over time. For them there is only a single standard, against which all forms of monastic life must be judged, and they are unwilling to accept that different forms may suit, and be authentic (to use one of their own favorite terms) for, different peoples and periods. The ritualisation to which Dekkers refers seems to have appeared later in the West than it did in the East, where the ceremony of entry to religious life was already to some extent sacramentalized, perhaps under the influence of similiar developments in baptism and holy communion, in the fifth and sixth centuries and where a monk was seen as a recipient of a gift from God more than as an active participant in a ceremony of self-oblation. According to Casel, « For the Easterners becoming a monk was a mystery and a consecration », and Oppenheim stressed that, « In an act of reception the essential concept is that of transfer » [28]. In the East, therefore, the rites of vesting and tonsure were central to the ceremony of entering religious life, whereas in the West, at least during the first centuries of monasticism, the rule and the personal com-

---

(27) ARMAND VEILLEUX, La liturgie dans le cénobitisme pachômien au quatrième siècle, Rome 1968 (Studia Anselmiana, 57), pp. XXIV, 161-166, and 195-197.

(28) ODO CASEL, Die Mönchsweihe, « Jahrbuch für Liturgiewissenschaft », V (1925), p. 20, see also p. 3, where he said that entry to monastic life was from the beginning considered « a holy grace-transferring act of consecration, which brought the monk into conformity with Christ and bound him to God and thus incorporated him into a new pneumatic community », and PHILIPP OPPENHEIM, Mönchsweihe und Taufritus. Ein Kommentar zur Auslegung bei Dionysius dem Areopagiten, in Miscellanea liturgica in honorem L. Cuniberti Mohlberg, I, Rome 1948 (Bibliotheca « Ephemerides liturgicae », 22), p. 260. On the distinctive character of the ceremony of profession in the East, see RAFFIN, Rituels, pp. 143-169, esp. 165-169, and on differences within the East, pp. 108, 125, and 133.

782

mitment of the monk to observe it were central. The works of Pachomius and Cassian show that the early eastern monks had a reasonably well-defined ceremony for admission to a monastery, but they make no reference to a written rule or a formal promise or profession, to which Basil referred only, it seems, in connection with the vow of celibacy [29]. The rule of the Master, on the other hand, was to be read through once during the noviciate, and that of Benedict three times, and the monk's commitment was called a *promissio* or *professio*, terms which were apparently used interchangeably in the early western monastic rules and legislation, and in Spain a *pactum* [30]. The concept of a sacrament appeared clearly in the West for the first time in the *ordo* for making a monk in the penitential of Theodore of Tarsus, or Canterbury, which was introduced into the West probably from the Greek East by way of Rome in seventh century [31]. *Ordinatio, benedictio* and *consecratio* were all used in connection with monastic profession in the pontificals and customaries of tenth and eleventh centuries, and they seem to have been more or less equated by Lanfranc in the late eleventh century [32].

---

(29) PACHOMIUS, Precept XLIX, in *Pachomiana latina*, ed. AMAND BOON, Louvain 1932 (Bibliothèque de la Revue d'histoire ecclésiastique, 7), pp. 25-26, see the Greek text on pp. 174-175 and the tr. in *Pachomian Koinonia*, II: *Pachomian Chronicles and Rules*, tr. ARMAND VEILLEUX, Kalamazoo 1981 (Cistercian Studies Series, 46), pp. 152-153, and notes on p. 187. DE VOGÜÉ, pp. 1324-1350, traced the development of the ceremony of admission from Cassian through the *R.M.* to the *R.B.*; see also RAFFIN, *Rituels*, pp. 151, who said that a formula of profession was found in the East only in the Armenian rite. The declaration (*homologia*) mentioned by BASIL in his Letter CXCIX, 18-19, ed. and tr. ROY J. DEFERRARI, III, Cambridge (Mass.)-London 1926-1934 (Loeb Library), pp. 104-110, apparently referred just to celibacy.

(30) VAN HAEFTEN, pp. 405-407 (IV, 5, 2), equated profession with *iuramenta et sacramenta, renuntiatio, pactum, dedicatio, promissio, sponsio*, and *petitio*, and in practice these terms may have been used interchangeably, even if incorrectly, at differing times. On the triple reading of the rule, which was unique to the *R.B.*, see MARTÈNE, col. 815BC.

(31) See n. 66 below.

(32) See, for example, the index (under *promissio* and *professio*) in *Initia consuetudinis Benedictinae*, ed. KASSIUS HALLINGER, Siegburg 1963 (*C.C.M.*, 1), p. 615, and LANFRANC,

Some of his contemporaries still maintained, however, that wearing the monastic habit and living a monastic life were alone enough to make a monk or nun, or profession without benediction or consecration [33]. In recent years there has again been a reaction against the idea of consecration to monastic life, and fewer monks and nuns wear habits than they did in the Middle Ages, let alone a century ago. On these points, therefore, there are no absolutes, and the only safe scholarly course is to try to concentrate on the conditions in specific communities at various times in the past.

II

Under the heading of entry to religious life I shall consider in particular (1) the promise or profession made by the new monk or regular canon, (2) the form of the ceremony of admission to the community, (3) the role of the abbot or other superior, (4) the symbolism of the ceremonies, and (5) their nature and necessity, as seen especially in the eleventh and twelfth centuries. I shall not attempt to survey the entire history of the question, for which the sources still lie to a great extend in unpublished liturgical manuscripts, of which I have seen only a few. Among published works, the scholar has to rely primarily on the two small collections of profession-rites made in the eighteenth century by Martène and Herrgott, which include ten and three orders respectively [34], and on editions

---

Decreta, 104, ed. DAVID KNOWLES, Siegburg 1967 (*C.C.M.*, 3), p. 88. MOLITOR, *Mönchsweihe*, pp. 586-588, lists the uses of *ordinare (ordinatio)*, *benedictio*, and *consecratio* in various monastic sources.

(33) See pp. 802-803 below.

(34) MARTÈNE, *De ritibus*, II, pp. 162-168, and HERRGOTT, *Disciplina*, pp. 589-592. On the manuscripts used by Martène, see AIMÉ-GEORGES MARTIMORT, *La documentation liturgique de Dom Edmond Martène*, Vatican City 1978 (Studi e testi, 279), pp. 366-369. Two of the three formulas printed by HERRGOTT are also found in ETIENNE BALUZE,

784

of individual pontificals, benedictionals, and customaries, which vary greatly with regard to accuracy and completeness. Two general preliminary points may be made on the basis of these sources. First, while most surviving orders were designed for the profession of a single man, many manuscripts have the plural and female forms as.interlinear additions, showing that the ceremonies for individuals and groups and for monks and nuns (as distinct from widows, virgins, and recluses, for whom there were separate orders) were essentially the same [35]. Second, the pontificals from England, where many bishops were also abbots, are especially useful because they include many ceremonies for making and blessing monks, unlike those from the continent, where the parallel orders are often found only in monastic customaries and liturgical books.

According to chapter LVIII of the rule of Benedict, a novice at the end of his noviciate came « into the oratory in the presence *(coram)* of all », which is also found in the rule of the Master, and made a promise « in the presence *(coram)* of God and his saints ». He then made a petition « concerning this promise of his », written or (if he was illiterate) marked by himself, « to the name *(ad nomen)* of the saints whose relics are there and of the present abbot » and placed it with his own hand on the altar [36]. From this

Capitularia regum Francorum, ed. PIERRE DE CHINIAC, II, Paris 1780, coll. 574-577, and reprinted in JEAN MABILLON, *Acta sanctorum O.S.B.*, V, Venice 1735, pp. 694-695 (at end of Saec. IV, 1). VAN HAEFTEN, pp. 408-410 (IV, 5, 4), and MARTÈNE, coll. 820A-821A, printed small collections of six and nine profession formulas respectively. HOFMEISTER, *Professriten*, p. 282, stressed the constant process of change.

(35) The same was true in the East: see RAFFIN, *Rituels*, pp. 61 and 106-107.

(36) See IVO ZEIGER, *Profession super altare*, « Analecta Gregoriana », VIII (1935), pp. 161-185, who said that putting the petition on the altar gave it the character of a vow (see n. 21 above). VAN HAEFTEN, pp. 438 (IV, 8, 1) and 681 (VII, 1, 2), held that the ceremony was normally but not necessarily in a church, whereas for MARTÈNE, col. 824C, it must be in a church.

it is clear that the promise and petition were distinct: [37] the former, in the presence of God and His saints, was essentially a personal commitment, whereas the latter, which was addressed to the patron saints of the monastery and to the abbot, probably created a legal obligation, since it was taken from the altar by the abbot and kept in the monastery in order to show, according to the Carolingian commentaries on the rule, that the novice had become a monk [38]. Rothenhäusler called the petition a *Bitturkunde* and considered it one of the most original features of the rule of Benedict [39]. In a ninth-century profession published by Baluze and Herrgott the monk promised to return to the monastery unless the barbarians held him against his will, and a fine was levied, as in a secular charter, against anyone who contravened the petition [40].

The two main features of the promise in the early rules and formulas of profession were obedience and stability. The addition of *conversatio morum*, or a change from a secular to a monastic way of life, was a distinctive mark of the spread of the rule of Benedict in the ninth and tenth centuries, [41] but the tripartite Benedictine formula never entirely replaced the single or double formulas. In a ninth-century profession which included a specific reference to the rule of Benedict, the novice promised « concerning my

(37) See YEO, *Profession*, pp. 148-149, on the views of the commentators on the *R.B.*, including MARTÈNE, col. 825A, who said that previous writers (among whom he probably included Van Haeften: see n. 30 above) tended to confuse the promise and the petition.

(38) SMARAGDUS, p. 299 (LVIII, 29), and HILDEMAR, p. 543; see MARTÈNE, coll. 838C-840A.

(39) ROTHENHÄUSLER, *Aufnahmeordnung*, pp. 10-12.

(40) HERRGOTT, *Disciplina*, pp. 591-592.

(41) See HERWEGEN, *Professformel*, p. 63, who attributed the addition of *conversatio morum* to Benedict of Aniane and regarded it as the heart of the cenobitic monastic obligation, and JEAN LECLERCQ, *Profession According to the Rule of St Benedict*, in *Rule and Life: An Interdisciplinary Symposium*, ed. M. BASIL PENNINGTON, Spencer 1971 (Cistercian Studies Series, 12), pp. 117-149, who stressed the continued variety of forms of profession in spite of the growing number of references to the *R.B.*

786

stability and obedience », and only concerning his *conversatio morum* in the formula in a Winchester-Worcester pontifical of the tenth-twelfth century, though the tripartite formula appears in the other contemporary English sources [42]. The profession from Beaulieu published by Martène included only stability , and a single promise of obedience was still used in Calabria, perhaps owing to Greek influence, in the fourteenth century [43]. The author of the twelfth-century treatise *On the professions of monks*, from Le Bec, believed that the standard elements were obedience and *conversatio morum* and that the early monastic legislators like Basil did not require stability, which was a special feature of the rule of Benedict [44]. The profession of regular canons was not formalized before the eleventh century, and in the twelfth-century customs of Marbach and St Rufus (in the Bamberg fragment) the novice gave himself to the church and promised obedience to the abbot or provost, and his successors, « according to the canonical rule of St Augustine » [45]. The earliest

(42) HERRGOTT, *Disciplina*, p. 590 (also p. 591); MS Cambridge, C.C.C., 146, p. 151. The tripartite formula is found in *The Benedictional of Archbishop Robert*, ed. H. A. WILSON, London 1903 (*H.B.S.*, 24), p. 131, and the eleventh-century Canterbury pontifical in MS Cambridge, C.C.C, 44, p. 309. On these two manuscripts, see MONTAGUE RHODES JAMES, *A Descriptive Catalogue of the Manuscripts in the Library of Corpus Christi College Cambridge*, I, Cambridge 1912, pp. 88-90 and 332-335.

(43) MARTÈNE, col. 820B, and PIERRE SALMON, *Analecta liturgica. Extraits des manuscrits liturgiques de la Bibliothèque Vaticane*, Vatican City 1974 (Studi e testi, 273), p. 318.

(44) MARTÈNE, *De ritibus*, II, pp. 169-170. On this work, which is found in MS Paris, Bibl. nat., Lat. 2342, ff. 146ᵛ-159ʳ (MARTIMORT, *Documentation*, p. 730) and of which the correct title is *De professionibus monachorum*, not *De professione monachorum*, as given by Martène, see ANDRÉ WILMART, *Les ouvrages d'un moine de Bec. Un débat sur la profession monastique au XIIᵉ siècle*, « Revue Bénédictine », XLIV (1932), pp. 21-46. It is followed in the manuscript by a treatise on the profession of abbots: see JEAN LECLERCQ, *Un traité sur la « Profession des abbés » au XIIᵉ siécle*, in *Analecta monastica*, VI, Rome 1962 (Studia Anselmiana, 50), pp. 177-191.

(45) JOSEF SIEGWART, *Die Consuetudines des Augustiner-Chorherrenstiftes Marbach im Elsass*, Fribourg S. 1965 (Spicilegium Friburgense, 10), pp. 169 and 296 (nos. 140 and 408), see intro. pp. 6 and 27-28, on the profession of regular canons.

known reference to the tripartite formula of poverty, chastity, and obedience is in the mid-twelfth-century *Letter on properly keeping the observance of the canonical profession* by Prior Odo of St Victor, who later became abbot of St Genevieve and who wrote, « In our profession, which we make, we promise three things, as you well know: chastity, common property (*communio*), obedience » [46]. He may have had in mind the content rather than the wording of the formula, but in an undated profession from St Denis published by Martène the monk specifically promised obedience, chastity, and poverty in addition to stability and *conversatio morum* [47].

Both the rule of the Master and the rule of Benedict emphasized the personal involvement and free choice of the new monk. The Master held that a monk could not even be restrained from evil, since he had free choice, and Benedict insisted that he write or mark the petition with his own hand and lay it on the altar [48]. An oblate was considered to have been given by the free gift of his parents when he was too young, as in baptism, to make a commitment for himself. In the interrogation of the novice prior to profession in the Romano-Germanic pontifical of the tenth century he renounced the world « by his own will » and « with a free spirit » [49]. The role of the abbot in these

(46) *P.L.*, CXCVI, col. 1399AB; see LUDWIG HERTLING, *Die professio der Kleriker und die Entstehung der drei Gelübde*, « Zeitschrift für katholische Theologie », LVI (1932), p. 171, who mentioned its distant roots in 1 John 2. 16 and in Carolingian monastic legislation.

(47) MARTÈNE, col. 820C. MARTÈNE, *De ritibus*, II, p. 166, published a late medieval profession from St Ouen at Rouen in which the three vows of religion were given as poverty, continence, and obedience.

(48) *R.M.*, LXXXVII, 35, LXXXIX, 17, and XC, 90-91, ed. DE VOGÜÉ, II, pp. 360, 374, and 396; *R.B.*, LVIII, on which SMARAGDUS, p. 296 (LVIII, 20), said that the monk promised to obey the abbot and observe the rules « propter aeternam libertatem ». According to the *Supplex libellus*, addressed to Charlemagne by the monks of Fulda, n. 9, in *Initia cons. Ben.*, p. 324, no monk could be made by force. Cf. RAFFIN, *Rituels*, p. 103, on the Syriac rite of profession.

(49) *Le pontifical romano-germanique du dixième siècle*, ed. CYRILLE VOGEL and REINHARD ELZE, I, Vatican City 1963 (Studi e testi, 226), p. 71 (XXVIII, 4-5). On the

proceedings was primarily as a witness and, in receiving the petition, as the administrative head of the community. In the rule of the Master the abbot specifically told the novice that the promise was not to him but to God and to the church or altar [50]. It was an aspect of the monk's commitment to God rather than a vow creating a juridical tie between the abbot and the monk, which in the early Middle Ages seems to have existed only in Hispanic pactual monasticism as a reciprocal agreement between the abbot and the monks as a group, not as individuals [51].

From at least the eighth century, however, there was a tendency, which has been attributed to the influence of Germanic law and custom, for the monk to be regarded as the abbot's man and the abbot, as the monk's lord. Herwegen found the concept of *fidelitas* in the early eighth-century *petitio monachorum* from Flavigny, where « The monk seems to have bound himself to the abbot like a follower to his lord or a subject to a king »; and Frank traced back to Pirmin the practice found in a late eighth-century profession from Reichenau of putting the petition before the profession, which may have reflected the secular institution of commendation, where the lord's acceptance of a man as his follower preceded the promise of fidelity [52].

freedom of oblation, see Peter of Blois, cited n. 105 below, and YEO, *Profession*, p. 41: « the voluntary offering by the parents of an immature child has the same effect as the voluntary self-offering by an adult ».

(50) *R.M.*, LXXXIX,11,ed. DE VOGÜÉ, II, p. 372.

(51) On these points (see n. 21 above), see COLOMBAN BOCK, *La promesse d'obéissance ou la « Professio regularis »*, Westmalle 1955, and CATHERINE CAPELLE, *La voeu d'obéissance des origines au XIIe siècle*, Paris 1959 (Thèse Strasbourg; Bibliothèque d'histoire du droit et droit romain, 2); also NICOLE HERMANN-MASCAUD, *Les reliques des saints. Formation coutumière d'un droit*, Paris 1975 (Société d'histoire du droit. Collection d'histoire institutionelle et sociale, 6), pp. 250-251, who said that in the thirteenth century the Gospels replaced relics in the profession of monks. On Hispanic pactual monasticism, see CAPELLE, *Vœu*, p. 240, and above all the articles of CHARLES J. BISHKO in his *Spanish and Portuguese Monastic History, 600-1300*, London 1984 (Variorum Reprint, CS188).

(52) HERWEGEN, *Professformel*, p. 27; FRANK, *Professliturgie*, pp. 107-111.

In the ninth century the monastic commitment was equated with a vow which created, by analogy with secular ceremonies, a personal tie between the abbot and monk [53]. The promise of *conversatio morum* in the Winchester-Worcester pontifical was made to God and His saints « in whose honor this oratory is consecrated and to you father N. », which conflated the prescriptions in the rule concerning the promise (« in the presence of God and His saints ») and the petition (« to the name of the saints whose relics are there and the present abbot ») [54]. Thus the promise of obedience, according to Bock, « became charged with the feudal sense of allegiance to a specific person », and by the twelfth century the ceremony for becoming a monk resembled in many respects that for becoming a vassal [55]. The author of the treatise *On the professions of monks* opposed this development, saying that the inclusion in the formula of profession of the words « in the presence of the lord abbot N. » was like that of a witness to a secular charter and that the profession was made to God and the church, not to the abbot, who should therefore not refer to « my monk » or « my professed » [56]. The wind was blowing the other way, however. Alexander III in *Consuluit* seems to have equated profession « on an altar » and « in the hand of a bishop, abbot, or abbess », and *professio in manus*, as it was called, became increasingly common in the twelfth century among both monks and regular canons, who (according to the customs of Marbach and St Victor) promised obedience to their superior and put their hands between his both when they became novices and

---

(53) CAPELLE, *Voeu*, pp. 236-237 and 241-242.

(54) MS Cambridge, C.C.C., 146, p. 151.

(55) BOCK, *Promesse*, pp. 34-44 (quotation on p. 35).

(56) MARTÈNE, *De ritibus*, II, p. 175. He cited the parallel with homage, in which a greater man might do homage for some property to a lesser man without becoming his « man ».

when a new superior was elected [57]. In the late medieval customary of Evesham, the profession was not put on the altar by the novice himself, as the rule required, but was given to the abbot, who put it on the altar [58].

Another sign of the participation of the superior was the questioning or *scrutinium* of the novice before profession. Both Basil and Ps-Dionysius mention some interrogation of the novice, and the practice may have originated in the East [59]. In the rule of the Master, the new monk before confirming his entry into the monastery was « questioned again by the abbot about what he had decided during the period of delay conceded to him » [60]; but there is no reference to it in the rule of Benedict, and it spread in the West probably on account of the parallel with baptism, which was always preceded by a series of questionings [61], and as a matter of common sense, to make sure that novices were aware of the consequences of their actions. In one of the ninth-century professions published by Herrgott, the abbot asked the novice before he made his promise whether

(57) GREGORY IX, Decr. c.4,X,IV,6 (*Consuluit*), in *Corpus iuris canonici*, ed. EMIL FRIEDBERG, II, Leipzig 1879, p. 685; *Marbach*, p. 256 (no. 348), see intro. p. 8 and the customs of St Nicholas at Passau, ibid., p. 306 (no. 447); see generally PHILIPP HOFMEISTER, *Der Handgang in der Kirche*, « Liturgisches Jahrbuch », XIII (1963), pp. 241-247.

(58) *Officium ecclesiasticum abbatum secundum usum Eveshamensis monasterii*, ed. H. A. WILSON, London 1893 (*H.B.S.*, 6), coll. 29-30.

(59) BASIL, Letter CXCIX, 19, ed. DEFERRARI, III, p. 111: « They should be questioned »; OPPENHEIM, *Mönchsweihe*, p. 266; see RAFFIN, *Rituels*, pp. 20, 23, 32-33, and 150-151, on the interrogation in other eastern rites. The fourteenth-century rite from Calabria published in SALMON, *Analecta*, p. 318, resembled that described by Ps-Dionysius and included a questioning.

(60) *R.M.*, LXXXIX, 2, ed. DE VOGÜÉ, II, p. 372.

(61) See the eighth-century *Interrogationes et responsiones baptismales* in *Capitularia regum Francorum*, ed. ALFRED BORETIUS and VICTOR KRAUSE, I, Hanover 1883 (*M.G.H.*, Leges, 2), p. 222; the Gelasian Sacramentary, in *Liber sacramentorum Romanae aecclesiae ordinis anni circuli*, ed. L. C. MOHLBERG, Rome 1960 (Rerum ecclesiarum documenta. Series maior. Fontes, 4), p. 74, and the seven *scrutinia* in H. A. P. SCHMIDT, *Introductio in liturgiam occidentalem*, Rome-Basel-Barcelona 1960, pp. 252-254. I owe these references to the Rev. Prof. Arnold Angenendt.

he had any other obligations in the world [62], and in the Romano-Germanic pontifical the abbot, after divesting the novice of his previous clothing,

> asks him whether by his own will (*propria voluntate*) he renounces the world and all the things that are of the world and, what is more, [his own] desires, and whether he is prepared to bear all injury and opprobrium for the love of our Lord Jesus Christ. And if he promises all of these things with a free spirit (*gratuito animo*) the abbot says to him: Put off the former man with his acts, and put on the new Lord Jesus Christ [63].

In the twelfth-century treatise *On the professions of monks*, the *scrutinium* came before the benediction and was treated as almost more important than the promise, and in the customs of Marbach the prelate questioned the novice about his desire in the presence of the entire chapter [64]. Although it never became a standard feature of the ceremony of entry, either in the East or in the West, it created in many religious houses another opportunity for the superior to intervene in the process of admission [65].

According to the *ordo* in the penitential of Theodore of Tarsus, which appeared in the West in the seventh century and was later incorporated into the Romano-Germanic pontifical,

(62) HERRGOTT, *Disciplina*, p. 590.

(63) See n. 49 above and WILMART, *Moine de Bec*, pp. 40-43, citing this passage from a tenth-century *ordo* from Mainz and a list of questions from an eleventh-century *ordo* from Monte Cassino.

(64) MARTÈNE, *De ritibus*, II, pp. 173-174 (see WILMART, *Moine de Bec*, pp. 38-39, on this point) and *Marbach*, pp. 183-184 (no. 128).

(65) See ODILO RINGHOLZ, *Wernher II, Abt und Dekan von Einsiedeln, seine « Constitutiones » und « Ordo ad faciendum Monachum »*, « Studien und Mittheilungen aus dem Benedictiner- und dem Cistercienser-Orden », VI (1885), p. 336, where the abbot questioned the novice after blessing the cowl, and the *ordo* from St Ouen at Rouen in MARTÈNE, *De ritibus*, II, p. 166, where the abbot was told to inquire concerning the life, morals, age, learning, ability to chant, and marital status of clerics seeking to enter the monastery.

792

In the ordination of a monk, the abbot should perform
the mass and complete three prayers over his head,
and he veils his head for seven days with his cowl and
on the seventh day the abbot removes the veil as in
baptism the priest is accustomed to remove the veil
of infants; thus the abbot should [do] for the monk,
since according to the judgment of the fathers, it is
a second baptism in which all sins are dismissed as
in baptism [66].

This *ordo* reflects a relatively developed ritual and symbolic interpretation and shows how the ceremony had
grown in the East between the time of Cassian, who
described a much less elaborate procedure, and the seventh
century. It spread rapidly in the West, where its only
serious rivals in the tenth and eleventh centuries were the
so-called English and Cluniac ceremonies, of which there
were so many forms that their classification may well be
modified by future research [67]. Frank distinguished two
versions of the English ceremony, which he considered to

---

(66) This *ordo* is published in F. W. H. WASSERSCHLEBEN, *Die Bussordnungen der
abendländischen Kirche*, Halle 1851, p. 204 (II, III, 3) and PAUL WILHELM FINSTERWALDER,
Die Canones Theodori Cantuariensis und ihre Überlieferungsformen, Weimar 1929 (Untersuchungen zu den Bussbüchern des 7., 8., und 9. Jahrhunderts, 1), p. 271; translated in
JOHN T. MC NEILL and HELENA M. GAMER, *Medieval Handbooks of Penance*, New York
1938 ([Columbia] Records of Civilization), p. 201; and incorporated into the *Pontifical
romano-germanique*, p. 72 (XXIX, 1). See CASEL, *Mönchsweihe*, pp. 32-37; FRANK, *Professliturgie*, pp. 115-123; DEKKERS, *Profession*, p. 95, n. 33; *The Claudius Pontificals*, ed.
D. H. TURNER, n.p. 1971 (*H.B.S.*, 97), pp. xxxiv-xxxv; and RAFFIN, *Rituels*, pp. 27-28.
    (67) On the English form, see Wilson's notes to *Archbishop Robert*, p. 191 (and the
text on pp. 131-135); CASEL, *Mönchsweihe*, p. 40; FRANK, *Professliturgie*, pp. 124-131; and
Claudius Pontificals, pp. xxxiii-xxxvi; and, on the Cluniac form, MOLITOR, *Mönchsweihe*,
pp. 558-591 and 601 (see YEO, *Profession*, pp. 261-265); FRANK, *Professliturgie*, pp. 131-132;
HOFMEISTER, *Professriten*; and my forthcoming article on *Entrance to Cluny in the Eleventh
and Twelfth Centuries, according to the Customaries and Statutes* to appear in the
Festschrift for Raymonde Foreville. On the four Cluniac prayers, see HERMANN J. GRÄF,
*Ad monachum faciendum. Die Mönchsprofess nach einem Fest-Sakramentar von Venedig
aus dem 11. Jh.*, « Ephemerides Liturgicae », LXXXVII (1973), pp. 353-369, and
CHRYSOGONUS WADDELL, *Sequantur IIII Collecte: A Letter to Brother Aidan about the
Cistercian Prayers for the Blessing of a Monk*, « Liturgy », XII (1978), pp. 99-130.

be of independent origin, and in one of which the vesting
with the monastic habit preceded the profession, as in the
Romano-Germanic pontifical [68], and in the other the profession preceded the vesting, as in the Cluniac ceremony
and the later Roman pontifical [69]. Turner, however, saw
a development within this second version, which he
distinguished from a later though simpler ceremony in the
pontificals of Archbishop Dunstan and Bishop Samson [70].
The Cluniac ceremony was characterized by four prayers
rather than three, as in Theodore's *ordo* and the English
ceremonies, and was followed by three rather than seven
days of veiling. There seems also to have been a distinction in the Cluniac rite both between the immediate petition and promise of obedience, accompanied by tonsure and
a change of clothing, made by the novice in the chapter
at the time of entry, and the later profession and benediction, or consecration, in the church and also, in certain circumstances, between the profession and benediction.
These distinctions may have arisen from the need to give
some formal status to monks who were received into
Cluniac priories before they could be the blessed by the abbot at Cluny, as the customs and statutes required, and also

(68) MS Cambridge, C.C.C., 146, pp. 150-152; *Pontifical romano-germanique*, p. 70
(XXVIII, 2).
(69) MS. Cambridge, C.C.C., 44, pp. 308-310; *Archbishop Robert*, pp. 131-135; *The
Missal of Robert of Jumièges*, ed. H. A. WILSON, London 1896 (*H.B.S.*, 11), pp. 283-284;
Pontificale Lanaletense, ed. G. H. DOBLE, London 1937 (*H.B.S.*, 74), pp. 45-48; *Claudius
Pontificals*, pp. 97-103; see also *Le pontifical romain du XII* siècle*, ed. MICHEL ANDRIEU,
Vatican City 1938 (Studi e testi, 86), p. 175 (XVI, 6-7).
(70) *Claudius Pontificals*, p. xxxv: « The Benedictional of Archbishop Robert, the
Missal of Robert of Jumièges and the Lanalet Pontifical all present the rite of monastic
profession in less developed forms than does Claudius II. The Benedictional and the Missal
have in fact the same and the least developed form. ...The next stage of the profession
rite is encountered in the Lanalet Pontifical. ...Finally, the Corpus Christi manuscript
[no. 44 from Canterbury, see n. 42 above] gives us a more developed form of the rite than
in Claudius II ». This conclusion is based largely on the form and order of the prayers
and does not take into account, among other elements, the order of vesting or the length
of veiling. As Turner says (p. xxxix), the picture is complex.

794

to cope with the problem of novices in distant dependencies who were in danger of dying or who had entered in order to die as monks *ad succurrendum*. The Cluniac ceremony was introduced at Canterbury by Lanfranc; elements of it are found at Monte Cassino under Abbot Desiderius in the late eleventh century; and it later became the predominant form of profession in houses not only of monks, including the Cistercians and other non-Cluniac orders, but also of regular canons, who substituted the name of Augustine for that of Benedict in the formula of profession [71].

The *ordo* of Theodore was combined with features from the Cluniac rite in an influential decree which was attributed to Pope Gregory I and was probably composed in Italy about the middle of the eleventh century:

A bishop should celebrate mass in the ordination of a priest and [likewise] an abbot in the consecration of a monk and say four prayers [according to the number of the four Gospels] over his head so that, as he is instructed by the four Gospels, so he is consecrated by four prayers, and so until the third day he should keep his head veiled with total silence and due reverence [to God], bearing the figure of the passion of the Lord. On the third day he [the abbot] takes the cowl from his head so that after the sadness of his ancient sin has been put down [as if resurrected according to the apostle] he may see the glory of the Lord with an unveiled face [and acting as on the day

(71) In addition to the references in n. 67, see, on its spread in England, *The Pontifical of Magdalen College*, ed. H. A. WILSON, London 1910 (*H.B.S.*, 39), pp. 79-81 (and the notes on p. 269); *Claudius Pontificals*, p. xxxvi; and *Evesham*, coll. 29-31; and on its spread among non-Cluniacs on the continent, PIERRE PHILIPPE GUIGNARD, *Les monuments primitifs de la règle cistercienne*, Dijon 1878 (Analecta Divionensia, 10), p. 221, and *Consuetudines canonicorum regularium Springiersbacenses-Rodenses*, ed. STEPHAN WEINFURTER, Turnhout 1978 (*C.C.:C.M.*, 48), pp. 138 and 143-144 (nos. 260-261 and 265-266).

of resurrection]. Therefore he has been baptized for a second time and cleansed [according to the judgment of the holy fathers] from all the sins [of his former life]. ...There are three days in silence [at the beginning of their ordination] like the apostles, who [after the passion of the Lord] lived in conclave for three days out of fear of the Jews, until on the third day the Lord rising said to them: Peace be with you. So the abbot should give [and communicate] peace to the monk, and remove from his head the cowl [which signifies shame and fear of punishment] [72].

Aside from the association with the ordination of a priest, and the differing number of prayers and days of veiling, and their symbolism, the three most important common points in this text and the *ordo* of Theodore are the celebration of mass, the covering of the head, and the parallel with baptism, all of which exercised a deep influence on the ceremony of entry to religious life in the West and emphasized its character as a sacramental transfer from one status of life to another.

Neither text mentioned the vesting with the monastic habit or the kiss of peace [73], nor the ceremonies, which

---

(72) The text in MS Munich, Bayerische Staatsbibliothek, Lat. 27129, is printed, with variants (put here in brackets) from MS Châlons-sur-Marne, Bibl. mun., 32, in my article *The Treatise « Hortatur nos » and Accompanying Canonical Texts on the Performance of Pastoral Work by Monks*, in *Speculum historiale* (Festschrift Johannes Spörl), ed. CLEMENS BAUER, LAETITIA BOEHM, and MAX MÜLLER, Munich 1966, pp. 575-576 and, on the manuscripts and diffusion, pp. 569-570. The remainder of the text justifies the performance of pastoral work by monks on the basis of their status. Dr Martin Brett has kindly sent me a list of seven canonical collections and some forty manuscripts in which the accompanying text *Sunt nonnulli*, attributed to Pope Boniface IV (see n. 152 below) is found, showing its wide diffusion. They were frequently cited together, as by RUPERT OF DEUTZ, *De trinitate et operibus eius*, XLI: *De operibus spiritus sancti*, VIII, 8, in *P.L.*, CLXVII, col. 1791BC (= *C.C.: C.M.*, XXIV, pp. 2082-2083).

(73) This kiss of peace was frequently used in the liturgy of the early church, especially at the beginning and end of ceremonies: see ANDRÉ CABASSUT, *Le baiser de paix*, « La vie et les arts liturgiques », III (1916-1917), pp. 145-158. It came at the end of the profession rite in the *R.M.*, LXXXIX, 26, ed. DE VOGÜÉ, II, p. 377, see I, p. 81, n. 2, on its

were of special importance in the East, of tonsure, laying-on of hands, and marking the new monk with (or giving him) a cross [74]. According to Casel, « The laying-on of hands and the putting-on of clothing were the principal elements of this consecration » in the Armenian, Coptic, and Syriac rites, and Raffin said that becoming a monk in the East was primarily a liturgical consecration « of which the tonsure and the clothing were the essential manifestations » [75]. Ps-Dionysius placed the tonsure between the mark of the cross and the divestment of secular clothing and considered it « the most essential element of the consecration of a monk » [76]. In the rule of the Master, tonsure and vesting took place after a year in the monastery, but in the rule of Benedict and other early western sources tonsure was not connected with the ceremony of profession [77]. Smaragdus expected novices to be tonsured while they were still in lay clothing, and Hildemar showed that there were still disagreements in the ninth century over whether a novice should be tonsured at the beginning of the noviciate, which might restrict his liberty to leave, or at a later stage, implying that he remained a layman during the noviciate [78]. It formed a part of the ceremony of

significance as a mark of the new monk's acceptance into the community. It is not mentioned in the R.B., perhaps because it was assumed, since it appears in SMARAGDUS, p. 297, and at various points in the ceremony in many later sources, including the English and Cluniac rites and in the customaries of regular canons: see YEO, Profession, pp. 133, 145, and 170-171.

(74) On the cross in eastern monastic profession ceremonies, see CASEL, Mönchsweihe p. 9; OPPENHEIM, Mönchsweihe p. 266 (on Ps-Dionysius, for whom marking with the cross was the fourth stage in making a monk); and RAFFIN, Rituels, pp. 106 and 13*-14*, n. 177, citing the pontifical commented upon by Bar Kepho (d. 903). See also p. 817 and nn. 147-148 below.

(75) CASEL, Mönchsweihe, p. 17 (and pp. 14-19 generally); see also RAFFIN, Rituels, pp. 144 and 152-154.

(76) OPPENHEIM, Mönchsweihe, pp. 266 and 273; see RAFFIN, Rituels, pp. 22-23.

(77) R.M., XC, 79-81, ed. DE VOGÜÉ, II, p. 392; DE VOGÜÉ, p. 1334; YEO, Profession, pp. 135-136.

(78) SMARAGDUS, p. 298 (LVIII, 26); HILDEMAR, p. 540; cf. FRANK, Professliturgie, pp. 97 and 102-107, and YEO, Profession, pp. 153-155. At Cluny and, later, at Monte Cassino,

admission in a few western sources from the ninth century on, but in some, as in the *ordo* from St Peter at Sens, it appears as a preliminary [79]. There is no reference to the celebration of mass in connection with admitting a monk in either the works of Pachomius or Cassian or the early eastern rite, which may date from about 700, in MS Barberini 336, nor in the rules of the Master or of Benedict, where the reception of a novice is a primarily legal matter, to which the laying of the petition on the altar may have given a quasi-sacramental character [80]. The practice spread in the West after the *ordo* of Theodore was incorporated into the Romano-Germanic pontifical and amalgamated with the Cluniac ceremony in the Ps-Gregorian decree. There are many references to a mass in association with the admission of novices in *ordines* of both the English and the Cluniac types from the ninth century on [81], but it seems never to have been a requirement, perhaps because not all abbots were ordained. In the late eleventh century Lanfranc said, « He [the abbot] should celebrate mass in the consecration of a monk, as the canons order, if it is suitable for him (*si ei commodum est*) » [82], and the specifications in

novices were tonsured and shaved at the beginning of the noviciate (ULRICH, *Consuetudines Cluniacenses*, II, 1, in *P.L.*, CXLIX, col. 701C, and n. 124 below), whereas at Cîteaux a lay novice was tonsured after the noviciate at the time of profession (GUIGNARD, *Monuments*, p. 220).

(79) MARTÈNE, *De ritibus*, II, p. 165; FRANK, *Professliturgie*, pp. 102-107.

(80) CASEL, *Mönchsweihe*, pp. 25 and 32-33, and RAFFIN, *Rituels*, pp. 26-28. According to HOFMEISTER, *Professriten*, p. 250, however, monastic ordination from the beginning took place at the offertory during mass.

(81) The opening words of the *ordo* of Theodore and the Ps-Gregorian decree, which refer to celebrating mass at the ordination or consecration of a monk, were cited in many profession rites, such as *Einsiedeln*, p. 334, and St Peter at Sens, in MARTÈNE, *De ritibus*, II, p. 165, and others in JEAN LECLERCQ, *Messes pour la profession et l'oblation monastiques*, « Archiv für Liturgiewissenshaft », IV. 1 (1955), pp. 93-96.

(82) LANFRANC, Decr. 104, ed. KNOWLES, p. 88. BERNARD OF CLUNY, I, 20, in HERRGOTT, *Disciplina*, p. 180, said that the benediction should take place after the gospel of the high mass «si domnus abbas cantat missam». This condition was omitted by ULRICH,

VII

798

the Cistercian statutes concerning profession that « if mass is to be celebrated afterwards » and « if he who is to be blessed will not go to mass » suggest that it was not regarded as an essential part of the ceremony [83]. The custom of veiling or covering the head with the cowl may also have originated in the East and have been introduced into the West by the *ordo* of Theodore [84]. In the eleventh-century Canterbury pontifical it came at the beginning of the ceremony, but it normally came at the end, as in Theodore's *ordo*, and varied in length from between one day and eight. The council of Aachen in 817 set the period at three days, which became standard after the spread of the Cluniac rite [85]. The veiling played a particularly important role in the consecration of women, for whom the veil was the symbol of chastity [86]. For men it probably originated as a confirmation of their admission to the community [87], but it was later given various symbolic meanings and was equated with a period of sleep, death, or burial, especially, as in the Ps-Gregorian decree, the passion and burial of Christ, and was commonly associated with the similiar periods of veiling during baptism [88].

II, 27, in *P.L.*, CXLIX, col. 713A, and WILLIAM of HIRSAU, I, 74, in HERRGOTT, *Disciplina*, p. 443, who later said «sive illam missam celebret sive non», which suggests that the point in question was not whether the benediction took place at mass but whether or not the abbot himself celebrated it.

(83) GUIGNARD, *Monuments*, pp. 220-221.

(84) CASEL, *Mönchsweihe*, pp. 29-37; FRANK, *Professliturgie*, p. 117; RAFFIN, *Rituels*, pp. 60-61; see PHILIPP OPPENHEIM, *Das Mönchskleid im christlichen Altertum*, Freiburg B. 1931 (Römische Quartalschrift für christliche Altertumskunde und für Kirchengeschichte, Supplementheft, 28), p. 165, stressing the importance of the veil in ancient religion and culture.

(85) II Aachen, 16, in *Initia cons. Ben.*, p. 476; see RAFFIN, *Rituels*, pp. 60-61 and esp. pp. 9*-10*, n. 114bis, and YEO, *Profession*, pp. 150-151.

(86) *Pontifical romain*, pp. 159-161 (XII, 20-25).

(87) CASEL, *Mönchsweihe*, p. 29.

(88) See PHILIPP OPPENHEIM, *Symbolik und religiöse Wertung des Mönchskleides im christlichen Altertum, vornehmlich nach Zeugnissen christlicher Schriftsteller der Ostkirche*, Münster W. 1932 (Theologie des christlichen Ostens. Texte und Untersuchungen, 2), pp. 68-72, also 21-22 and 126, and YEO, *Profession*, pp. 348-349, who associated replacing

It was customary since the earliest days of monasticism to equate entry to religious life with baptism, and the parallel cannot be dismissed, as it was by Protestants in the sixteenth century and more recently by scholars who want to defend the uniqueness of baptism, simply as a metaphor or a way of saying that monastic profession is an imitation or fulfilment of baptism [89]. Although some of Van Haeften's nine points of similarity may seem far-fetched today, and he denied that profession was equal or superior to baptism, because it lacked any power of its own and worked not *ex opere operato* but *ex vi et merito ipsius operantis*, his defense of the parallel was firmly based on tradition [90]. It is possible that when Jerome said that Blesilla by entering religious life « washed herself by the second baptism of her undertaking (*propositum*) » he had in mind a baptism of blood or martyrdom [91], but the

the symbolism of baptism by that of death with the reduction of the period of veiling from seven to three days. The triple immersion at baptism was compared with the three-day discipline of Christ, however, by HAMELIN OF ST ALBANS, *De monachatu*, in *Thesaurus novus anecdotorum*, ed. EDMOND MARTÈNE and URSIN DURAND, V, Paris 1717, p. 1453.

(89) In addition to the works cited in nn. 22-23 above, see HERIBERT ROSWEYDE's notes to his edition of the *Life* of Anthony, XXXVII, rp. in *P.L.*, LXXIII, coll. 182A-183A; CASEL, *Mönchsweihe*, pp. 5-6; OPPENHEIM, *Symbolik*, pp. 21-22, and *Mönchsweihe*, pp. 263-266; FRANK, *Professliturgie*, p. 122; EDWARD E. MALONE, *Martyrdom and Monastic Profession as a Second Baptism*, in *Vom christlichen Mysterium* (Festschrift Odo Casel), ed. ANTON MAYER, JOHANNES QUASTEN, and BURKHARD NEUNHEUSER, Düsseldorf 1951, pp. 115-134; JEAN LECLERCQ, *Profession monastique, baptême et pénitence d'après Odon de Cantorbéry*, in *Analecta monastica*, II, Rome 1953 (Studia Anselmiana, 31), pp. 127 and 136-139, and *La vêture « ad succurrendum »* d'après le moine Raoul, in *Analecta monastica*, III, Rome 1955 (Studia Anselmiana, 37), p. 160; RENÉ ROQUES, *Eléments pour une théologie de l'état monastique selon Denys l'Aréopagite*, in *Théologie de la vie monastique*, Paris 1961 (Théologie. Etudes publiés sous la direction de la Faculté de Théologie S.J. de Lyon-Fourvère, 49), pp. 285-296; JULIEN LEROY, *Saint Théodore Studite*, ibid., pp. 431-433; RAFFIN, *Rituels*, pp. 108-109 and 165-169; and WOLLASCH, *Mönchsgelübde*, pp. 535-537.

(90) This distinction was based on the argument of Cajetan and Bellarmine that baptism removed both the crime and the punishment but profession removed only the punishment: see VAN HAEFTEN, p. 441 (IV, 8, 2).

(91) JEROME, Letter XXXIX, 4: « nunc vero, cum propitio Christo ante quattuor ferme menses secundo quodam modo se propositi baptismo lauerit et ita deinceps vixerit », ed. ISIDORE HILBERG, I, Vienna-Leipzig 1910 (*C.S.E.L.*, 54), p. 299; see DEKKERS, *Profession*, pp. 91-97, and NEUNHEUSER, *Profession*, pp. 11-12.

800

distinction would probably have been lost on the early monks, such as the desert father who said, « I have seen the power which I have seen standing over baptism also over the vestment of a monk when he received the spiritual habit » [92]. The words of Theodore's *ordo* (and the Romano-Germanic pontifical) calling monastic ordination « a second baptism in which all sins are dismissed as in baptism » and of the Ps-Gregorian decree saying that the new monk « has been baptized for a second time and cleansed from all sins » were cited and echoed in countless pontificals and customaries, and in many other types of works [93], and influenced the imagery of renewal and regeneration used in the profession prayers, like those in the Romano-Germanic and Roman pontificals, which called on God to look on the new monk with favor « by which he may, renewed in the spirit of his mind, deserve to put off the former man with his actions and put on the new one who is created in accordance with God » [94]. Although the parallel of profession and baptism is not found in the rule of Benedict or other western sources before the seventh century [95], it spread rapidly and there can be no doubt that entry to monastic life was almost universally regarded in the Middle Ages as truly a second baptism or regeneration [96].

(92) *Verba seniorum*, I, 9, in *P.L.*, LXXIII, col. 994B; see CASEL, *Mönchsweihe*, pp. 5-6; FRANK, *Professliturgie*, p. 122; LECLERCQ, *Profession*, p. 137, who cited three allusions to this story from the ninth to the twelfth century; and RAFFIN, *Rituels*, p. 109.

(93) See MS Cambridge, C.C.C., 44, pp. 308 and 316; MARTÈNE, *De ritibus*, II, p. 165; and the work of Rupert of Deutz cited n. 72 above.

(94) *Pontifical romano-germanique*, p. 71 (XXVIII, 5) and *Pontifical romain*, p. 174 (XVI, 3).

(95) The wording of Theodore's *ordo* is echoed in HILDEMAR, p. 539, of which YEO, *Profession*, p. 149, said, « In the literature we have been studying [the rules and commentaries], this is the first mention of baptism in the context of monastic profession ».

(96) In addition to the works cited in nn. 72 and 93, which used the Ps-Gregorian decree, see GEOFFREY OF VENDÔME, Letter IV, 12, in *P.L.*, CLVII, col. 158A, who said that a fugitive monk had rejected the « stola secundae regenerationis », and the *De professionibus monachorum*, in MARTÈNE, *De ritibus*, II, p. 171, which argued that unlike other

Peter Damiani in his treatise against a bishop who recalled monks to the world asserted strongly that entering monastic life was a second baptism and carried the same consequences as the first [97]. In an interesting story found in two differing versions in Eadmer's *Life* of Anselm and in the Ps-Anselmian *On likenesses* or *On analogies* a dead monk named Osborn appeared to Anselm and described how during his lifetime the Devil had attacked him and been defeated three times: according to the *Life*, first when the sins he had committed in the world were removed by his parents' faith in offering him to God, second when the sins committed in the monastery before his profession were removed by profession, and third when his sins as a monk were removed by confession and penance; and according to the *On likenesses*, first by baptism, which abolished his pre-baptismal sins, second by profession, which abolished the sins « which he had committed in the world or in the monastery before his profession », and third by confession for the sins committed after he became a monk [98]. Bernard of Clairvaux discussed the question of « Why the monastic discipline is called a second baptism ? » in his treatise *On precept and dispensation*, where he said that those who professed and loved a life of perfect renunciation were like angels and unlike men, since it « reformed the divine image in man, making us like Christ in the man-

---

orders, which required a man already to be holy, the monastic order « makes a man holy, like baptism ». The superiority of monks to other orders in society was also asserted by HUGH OF ROUEN, *Dialogi*, VI, 1-2, in *Thesaurus novus*, V, pp. 971-972, and HAMELIN OF ST ALBANS, *De monachatu*, ibid., p. 1456.

(97) PETER DAMIANI, *Opusc.* XVI, 8, in *P.L.*, CXLV, coll. 376C and 377A; see GIOVANNI MICCOLI, in *Théologie de la vie monastique*, pp. 469-472.

(98) EADMER, *The Life of Anselm, Archbishop of Canterbury*, I, 10, ed. RICHARD W. SOUTHERN, London-Edinburgh 1962 ([Nelsons's] Medieval Texts), pp. 18-19, and *De similitudinibus*, CXCII, in *P.L.*, CLIX, col . 720A; see on the composition and date of the *De similitudinibus*, RICHARD W. SOUTHERN and F. S. SCHMITT, *Memorials of St. Anselm*, London 1969 (Auctores Britannici Medii Aevi, 1), pp. 12-13 and 18-20.

ner of baptism. And as if he has been baptized for a second time, ...we again put on Christ ». As a man is raised in baptism from the power of darkness to the realm of light, so in this second regeneration he rises into the light of the virtues from the darkness not of one original sin but of many present sins [99]. Bernard's use of *dicatur* and *quasi* in this passage suggests that he regarded baptism and profession as analogous rather than identical, but in his sermon *On double baptism* he specifically referred to profession as a rebaptism, in which « It is not enough now to renounce the Devil and his works [as in first baptism]; it is necessary to renounce likewise the world and one's own will » [100].

Although the parallel between baptism and profession was probably the single most important factor in promoting the view of entry to religious life as a sacrament, there was considerable disagreement in the eleventh and twelfth centuries over whether benediction or consecration, or even formal profession, was required to make a monk. Ivo of Chartres wrote to Abbot Geoffrey of Vendôme in 1094 that « No exterior addition other than contempt of the world or complete love of God makes a true monk » and that « The benediction of a monk is not the imposition of hands or the celebration of any sacrament from apostolic tradition ». It can be performed by either an abbot or another monk and was, like profession, a guarantee against backsliding, « because all religious stability grows and flourishes when it is recent and scarce but grows cold and worthless when it is old and frequent, unless it is strictly bound and

---

(99) BERNARD OF CLAIRVAUX, *De praecepto et dispensatione*, XVII, 54, in *Sancti Bernardi opera*, ed. JEAN LECLERCQ a.o., III, Rome 1957-1981, pp. 288-289. On this and other passages concerning profession as second baptism in the works of Bernard, see PLACIDE DESEILLE, in *Théologie de la vie monastique*, p. 515.

(100) BERNARD OF CLAIRVAUX, *De diversis* XI, ed. LECLERCQ, VI.1, p. 126.

preserved » [101]. At about the same time Anselm of Canterbury wrote to King Harold's daughter Gunnilda, who had abandoned the religious habit,

> For although you were not consecrated (*sacrata*) by a bishop and did not read a profession in his presence, the fact that you publicly and privately wore the habit of the holy way of life (*habitum sacri propositi*), by which you proclaimed to all who saw you that you were dedicated to God no less than by reading a profession, is in itself a manifest and undeniable profession. ...You are therefore without an excuse if you desert the holy way of life, which you have long professed by your habit and life, although you did not read the profession which is now used and were not consecrated (*consecrata*) by a bishop [102].

Both Ivo and Anselm appealed to history, pointing out that the early monks and nuns made no profession and received no benediction and yet obtained « the reward of their labor » and « the height and crown » of the monastic life, as Ivo and Anselm respectively put it. Profession and benediction or consecration came « later when the congregations of monks multiplied », said Ivo, and were said to be « used now (*nunc usitata*) » by Anselm, though he surely knew that they had existed for centuries.

The views of a lawyer like Ivo and a theologian like Anselm, who was also a monk, cannot to taken lightly, but

---

(101) IVO OF CHARTRES, Letter 41, ed. JEAN LECLERCQ, I, Paris 1949 (Les classiques de l'histoire de France au Moyen Age, 22), pp. 164-166; see also Letter 73 in *P.L.*, CLXII, col. 94A, where Ivo wrote to the abbot of Marmoutier that abbatial benediction was a simple prayer, not a laying-on of hands or a consecration, and that many early monks received no benediction. CASEL, *Mönchsweihe*, p. 46, deprecated this view as that of a non-monastic lawyer.

(102) ANSELM OF CANTERBURY, Letter 168, in *Opera omnia*, ed. F. S. SCHMITT, IV, Edinburgh 1946-1961, pp. 44-45, where this letter is dated after Anselm became archbishop in 1093.

they represented a reaction against a more formal and legalized view of monasticism which was already established at the time they were writing. Two monks from Anselm's own abbey of Le Bec, both writing in the early twelfth century, took somewhat different positions. One, named Boso, stressed the need for profession, which made a monk's gift of himself and his property to God permanent and therefore more worthy than self-donation without profession. No one to whom God has given the major grace of being a monk should remain in a lower grade [103]. The other was the author of *On the professions of monks,* who argued that benediction or consecration, although not found in any rule, were essential to the dignity of the monastic order « because there is no sacred order in the holy church which does not have its own benediction ». While he recognized that there were differing opinions on the subject, and that some people thought that a monk was made only by profession and others only by benediction, he himself believed that benediction irrevocably bound a monk to God and the monastic order and that he must therefore (unlike a hermit, who was free to return to the world) maintain the habit « which is the greatest and most particular bond of the holy order ». « The sole assumption of the holy habit with benediction makes a monk ». He put less emphasis on the *subscriptio* or profession, which bound but did not make a monk. He agreed with Ivo that it held the monastic order together when its fervor cooled, but said that there were many monks, including those *ad succurrendum,* who had made no profession. « For whether or not he subscribes, he will certainly be a monk if he strives to carry out » Christ's command to deny himself, take up

(103) H. -M. ROCHAIS, *Textes anciens sur la discipline monastique,* « Revue Mabillon », XLIII (1953), pp. 45-46.

His cross, and follow Him, « since in these is the sum of the monastic religion » [104]. Idungus of Regensburg, writing in the middle of the twelfth century, said that « Nothing makes a monk except lawful profession », and in a letter concerning a woman who claimed to have been forced to become a nun Peter of Blois wrote that « The authority of the canons declares that one's own profession or paternal devotion [i.e. oblation] makes a monk or nun » [105].

Peter went on in this letter to stress the voluntary character of entry to religious life, saying that the freedom of a spiritual marriage should be no less than that of a carnal marriage, but he did not suggest that even someone who had been forced to enter religious life was entitled to leave, because the obligation, once entered, was universally regarded as irrevocable, inviolable, and overriding, since it subsumed all lesser obligations. Anselm in his letter to Gunnilda said that anyone who abandoned the habit, even if taken without profession or consecration, was an apostate, and for Ivo, Boso, and the author of *On the professions of monks* the purpose of profession was not to make a monk but to bind him legally [106]. Smaragdus and Hildemar in the ninth century said that the petition written (or marked) by the monk himself was kept as evidence that he must return to the monastery if he left [107]. The only reasons a monk might leave were improvement, salva-

---

(104) MARTÈNE, *De ritibus*, II, pp. 170-173.

(105) ROBERT B. C. HUYGENS, *Le moine Idung et ses deux ouvrages: « Argumentum super quatuor questionibus » et « Dialogus duorum monachorum »*, « Studi Medievali », 3rd ser., XIII (1972), p. 412, and PETER OF BLOIS, Letter 54, in *Opera omnia*, ed. J. A. GILES, I, Oxford 1846, p. 162.

(106) According to an anonymous follower of Anselm, in LECLERCQ, *Vêture*, p. 164, « A monk can in no way leave his order », though a layman or cleric might leave his order to become a monk, and the author of the *De professionibus monachorum*, in MARTÈNE, *De ritibus*, II, p. 176, said that a monk was bound by the obligations of his profession and could be released even from the obedience promised in the *scrutinium* only if the superior was a simoniac, the church was deconsecrated, or the monk was persecuted.

(107) See n. 38 above.

tion, or obedience, according to Hildemar, who explained that improvement (*melioratio*) was not really leaving because, « He [the monk] subjects himself more to the rule if he goes either into a deserted place or to another monastery for the sake of improvement » [108]. This later developed into the accepted view that *transitus* was allowed to a stricter but not to a less strict form of life, so that departure from a strict monastery was always prohibited. Even a promise made in ignorance as a child was binding according to a text attributed to Urban II concerning the obligation of all members of a religious community, whether or not they had taken a vow of poverty, to lead a common life like that of the apostles.

> But someone may say, « I did not promise the apostolic life but to live according to the recent customs of such and such a monastery and according to the tradition of those fathers ». Behold you have heard [the words of the Lord in Jer. 3. 5], since you were not able to do this [evil thing]. But you may say, « I did not understand thus, since I was a boy ». But if you did not understand, none the less he made the vow. ...Search the Scriptures, search the rule, and see what you promised [109].

Urban cited the parallel of a child who in baptism is put under obligations which later have to be fulfilled and which, like the obligations of religious life, cannot be set aside.

This view of entry to religious life as an irrevocable and once-in-a-lifetime ceremony, like baptism (and, in the early church, penance and marriage), raised serious questions about whether or how it could be repeated, especially in

---

(108) HILDEMAR, pp. 543-544.

(109) HORST FURHMANN, *Papst Urban II. und der Stand der Regularkanoniker*, Munich 1984 (Bayerische Akademie der Wissenschaften. Phil-hist. Kl., 1984.2), pp. 42-44.

the case of monks who moved from one religious community to another, or who joined a house that was a dependency (and legally part of) another house, or who had been
clothed in the monastic habit, and sometimes made a profession and been blessed, when they were ill or in danger
of death [110]. Ivo of Chartres, in spite of his conviction
that the benediction of a monk was not a sacrament and
had no more power than an absolution or prayer, none the
less conceded in his letter to Geoffrey of Vendôme that
« If the benediction of a monk is a consecration among the
Cluniacs, among whom as you say this is the custom, absolutely no repetition of the benediction could be
made » [111]. One of the most strongly worded charges
against the Cluniacs to which Peter the Venerable replied
in his Letter 28 to Bernard of Clairvaux was that they
allowed monks who had professed stability, *conversatio
morum*, and obedience in one place to swear them again
in another. Peter replied that there was no harm in
repeating a vow that was neither inferior nor contrary to
a previous vow and cited the permission given in the rule
of Benedict for a wandering monk to confirm his stability
(which Peter regarded as a second profession) in a
monastery [112]. The Cluniac customaries and other sources
show that the benediction (or consecration) was not
repeated and that monks who came to Cluny after they had
been blessed elsewhere repeated only their profession [113]. The precise status of those who had made only
a profession, or simply wore the monastic habit without
having either made a profession or been blessed, was a mat-

---

(110) See p. 816 below.
(111) Ivo, Letter 41, ed. LECLERCQ, pp. 166-168. He compared this to the consecration of virgins, which could not be repeated.
(112) PETER THE VENERABLE, Letter 28, ed. GILES CONSTABLE, I, Cambridge (Mass.)
1967 (Harvard Historical Studies, 78), pp. 55 and 76-78.
(113) See n. 67 above.

808

ter of doubt, but there is no question that as the twelfth century progressed they were not considered to be fully monks [114].

III

The increasingly formal character of entry to religious life, and the requirement of both profession and consecration, was an important aspect of the development of monasticism in the eleventh and twelfth centuries, but it did not obliterate the traditional view of the monastic habit as the principal sign and symbol of religious life or the significance attached to the ceremony of vesting, which in some early sources was considered to be the single most important element in making a monk. The power that was seen by the desert father whose words were reported in the *Sayings of the Fathers* was over the habit with which a new monk was vested, and for Cassian every part of the habit was imbued with symbolic meaning, starting with the cowl which resembled a child's hood and stood for the innocence and simplicity of children [115]. This and other allegorical interpretations of the habit have been studied especially by scholars who see the vesting as a sacramental action through which, as Casel said, « Christ the crucified lived in the monk » [116].

The ceremony of putting off secular clothes and put-

(114) This seems to have been the status of lay-brothers (*conversi* of the new type), on which see HOFMEISTER, *Handgang*, p. 242, and *Marbach*, pp. 28-29, with references to earlier literature. According to the Cistercian *Capitula* XXI-XXII, the *conversi* made a profession in chapter after a year but were not allowed to become monks, which would have required benediction: JEAN DE LA CROIX BOUTON and JEAN BAPTISTE VAN DAMME, *Les plus anciens textes de Cîteaux*, Aachel 1974 (Cîteaux-Commentarii Cisterciensis. Studia et documenta, 2), p. 124.

(115) CASSIAN, *De institutis coenobiorum*, I, 3-7, ed. MICHAEL PETSCHENIG, Prague-Vienna-Leipzig 1888 (*C.S.E.L.*, 17), pp. 11-12; see OWEN CHADWICK, *John Cassian*, Cambridge 1950, pp. 60-61, who said that these interpretations were allegorical rather than practical in intent.

(116) CASEL, *Mönchsweihe*, pp. 6-7; see also OPPENHEIM, *Symbolik*, esp. pp. 1-27.

ting on the monastic habit was described by Pachomius, who said that after a novice had been instructed in good works he should join the brothers and be stripped of his secular clothing and clad in the habit of a monk [117], and by Cassian, who said that after the novice had been kept waiting in order to test his resolution he should be taken into the council of monks and

> should put off his own [clothes] and be dressed in the clothes of the monastery by the hand of the abbot, so that by this he will know not only that he has been despoiled of his former things but also that he has put aside all worldly pomp and descended into the poverty and necessity of Christ and that he should now be supported not by works sought in a secular manner and held over from his former infidelity but that he will receive the stipend of his service from the holy and pious grants of the monastery and, knowing that he will henceforth be clothed and fed therefrom, he will have nothing and yet will not be solicitous for the morrow [118].

The ceremony of vesting and divesting was thus for Cassian primarily a sign of the monk's dependency on the monastery and break with his former life. It was discussed in the rule of the Master, however, not in the chapters on dispropriation or profession but in that on the year of probation, at the end of which the novice was tonsured and changed from his secular clothes to « the holy clothes or sacred habit » [119]. In the rule of Benedict it was

---

(117) PACHOMIUS, Precept XLIX, ed. BOON, p. 26 (Greek text on pp. 174-175), and tr. VIELLEUX, p. 153, with notes on p. 187. The secular clothes were taken to the storeroom and kept « in the power of the ruler of the monastery ». On the ceremony of vesting in the East, see RAFFIN, Rituels, pp. 13-15, 17-19, and 154.

(118) CASSIAN, De institutis, IV, 5, ed. PETSCHENIG, pp. 50-51. Part of this passage was incorporated into the customs of Marbach, p. 102 (no. 2).

(119) R.M., XC, 79-80 and 83-86, ed. DE VOGÜÉ, II, pp. 392-394.

810

associated with dispropriation but took place immediately after the novice placed his petition on the altar. The fact that he kept his secular property and clothing during the noviciate and changed into the monastic habit only after making his promise and petition linked it more closely with the ceremony of admission than in either Cassian or the rule of the Master [120]. The habit became a symbol of the monk's new life, which as time went on was emphasized in specific ceremonies for blessing the vestments and in the accompanying prayers.

Putting on the monastic habit increasingly took on the character of an implicit vow [121]. It sometimes came before profession, as in the Romano-Germanic pontifical and the Winchester-Worcester pontifical and in a late eleventh- or early twelfth-century *ordo* for receiving canons from St Nazarius at Carcassonne, where the candidate after being examined for three months was led into the chapter and changed from secular to regular clothing before making his profession [122]. The vesting usually followed the profession, as in the rule of Benedict, but the exact nature and timing of the change of clothing varied from time to time and place to place [123]. Scholars are in particular disagreement over the type of clothes worn by novices in different houses at different periods. Bernard Ayglier of Monte Cassino in the thirteenth century referred

(120) According to DE VOGÜÉ, p. 1333, « La sequence déappropriation-vêture mérite particulièrement d'être soulignée, parce qu'elle trouve déjà chez Cassien », who established in *De institutis*, IV, 6 (ed. PETSCHENIG, pp. 51-52), that the secular clothes would be kept until it was clear that the new monk would stay in the monastery. According to *R.B.*, LVIII, it was to be kept in case he left either willingly or unwillingly.

(121) BOCK, *Promesse*, pp. 33-34.

(122) ELISABETH MAGNOU-NORTIER, *La société laïque et l'église dans la province ecclésiastique de Narbonne (zone cispyrénéenne) de la fin du VIIIᵉ à la fin du XIᵉ siècle*, Toulouse 1974 (Publications de l'Université de Toulouse-Le Mirail, A 20), pp. 635-636.

(123) VAN HAEFTEN, pp. 463-464 (V, 2, 2).

to the custom of vesting novices as modern [124], but long before this time many novices in both East and West wore some sort of habit, often without the cowl or scapular [125]. The practice of clothing novices with the entire monastic habit except the cowl may have originated with the Cluniacs [126], and it was rejected by the early Cistercians, whose novices were said to resemble the monks in all things except the monastic habit. When Bernard of Clairvaux's cousin Robert became a Cistercian monk, he put off his secular costume and received the habit of religion only at the time of profession, after a year as a novice [127]. In many houses, the cowl took on the significance with which the habit had previously been endowed, and the blessing of the habit was referred to as the blessing of the cowl [128]. At Marbach in the twelfth century the novice, who had taken off his own clothes and put on those of the monastery at the beginning of his noviciate, put on his secular clothing again so that he could be cloth-

---

(124) Differing versions of Bernard's text (of which the edition by A. CAPLET, Monte Cassino 1894, was unavailable to me) are printed by VAN HAEFTEN, p. 464 (« Nos autem de consuetudine moderna, utinam rationabili, in ipso ingressu probationis, et radimus et tonsuramus, et habitum induimus, non tamen benedictum ») and MARTÈNE, col. 837C (« Nos autem moderni de consuetudine, o utinam rationabili, in ipso ingressu probationis, et radimus, et tonsuramus, et habitum induimus, non tamen habitum benedictum »).

(125) MARTÈNE, coll. 837B-838D, collected various texts on the clothing of novices. On the practice in the East, see OPPENHEIM, *Symbolik*, pp. 1, 5, and 89, and the criticisms of PLACIDE DE MEESTER, *Autour de quelques publications récentes sur les habits des moines d'Orient*, « Ephemerides liturgicae », XLVII (1933), p. 450, who said, « Les novices eux-mêmes n'ont pas d'habits particuliers à leur condition ». On the different types of habits worn by Byzantine monks at various stages of monastic life, see RAFFIN, *Rituels*, pp. 31-32.

(126) BERNARD OF CLUNY, *Ordo Cluniacensis*, I, 15, in HERRGOTT, *Disciplina*, p. 165; ULRICH, *Cons. Clun.*, II, 1, in *P.L.*, CXLIX, col. 701C; LANFRANC, Decr. 102, ed. KNOWLES, p. 86: « Dehinc uestibus saecularibus exuatur et rebus monasterii regularibus praeter cucullam capitio assuto tunicae induatur »; see YEO, *Profession*, p. 204, citing Calmet's commentary on the *R.B.*.

(127) GUIGNARD, *Monuments*, p. 219, and BERNARD, Letter 1, ed. LECLERCQ, VII, p. 7.

(128) See *Lanalet*, pp. 46-47, and GEBHARD HÜRLIMANN, *Das Rheinauer Rituale* (Zürich Rh 114, Anfang 12. Jh.), Fribourg S. 1959 (Spicilegium Friburgense, 5), p. 147 (XXXIII). On the blessing of the cowl, see GRÄF, *Ad monachum faciendum*, p. 358, and WADDELL, *IIII Collecte*, pp. 127-129.

812

ed in the religious habit after it was blessed, and at Evesham and Bury in the thirteenth century the novices made their professions wearing tunics and frocks and carrying the cowls, which after their professions they laid before the abbot who blessed and asperged them and put them on the novices, raising them so as to cover their faces for the period of veiling [129].

The prayer in the *ordo* in the Romano-Germanic pontifical called on God, who promised to give the faithful « the vestment of salvation and the clothing of eternal joy », to bless « this clothing which signifies humility of heart and contempt for the world » and « the habit of blessed chastity » and to grant « that he whom You temporarily clothe with the vestments of the venerable promise may be clothed in blessed immortality ». In the second prayer the novice was said to put on the monastic habit « as a sign of the religious life which should be known » and « in order that he may be known among other men to be dedicated to You ». After being told by the abbot to put off the former man and put on the Lord Jesus Christ, he received from the abbot the clothing which Benedict had kept unimpaired « so that by imitating him you may be gathered into his assembly and come in perpetuity before the tribunal of Christ » [130]. The history and development of these prayers, some of which may have originated in the prayers for blessing the clothing of virgins, needs further study. In different versions of the prayer *Deus bonarum virtutum*

---

(129) *Marbach*, pp. 102 and 164 (nos. 2 and 130), see intro. pp. 21-22 and 33-34; *Evesham*, coll. 28 and 32-33; *The Customary of the Benedictine Abbey of Bury St Edmunds in Suffolk*, ed. ANTONIA GRANSDEN, n.p. 1973 (*H.B.S.*, 99), pp. 72-73. On the vesting of novices in the Premonstratensian order, see PLACIDE LEFÈVRE, *A propos du cérémonial de la vêture dans l'ordre de Prémontré*, « Analecta Praemonstratensia », XXXIII (1957), pp. 147-156, who maintained that there was a double vesting, of both postulants and novices, in opposition to G. Van den Broeck's view that there was no vesting at the time of entry, before the noviciate.

(130) *Pontifical romano-germanique*, pp. 70-71 (XXVIII, 2-6).

dator the habit was called « a sign of conserving chastity » (Alcuin), « a sign of conserving the monastic state and of blessed obedience » (the Dunstan, Lanalet, and Winchester-Worcester pontificals), and « a sign of conserving the rule» in the benedictional of Archbishop Robert and the missal of Robert of Jumièges, which went on to call it « the clothing signifying mortification of the flesh, humility of heart, and remorse and contempt for the world » [131]. This is an expanded version of the formula in the Romano-Germanic pontifical and also appears (without the reference to remorse) in the Canterbury pontifical, which also described the clothing as formed in figure of a cross:

Just as this clothing is an assimilation of Your blessed cross in our externals, so may it also be a crucifixion of the world in [our] interior things. ...Just as he [the novice] bears the manner of the holy cross external-ly in his clothing, so may he bear the memory of the same mystery internally in his mind [132].

At Einsiedeln in the late twelfth century the vestment was called « a salutary protection, mark of religion, beginning of sanctification, and powerful defense against all the enemy's darts », and in the Roman pontifical and many later *ordines* the prayer for the blessing of the habit (or cowl) referred to « this type of vestment which the holy fathers authorized those who renounce the world to wear as a sign of innocence and humility » [133].

---

(131) MARTÈNE, *De ritibus*, II, p. 162; *Lanalet*, pp. 46-47; MS Cambridge, C.C.C., 146, p. 151; *Archbishop Robert*, pp. 132-133; *Robert of Jumièges*, p. 284; see also GRÄF, *Ad monachum faciendum*, pp. 359-361.

(132) MS Cambridge, C.C.C., 44, pp. 314-315 and 320-321, where the habit was later referred to as « formam ...sanctissime et uenerande crucis » and « humilitatem sine simulatione » (p. 325).

(133) *Pontifical romain*, p. 175 (XVI, 6); *Marbach*, p. 165 (no. 131); *Rheinau*, p. 147 (XXXIII); *Einsiedeln*, p. 336; *Evesham*, col. 32. WADDELL, *IIII Collecte*, pp. 127-129, considered that it related exclusively to the cowl and traced it to the imagery of Cassian (n. 115 above).

814

The monastic habit thus came to be seen as the mark of religious life and the principal distinction between monks and other members of society. Oppenheim in his book on monastic clothing said that « the clothing of a monk is the clothing of an order », and later, in his book on the significance of monastic clothing, that « The clothing of a monk is not only the clothing of an order but also a holy clothing » [134]. Gregory the Great in the second book of the *Dialogues* wrote that Benedict « seeking to please God alone sought the habit of holy conversion (*conversio*) » and that he gave Romanus « the habit of the holy way of life (*conversatio*) » [135]. For some monks and nuns the habit was their only claim to lead a religious life. The early tenth century canonical collection in Vatican Lat. 1349, which comes from around Naples or Benevento, includes a canon « Concerning monks who exist only in habit (*solo habitu*) and will not avoid that » [136], and the tenth century hagiographer Letaldus of Micy referred to himself as « unworthy and a monk only in habit (*solo habitu*) » [137].

(134) OPPENHEIM, *Mönchskleid*, p. 247, and *Symbolik*, p. 145. See also M.-ANSELME DIMIER, *Observances monastiques*, « Analecta sacri ordinis Cisterciensis », XI (1955), pp. 178-182, who stressed the devotion of medieval monks to their habits, and WOLFGANG BRÜCKNER, *Sterben im Mönchsgewand. Zum Funktionswandel einer Totenkleidsitte*, in *Kontakte und Grenzen... Festschrift für Gerhard Heilfurth*, Göttingen 1959, pp. 264 and 268: « Das Mönchsgewand hat einen neuen Menschen geschaffen. ...Die Cuculle ist wie in der Sakramentenlehre das sichtbare Zeichen des quasi sakramentalen Aktes der Mönchwerdung ».

(135) GREGORY THE GREAT, *Dialogi*, II, prol., and II, 1, ed. UMBERTO MORICCA, Rome 1924 (Fonti per la storia d'Italia, 57), pp. 72 and 76.

(136) MS Vatican, Lat. 1349, f. 98ᵛ. The canon requires such monks to return to their monasteries or to join one where they will lead a regular life. I am indebted to Professor Stephan Kuttner and Dr Frederick Paxton for sending me photographs of this manuscript, of which only the headings were published by ANGELO MAI, in *P.L.*, CXXXVIII, col. 416C; see on this collection PAUL FOURNIER and GABRIEL LE BRAS, *Histoire des collections canoniques en occident depuis les fausses décretales jusqu'au Décret de Gratien*, I, Paris 1931, pp. 341-347.

(137) LETALDUS OF MICY, *Miracula sancti Martini Vertavensis*, prol., in *M.G.H., Scriptores rerum Merovingicarum*, ed. BRUNO KRUSCH, III, Hanover 1896, p. 567. I owe this reference to Dr Thomas Head.

Manegold of Lautenbach equated taking the habit of
religion with becoming a monk [138], and Anselm in his letter to Gunnilda said that before profession and consecration became customary any number of men and women
showed that they were monks or nuns only by their habit
(*solo habitu*) and were considered apostates if they gave
up « the habit which had been taken without profession or
consecration » [139]. In a letter entitled *That a monk cannot be saved when his habit has been abandoned* Franco
of Afflighem wrote, « A monk cannot cast off the habit of
his profession and take on the habit of a cleric without losing salvation; any habit other than that in which he was
professed has been made illicit for him » [140].

Canon lawyers also recognized the binding character of
wearing a religious habit and of living like a monk, even
without profession and consecration. The views of Ivo of
Chartres have already been studied. Alexander III in two
important decretals concerning marriage distinguished between a monk « who vowed himself to religion and made
a profession after the habit had been received » and one
who « neither received the habit nor made a profession but
only a vow and a promise to transfer to religion » and
decided, more explicitly, in a case concerning a widow who
remarried after changing her clothing and receiving the veil
(but without giving up her property, entering a cloister, or
making a formal profession or promise of obedience) that
« just as a simple vow prevents contracting a marriage but

---

(138) MANEGOLD OF LAUTENBACH, *Ad Gebehardum liber*, X, in *M.G.H.*, *Libelli de lite
imperatorum et pontificum*, ed. ERNST DÜMMLER a.o., I, Hanover 1891-1897, p. 329.

(139) See n. 102 above; *Marbach*, p. 21; and HILDEGARD OF BINGEN, Vision II, 5, 41,
in *Scivias*, ed. ADELGUNDIS FÜHRKÖTTER and ANGELA CARLEVARIS, Turnhout 1978
(*C.C.:C.M.*, 43), p. 209, where she referred to men who entered religious life « rejecting
not their own will but only their secular clothing ».

(140) FRANCO OF AFFLIGHEM, *Epistola*, in *P.L.*, CLXVI, col. 810C.

does not dissolve one already made, so a habit received without profession prevents its being contracted but does not dissolve one that has been made » [141]. Wearing a religious habit was considered a tacit profession down until the nineteenth century, in spite of Clement III's decree that « It is not the habit but the profession that makes a monk » [142]. This created particular difficulties for monks who had received the habit in the expectation of death in order to enter the next world clad as monks, but who subsequently recovered. Occasionally they were allowed to leave or to buy their way out of their obligations, or live as hermits, but as a rule they had to remain monks, showing that the habit taken *ad succurrendum* was no less binding than other ways of entering religious life [143]. At Springiersbach and Rolduc anyone who became a canon when he was either « apparently or truly » dying and who later recovered was required to go through the normal admission procedure [144]. There may also have been some uncertainty over the status of men who had been tonsured and clothed in the monastic habit against their wills, like the last Merovingian king, Childeric III. It is probable that deposed rulers were more frequently made clerics than monks in order to prevent their exercising secular power, but there is no reason to doubt that those who were put in monasteries remained there [145].

Every aspect of the monastic habit, in view of its importance, was given a special meaning and interpreta-

---

(141) GREGORY IX, Decr. cc. 3-4, X, IV, 6, ed. FRIEDBERG, II, p. 685.

(142) YEO, *Profession*, pp. 44-48 and 177-178.

(143) See LECLERCQ, *Vêture*, pp. 155-168, and JACQUES DUBOIS, *Une œuvre littéraire à Saint-Aubin d'Angers au XIIᵉ siècle: « La vie de saint Girard »*, in *La littérature angévine médiévale. Actes du colloque du samedi 22 mars 1980*, Angers 1981, p. 53.

(144) *Springiersbach-Rolduc*, pp. 148-149 (nos. 277-278).

(145) I am indebted for this to Professor Walter Goffart, who informs me that Childerich III is the only unambiguous instance of a ruler's disappearing into a monastery.

tion [146]. As a whole it was assimilated to the cross, though the sources are often unclear whether the cross was allegorical or whether it was literally given to a monk at the time of his profession or marked on his clothing, as with crusaders and in some religious orders in the West [147]. In the East Syriac rite of the ninth century, the monk bore a cross on his shoulder; William of Gellone when he became a monk was said to have put on « the apostolic vestment in the likeness of a cross »; and the prayer from the Canterbury pontifical stressed the interior assimilation of the monk to the exterior form of the cross symbolized by his clothing [148]. In the Ps-Anselmian *On likenesses* the cross-like shape of the habit was said to remind the monk of the Lord's passion and the fact that it stretched from head to foot to indicate his entire life [149]. In the *Book on conserving the unity of the church*, which was probably written by a monk of Hersfeld in the early 1090s, the cross of Christ was said to represent His whole life as well as His Passion. « In the sign of the cross is therefore described not only the entire life and institution of the monk but also every Christian action ». It compared the monastic habit to the mysteries of the cross: its breadth to the love of behaving

---

(146) See VAN HAEFTEN, pp. 542-546 (V, 10); OPPENHEIM, *Symbolik;* and RAFFIN, *Rituels,* p. 48, on the East, where SYMEON OF THESSALONICA (d. 1429), *De penitentia,* CCLXXIV, in *P.G.,* CLV, col. 499BC, compared the chlamys to the grave and the scapular and other vestments to the passion. The names of the various parts of the monastic costume changed during the early Middle Ages, and SMARAGDUS, p. 285, commenting on *R.B.,* LV, remarked on the various meanings of the terms *cuculla, cappa, casula* (with one and two l's), and *scapulare.*

(147) On the hand-cross used in profession ceremonies in the East, see FRANZ J. DÖLGER, *Das Kreuz bei der Mönchsweihe,* « Antike und Christentum », V (1936), pp. 291-292. See also n. 74 above.

(148) See nn. 74 and 132 above; *Vita* of William of Gellone, II, 23, in *AA. SS.,* 28 May VI, p. 817A; also VAN HAEFTEN, pp. 480-483 (V, 3, 5-6). HAMELIN OF ST ALBANS, *De monachatu,* in *Thesaurus novus,* V, p. 1454, said that the extension of the sleeves and cowl represented the cross.

(149) *De similitudinibus,* XCII, in *P.L.,* CLIX, col. 661B; see n. 98 above.

well, its length to the perseverance of adhering firmly, and its height to the contemplation of celestial life. « Just as [the term] monk is a certain word of mystery, so is the cowl also a certain strength of sacrament » [150]. The author of *On the professions of monks*, calling the cowl « a sign of innocence », said that the hood and hair-shirt indicated respectively the monk's abstention from love and worldly acts and the mortification of his flesh [151].

Another widely-used image for the clothing of monks was that of wings. Cassian in the *Institutes* compared the vestment of the monk to two wings, and the decree attributed to Pope Boniface IV on the monastic performance of pastoral work, which was probably written at the same time as the Ps-Gregorian decree, and is often found with it, asked, « Are not monks, like cherubim, covered by six wings ? » [152]. Peter Damiani cited both this decree and Isaiah 6.2, describing the six wings of the seraphim, in his *Apology of the monks against the canons*, where he argued that the costume of monks followed not only the fathers but also « the highest court of the heavens », since monks were covered by six wings, « two on the head, two to right and left, and two in front and behind » [153]. The image

---

(150) *Liber de unitate ecclesiae conservanda*, II, 42, in *M.G.H., Libelli de lite*, II, p. 278; see ZELINA ZAFARANA, *Ricerche sul « Liber de unitate ecclesiae conservanda »*, « Studi Medievali », 3rd ser., VII (1966), pp. 626-629, on the date and provenience.

(151) MARTÈNE, *De ritibus*, II, pp. 171-172.

(152) See n. 115 above on Cassian and n. 72 on the Ps-Bonifacian decree, which is edited in CONSTABLE, « *Hortatur nos* », pp. 574-575, and continued: « Due in capitio quo caput tegitur, ueris assertionibus demonstrat [demonstrantur]. Illud uero quod brachiis extenditur, alas duas esse dicimus; illud quo corpus absconditur [conditur, tegitur], alas duas. Sic sex alarum numerus certissimae conficitur ». This is the earliest known reference to this comparison, of which the sources are unknown. The phrase « ueris assertionibus demonstrat » shows that there was a traditional source for the first two wings, while « dicimus » suggests that the other two sets were less familiar and were perhaps new here. On this imagery, see VAN HAEFTEN, pp. 478 and 550 (V, 3, 3 and V, 10, 4), citing various sources, and JEAN LECLERCQ, *The Life of Perfection*, tr. LEONARD J. DOYLE, Collegeville 1961, p. 16.

(153) PETER DAMIANI, *Opusc.* XXVIII, 2, in *P.L.*, CXLV, col. 515AB.

was also cited by various writers in the twelfth century, including Conrad of Brunwiler, Rupert of Deutz, Honorius of Augsburg, and Otto of Freising, who said of the Cistercians:

> They place rough tunics next to their skin and over these other broader tunics with cowls consisting of six parts like as many wings, on the model of the seraphim. Covering their heads with two of these, those of the cowl; flying to supernatural things with two, those of the sleeves ...; covering the rest of their bodies with two, in front and behind ...they present themselves armed against all the fierce darts of the tempter [154].

The chronicler of Petershausen, who went down to 1156, compared the six wings respectively to contempt for the world, obedience, secrecy of life, silence, meditation, and assiduous prayer, each of which derived from the life of the apostles [155]. In the *Dialogue of two monks* by Idungus of Regensburg, the Cistercian criticized the Cluniac for having only four wings, lacking the sleeves or middle wings, and praised the Cistercian cowl for being in the shape of a cross [156].

The two images of a four-armed cross and a six-winged seraph were not entirely compatible and led to some disputes, since the more closely the monastic habit was identified with the life of religion, the more important any difference or change appeared to be. The strong feelings

---

(154) OTTO OF FREISING, *Chronica sive historia de duabus civitatibus*, VII, 35, ed. ADOLF HOFMEISTER, 2nd ed., Hanover-Leipzig 1912 (*M.G.H., Scriptores in usum scholarum* [45]), p. 372.

(155) *Die Chronik des Klosters Petershausen*, ed. and tr. OTTO FEGER, Landau-Constance 1956 (Schwäbische Chroniken der Stauferzeit, 3), p. 18.

(156) IDUNGUS OF REGENSBURG, *Dialogus*, III, ed HUYGENS, p. 465, see also p. 460, where he said, « The life of monks is apostolic, their habit is angelic, and the crown [tonsure] which they wear is the sign of perfection and the clerical sign ».

820

aroused by the differences in clothing among the various groups of reformed monks in the tenth and eleventh century, especially in the Empire, were studied by Kassius Hallinger in *Gorze-Kluny*. The monks in older reformed houses like Hersfeld used the knee-length scapular cowl, without arms, for work and the ankle-length robe cowl for ceremonies, whereas in Cluniac and neo-Cluniac houses like Hirsau, they were combined into what was known, perhaps echoing Isidore's *Etymologies*, as the *duplex vestis*, and the monks wore a distinctive type of long and full frock called a *laxa vestis*, which has long and wide arms [157]. According to the *Book on conserving the unity of the church*, which represented the older point of view,

> There has therefore been a long quarrel and discord among monks over the monastic clothing, and among those who seem to be more religious in their display, among these, I say, the name of the double costume is so solemn and celebrated and so holy and venerable that other monks living in monasteries are thought to be without merit and moment by these men, unless they wear this double robe of confusion.

He went on to compare the traditional habit to the cross and say that the short type of monastic costume, with bare arms, was previously used for work:

> This type of costume is now rare and unused among monks, however, since few or altogether no monks of this time strive in the manner of the fathers in labor or the exercise of work, as used to be done among the ancient fathers, so that they would receive into

---

(157) KASSIUS HALLINGER, *Gorze-Kluny. Studien zu den monastichen Lebensformen und Gegensätzen im Hochmittelalter*, II, Rome 1951 (Studia Anselmiana, 24-25), pp. 661-734. According to ISIDORE OF SEVILLE, *Etymologiae*, XIX, 24, 11, ed. W. M. LINDSAY, Oxford 1911, the *duplex amictus* was a Greek military costume.

their company no one unless he showed himself worthy of it by the exercise of works [158].

Religious clothing had a moral and historical as well as a spiritual significance, and the differences between the various types of religious life were indicated by their clothes. The hermit Wulfric of Hazelbury was given a corselet of chain-mail by a knight « as to a stronger knight » and wore it as a mark of his spiritual battle as well as a physical mortification until it slipped off his shoulders in old age [159]. The regular canon Ailbert, who founded Rolduc, wore « a moderate habit, neither poor nor rich, but tighter and shorter than is the modern use, hardly touching the top of his foot, such as the clergy used when religion was still flourishing in ancient times ». Under his tunic he wore a hair-shirt, and he put on shoes only when he celebrated mass [160]. This costume associated him with the ancient and, as he believed, apostolic custom and distinguished him, on the one hand, from the contemporary clerics and monks who wore long and flowing robes and, on the other, from the ostentatious poverty and raggedness of some of the reformers, like Robert of Arbrissel, who according to Marbod of Rennes entirely rejected the regular habit and dressed in skins and a cloak, with half-covered legs, bare feet, a long beard, and his hair cut across his forehead, « so that they say that you lack only a staff to make up the attire of a lunatic » [161]. This may have been

(158) *De unitate*, II, 42, in *Libelli de lite*, II, p. 276 and 279. See also the criticisms of the Cluniac costume and tonsure by the monks of Monte Cassino in *Die ältere Wormser Briefsammlung*, ed. WALTHER BULST, Weimar 1949 (*M.G.H., Die Briefe der deutschen Kaiserzeit*, 3), pp. 13-18, and in the chronicle of Lorsch, CXLII, in *Codex Laureshamensis*, ed. KARL GLÖCKNER, I, Darmstadt 1929. p. 420.

(159) JOHN OF FORD, *Wulfric of Hazelbury*, ed. MAURICE BELL, [Frame-London] 1933 (Somerset Record Society, 47), pp. 100, 124, and 143-146.

(160) *Annales Rodenses* (facsimile ed.), ed. P. C. BOEREN and G. W. A. PANHUYSEN, Assen 1968, p. 30 (f. 3^r).

(161) MARBOD OF RENNES, Letter 6, in *P.L.*, CLXXI, col. 1483CD; see JOHANNES VON

822

the usual costume of hermits and of penitents, pilgrims, and beggars, but not of monks, who were supposed to be set off by the sobriety as well as the simplicity of their dress and appearance [162].

Of all the disputes over monastic clothing, the most bitter was that which arose in the twelfth century over the type of cloth and, above all, its color. Since the beginnings of monasticism, different types of holy men and women had worn clothing of various colors and of natural and undyed cloth, and it is probable that many of the reformers at first paid little or no attention to the matter, since they wore clothes which were variously described as white, brown, or grey depending presumably on the color of the hair from which the cloth was woven and the cleanness of the garment [163]. After Otto of Freising cited the symbolism of the six parts of the monastic habit, he said of monks that

> They differ in this, however, that some in order to express contempt for the world wear only the same black clothing, but others who want no disputes over the color or thickness are accustomed to wear white or grey or other [colors], but lowly and rough [164].

WALTER, *Die ersten Wanderprediger Frankreichs*, I: *Robert von Arbrissel*, Leipzig 1903 (Studien zur Geschichte der Theologie und der Kirche, IX.3), p 186.

(162) See, generally, HENRI PLATELLE, *Le problème du scandale. Les nouvelles modes masculines aux XIe et XIIe siècles*, « Revue belge de philologie et d'histoire », LIII (1975), pp. 1071-1096, and, on beards, my intro. to BURCHARD OF BELLEVAUX, *Apologia de barbis*, ed. ROBERT B. C. HUYGENS, Turnhout 1985 (*C.C.:C.M.*, 62), pp. 114-130.

(163) VAN HAEFTEN, pp. 506-508 (V, 6, 1); OPPENHEIM, *Mönchskleid*, pp. 69-70 (and the criticisms of DE MEESTER, p. 448); and [MAURICE LAPORTE], *Aux sources de la vie cartusienne*, VI: *Sources des Consuetudines Cartusiae* (2), La Chartreuse 1967, pp. 473-479. See also B. JOLIET, *Essais d'iconographie monastique. De la couleur du vêtement de saint Benoît*, « Revue liturgique et bénédictine », I (1911), pp. 449-455, showing that Benedict himself was portrayed in various colors, and BRUNO SCHNEIDER, *Eine zeitgenössische Kritik zu Janauscheks « Originum Cistercensium tomus I »*, « Analecta Cisterciensia », XXI (1965) pp. 271-278, with references to previous literature.

(164) See n. 154 above. The *R.B.*, LV, established that « de quarum rerum omnium colore aut grossitudine non causentur monachi ».

The monks shown in the early Cistercian manuscripts in the municipal library at Dijon are wearing both brown and grey clothes, and Idungus in his *Dialogue of two monks* said that the Cistercian habit was neither black nor white but grey [165]. When Geoffrey of Savigny moved from one religious house to another, said his biographer, « He was clothed in the manner of the monastery of Savigny, where the monks use garments of grey color, after the black habit of his previous order had been changed », and Hamo of Savigny had a vision of the entire order of Savigny divided into three groups, one on the ground dressed in black, one above the ground in various colors, and one higher up in bright clothing [166]. Religious women also wore clothes of various colors. Guibert of Nogent's mother had clothes « of a natural color »; the use of expensive white clothing was condemned in the *Mirror of virgins*; and simple clothing of white, brown, or black was prescribed in the statutes of the hospital at Aubrac, which date from 1162 [167]. Black was worn by some of the reformed regular canons, as at Rolduc [168], and also at St Pierremont

---

(165) IDUNGUS OF REGENSBURG, *Dialogus*, III, ed HUYGENS, p. 460. The Cistercians were still referred to as « grey » and « the order of grey men » in REGINALD OF DURHAM, *Libellus de vita et miraculis S. Godrici de Finchale*, ed. J. STEVENSON, London-Edinburgh 1847 (Surtees Society, 20), pp. 174 and 185 (LXXVI, 164, and LXXXIV, 177), and by WILLIAM OF AEBEHOET, Letters, II, 46 and 48, writing in Denmark in the late twelfth century, in *Scriptores rerum danicarum Medii Aevi*, ed. J. LANGEBEK, VI, Copenhagen 1786, pp. 60-61.

(166) *Vitae BB. Vitalis et Gaufredi*, ed. E. P. SAUVAGE, Brussels 1882 (offprint from *Analecta Bollandiana*), p. 49, and *Vitae B. Petri Abrincensis et B. Hamonis monachorum coenobii Saviniacensis*, ed. E. P. SAUVAGE, Brussels 1883 (offprint from *Analecta Bollandiana*), pp. 87-88.

(167) GUIBERT OF NOGENT, *De vita sua*, ed. GEORGES BOURGIN, Paris 1907 (Collection de textes pour servir à l'étude et à l'enseignement de l'histoire), p. 50; MATTHÄUS BERNARDS, *Speculum virginum. Geistigkeit und Seelenleben der Frau im Hochmittelalter*, Cologne-Graz 1955 (Forschungen zur Volkeskunde, 36-38), pp. 161-163; LÉON LE GRAND, *Statuts d'hôtels-dieu et de léproseries*, Paris 1901 (Collection de textes pour servir à l'étude et à l'enseignment de l'histoire), p. 17 (c. 3).

(168) *Annales Rodenses*, p. 28 (f. 2ʳ).

824

in Lorraine, where the decision of Pope Eugene III allowing the canons to keep their black clothing even after a
Premonstratensian became abbot was confirmed by
Hadrian IV in 1155 after the abbot « did not fear to violate
the union of love among you by changing the costume, since
he presumed to expel some of your brothers from the
cloister, as they said, because they did not wish to receive
the vestments of the Premonstratensians or to change the
habit which they had assumed » [169].
The black habit was so well established in many
monasteries that the very act of changing the color was
seen as a mark of reform and as an implied criticism of the
previous type of life [170]. After Rupert of Deutz in his
commentary on the rule of Benedict said that the new
monks wore clothes of « off-white and of doubtful and
uncertain color » (which may be the earliest reference to
the reformers' change of color), he added somewhat bit-
terly, « Perhaps if we had used white clothes they would
now use black », and Orderic Vitalis said, « Modern monks
and regular clerics in order to show their greater
righteousness now reject the blackness which the early
fathers used as a mark of humility for both the cloaks of
the regular clerics and the cowls of the monks, and they
also seek to separate themselves from others by the unac-

---

*   (169) Augustin Calmet, *Histoire de Lorraine*, 2nd ed., IV, Nancy 1752, preuves p.
cccxlii (= *P.L.*, CLXXXVIII, col. 1372); Jaffé-Löwenfeld, no. 9969; see Michel Parisse,
Les chanoines réguliers en Lorraine. Fondations, expansion (XIᵉ-XIIᵉ siècles), « Annales
de l'Est », 5th ser., XX (1968), p. 362. On the Premonstratensian habit, see François
Petit, *Les vêtements des Prémontrés au XIIᵉ siècle*, « Analecta Praemonstratensia », XV
(1939), pp. 17-24, esp. p. 20 on the color. There is an account in the *Histoire littéraire
de la France*, XII, Paris 1763, of a letter of Hugh Farsit of Soissons in MS Paris, Bibl. nat.,
Lat. 2842, attacking the innovations of the Premonstratensians, including their clothing:
see *Bibliothèque nationale. Catalogue générale des manuscrits latins*, III, Paris 1952,
p. 145.
   (170) Van Haeften, p. 509 (V, 6, 3), traced the use of the term « black monk » to
England in the eighth century, when it was used to distinguish the continental from the
« white » Irish monks, but he said that it may have been used earlier on the continent.

customed cut of their clothes » [171]. Orderic mentioned in this connection a canon of Chartres named Pagan Bolotinus, who wrote a poem against the hypocrisy of the false hermits, associating their white clothing with their claim to novelty, and he later referred to hypocrites who « clad in white and varied garments deceive men and make a great spectacle to the people » [172]. The difference in color become a distinguishing point between the various orders, both monastic and clerical [173], and Peter the Venerable in his Letter 28 criticized the Cistercians for their white clothing:

> You saints, you singular men, you only true monks in the whole world, since all others are false and corrupt, you set yourselves alone among all according to the interpretations of the name, whence you also arrogate a habit of an unaccustomed color, and in distinction from all monks of almost the entire world, you present yourselves in white among those who are in black [174].

Thus the tables were turned within just over a generation, and the charge of self-righteousness in their costume that

(171) Rupert of Deutz, *In regulam sancti Benedicti*, III, 13, in *P.L.*, CLXX, col. 521; *The Ecclesiastical History of Oderic Vitalis*, VIII, 26, ed. Marjorie Chibnall, IV, Oxford 1969-1981 (Oxford Medieval Texts), pp. 311-312.

(172) Jean Leclercq, *Le poème de Payen Bolotin contre les faux ermites*, « Revue Bénédictine », LXVIII (1958), p. 56; Orderic Vitalis, *Historia*, VIII, 26, ed. Chibnall, IV, p. 327. Lambert of Ardres, *Historia comitum Ghisnenium*, CXLIII, in *M.G.H.*, *Scriptores* in fol., XXIV, Stuttgart 1879, p. 634, described a pseudo-pilgrim at Douai in 1176 who went around in white clothing and with white hair and beard, giving him an appearance of holiness.

(173) Herman of Tournai, *Liber de restauratione monasterii sancti Martini Tornacensis*, XXXVIII, in *M.G.H.*, *Scriptores* in fol., XIV, Stuttgart 1883, p. 290, commented on the dislike of clerics for the black monastic habit, and the author of a sermon attributed to Peter of Poitiers in MS Paris, Bibl. nat., Lat. 13575, distinguished the order of monks « qui propter colorem uestis niger uoceatur » from those who wore white: see Barthélemy Hauréau, *Notices et extraits de quelques manuscrits latins de la Bibliothèque nationale*, II, Paris 1890-1893, pp. 227-228.

(174) Peter the Venerable, Letter 28, ed. Constable, I, p. 57, see notes in II, p. 116.

826

was brought against the Cluniacs in the *Book on conserving the unity of the church* was now brought by the Cluniacs against the Cistercians. A few years later, in Letter 111, Peter the Venerable wrote, again to Bernard of Clairvaux:

> I have seen I know not how many black monks laughing at a white monk whom they meet as if he were a monster and showing by their voices and gestures they are amazed as if a chimaera or centaur or some travelling monster came before their eyes. I have on the other hand seen white monks who were previously talking and constantly telling each other what was going on suddenly become quiet when a black monk comes by and take the precaution of silence for themselves as if from enemy spies who are searching for the secrets of enemies [175].

The rule of Benedict forbade monks to dispute over the color or thickness of their clothes, and many well-meaning efforts were made to defuse the issue in the twelfth century. « Different people say different things about the difference in vestments », wrote the regular canon Hugh of Fouilloy, who stressed that in clothing the four evils of « baseness and superfluity, poverty and richness » should be equally avoided [176]. It became a topos that virtue and salvation did not depend on clothing. « The chalor [of faith] not the color of clothes is considered in it [the rule of Benedict] » [177]; « It should be known above all that the sign of religion rather than the virtue of holiness is in the habit » [178]; « Religion is not in the clothing but in the

---

(175) PETER THE VENERABLE, Letter 111, ed. CONSTABLE, I, pp. 285-286.

(176) HUGH OF FOUILLOY, *De claustro animae*, II, 8, in *P.L.*, CLXXVI, col. 1056BC.

(177) HUGH OF KIRKSTALL, *Narratio de fundatione Fontanis monasterii*, in *Memorials of the Abbey of St. Mary of Fountains*, ed. JOHN R. WALBRAN, I, Durham 1863 (Surtees Society, 42), p. 16.

(178) GODWIN OF SALISBURY, *Meditationes*, in MS Oxford, Bodleian Library, Digby 96, f. 22ᵛ. On Godwin, who was precentor of Salisbury in the early twelfth century and

heart » [179]; « The Kingdom of God is not the pallium or the tunic but justice and peace and joy in the Holy Spirit » [180]; « He who makes no distinction between Jew and Greek does not distinguish between the white and the black habit; the Lord considers the mind not the vestment, merits not color » [181]; and religion in the *Ancrene Riwle* lay in keeping oneself unspotted by the world, « not in a wide hood or a black cape, nor in a white mantle or a grey cowl » [182]. According to Norbert of Xanten, the rule of Augustine covered all that was necessary for salvation,

> Because if there is a controversy among some spiritual men concerning the color or thickness or softness of clothing, let those who take the opportunity of disparaging [others] on this account indicate from this rule — let them, I say, indicate from the institution of the Gospel and the apostles — where the whiteness, blackness, softness, or thickness is described in giving a precept, and then they should be believed [183].

It was not easy to ignore the change, however, or the significance attached to various types and color of cloth. Bonizo of Sutri in his *Book of Christian life*, written at the end of the eleventh century, criticized monks who loved

whose « meditations » are really a series of sermons, see KATHLEEN EDWARDS, *The English Secular Cathedrals in the Middle Ages*, 2nd ed., Manchester-New York 1967, pp. 4, 7, and 183 n.

(179) ANDRÉ WILMART, *Une riposte de l'ancien monachisme au manifeste de saint Bernard*, « Revue Bénédictine », XLVI (1934), p. 343; cf. *De vita vere apostolica*, II, in *Veterum scriptorum et monumentorum ... amplissima collectio*, ed. EDMOND MARTÈNE and URSIN DURAND, IX, Paris 1724-1733, p. 992; and SIMEON OF DURHAM, *Vita Bartholomaei Farnensis*, IX, in *Opera omnia*, ed. THOMAS ARNOLD, London 1882 (Rolls Series, 75), p. 301: « Non in veste scilicet sed in corde monachi omnem vigere consummationem mandatorum Dei ».

(180) H.-M. ROCHAIS and R. M. IRÈNE BINONT, *La collection de textes divers du manuscrit Lincoln 201 et Saint Bernard*, « Sacris Erudiri », XV (1964), p. 143 (Lc 32), citing Rom. 14.17.

(181) PETER OF BLOIS, Letter 97, ed. GILES, I, p. 305.

(182) *The Ancren Riwle*, ed. and tr. JAMES MORTON, London 1853 (Camden Society, 57), p. 11, and tr. M. B. SALU, London 1955, p. 5.

(183) *Vita B* of Norbert of Xanten, IX, 52, in *P.L.*, CLXX, col. 1293A.

themselves more than God and enjoyed sumptuous meals and gloried in « rich although dark-colored clothes » [184], and Philip of Harvengt praised the Cistercians who « assumed a coarser [clothing] of another color », unsoftened and un-dyed, in contrast to the modern monks who « have turned the style and color of the habit, which earlier monks adopted to show the grief of penance or sadness, into comforts and arrogance » [185]. According to one of the replies written (perhaps by Hugh of Rouen) to refute the charges against Cluny, the monks of Tiron wore grey and the Cistercians white « either because they found nothing cheaper to buy in their regions or because whiteness in clothing might indicate chastity of the body » [186], and a prior of Ste-Barbe who became a Cistercian said that his white clothes were no better than his old black ones except that, being humbler and cheaper, they professed « a stricter life than that of the people living comfortably in the world » [187]. Even Norbert, after trying to calm the controversy, went on to say that the regular canons wore white like the angels, wool like penitents, and linen in the sanctuary, though he denied that they did so in order to disparage others.

The symbolism of black and white was too deeply embedded to be easily eradicated or overlooked. « Symbolize whatever grand or gracious thing he will by whiteness », wrote Melville in *Moby Dick*, « no man can deny that in its profoundest idealized significance it calls up a peculiar apparition to the soul » [188]. Christ appeared

(184) BONIZO OF SUTRI, *Liber de vita christiana*, X, 78, ed. ERNST PERELS, Berlin 1930 (Texte zur Geschichte des römischen and kanonischen Rechts im Mittelalter, 1), p. 333.

(185) PHILIP OF HARVENGT, *De institutione clericorum*, IV: *De continentia clericorum*, 125, in *P.L.*, CCIII, col. 836BC.

(186) WILMART, *Riposte*, p. 340.

(187) *Amplissima collectio*, I, p. 783B, see also 786CD.

(188) HERMAN MELVILLE, *Moby Dick*, ch.. 42; cf. ch. 8 on « Snow, and the Quality of Whiteness » in W. H. HUDSON, *Idle Days in Patagonia*. On the symbolism of colors in the Middle Ages, see M.-D. CHENU, *La théologie au douzième siècle*, Paris 1957 (Etudes de philosophie médiévale, 45), p. 163.

in a white robe at the Transfiguration, and white was worn by the angels and by Christ, the elders, and those who win victory in the Apocalypse [189]. White was thus associated with resurrection, exaltation, glory, and victory, and also with purity, innocence, chastity, and love, and with success, joy, happiness, and goodness [190]. The white robes of the Premonstratensians, said Philip of Harvengt, showed « the grace of remission that has been received » and « the hoped-for glory of celestial joy », and Walter Daniel in his *Life* of Ailred of Rievaulx said that the Cistercians were « white in clothing and in name, for they took the name from the fact that they were clothed in angelic fashion in pure wool spun into thread and woven into cloth without dye of any color » [191]. Black on the other hand was associated with abjection, contempt for the world, penance, adversity, self-abasement, consciousness of sin, humility, sadness, and death [192]. Abelard wrote, « The blackness, that is of bodily tribulations, easily turns the minds of

---

(189) PER BESKOW, *Rex Gloriae: The Kingship of Christ in the Early Church*, Uppsala 1962, pp. 151-152.

(190) See ANDRÉ G. OTT, *Etude sur les couleurs en vieux français*, Paris 1899, pp. 1-18; OPPENHEIM, *Symbolik*, pp. 33-43 and 100; *Marbach*, pp. 47-48; and, in addition to the sources cited elsewhere, the letter to the prior of La Charité in *P.L.*, CCXIII, col. 718D; ANSELM OF HAVELBERG, *De ordine canonicorum*, X, in PEZ, *Thesaurus*, IV.2, p. 89; LÉOPOLD DELISLE, *Rouleaux des morts du IXe au XVe siècle*, Paris 1866 (Société de l'histoire de France, 11), p. 333 (XXXVIII, 173).

(191) PHILIP OF HARVENGT, *De institutione clericorum*, IV: *De continentia clericorum*, CXXVII, in *P.L.*, CCIII, col. 838D (and 838-840 on the symbolism of white), and WALTER DANIEL, *The Life of Aelred of Rievaulx*, tr. F. M. POWICKE, London-Edinburgh 1950 ([Nelson's] Medieval Classics), p. 10. ADAM OF DRYBURGH, *Liber de ordine*, Serm. III, 10, and IV, 2, in *P.L.*, CXCVIII, coll. 468AC and 470D, said that white robes were worn by the elect « in the brightness of future remuneration » and as evidence that they would pass « from whiteness to whiteness ... from the merit to the reward, so that we may confidently hope that if in the present we wear the albs of justice we may in the future wear the albs of glory ».

(192) See VAN HAEFTEN, pp. 545-548 (V, 10, 2); OTT, *Couleurs*, pp. 19-33; OPPENHEIM, *Symbolik*, pp. 29-33 and 100; and in addition to the sources cited elsewhere, *De similitudinibus*, XCII, in *P.L.*, CLIX, col 661B; ORDERIC VITALIS, *Historia*, VIII, 28, ed. CHIBNALL, IV, pp. 311-312; and *The Customary of the Benedictine Abbey of Eynsham in Oxfordshire*, ed. ANTONIA GRANSDEN, Siegburg 1963 (*C.C.M.*, 2), p. 55 (no. 49).

830

faithful men from the love of worldly things, raising them
to the desires of eternal life, and often draws them from
the tumultuous life of the world towards the secret of contemplation » [193]. And Philip of Harvengt, in spite of his
praise for the white clothing of the canons, also praised the
desire of the black monks to keep their habit, which expelled darkness from their minds by reminding them of the
ancient blackness and makes them glory in the present « as
much more securely as more humbly. Thus [they are] dark
externally in a black and rough habit but filled with the
internal light of the mind » [194].

These examples show that the comparisons of the two
colors and of the types of religious life for which they stood
were usually disparaging to one or the other. « Useful
black is better than useless white », said Hamelin of St
Albans, and the monk who replied to Theobald of Etampes
compared clerics to white salt and monks to black pepper,
which he said « is costlier and more rarely found [than
salt] » [195]. Nicholas of Montiéramey on the other hand contrasted « the shade of the Cluniacs » with « the purity of the
Cistercians » [196]. As time went on, the comparisons
became more fanciful, as when Walter Daniel compared the
Cistercians to flocks of quail and the whiteness of snow and

---

(193) ABELARD, Letter IV to Heloise, ed. J. T. MUCKLE, in « Medieval Studies », XV
(1953), p. 85, see p. 84 on the significance of black. In Letter VI, ibid., XVIII (1956), p.
281, Abelard used the phrase « nulli vero panni magis quam nigri lugubrem paenitentiae
habitum decent », which with one change of word order appears in Serm. 15 of Geoffrey
of St Thierry in MSS Paris, Bibl. nat., Lat. 3563, f. 20ᵛB, and 13586, p. 46, for photographs
of which I am indebted to the Rev. Dr Robert Sullivan. Since Abelard and Geoffrey were
probably writing independently, they must have drawn on a common source.
(194) PHILIP OF HARVENGT, De institutione clericorum, IV: De continentia clericorum,
C, in P.L., CCIII, col. 803BC.
(195) HAMELIN OF ST ALBANS, De monachatu, in Thesaurus novus, V, p. 1454, and
RAYMONDE FOREVILLE and JEAN LECLERCQ, Un débat sur le sacerdoce des moines au XIIᵉ
siècle, in Analecta monastica, IV, Rome 1957 (Studia Anselmiana, 41), p. 90.
(196) NICHOLAS OF MONTIÉRAMEY, Letter 7, in P.L., CXCVI, col. 1603BC.

Joachim of Fiore called the Cistercians doves and the black monks crows [197]. In the early thirteenth century William the Breton in the *Philippides* compared the white and black monks to the lilies and nettles of the prophecy of Merlin, and Matthew of Rievaulx called the Cistercians gold and the black monks silver [198]. In Odo of Cheriton's fable « Concerning the quarrel of the white sheep, the black sheep, the donkey, and the goat », each of whom claimed to be holier than the others, the white sheep stood for those who wore the white vestments of cleanness and innocence, like the Cistercians, Premonstratensians, and Trinitarians; the black sheep for those who wore black and claimed, echoing the Song of Songs, to be black outside but beautiful inside; the donkey with a cross on its shoulders, like Christ, for the Hospitalers and Templars; and the goat, with a hair-shirt and beard, for the Grandmontines and Cistercian lay-brothers. External appearances make no one holy, however, Odo said, unless « they have grace in their hearts and a good life before God and men », and he ended with a verse which can be very approximately rendered:

If bearded men by beards are blessed,
The goat's more holy than the rest.
No saint was made by white or black
Or donkey's cross upon his back [199].

(197) In the edition of Walter Daniel cited n. 191 above, Powicke translated *conturnix* as « sea-gull »; CIPRIANO BARAUT, *Un tratado inédito de Joaquín de Fiore: De vita sancti Benedicti et de officio divino secundum eius doctrinam*, « Analecta sacra Tarraconensia », XXIV (1951), pp. 48-50 (c. 4).

(198) WILLIAM LE BRETON, *Philippides*, VIII, 904-905, in *Oeuvres de Rigord et de Guillaume le Breton, historiens de Philippe-Auguste*, ed. H. FRANÇOIS DELABORDE, II, Paris 1885 (Société de l'histoire de France), p. 244, and ANDRÉ WILMART, *Les mélanges de Mathieu préchantre de Rievaulx au début du XIIIᵉ siècle*, « Revue Bénédictine », LII (1940), pp. 63-64.

(199) ODO OF CHERITON, Fable LII, in LÉOPOLD HERVIEUX, *Les fabulistes latins*, IV: *Eudes de Cheriton et ses dérivés*, Paris 1896, pp. 223-224.

832

IV

This fable forms a suitable conclusion for my paper because it shows at the same time the continued importance attached to the habit and the outward signs of religious life, which for many people still summed up what it meant to be a member of a religious community, and also the waning confidence put in them not only by satirical moralists like Odo of Cheriton but also by serious churchmen and religious reformers, who looked back after almost a thousand years of change and development to the age of the primitive church when, as they believed, monks and nuns were esteemed for their simplicity of life and inner holiness rather than for their outward appearance and behaviour. In the early Middle Ages, when appearance not only represented but was identified with reality, many of the deepest values of society were expressed in its rituals, which gave continuity and meaning to human behaviour by bringing the relevant past into the present and linking it to a divinely-ordained future. During the great age of medieval monasticism, from the ninth to the twelfth century, the highest standard of Christian life, and the aspiration of innumerable individual monks and nuns, were embodied in the liturgy of the church and the framework of monastic life. Every detail of the ceremony of entry to a religious community and of the monastic habit was related both to the life of the community, and its ultimate purpose, and to the role and position of the individual within it. Entering a monastery and putting on the habit was a second baptism which mediated between the novice's previous life and the new life which he entered, cleansed of sin and reformed in the image of God. It was a ritual of reconciliation, or of resolution of conflict, and the monastic habit transmitted the experience of the divine. Wearing it was to conform to the life of the angels, the seraphim, and the cherubim, and to lead the life of Christ on the cross, which gave meaning and hope to the individual as it did to society as a whole. The inner *persona* of the monk or nun was shaped by the outer ceremonies and signs, and the essence of their religious life was expressed by its symbols.

Some time after the turn of the millenium, for reasons which are far from clear, this confidence in the meaning and efficacy of ritual began to wane. There are signs of a sense of division between the essence and the forms of religious life, and a growing belief that to be a monk it was no longer enough to live and look like one. This was reflected both in the emphasis on formality in the entry to religious life, as in the requirement of profession and consecration, and in the concentration on the inner feelings of which the outer actions and appearances should be an expression. In prayer, the mind was no longer expected to conform to the words so much as the words to the mind and heart, where God's real concern lay [200]. An ideal of inner conformity did not replace one of outer conformity, since there had been no clear division between the two in the early Middle Ages, but there was a realization in the eleventh and twelfth centuries of the distinction between them. The outward forms of monastic life did not disappear, and are still of importance today, but they took on a new significance as they were seen as distinct from, and sometimes at variance with, the inner life of monks and

(200) See the articles by DE Boer and Szövérffy cited n. 8 above and my article on *The Concern for Sincerity and Understanding in Liturgical Prayer, especially in the Twelfth Century*, in *Classica et Mediaevalia: Studies in Honour of Joseph Szövérffy*, ed. IRENE VASLEF and HELMUT BUSCHHAUSEN, Washington-Leyden 1986 (Medieval Classics: Texts and Studies, 20), pp. 17-30.

834

nuns. The breakdown of the early medieval sense of coherence between inner and outer forms, and its expression in ritual, marked a turning point in the history of monasticism as it did in the history of the church and of Christian society as a whole.

VIII

The diversity of religious life and acceptance of social pluralism in the twelfth century*

When the prelates at the Fourth Lateran Council forbade the foundation of new religious orders and required anyone who wanted to enter religious life to choose a house of an approved order and any new religious house to follow the rule of an approved order, they gave as the reason 'lest the excessive diversity of religions should introduce grave confusion into the church of God'.[1] This decree reflected a widespread concern in the late twelfth and early thirteenth centuries, but it tried to close the stable door after the horse was out. The creation of new religious houses and orders had already for over a century presented an unprecedented challenge to the values and order of the medieval church. The reformers of the eleventh and twelfth centuries, as Knowles put it,

split the single traditional version of the monastic life into twenty different divisions, as it were the colours of the spectrum, each realizing a potentiality implicit in the monastic life but neglected by most contemporary manifestations, and thus meeting a need in the more complex and articulated society of the later Middle Ages.[2]

* This essay is a revised version of a paper presented at the conference on 'Consciousness and Group Identification in High Medieval Religion' at York University, Toronto, on 7–9 April 1978. It benefited from the comments of several participants, especially Professor Caroline Bynum and the Rev. Leonard Boyle. The abbreviations *PL* and *MGH* will be used in the notes for, respectively, the *Patrologia latina* and *Monumenta Germaniae historica*.

[1] IV Lateran (1215) can. 13, in Giuseppe Alberigo (ed.), *Conciliorum oecumenicorum decreta*, 3rd edn (Bologna, 1973), p. 242. See Raymonde Foreville, *Latran I, II, III et Latran IV* (Histoire des conciles oecuméniques, VI; Paris, 1965), pp. 296–7: 'Il concerne seulement l'organisation élémentaire de toute maison religieuse, et la Règle fondamentale susceptible d'orienter toute nouvelle fondation soit vers l'*ordo monasticus*, soit vers l'*ordo canonicus*.'

[2] David Knowles, *From Pachomius to Ignatius: A Study in the Constitutional History of the Religious Orders* (Sarum Lectures, 1964–5; Oxford, 1966), p. 16. The shift is reflected in the titles of the successive parts of Knowles's history of monasticism in England, of which the first volume, which goes to 1215, was entitled *The Monastic Order in England* and the following volumes, *The Religious Orders in England*.

The unity of the monastic order and pre-eminence of the religious way of life were so widely accepted in the early Middle Ages that it was hard for people to accept this diversity in the forms of religious life, each claiming to embody the highest ideal of Christian life on earth and to be the surest way to salvation. Out of this confusion, which the Council sought to avert by prohibiting new orders, there developed a tolerance and, later, approval of religious diversity, which was an important aspect of the pluralism of modern European society and of the ever-accelerating movement, as Henry Adams saw it, from unity to multiplicity.[3]

Differences in ideas and customs were recognized in the early Middle Ages but were commonly fitted into a framework of underlying unity. The lapidary formula *diversi sed non adversi*, which at least one scholar has called magical, was first used by Anselm of Laon in 1117, but the idea behind it is found in the Church Fathers and in writers of classical antiquity.[4] Quintilian's view of the difficulty of choosing between the differing opinions of earlier writers may have inspired Ambrosiaster, when he said that the apparently contradictory words of the Evangelists did not disagree in meaning, and Ambrose, who wrote, 'Although the Evangelists do not seem to have said contrary things, they said diverse things.'[5] Cassiodorus applied this principle to the writings of the Church Fathers, who 'said not contrary but diverse things';[6] and Gregory the Great used it to accommodate the differences in ecclesiastical customs and liturgical usages of the early medieval

---

[3] See the last paragraph of chapter 34, entitled 'A Law of Acceleration (1904)', of Henry Adams, *The Education of Henry Adams*: 'The movement from unity into multiplicity, between 1200 and 1900, was unbroken in sequence, and rapid in acceleration. Prolonged one generation longer, it would require a new social mind.' I am indebted for this reference to Professor Charles Connell of West Virginia University.

[4] There is a considerable scholarly literature, and some disagreement, on this subject: see especially J. de Ghellinck, *Le Mouvement théologique du XIIe siècle*, 2nd edn (Museum Lessianum: Section historique, x; Brussels – Paris, 1948), pp. 517–23; Henri de Lubac, 'A Propos de la formule: *Diversi, sed non adversi*', *Recherches de science religieuse*, XL (1952), pp. 27–40; Paul Meyvaert, 'Diversity within Unity, a Gregorian Theme', *Heythrop Journal*, IV (1963), pp. 141–62, reprinted in his *Benedict, Gregory, and Others* (Variorum Reprint CS61; London, 1977); and Hubert Silvestre, 'Diversi sed non adversi', *Recherches de théologie ancienne et médiévale*, XXXI (1964), pp. 124–32, and *Revue d'histoire ecclésiastique*, LX (1965), pp. 987–8. Carolly Erickson, *The Medieval Vision* (New York, 1976), pp. 53–4, commented on its use by Hugo Metellus and by Abelard, saying that 'Clearly the motto meant different things to them.'

[5] Silvestre, 'Diversi', pp. 130–1, who also suggested that Martianus Capella's definition of *differentia* 'quae res inter se diversas, non adversas ostendit' (which derives from Cicero) may have inspired the formula of Anselm of Laon.

[6] Cassiodorus, *De institutione divinarum litterarum*, XIV, ed. R. A. B. Mynors (Oxford, 1937), p. 40, cited by Silvestre, 'Diversi', p. 131. Cassiodorus mentioned Hilary of Poitiers, Rufinus, Epiphanius, and the councils of Nicaea and Chalcedon.

Religious life in the twelfth century

church. Among the questions addressed in Gregory's *Libellus responsionum* was: 'Are there varying customs in the churches, even though the faith is one, and is there one form of mass in the Holy Roman Church and another in the Gallic churches?'[7] In his reply, and also in the *Regula pastoralis* and *Moralia* on Job, Gregory stressed the theme of diversity within unity, basing it on Christ's description of the many mansions in His Father's house and on the principle of the diversity of individual gifts. For Gregory the universal church itself, Meyvaert said, 'consisted of a plurality or diversity of churches'.[8]

Isidore of Seville expressed the same view, in a negative way, when he commented, referring to how monks wore their hair, that 'It is wrong to have a different style, where there is not a different way of life.'[9] He thereby implied that people who lived differently might wear their hair differently. Hair-style was in fact an important mark of social, ethnic, and regional diversity in the early Middle Ages. In the ninth century the question of whether or not priests should shave became a major point of controversy between the Greek and Latin churches. Ratramnus of Corbie in his *Contra Graecorum opposita Romanam ecclesiam infamantium* said: 'This usage of clerics [cutting the hair and beard] is not uniform in all churches and varies and diverges according to the custom of the greater ones', and his contemporary Bishop Eneas of Paris argued that different peoples might follow different customs 'so long as it does not depart from the catholic faith'.[10] Two centuries later Pope Leo IX made the same point in a letter to the patriarch of Constantinople: 'For it should be known that differing customs according to time and place are no obstacle to the salvation of believers, provided one faith...commends all people to one God.'[11] Regino of Prüm in the preface to his *De synodalibus causis*, written about 900, said:

Just as different nations of peoples differ from each other in descent, customs, language, [and] laws, so the holy universal church diffused over the whole world of lands, though joined in the unity of faith, differs within itself in ecclesiastical customs. Various customs in ecclesiastical offices are found in the kingdoms of the Gauls and of Germany, others in the eastern kingdoms, [and] in the lands across the sea.[12]

---

[7] Bede, *Historia ecclesiastica gentis Anglorum*, I, 27, ed. Bertram Colgrave and R. A. B. Mynors (Oxford Medieval Texts; Oxford, 1969), p. 80. Colgrave translated this as two separate questions; Meyvaert, 'Diversity', p. 144, made it into a single statement.

[8] Meyvaert, 'Diversity', p. 155, who said later (p. 162) that 'the era of unity on the basis of uniformity' began in the eighth century, when there was 'a deliberate policy of unification in the domain of the liturgy'.

[9] Isidore of Seville, *Regula monachorum*, XII, 4, in *PL*, LXXXIII, 883A.

[10] Ratramnus of Corbie, *Contra Graecorum opposita*, IV, 5, in *PL*, CXXI, 322C; Eneas of Paris, *Liber adversus Graecos*, CLXXXVI, *ibid.*, 747C.

[11] *PL*, CXLIII, 764B.

[12] Regino of Prüm, *De synodalibus causis*, pref., ed. F. G. A. Wasserschleben (Leipzig, 1840), p. 2.

This acceptance of diversity with regard to ideas and customs did not extend to religious beliefs and standards of perfection, concerning which there was a wide measure of agreement in the early Middle Ages.[13] A life of prayer, withdrawal from secular life, and dedication to God was almost universally regarded as the highest ideal of life on earth, and monks and nuns were seen as a distinct order of society, superior to both the clergy and the laity. This professional division of society into monks, clerics, and laymen, as well as the later occupational division into those who prayed, fought, and worked, regarded monks as primarily responsible for the spiritual welfare of society. Most monks at that time were not in holy orders and were forbidden to perform clerical duties without special permission. Their function was to do the work of God, and above all to pray. The concern of the Carolingian rulers for monastic regularity was largely owing to their desire to win the favour of God for themselves and for their realm.[14] William of Aquitaine founded the abbey of Cluny, according to his foundation charter, out of love for God and concern for the souls of the king, himself, his family and followers, 'and for the state and integrity of the catholic religion'.[15] The caritative activities of monks, though mentioned in the charter, were secondary in William's mind.

This unity in theory and purpose was compatible with a high degree of variety in practice. Especially in the so-called period of the mixed rule, from the sixth to the eighth centuries, every house had in effect its own rule and was held together by loyalty to the memory of the founder, adherence to its own traditions, and dependence on its own special spiritual and secular patrons. Even after the general acceptance of the Rule of Benedict in the ninth century, there was probably less uniformity between individual houses than many contemporary reformers, and some later scholars, have claimed. During this period, however, the first signs of a stress on uniformity of

[13] See Silvestre, in *Rev. d'hist. ecc.*, LX, p. 987: 'Celle-ci connut un grand succès au moyen âge et déjà, sous des formes approchantes, à la période patristique, soit qu'on l'appliquât aux divergences constatées dans la Bible, soit qu'elle visât les désaccords entre les Pères eux-mêmes, soit qu'on y eût recours à propos d'une différence d'opinions plus apparente que réelle sur un sujet quelconque.'

[14] Charlemagne's famous capitulary *De literis colendis* is concerned not with the general level of education among his subjects, as is often said, or even of teachers and preachers, but specifically with the education of monks – 'our faithful orators' – upon the correctness of whose prayers the welfare of the empire depended: *MGH, Leges: Capitularia regum Francorum*, 2 vols. (1883–97), I, p. 79, no. 29. See F. L. Ganshof, *Recherches sur les capitulaires* (Paris, 1958), pp. 45–6, and Luitpold Wallach, *Alcuin and Charlemagne: Studies in Carolingian History and Literature* (Cornell Studies in Classical Philology, XXXII; Ithaca, NY, 1959), p. 214.

[15] *Recueil des chartes de l'abbaye de Cluny*, ed. A. Bernard and A. Bruel, 6 vols. (Collection de documents inédits sur l'histoire de France; Paris, 1876–1903), I, p. 125, no. 112.

Religious life in the twelfth century

practice among special groups of monasteries, often to the exclusion of other houses, can be seen in the emergence of systematized collections of customs.[16] Cluny in the late tenth and eleventh centuries produced four distinct customaries, which established the type of monasticism known as Cluniac and defined the order of Cluny and later orders which were influenced by it.[17] The interdependence of the three orders of society is emphasized in two speeches attributed respectively to Bishops Burchard of Worms and Gerard of Cambrai in the early eleventh century. When Burchard saw the number of clerics entering monasteries in his diocese, he allegedly brought together monks from several houses and told them

that everyone who fears God and acts justly is acceptable to Him, not only the monk but also the canon and likewise the layman. It is not good for all who work on a ship to insist on the same occupation, as if there were either all pilots and no sailor or all sailors and no pilot... We should likewise recognize, brothers, that we cannot all do everything. For if everyone were monks and canons, where would be the laymen? ... For the family in the church of God is diverse, [including] not only monks but also canons and faithful laymen... A canon may not therefore leave his monastery for the monastic life without permission; but he should labour in common with his brothers; and if he desires to lead a stricter life, let him attend to works pleasing to God within his own monastery.[18]

Burchard here had in mind the professional orders of monks, clerics (whom he called canons), and laymen. Gerard of Cambrai referred to the occupational orders of prayers, fighters, and tillers in a speech delivered in 1036, following a decree of the Frankish bishops concerning the truce of God. The tillers were 'raised to God by the prayers of the orators and defended by the army of the fighters', he said. The fighters in turn collected revenues from agriculture and tolls and were supported by the prayers of holy men. As was proper in a speech concerning the truce of God, Gerard emphasized that the office of fighting was not blame-worthy 'if there is no sin in the

---

[16] See the *Corpus consuetudinum monasticarum*, ed. Kassius Hallinger, 9 vols. to date (Siegburg, 1963–), esp. the general introduction to vol. I. The increasing use of common bodies of written customs, which was an aspect of the transfer from oral and mimetic tradition to reliance on texts, is discussed by Brian Stock, *The Implications of Literacy: Written Language and Models of Interpretation in the Eleventh and Twelfth Centuries* (Princeton, 1983).

[17] On the issue of clothing, see Kassius Hallinger, *Gorze-Kluny. Studien zu den monastischen Lebensformen und Gegensätzen im Hochmittelalter*, 2 vols. (Studia Anselmiana, XXII–XXV; Rome, 1950–1), II, pp. 696–701, and, on the emphasis on uniformity within individual orders, Gerd Zimmermann, *Ordensleben und Lebensstandard. Die Cura corporis in den Ordensvorschriften des abendländischen Hochmittelalters* (Beiträge zur Geschichte des alten Mönchtums und des Benediktinerordens, XXXII; Münster West., 1973), pp. 115–16, 207–8.

[18] *Vita Burchardi episcopi*, XVII, in *MGH, Scriptores: Scriptores* in fol., 34 vols. (1826–1980), IV, p. 840. Burchard used the term *monasterium* here to refer to a house of canons.

consciousness', and he justified the variety of occupations in society by referring to the many mansions in God's house.[19]

These texts also show that by the early eleventh century the lines between the clerical and monastic orders were becoming blurred. The distinction broke down further in the eleventh and twelfth centuries, when an increasing number of monks entered holy orders and when ecclesiastical reformers applied to clerics the rules of celibacy and community life that had previously characterized monks and nuns. Many groups of canons adopted rules resembling those of monks, and sometimes derived from them. Their houses were called monasteries, and they themselves were called regular canons in order to distinguish them from secular canons, who like other clerics owned property and lived in separate households.

The distinction between the monastic and lay orders was similarly blurred by the two new institutions of lay brothers and military orders. Scholars are still uncertain precisely when and where the old type of monastic *conversi* – illiterate and unordained monks who had entered a monastery as adults but who could, and often did, learn to read and write and take holy orders – were replaced by the new type of *conversi*, who constituted a closed category in a monastery, from which no graduation was possible, and who performed special, and usually menial, duties.[20] The new type is found especially in Italy and south Germany in the last quarter of the eleventh and first quarter of the twelfth centuries, and it spread rapidly among the new religious orders, which were thus freed from dependence on lay servitors. They were referred to as *conversi laici, fratres,* and frequently *barbati,* from their beards which distinguished them from the unbearded clerical monks.[21] Contemporaries disagreed over whether they were monks or laymen, and in practice they constituted a group whose way of life resembled in many respects that of laymen.

The new military orders also formed a bridge between the monastic and lay orders, since their members were both soldiers and monks. Bernard of Clairvaux stressed the novelty of this combination in his *De laude novae militiae,* written between 1128 and 1136 for the Knights of the Temple.

A new type of fighting force may be said to have arisen upon earth... A new type of fighting force, I say, unknown to earlier ages, which fights equally and unceasingly in the twofold war both against flesh and blood and against 'the spirits of wickedness in the high places'.

[19] *Gesta episcopum Cameracensium,* III, 52, in *MGH, Scriptores* in fol., VII, p. 485.

[20] See the references in my article on '"Famuli" and "Conversi" at Cluny: A Note on Statute 24 of Peter the Venerable', *Revue bénédictine,* LXXXIII (1973), pp. 326–50, reprinted in *Cluniac Studies* (Variorum Reprint CS109; London, 1980).

[21] See my introduction to the forthcoming edition by R. B. C. Huygens of Burchard of Bellevaux, *Apologia de barbis.*

Religious life in the twelfth century

There was nothing remarkable, Bernard continued, in waging either physical war against enemies or spiritual war against sins, but for the same person to engage in both wars was new and noteworthy. The Templars, he said, 'seem milder than lambs and fiercer than lions, so that I should be in doubt whether to call them monks or soldiers were it not suitable to call by both those names those in whom neither the mildness of the monk nor the fortitude of the soldier is lacking'.[22]

The idea that monks could be soldiers or laymen would have been unthinkable in the early Middle Ages, when the special status of the monastic order was universally recognized, in spite of the loose usage of referring to monks as lay because they were not in holy orders. Hermits also to some extent cut across the established typology of forms of religious life.[23] Many twelfth-century religious leaders, such as Norbert of Xanten, Robert of Arbrissel, and Bernard of Tiron, spent parts of their lives as hermits, pilgrims, and wandering preachers. When Stephen of Muret, the founder of the Grandmontines, was asked by two visiting cardinals whether he was a monk, hermit, or canon, he replied that his glory was nothing, thus showing not only his humility but also his desire to avoid the established categories of religious life.[24] Unlike a canon, he said, he could not rule a church; he was not called a monk, which was a term of sanctity and singularity, 'although all Christians can be called monks'; and he did not avoid worldly affairs and stay in his cell like a hermit.

New and anomalous types of religious life sprang up all over Europe. Bands of laymen were attached to religious houses, like those described by Bernold of Constance in his chronicle under the year 1091,[25] and independent groups of lay penitents lived together in north Italy in the second half of the twelfth century.[26] The lost (or perhaps unwritten) second book of the *Libellus de diversis ordinibus et professionibus qui sunt in aecclesia*, which was written in the fourth or fifth decade of the twelfth century, probably in the

---

[22] Bernard of Clairvaux, *Opera*, ed. Jean Leclercq a.o., 8 vols. in 9 (Rome, 1957–77), III, pp. 216, 221, tr. Conrad Greenia (Cistercian Fathers Series, XIX; Kalamazoo, Mich., 1977), pp. 129–30, 140.

[23] The three sections of the first book of the *Libellus de diversis ordinibus et professionibus qui sunt in aecclesia*, ed. G. Constable and B. Smith (Oxford Medieval Texts; Oxford, 1972), are devoted to hermits, monks, and canons.

[24] *Vita venerabilis viri Stephani Muretensis*, XXII, and *Vita ampliata*, XXXIV, in *Scriptores ordinis Grandimontensis*, ed. Jean Becquet (Corpus Christianorum: Continuatio Mediaevalis, VIII; Turnhout, 1968), pp. 121–3, 141.

[25] Bernold of Constance, *Chronicon*, *sub anno* 1091, in *MGH*, *Scriptores* in fol., V, pp. 452–3; see also *sub anno* 1083, *ibid.*, p. 439.

[26] See in particular the articles of G. G. Meersseman collected in vol. I of his *Ordo Fraternitatis. Confraternite e pietà dei laici nel Medioevo*, ed. G. P. Pacini, 3 vols. (Italia sacra, XXIV–XXVI; Rome, 1977).

diocese of Liège, was devoted to the 'worshippers of God', as the author called them, both men and women, who were neither canons, monks, hermits, nor recluses.[27] Much work remains to be done on lay religious confraternities and corporations, on lay *familiares* who were associated with religious houses where prayers were offered for their salvation, and on the men who became monks *ad succurrendum*, at the end of their lives, in order to enter the next world clothed in the monastic habit. Crusaders, pilgrims, and penitents all had a recognized legal status, if only for a limited time, and added to the complexity of the typology of forms of consecrated life.

Some of the new religious houses and orders of the twelfth century likewise defy any easy classification. Most of them claimed to follow the Rule of Benedict, but usually interpreted in the light of various customs, which formed the real basis of new orders. Scholars are not agreed over whether or not the Carthusians followed the Rule of Benedict or whether they should be called hermits or monks, since they lived alone in cells gathered around a common cloister.[28] At the same time, the uniformity of observance within each order tended to be tightened, so that the sense of belonging to a religious order, in any house of which a similar way of life was followed, increasingly replaced the sense of belonging either exclusively to an individual community or to the monastic order in general. Some houses of regular canons were indistinguishable from those of monks and had abbots as superiors. Even more confusing for contemporaries were the so-called double houses of men and women, like those founded by Gilbert of Sempringham, who gathered together nuns, canons, lay sisters, and lay brothers into single communities.

The sense of competition fostered by this diversity of forms of religious life showed itself not only in polemical writings but also in outright conflicts between religious houses. Rivalry for property, patronage, and recruits had always to some extent existed, but it was sharpened by the emergence of rival standards and ideals of religious life. Writing to Bernard of Clairvaux in 1144, Peter the Venerable deplored 'the hidden and execrable variety of minds' which alone, he said, divided men who were joined in the Christian name and unified in the monastic profession and which kept them 'from the sincere unity of hearts in which they seem to be congregated'.[29]

---

[27] *Libellus*, pref., ed. Constable, p. 5. See introduction, pp. xix–xx.

[28] See Bernard Bligny, *L'Église et les ordres religieux dans le royaume de Bourgogne aux XIe et XIIe siècles* (Collection des cahiers d'histoire publiée par les Universités de Clermont, Lyon, Grenoble, IV; Paris, 1960), pp. 268–9, and Jacques Dubois, 'Quelques problèmes de l'histoire de l'ordre des chartreux à propos de livres récents', *Revue d'histoire ecclésiastique*, LXIII (1968), pp. 34–7.

[29] Peter the Venerable, Ep. 111, *The Letters of Peter the Venerable*, ed. Giles Constable, 2 vols. (Harvard Historical Studies, LXXVIII; Cambridge, Mass., 1967), I, p. 277:

Religious life in the twelfth century

Religious houses in the twelfth century, like those in earlier times, fought for the favour of supernatural and secular patrons, and for the privileges and economic favours which came from both. The Virgin was expected to defend the new Cistercian houses dedicated to her just as much as Sts Peter and Paul were expected to look after their rights and property at Cluny. Perhaps the principal rivalry, however, was for recruits, without whom no religious house can survive. Some of the sharpest controversies arose over the transfer, or *transitus*, as it was called, of members from one religious community to another. Such moves were technically forbidden without the permission of the superior, but they became increasingly common. Some houses were populated primarily by fugitives from other houses, and many prominent figures moved from one house to another. The practice in canon law of allowing moves to stricter but not to less strict houses did little to help the situation, since there was no accepted hierarchy of strictness. It led in particular to some acerbic exchanges between monks and regular canons, who often asserted the superiority of their ideal of a life both in and out of the world to the monastic ideal of withdrawal and prayer. The regular canon Anselm of Havelberg said in his *Epistola apologetica pro ordine canonicorum regularium*, written about 1150, that 'The order of canons is higher (*sublimior*) in the church than [that] of monks' and argued that clerics, like Christ, combined the active and contemplative lives into a true *vita apostolica*. 'Just as a good and perfect monk should be loved and imitated more than an inept cleric,' he wrote, 'so a cleric living well and regularly is without doubt always to be preferred even to the best monk.'[30]

Contemporary observers of the religious scene were aware of these developments. The author of the *Libellus de diversis ordinibus* worked out what

'Et cum eos ut dixi Christianum nomen coniungat, cum monastica professio uniat, sola eos mentium nescio quae occulta et nefanda varietas separat, et ab illa sincera cordium unitate in quam videntur congregati disgregat.'

30 Anselm of Havelberg, *Epistola apologetica pro ordine canonicorum regularium*, in PL, CLXXXVIII, 1125C, 1136C; see Georg Schreiber, 'Studien über Anselm von Havelberg zur Geistesgeschichte des Hochmittelalters', *Analecta Praemonstratensia*, XVIII (1942), p. 38; Kurt Fina, 'Anselm von Havelberg [I]', *ibid.*, XXXII (1956), p. 85; Gabriella Severino, 'La discussione degli "Ordines" di Anselmo di Havelberg', *Bullettino dell'Istituto Storico Italiano per il Medio Evo*, LXXVIII (1967), pp. 86–7, 107, stressing that canons, unlike monks, have a role in the world. See also the *Coutumier du XI siècle de l'ordre de Saint-Ruf*, ed. A. Carrier [de Belleuse] (Etudes et documents sur l'ordre de St-Ruf, VIII; Sherbrooke, Que., 1950), p. 97, no. 69: 'Et scorum Patrum inexpugnabili sentencia sancitur, canonicum ordinem omnibus ecclesie ordinibus preponendum merito. Nec mirum, cum Xpo et apostolis eius succedat, in predicacionis, baptismatis ac reliquorum ecclie sacramentorum officium subrogatus.' This customary in fact dates from the second half of the twelfth century: see Charles Dereine, in *Revue d'histoire ecclésiastique*, XLVI (1951), p. 356, and *Scriptorium*, V (1951), p. 109, and XIII (1959), p. 244.

was perhaps the first typology of forms of religious life, showing the parallels between the various types of monks and canons who lived, respectively, close to, far from, and among other men and finding biblical prototypes for each. Otto of Freising in the seventh book of his *Chronica*, which goes to 1146, stressed the variety of types of religious life and praised them all for leading pure and holy lives and for living together in monasteries and churches with one heart and one soul. They glowed internally, he said, with the varied splendours of the virtues and wore externally clothes of diverse colours, fulfilling the words of the Psalmist: 'All the glory of the king's daughter is within in golden borders, clothed round about with varieties.'[31] In the description of various types of religious life in the chronicle of Petershausen, which ends in 1156, the monks, canons, bishops, and priests are followed by virgins, solitaries, recluses, wandering preachers, pilgrims, and beggars, who will also be carried by the angels 'with Lazarus into the bosom of Abraham'.[32]

These writers all turned to the Bible to justify the various forms of religious life they saw around them. The author of the *Libellus* found a prototype in both the Old and New Testaments for every type of life except that of the so-called secular monks, who did not observe the monastic profession. The life of hermits, for instance, was exemplified by Abel in the first age, by the patriarchs in the second age, and by Christ when He withdrew 'Himself alone' into the mountain in John 6. 15.[33] Otto of Freising cited both the variegated robe of the princess in Psalm 44 and the description of the primitive church in Acts 4. 32 – 'The multitude of believers had but one heart and one soul' – which was a key text for twelfth-century religious reformers and had far-reaching implications for the organization of religious institutions and of society as a whole. The Petershausen chronicler used the account in Luke 16. 22 of how the dead beggar 'was carried by the angels into Abraham's bosom', an image also used by contemporary artists to depict the salvation of various types of people. The many mansions of John 14. 2, which were cited in support of diversity by Gregory the Great and Gerard of Cambrai, were also often used to show the legitimacy of varying types of religious life.

The themes of celestial harmony and social unity were likewise cited as evidence that God intended people to be saved in different ways. Otloh of

---

[31] *MGH, Scriptores rerum Germanicarum in usum scholarum separatim editi:* Otto of Freising, *Chronica*, ed. A. Hofmeister (1912), pp. 370–1, tr. Charles C. Mierow (Records of Civilization; New York, 1928), pp. 446–7.

[32] *Die Chronik des Klosters Petershausen*, ed. Otto Feger (Schwäbische Chroniken der Stauferzeit, III; Lindau – Constance, 1956), pp. 30–6.

[33] See *Libellus*, intro., p. xxiv.

Religious life in the twelfth century

St Emmeram in the eleventh century said: 'Almighty God has in His hand all men predestined to the harmony of the celestial life, like a lute arranged with suitable strings, and He destines some indeed to the sharp sound of the contemplative life and assigns others by regulating to the depth of the active life.'[34] The author of the *Libellus*, after stressing the differences among hermits, said: 'If it displeases you that all men in this calling do not live in the same way, look at the Creation fashioned by the good Creator in various ways, and how a harmony has been achieved from different chords.'[35] Goscelin of St Bertin wrote in his *Liber confortatorius*:

The palm of Christ is denied to no sex, no age, no condition. Every earthly being and child of man, one and the same rich and poor, kings and princes, young men and virgins, old and young, boys, girls, sucking and crying babes, are crowned either with martyrdom, virginity, or continence... In that unanimity of peace, the distinctions of differing qualities will not exist for division or dissonance, but for a most beautiful harmony of varied ornaments, just as a field is decorated with various flowers, a picture with various colours, and a basin with various stones.[36]

These themes of harmony and unity, derived from the sphere of aural and visual aesthetics, were rhetorical topoi, but they reflected a serious concern for the relation of differing groups and individuals in the church and helped to lay the basis for an acceptance of religious diversity. It was also a commonplace to stress the universality of God's love. 'In everyone He duly regards not grade or sex but sanctity of life', said Sigiboto in his *Vita* of St Paulina, the founder of Paulinzelle.[37] Ivo of Chartres in his letter to the monks of Coulombs in effect denied the traditional hierarchy of forms of religious life by stressing the universality of the church and criticizing those who claimed that it belonged to just a few wandering ascetics, forgetting that 'Each person has their own gift from God and that in the house of God one person walks this path and another that and that all branches do not behave in the same way.'[38] The author of the *Libellus*, after mentioning the differences in monastic customs concerning food, clothing, and manual

---

[34] Otloh of St Emmeram, *In Psalmum LII commentarius*, in *PL*, XCIII, 1110A.

[35] *Libellus*, I, ed. Constable, p. 17. On the freedom of hermits to live as they pleased, see my paper on 'Liberty and Free Choice in Monastic Life and Thought', to appear in the proceedings of the fourth Pennsylvania – Paris – Dumbarton Oaks Colloquium.

[36] Charles Talbot, 'The Liber confortatorius of Goscelin of Saint Bertin', *Analecta monastica*, III (Studia Anselmiana, XXXVII; Rome, 1955), pp. 55, 113.

[37] Sigiboto, *Vita Paulinae*, pref., in *MGH*, *Scriptores* in fol., XXX, 2, p. 911: 'Amat Christus doctores, amat coniugatos, amat continentes: in his fructum sapientiae, in illis de sobole matris ecclesiae fedus coniugale, in illis gratiam continentiae, virginale meritum, coniugale consortium, viduale votum et meritum sic remunerans, ut in omnibus non gradum vel sexum sed vitae sanctitatem mercede compenset.'

[38] Ivo of Chartres, Ep. 192, in *PL*, CLXII, 201C.

labour, said: 'I desire to show that although they live differently they aspire from the one beginning to the one end that is Christ.'[39]

The phrase *diversi sed non adversi*, first formulated by Anselm of Laon, was often used in twelfth-century theological and legal writings. In similar and analogous forms it was also applied to the differences in religious life. In the *Altercatio monachi et clerici utrum monacho liceat praedicare* of Rupert of Deutz, the monk said: 'For you [are] only a cleric; I am both a monk and a cleric. These are diverse... but not contrary.'[40] Idungus of Regensburg in his *Argumentum super quatuor questionibus*, written about 1142/5, also said: 'The clericate and the monachate go together very well in the same person, since they are not opposed although diverse (*non sint opposita, licet diversa*).'[41] Peter the Venerable ended a letter written to Bernard in 1149, stressing the need for unity of faith: 'May the divided hearts be slowly united by this remedy, and when they shall see nothing separated between them, let them learn at the inspiration of Him who "breatheth where He will" to be one concerning things that are different but not opposed (*de diversis ne dicam adversis*).'[42]

Arguments of this sort were particularly used by defenders of the old black Benedictine houses, who stressed the traditional unity of the monastic order against the divisive tendencies of the reformers. Guibert of Nogent discounted differences in fasting and singing in his *De pignoribus sanctorum* because, 'Although they differ in act they do not disagree from the sense of faith.'[43] Rupert of Deutz compared the church to Noah's ark, with differing dimensions, in his discussion of the issue of *transitus* in the commentary he wrote on the Rule of Benedict in 1124/5. Although he distinguished the professions of monks and clerics, and regarded the former as stricter and higher than the latter, he attached no moral value to this difference, saying that 'Each person is blessed in his own order.'[44] The author of the so-called

[39] *Libellus*, II, ed. Constable, p. 28.
[40] *PL*, CLXX, 540B; see Silvestre, 'Diversi', p. 126n., and John H. Van Engen, *Rupert of Deutz* (Publications of the UCLA Center for Medieval and Renaissance Studies, XVIII; Berkeley – Los Angeles – London, 1983), pp. 310–12, dating it 'ca. 1120–1122'.
[41] R. B. C. Huygens, *Le Moine Idung et ses deux ouvrages: 'Argumentum super quatuor questionibus' et 'Dialogus duorum monachorum'* (Biblioteca degli 'Studi Medievali', XI; Spoleto, 1980), p. 59. Idungus used 'diversa quamvis non adversa' in his *Dialogus*, II, *ibid.*, p. 139.
[42] Peter the Venerable, Ep. 150, *Letters*, ed. Constable, I, p. 371. Silvestre, 'Diversi', p. 126n., cited this and another use, in the *Vita* of Norbert of Xanten, in *MGH, Scriptores* in fol., XII, p. 683.
[43] Guibert of Nogent, *De pignoribus sanctorum*, I, 1, in *PL*, CLVI, 612D.
[44] Rupert of Deutz, *Commentarium in regulam Benedicti*, IV, 13, in *Opera omnia*, 4 vols. (Venice, 1748–51), IV, p. 319. See Van Engen, *Rupert*, pp. 237 n. 55, and 313, on the date.

Religious life in the twelfth century

Riposte to Bernard's criticisms of the old monasticism (who may have been the Cluniac abbot and archbishop, Hugh of Rouen) vigorously defended variety. 'The holy fathers established many ways of living in the church, so that ordinary men of the world, living according to them, might offer to God the multiple proofs of the virtues... Religion is not in the clothing but in the heart.'[45] The variety of vocations in the church was also stressed by the author of the *Nouvelle réponse*, written about the middle of the twelfth century, who said that 'Everyone has his own gift from God.'[46]

Peter the Venerable returned repeatedly to these issues in his letters to Bernard of Clairvaux, especially the long letter written in 1144, defending the diversity of observances and customs within the monastic order. According to Peter, communities that change their customs, or follow different customs, do not thereby lose their love or cease to be Christians. He defended diversity even within a single order, which should be united by a single purpose. It is a matter of no concern, he said, 'if one comes to the same place by a different path, to the same life by different roads, to the same Jerusalem, which is above, that is our mother, by various journeys'. Both here and in his letter of 1149 he stressed the need for unity of faith among monks who differed in their ways of life.[47]

This point of view was shared by many clerics and canons, including some regular canons. Master Hilary of Orléans, writing in 1117/25 to a monk of the abbey of St Albinus at Angers, said that the Lord's command for men to deny themselves, carry His cross, and follow Him could be obeyed in various ways, each of which was good so long as it was sincerely followed. 'Take on the life as well as the habit of your order,' he urged.[48] After the

---

[45] André Wilmart, 'Une riposte de l'ancien monachisme au manifeste de saint Bernard', *Revue bénédictine*, XLVI (1934), pp. 324, 343. Between these quotations he said, among other things, that monks resembled the various types of soldiers mentioned in the Bible. On the author and date, see Charles Talbot, 'The Date and Author of the "Riposte"', in *Petrus Venerabilis, 1156–1956*, ed. Giles Constable and James Kritzeck (Studia Anselmiana, XL; Rome, 1956), pp. 72–80. In his *Dialogi*, VII, 6, Hugh wrote that monks and clerics were joined by the same faith and grace in Christ, 'quorum diversus est habitus, sed unus in eis est Christus. Diversa membra in uno corpore non eumdem habent actum, sed eumdem habent spiritum; pro quo uno diversa illa dicimus corpus unum': E. Martène and U. Durand, *Thesaurus novus anecdotorum*, 5 vols. (Paris, 1717), V, col. 973E.

[46] Jean Leclercq, 'Nouvelle réponse de l'ancien monachisme aux critiques des Cisterciens', *Revue bénédictine*, LXVII (1957), p. 90; see *ibid.*, intro., pp. 80–1.

[47] Peter the Venerable, Epp. 111 and 150, *Letters*, ed. Constable, I, pp. 277–80, 294, 368–9. See Raphael Molitor, *Aus der Rechtsgeschichte benediktinischer Verbände*, 3 vols. (Münster West., 1928–33), I, pp. 47–8, on Peter's stress on love, and Zimmermann, *Ordensleben*, pp. 223–4.

[48] Nikolaus M. Häring, 'Hilary of Orléans and his Letter Collection', *Studi Medievali*, 3rd ser., XIV (1973), p. 1097, no. 10.

prior of La Charité had admitted a canon on the grounds that monastic was superior to canonical life, he received a letter from an anonymous canon saying that neither order was better than the other. Black was the colour of humility and abjection; white, of purity and exaltation. 'We are all evil,' the letter concluded, 'and where all are evil, none are better.'[49] When the prior of St Barbe resigned in order to become a Premonstratensian canon, thus leaving a moderate monastery for a strict canonical house, he stressed that his change of place and colour was worthless without a change of life. Although he had departed in order to serve God in a particular place and way, he said, God is served in all parts of the world, and men fight for the same king.[50] The image of an army united in leadership and purpose but differing in appearance and usages was also used by Hugh of St Victor and Peter the Venerable.[51]

The ideals of harmony and diversity within unity were accepted even by reformers who promoted new and, in their view, superior ways of religious life and who encouraged *transitus* from less strict houses to their own. Bernard of Clairvaux, in spite of his belief in the superiority of the Cistercian to all other forms of monastic life,[52] none the less defended the legitimacy of diversity. In his *Apologia*, where he strongly criticized the Cluniacs, he deplored the quarrels between various groups of monks and canons and said that the church was made up of different orders united in a single love and faith, like the princess 'clothed round about with varieties', Joseph's seamless coat of many colours, and the many mansions in the house of God. 'Diverse men receive diverse gifts, one this and the other that, whether they be Cluniacs, or Cistercians, or regular clerics, or even faithful laymen, in fact every order, every language, every sex, every age, every condition, in every place, for every time, from the first man to the last.' 'Let each man observe by which way he walks,' Bernard continued, referring to the many

---

[49] *Cujusdam canonici regularis epistola ad priorem Charitatis*, in *PL*, ccxiii, 718D–719A. See also the discussion of the ways of unity in the letter by Hugh Farsit (d. after 1143) to the Premonstratensians translated in the *Histoire littéraire de la France*, xii (Paris, 1763), p. 296, and published in G. van Elsen, *Beknopte Levengeschiedenis van den H. Norbertus* (Averbode, 1890), pp. 390–5, which I have not seen.

[50] E. Martène and U. Durand, *Amplissima collectio*, 9 vols. (Paris, 1724–33), I, col. 784B.

[51] Peter the Venerable, Ep. 4, *Letters*, ed. Constable, I, p. 145; Hugh of St Victor, *On the Sacraments of the Christian Faith* (*De Sacramentis*), tr. Roy J. Deferrari (Mediaeval Academy of America Publication lviii; Cambridge, Mass., 1951), p. 4. See also n. 45 above.

[52] Bernard of Clairvaux, *De praecepto et dispensatione*, xlvi, in *Opera*, ed. Leclercq, iii, p. 285; *Sermo de diversis*, xxii, 2 and 5, *ibid.*, vi, 1, pp. 171, 173, etc. According to M. Anselme Dimier, 'Saint Bernard et le droit en matière de *Transitus*', *Revue Mabillon*, xliii (1953), p. 80, Bernard suggested more than once that Cîteaux was the only true way to heaven.

Religious life in the twelfth century

mansions, 'so that a diversity of ways may not lead him from a single just way, for whatever mansion he reaches he will not be excluded from his Father's house.'[53] In *De praecepto et dispensatione* he specifically defended the diversity of observance within the monastic order, saying that although all monks make a single profession according to the Rule, 'since not everyone has a single intention in his heart, a non-single [i.e. diverse] observance can undoubtedly be celebrated in different places without losing salvation and without damaging one's profession'.[54] Bernard was therefore ready to accept that motives as well as behaviour varied and that different types of religious life were suited to different people, all of whom would be saved.[55]

This attitude also showed itself in the widespread concern in the twelfth century for the religious life of women. Gaucherius of Aureil, according to his biographer, knew 'that neither sex is excluded from the kingdom of God. Wherefore he tried to build the heavenly Jerusalem out of the double wall, that is, of men and of women, and he constructed the habitation for women a stone's throw from his cell, distributing what little he had to both men and women.'[56] The biographer of Gilbert of Sempringham compared his order, with its double houses, to the chariot of God, 'which has two sides, that is, one of men and the other of women; four wheels, two of men, clerics and laymen, and two of women, literate and illiterate; two beasts dragging the chariot, the clerical and monastic disciplines'. He went on to praise 'this marvellous unity of persons and churches and this unheard-of community of all things, which made all things one and one thing all in the diversities of so many hearts and such great monasteries'. The ideal here was paradisiacal harmony in which men and women lived side by side united in spiritual love.[57]

---

[53] Bernard of Clairvaux, *Apologia*, VI and IX, in *Opera*, ed. Leclercq, III, pp. 86–7, 89.

[54] Bernard of Clairvaux, *De praecepto et dispensatione*, XLVIII, in *Opera*, ed. Leclercq, III, p. 286.

[55] On Bernard's attitude toward diversity, see Jean Leclercq, 'Saint Bernard of Clairvaux and the Contemplative Community', in *Contemplative Community*, ed. M. Basil Pennington (Cistercian Studies Series, XXI; Washington, D.C., 1972), pp. 88–97, and, in intellectual matters, the introduction by Bernard McGinn to *On Grace and Free Choice*, tr. Daniel O'Donovan (Cistercian Fathers Series, XIX; Kalamazoo, Mich., 1977), pp. 32–3, citing Bernard's Sermon 81 on the Song of Songs. Some of these points are discussed, and the same sources cited, in my article, 'Cluny – Cîteaux – La Chartreuse. San Bernardo e la diversità delle forme di vita religiosa nel XII secolo', *Studi su S. Bernardo di Chiaravalle. Convegno internazionale, Certosa di Firenze, 6–9 novembre 1974* (Rome, 1975), pp. 93–114, reprinted in *Cluniac Studies*.

[56] *Vita beati Gaucherii*, in P. Labbe, *Nova bibliotheca manuscriptorum librorum*, 2 vols. (Paris, 1657), II, p. 562.

[57] *Vita s. Gileberti confessoris*, in William Dugdale, *Monasticon anglicanum*, eds. John Caley, Henry Ellis, and Bulkeley Bandinel, 6 vols. in 8 (London, 1846), VI, 2, pp. *ix–x (after p. 945).

By the middle of the twelfth century the variety and multiplicity of forms of religious life were accepted facts, and there were signs of a change in attitude from tolerance to approval. Anselm of Havelberg gave a famous defence of diversity and innovation in the first book of his *Dialogi*, where he said that in the six ages between the coming of Christ and the Day of Judgment, 'in which one and the same church is innovated, the Son of God being present, not a single and uniform [status] but many and multiform statuses are found'. He described this variety, which included the new monastic and canonical orders, the military orders, and the Greek religious orders.

Let no one be astonished or dispute that the church of God is divided by an unchanging God into various laws and observances before the law, and under the law, and under grace, for it is fitting that as the ages proceed the signs of the spiritual graces should grow, making the truth itself increasingly clear, and thus the knowledge of truth with its effect of salvation grows from age to age; and so at first good things, then better things, and finally the best things were proposed. This variety was created not on account of the mutability of an unchanging God, Who is 'always the selfsame' and Whose 'years shall not fail', but on account of the changing infirmity of the human race and the mutation in time from generation to generation.

In the title to the last chapter Anselm again asserted that 'The church of God, which is one in faith, one in hope, one in charity, is multiform in the variety of its diverse statuses.'[58]

The differences between the various ways of life open to Christians were seen as of relatively little importance. The one and only rule for Stephen of Muret was the Gospel of Christ, according to the *Liber de doctrina* or *Liber sententiarum* compiled by his disciples before 1157.

All Christians who live in unity can be called monks, especially those who according to the apostle are more removed from secular affairs and think only about God (2 Tim. 2. 4)... There would be an infinite number of rules if they were made by men, for each of the doctors in his time taught either by speaking or by writing how a person should go to God. If they made a rule, therefore, it could be said: '[There are] as many rules as prophets; as many rules as apostles; as many rules as doctors.'... Whoever holds to the rule of God can be saved, with or without a wife, which cannot be done under the rule of St Benedict; for it is of great perfection, but the rule of

---

[58] Anselm of Havelberg, *Dialogi*, I, 6 and 13, ed. Gaston Salet (Sources chrétiennes, CXVIII; Paris, 1966), pp. 64, 114, 116 (= *PL*, CLXXXVIII, 1148BC, 1159AB, 1160AB). Various scholars have studied Anselm's views on the diversity of religious orders: Schreiber, 'Studien', pp. 55–6; Ernest W. McDonnell, 'The *Vita Apostolica*: Diversity or Dissent', *Church History*, XXIV (1955), pp. 21–2; Kurt Fina, 'Anselm von Havelberg [V]', *Analecta Praemonstratensia*, XXXIV (1958), pp. 13–41; Amos Funkenstein, *Heilsplan und natürliche Entwicklung. Formen der Gegenwartsbestimmung im Geschichtsdenken des hohen Mittelalters* (Munich, 1965), pp. 60–7; Severino, 'Discussione degli "Ordines"', pp. 100–1.

Religious life in the twelfth century

St Basil is of greater perfection. It is all taken from the common rule, however, that is, from the Gospel.[59]

Peter of Celle spoke with approval of the *seminaria* of every type of religious order that were planted by Archbishop Eskil of Lund in his diocese, and he stressed that the differences between monks and canons were *accidentalia*.[60] The Carthusian Adam of Dryburgh condemned the quarrels between religious houses, saying that 'The entire ordained custom of any church is religious and good.'[61] In the early thirteenth century Peter of Blois wrote to the abbot of Evesham: 'All works, devotions, and counsels come down to one thing... The order of the Cluniacs is holy, so is the order of the Cistercians, and the Lord entrusted to both the ministry of reconciliation and the business of salvation. No one should be disturbed', he concluded, in terms resembling those used in the *Libellus* about the diversity of hermits, 'by the diversity of orders among men, for there is order also in the stars.'[62]

James of Vitry gave a classic picture of the pluralistic nature of Christian society in his *Historia occidentalis*, which was completed a few years after the Fourth Lateran Council. 'We consider to be regulars', he wrote, using the term in the sense of members of religious houses, 'not only those who renounce the world and go over to a religious life, but we can also call regulars all the faithful of Christ who serve the Lord under the evangelical rule and live in an orderly way under the one highest and supreme Abbot.' He went on to list clerics, priests, married people, widows, virgins, soldiers, merchants, peasants, craftsmen, 'and other multiform types of men', each having its own distinct rules and institutions 'according to the diverse types of talents' and making up collectively the single body of the church.[63] For James the entire body of the faithful was, as it were, a gigantic religious community under the Abbot God. Those dedicated to a formal religious life were no longer at the top of the scale of perfection for James, who said that no religious order or type of life, however strict, was more pleasing to God than the order of priests who cared for the spiritual needs of the faithful.

The author of the thirteenth-century customary of the Augustinian canons of Barnwell shared this view, without going as far as James of Vitry. There

[59] *Scriptores ord. Grand.*, pp. 5–6. See also the references in n. 24 above.
[60] Peter of Celle, Ep. I, 20, in *PL*, ccII, 423AB, and *De disciplina claustrali*, II, *ibid.*, 1103D–1104B.
[61] Adam of Dryburgh, Sermon 3, in *PL*, cxcVIII, 464D–465A.
[62] Peter of Blois, Ep. 97, in *Opera omnia*, ed. J. A. Giles, 4 vols. (Oxford, 1847), I, p. 306.
[63] James of Vitry, *Historia occidentalis*, xxxIV, ed. John F. Hinnebusch (Fribourg, 1972), pp. 165–6. See Joseph Greven, *Die Anfänge der Beginen* (Vorreformationsgeschichtliche Forschungen, VIII; Münster West., 1912), pp. 201–2, and McDonnell, '*Vita Apostolica*', pp. 21–2.

VIII

were many paths to the celestial Jerusalem, he said, of which some were
stricter and some less strict. The important thing was for men to persevere
in the calling to which God summoned them. 'Let those who lead a religious
life learn, not only these and those but also all and each, of whatever habit
or profession, province or region, dignity or order; let them learn, I say,
and keep to the straight way that leads to the city, not to vanity but the way
of his calling to which the Holy Spirit calls him.' The author went on to
describe, among these ways, the one by which the regular canons walked to
the city.[64]

In the course of the twelfth century there was thus a dramatic change in
social and religious values. The monastic life came to be regarded as only
one, and not necessarily the best, way to salvation. The acceptance of the
legitimacy of various callings opened the way for the emergence of new
ideals of religious life. Some of these developed within and to some extent
at the expense of the older institutions but did not replace them, and eventually,
like the Cistercians, conformed to their standards. Others, like the regular
canons and later the mendicant orders, challenged the older scale of values
and prepared the way for an age of pluralism which accepted not only
various forms of religious life but also diversity of belief, which was seen as
essential for the instruction and purification of true believers and, later, as a
social ideal in itself.[65]

This development can be traced in the successive versions of the story of
the three rings, which first appeared in a sermon of the thirteenth-century
Dominican preacher Stephen of Bourbon, where the true ring won the
legitimate daughter her rightful inheritance.[66] In the Gesta Romanorum the ring
belonging to the third son represented Christianity and proved its authenticity by performing various miracles, but the similar rings belonging to the
two older brothers, and representing Judaism and Islam, were not without
value, since God the Father gave land to the Jews and power to the Saracens.[67]
The rings in The Decameron, a century after their first appearance, were indistinguishable, like the three religions they represented. 'Each of them
considers itself the legitimate heir to His [the Father's] estate', said Boccaccio;

[64] John Willis Clark, The Observances in Use at the Augustinian Priory of S. Giles and
S. Andrew at Barnwell, Cambridgeshire (Cambridge, 1897), pp. 32–5.
[65] See Herbert Grundmann, 'Oportet et haereses esse', Archiv für Kulturgeschichte, XLV
(1963), pp. 129–64, and C. N. L. Brooke, 'Heresy and Religious Sentiment: 1000–
1250', Bulletin of the Institute of Historical Research, XLI (1968), pp. 115–31, esp. 121–3.
[66] A. Lecoy de la Marche, Anecdotes historiques, légendes et apologues tirés du recueil
inédit d'Etienne de Bourbon (Société de l'histoire de France; Paris, 1877), pp. 281–2,
no. 331. See Stith Thompson, Motif-Index of Folk-Literature, 2nd edn, 6 vols. (Bloomington, Ind. – London, 1975), IV, pp. 40–1, nos. J462.3.1f.
[67] Gesta Romanorum, ed. Hermann Oesterley (Berlin, 1872), pp. 416–17, no. 89.

46

Religious life in the twelfth century

'each believes it possesses His one true law and observes His commandments. But as with the rings, the question of which is right remains in abeyance.'[68]

The acceptance of a variety of forms of religious life in the twelfth century did not mean that all types of life were regarded as equally valuable. Many of the writers cited in this article had firm views about the respective merits of the religious houses and orders about which they were writing. Peter the Venerable defended the Cluniacs and old black Benedictine monasticism; Bernard of Clairvaux was the champion of the Cistercians; and Anselm of Havelberg, of the regular canons. Yet each in his own way was ready to accept, and even to praise, the others. By the early thirteenth century the old monastic order had lost its consciousness of unity as well as its position of superiority and had been replaced by a multiplicity of religious orders representing different ideals of Christian life on earth. The confusion which the Fourth Lateran Council hoped to avert by prohibiting new religious orders already existed, and it had already changed the view of monasticism and of its role in the church and in society generally.

[68] Giovanni Boccaccio, *The Decameron*, I, 3, tr. G. H. McWilliam (Harmondsworth, 1972), pp. 86–7. See A. C. Lee, *The Decameron, Its Sources and Analogues* (London, 1909), pp. 6–13, citing other versions in vernacular literature and earlier secondary works on this tale.

IX

ATTITUDES TOWARD SELF-INFLICTED SUFFERING
IN THE MIDDLE AGES

The subject of this paper may seem at first sight to be a long way from contemporary concerns. The practice by many people in the Middle Ages, and the approval by almost all, of voluntary, often self-inflicted, physical mortifications, such as fasting, celibacy, and flagellation, are today among the strangest and least attractive aspects of medieval life, with regard to which we are inclined to agree with Gibbon that the sufferings and devotions of the early monks must have destroyed, as he put it, 'the sensibility both of the mind and of the body.' This is not to say that we approve of unrestrained indulgence of our bodily desires but that we tend to regard self-inflicted punishment as a sign of spiritual and psychological disorder and not, as was believed in the Middle Ages, of a proper and praiseworthy attitude toward oneself and God.

Upon closer consideration, however, it becomes clear that, while the causes for which people are prepared to suffer now are different than they were then, the desire, and perhaps even the need, to suffer is also present in modern society. I have a file of clippings from popular works showing that we no less than our ancestors believe that merit, achievement, and a sense of personal worth can be acquired only by effort and, frequently, suffering. I am thinking not only of those in risky professions, like soldiers and athletes, whose determination to win and break records often involves suffering and even physical damage, but also of creative artists, scholars, and anyone who tends to feel, with the traveller, Wilfred Thesiger, that 'the harder the way the more worthwhile the journey.' Many people feel a need to toughen themselves for possible future suffering. The ascetic element in social revolutions can be clearly seen in Savonarola, Calvin, and Robespierre and is far from dead in our own times. Modern social activism is likewise often inspired by a desire to do something, preferably something hard and dangerous, in order to express one's deepest convictions and to bear witness, in an unmistakeably religious sense, against some of the most flagrant abuses in modern society.

The psychological basis of this attitude is still not fully understood, but it is found in most major religious systems. There is nothing peculiarly Christian, either medieval or, as has been said, Protestant,[1] in the belief that pain may be a source of power and grace and thus of value to human beings. Emile Durkheim, the pioneer sociologist of religion, regarded asceticism as an essential element in religious life and said that both in the higher and in primitive religions, 'The positive cult is possible only when a man is trained to renouncement, to abnegation, to detachment from self, and consequently to suffering.' This attitude is found in Buddhism and Islam and at certain times even in Judaism, which among the world religions is perhaps the least sympathetic to asceticism. Students of anthropology and folklore have also stressed the importance of voluntary suffering in rites of purification, initiation, and atonement. There is evidence that animals, under some circumstances, will impose sufferings on themselves in the same manner as human beings. Fasting and rigorous exercise are known to have psychological as well as physiological effects, including a tendency towards introversion and a reduction of sexual desire. Recent research suggests that great physical exertion may indeed produce hormonal changes that account not only for an oblivion to pain but also for the sense of well-being known among athletes as 'runner's high.'

William James in his book entitled *Varieties of Religious Experience* distinguished six motives, or psychological levels as he called them, for ascetic practices: first, 'a mere expression of organic hardihood, disgusted with too much ease'; second, 'the love of purity, shocked by whatever savors of the sensual'; third, 'the fruits of love, that is, they may appeal to the subject in the light of sacrifices which he is happy in making to the Deity whom he acknowledges'; fourth, they 'may be due to pessimistic feelings about the self, combined with theological beliefs concerning expiation'; fifth, ' in psychopathic persons, mortifications may be entered on irrationally, by a sort of obsession or fixed idea'; and sixth, 'ascetic exercises may in rarer instances be prompted by genuine perversions of the bodily sensibility,' that is, by what would today be called masochism, a term that had not been invented at the time James was writing. Even masochism, however, according to Freud and his followers, is not totally irrational or without some expectation of personal benefit.[2] To these motives should be added, according to Kenneth Kirk in the *Vision of God,* the spirit of competition, of which the psychological basis is also very unclear. Not all these motives apply as well to the Middle Ages as to the post-Reformation period, with which James was principally concerned. The title of his book shows that he emphasized that religious motives varied and often overlapped in individual cases. He also stressed that physical pain was taken for granted by our ancestors and that attitudes toward it have changed in recent times, when freedom from pain has come to be considered almost a right.

Orthodox Christianity has traditionally taken a relatively positive attitude toward the material world and the human body. The reasons for this are not my primary concern in this paper, but I might mention three relevant points. First, and most important, Christianity took over from Judaism the inheritance of monotheism, with its belief in one transcendent and omnipotent God and consequent belief in the goodness of the created world. Second, the classical emphasis on the integrity of the individual was never entirely lost in Christianity. And third, the doctrine of justification by faith (which is today associated primarily with the Reformation but which had important early roots, especially in the works of St. Augustine) tended to play down the significance of voluntary works and especially of ascetic practices.[3] Dualism as a philosophical or metaphysical doctrine, holding that good and evil, or mind and matter, are two radically distinct and rival principles in the world, has always been rejected by Christians, especially during the early centuries, in opposition to the beliefs of the Manichaeans. As a religious temper, however, dualism has played an important part in the history of Christian asceticism and apocalypticism. The sources of this practical dualism in Christianity are obscure. It certainly does not derive from Judaism and is more strongly marked in the New than in the Old Testament. Christ called on man to deny himself in Matthew 16.24-26, Mark 8.34-36, and Luke 9.23-25, and St. Paul in Colossians 3.5 said that Christians should 'Mortify . . . your members which are upon earth.' There are many other biblical passages and examples, including the Old Testament prophets and John the Baptist, which were cited in the Middle Ages to encourage, if not command, self-denial and voluntary physical mortifications.

These precepts fell on receptive ears in Late Antiquity, when a 'wave of pessimism' swept over pagans as well as Christians, almost all of whom practiced asceticism in one form or another. 'Contempt for the human condition and hatred of the body,' wrote E. R. Dodds, 'was a disease endemic in the entire culture of the period...an endogenous neurosis, an index of intense and widespread guilt-feelings.'[4] It may be that a broad socio-psychological explanation, still to a great extent unexplored by scholars, underlies the origins of the attitudes we are studying. Among Christians, these attitudes found a specific institutional framework in monasticism. The monks of Egypt, Syria, and the Holy Land in the third and fourth centuries were among the most heroic exponents of a life of complete renunciation and voluntary physical suffering. The monks who lived in the Nitrian desert in Egypt were looked upon as models of ascetic practice. They were called 'athletes of Christ' and were filled with a spirit of individualism and competition. As Cuthbert Butler put it, 'They loved to "make a record" in austerities, and to contend with one another in mortifications; and they would freely boast of their spiritual achievements. ...The practice of asceticism constituted a predominant feature of this type of Egyptian monachism. Their prolonged fasts and vigils, their combats with sleep, their exposures to heat and cold, their endurance of thirst and bodily fatigue, their loneliness and silence, are features that constantly recur in the authen-

9

tic records of the lives of these hermits, and they looked on such austerities as among the essential features of the monastic state.'

It is not my intention to enter at length in this paper into a description of the specific types of self-imposed sufferings practiced by monks and nuns, and occasionally by members of the clergy and laity, in the Middle Ages. They may be divided, broadly speaking, into negative and positive mortifications, that is, into forms of deprivation and the active imposition of suffering. Among the former are chastity, poverty, and obedience, which are respectively the renunciation of sexual satisfaction, including marriage, of property, and of self-will. Fasting involves giving up the pleasures of the table; solitude, of human company; silence, of conversation and, as St. Basil stressed, laughter. Humility requires the subordination of one's own wishes and ideas to those of another. These are all aspects of temperance. Among the positive asceticisms, which are the most incomprehensible to us, are the wearing of chains and iron plates and shirts known as *lorica*, immersions in cold water, rolling in thorn bushes and nettles, living on pillars, flagellation and the discipline of whips, and liturgical exercises involving long and painful practices such as standing in a particular position for a long time or repeated genuflexions. Even the kiss, as of the earth, the diseased, or the feet of the poor, was considered an ascetic act of mortification and humiliation. Some of these practices, such as wearing no clothes or shoes, were both negative and positive. Illness or infirmity was likewise considered not only a deprivation of health but also a test by God of His servitors. Ascetic homelessness or expatriation was both a renunciation of home and family and an assumption of a harsh life of solitude and wandering.

The *Vitae patrum* and lives of later medieval saints, and other contemporary sources, dwell at length on the nature of these practices, but they shed little light on the motives behind them, with which I am principally concerned here. The three most prominent motives were the expiation of sin, the expression of devotion, and the avoidance of temptation, which doubtless mingled with less clearly perceptible survivals of ancient elements of purification and atonement. It is no accident that these practices developed, among pagans as well as Christians, at a time when society was pervaded with a sense of failure and guilt, which expressed itself in dislike of the material world and especially of the human body. Suffering was seen as a means not only of expiating guilt in the present world but also of averting punishment in the next. The term 'punishment' today refers principally to retribution, and the term 'penance' to expiation, but they both derive from the Latin *poena.*

The willing acceptance of suffering was also a way of expressing devotion, especially to Christ, Who voluntarily suffered on the cross for the sake of mankind. The question of whether monasticism, historically considered, should be seen as a substitute for martyrdom is disputed by scholars, but there is no doubt that many of the early monks regarded themselves, and were regarded by others, as the successors of the martyrs and confessors and that the desire to suffer with and for Christ inspired their self-inflicted austerities. The example of Christ Himself, according to the biographer of Daniel the Stylite, shows that man can please God by suffering.

Ascetic practices also served the more immediate purpose of warding off temptations to sin. Nearly all the devils and demons who attacked men and women in the Middle Ages (and who can be seen in representations of the temptations of St. Anthony and in the paintings of Hieronymus Bosch) were personifications of sensual desires. In the early centuries they may also have stood for the tendencies to revert to pagan beliefs and practices. Pliny in his *Natural History* recommended tying lead plates to the loins and hips as an antiaphrodisiac, and the countless monks who wore *lorica,* and the more familiar hair-shirts or *cilicia,* were motivated less by a desire to suffer than to avoid fleshly temptations. The Egyptian hermit who thrust his fingers into the flame of a candle when he was tempted by a woman—and whose example was being cited, and followed, a thousand years later—took no satisfaction in the suffering but saved his chastity thereby. (The woman, incidentally, died of the shock, but she was later revived by the hermit's prayers and lived a virtuous life.) The mortification of immersion in cold water, of which examples can be found in the twentieth century, had the same purpose. Gregory the Great specifically said that St. Benedict changed his lust into pain by rolling in nettles and thorns.

There may have been in some of these practices an element of genuine dualism in the sense of an almost instinctive rejection of anything material or fleshly. Theologically, this feeling found its clearest expression in some of the early rivals of Christianity, such as Manichaeism, and in puritanical heresies like Montanism and, later, Catharism, which can be considered both as a rival religion to Christianity and as a heresy. Many monastic leaders, including Basil of Caesaria, were influenced by philosophical dualism and held that monks must dematerialize themselves by cutting themselves off from the physical world as much as possible. This dematerialization could take either one of two basic forms, which in practice doubtless overlapped. The first of these, which is still with us today (to judge from the passages I have cited), is the result of a desire for mastery over the body and a determination not to be governed by purely material needs, either for food, warmth, sleep, or other lower, as they were called, desires.

The second, and more interesting, form of dematerialization was based on the belief that man is placed between the animals and the angels on the scale of created beings and is therefore in a position of constant tension between the material and spiritual natures. The body, according to this view, while good in itself and essential for life in this world, is something to be left behind, so that man can be as free as possible from material needs and desires. Many monks in the East strove to attain a state of impassivity, apathy, or *theoria,* as it was called, which approximated in its extremes a Yoga-like superiority to physical suffering. Their object was to achieve the *bios angelikos,* the life of the angels, who were by their nature immaterial and above physical needs. To live above the requirements of the body was at the same time to recover the perfect peace and contentment of the Garden of Eden and to anticipate the pleasures of paradise. *Askesis* for them was a process of training and exercise, not unlike that of the athlete, and led to a higher end. The great Alexandrian theologians Clement and, above all, Origen formulated the bases of an ascetic theology in which the Christian way of life was seen as a school for sinners and training ground for souls. Their ideas were used by Evagrius Ponticus in the late fourth century in the first real system of monastic spirituality, with steps leading up to the pure intellect of God by a progressive stripping of the soul and removal of sin. Action and contemplation were, for Evagrius, closely associated and interactive stages of a single monastic life. These ideas were transmitted to the West especially by John Cassian, who in the early fifth century established two monasteries in southern France which were for over a century the spiritual centers of western monasticism. Cassian, like Evagrius, regarded the *vita actualis,* or active life, not as a life of work in the world but as the practice within a monastery of ascetic virtues which prepared the way for a life of contemplation.

St. Augustine examined some of these ideas in his sermon *On the Usefulness of Fasting,*[6] which is concerned not so much with the material aspects of fasting, or its scriptural justification, as with abstention generally not only from food but also from sin, love of the world, discord, and even heresy. Only man, who is in a middle position between animals and angels, can make this offering to God. 'If then the flesh bending toward the earth is a burden to the soul,' Augustine wrote, '. . . so far as every man delights in his own higher life, so such a degree does he lay aside his earthly burden. This is what we do by fasting.' Later he went on to say that, 'By abstaining from the joy of the flesh, joy of the soul is acquired. . . . Accordingly, for us the purpose (*finis*) of our fastings is for our journey.' Here too, therefore, ascetic practices are seen as a means to

12

the end of man's journey away from this world toward the next. St. Jerome popularized the concept of spiritual nudity in the phrase, much cited later, 'naked to follow the naked Christ.' In the East the concept was put more simply by the great Byzantine hymnwriter Romanos, who said that, 'Fasting gives men eternal life.'

For western monks these ideas were embodied in the Rule of Benedict, of which the full debt to eastern monastic spirituality has only recently been proved by the researches showing its dependence on the earlier rule known as the *Regula Magistri*.[7] It is now known that Benedict (or whoever wrote the rule that goes under his name) was much less original as a monastic theorist than was once believed, though his stature as a legislator and administrator has emerged unscathed. The earlier views stressing the contrast between pre-Benedictine and Benedictine monasticism, especially with regard to ascetic practices, have been revised. His rule has been described as 'unintelligible without the Cassianic and Basilian thought behind it' and as providing a framework for 'Evagrian spirituality as interpreted by Cassian.' Although the principal emphasis of the rule, as in the works of Basil and Cassian, is on privative rather than active mortifications, and especially on poverty, chastity, obedience, and silence, self-inflicted suffering was not excluded, and life in a strict Benedictine house was one of great, and sometimes extreme, physical hardship.

Monastic life in the West in the early Middle Ages was not led exclusively according to the Rule of Benedict, however, and during the so-called period of the *Regula mixta*, or mixed rule, from the sixth to the ninth century, every religious house had its own way of doing things, and many types of monastic life, some of great severity, were found in western Europe. Eastern influences persisted in southern France and in Burgundy, especially in the 'perpetual prayer' (*laus perennis*) monasteries, where the monks served in shifts worshipping God twenty-four hours a day. The monks in Ireland were famous at this time for their austerities, which included rigorous fasting, ascetic immersions and tests of chastity, and praying in painful positions. Another form of asceticism that was popular among Irish monks, and of which the character and historical importance have only recently been fully recognized, was penitential pilgrimage or exile. Solitude in the sense of separation from the world had always been recognized as an essential element in monastic life, and St. Basil, among others, stressed the need to break all familial ties. The state of being a stranger, without a home, was considered an ascetic ideal comparable to poverty and humility and was eagerly sought by Irish monks, who set out from their homeland as expatriates, sometimes entrusting themselves to the sea in boats without either sails or oars. Their wanderings, which had such important results for the foundation of new monasteries and the conversion of large areas of Europe, were basically ascetic rather than missionary in purpose.

Some of these wanderers, and other monks all over Europe, settled down as hermits, living either a classical eremitical life in the woods or a cave, alone or with a few companions, or as a recluse, walled up in a cell or small house usually in close proximity to a church or monastery. These forms of solitary life were in principle — and often in fact, since recluses, and frequently also hermits, depended for food on the surrounding community — no more cut off from the world than life in a monastery, but they involved a higher degree of physical hardship and presented a greater opportunity for ascetic practices.

This was the heroic age of monasticism in the West, and many monks endured suffering in order to show their devotion to Christ and bear witness to the superiority of Christianity over paganism. For Bede, a willingness to suffer and even to die for the sake of truth was a characteristic of the monastic life or, as he called it, apostolic life, referring to the common life of the apostles in Jerusalem after the death of Christ. Asceticism was regarded as pleasing to God, and Gregory of Tours in his *History of the Franks* cited examples of tortures imposed on themselves by monks simply in order to increase their suffering. Jonas said that the fastings and mortifications of St. Columban propititated Christ and atoned for evil thoughts. The Irish monks in particular adopted many practices designed to test their virtue and endurance. Among these was a type of spiritual marriage which was known in the early church, and appeared again in the eleventh and twelfth centuries, by which a male and a female ascetic lived together, and even shared the same bed, in a chaste union. Many years later James of Vitry told of a departing crusader who had his children brought to him in order to increase his suffering and hence his merit.

Self-inflicted suffering also served some practical functions in society. For the holy man, it was a source of power, as the biographer of Daniel the Stylite realized when he stressed the amazement of those who saw him. To the extent that he was outside secular society, and not bound by its standards, he could act as an arbiter and impose his decisions. Few people are unaffected by the sight of suffering, especially when it is self-imposed, and in Ireland particularly fasting was used in the Middle Ages (as it is today) as a means of bringing pressure and of righting a perceived wrong. The *Liber vitae* of Durham records that some sons prostrated themselves for the sake of their mother, with bare feet and tears in the middle of the night, seeking divine aid against one Gasbert, 'since there was no human aid.' Something like this probably happened at Canossa in 1077, when the pope was morally unable to keep the barefoot and penitent emperor waiting in the snow for more than three days, and Henry IV in essence got what he wanted. The sacramental efficacy of blood was universally recognized at that time, and the crusades have been described as a sacrifice, in the biblical sense, enlarged to the dimensions of the entire world. Ascetic practices were also used as a means of exorcism, and both Bede and Walafrid Strabo, in his *Life of St. Gall,* describe how places were consecrated by fasting.

As the Middle Ages progressed, there was a tendency for these austerities to become even more severe and emotional in character, and to spread outside monastic circles. Around the turn of the millenium a number of ascetic and devotional exercises appeared, or became more general, which were a standard aspect of spiritual life in the late Middle Ages. These included all-night vigils; copious weeping; ascetic recitations from the Bible, especially the Psalms, often accompanied by prostrations, genuflexions, breast-beating, and whipping; penitential foot-washing; the wearing of hairshirts, chain-mail, and plates of metal; flagellation; praying with outstretched arms and in other painful positions, which had previously been a specialty of Irish monks; and processions and pilgrimages dressed in sack-cloth, with bare feet or on the knees, and burdened with metal weights or a wooden cross. I do not intend to trace the history of each of these practices in detail. I shall rather look at a few practitioners of these types of asceticism and study some characteristic manifestations of this ascetic spirit in order to discover the attitudes and motives behind it.

The first figure I shall discuss is one of the most celebrated and extravagant ascetics of the entire Middle Ages, Dominic *Loricatus,* a monk of Camaladoli who died in 1060 and whose *Life* was written by Peter Damiani, who was himself a fierce ascetic and an influential friend and advisor of Pope Gregory VII. Dominic derived his name *Loricatus* from the *lorica* or metal plates which he hung on his body and which by the time of his death had grown in number to eight, hanging around his neck, hips, and legs. He also prayed for long periods with his arms extended and performed numerous penitential genuflexions or *metanea,* as they were called. But he is most famous for his heroic self-flagellation. According to Damiani, he was in the habit of beating himself while reciting the Psalms and gave himself a thousand blows for each ten Psalms and performed a hundred *metanea* for each fifteen, making a total of fifteen thousand blows and a thousand *metanea* for each full recitation of the Psalter. He regularly recited twenty Psalters in six days and once reached nine (though never, Damiani says, ten) Psalters in a single day. Some scholars have said that he and Damiani originated the practice of penitential flagellation. This is not true, since earlier examples of the practice can be found. The discipline of whips, or simply the discipline, had long been used in monasteries as a punishment. Dominic and Damiani contributed greatly, however, to the spread of voluntary flagellation, 'this discipline of the new rite,' as Damiani's biographer John of Lodi called it. In the twelfth century it became a regular observance in many monasteries, in spite of the warnings and occasional opposition of monastic leaders, and it culminated in the thirteenth century with the foundation of the order of Disciplinati specifically for the purpose of flagellation. Long processions of flagellants were a familiar sight in the late Middle Ages and can still be seen, I am told, in some parts of the American continent today.

The second figure I shall look at is Stephen of Obazine, who died in 1159, almost exactly a century after Dominic. He started life as a well-to-do layman and then became a secular priest and a popular preacher, practicing various austerities such as hair-shirts, rigorous fasts, and ascetic immersions, when necessary breaking the ice with an axe. Finally he decided to renounce the world entirely and having left his native soil, as his biographer says, began to go with bare feet into exile. After a while he settled down with a single companion at Obazine, in the Limousin, leading a life of rigid poverty, manual labor, and ascetic mortification. They beat each other whenever they felt sleepy, and they wore their clothes in winter frozen stiff, not because they needed washing, the biographer says, 'but for the sole desire of suffering.' Stephen travelled barefoot and, like Dominic *Loricatus,* wore metal plates next to his skin. He kept strict silence, except when celebrating the holy offices, and practiced intensive prayer and psalmody, accompanied by many genuflexions. This discipline relaxed somewhat as disciples gathered aroung him, but I am not concerned here with the later history of Obazine, interesting as it is, except to note that in 1142 the brothers officially adopted the Benedictine rule and became monks and in 1147 joined the Cistercian order.

It is no accident that both Dominic and Stephen were members of reformed monastic orders, because the winds of asceticism blew strongly through the monasteries of the eleventh and twelfth centuries and affected many of the old as well as most of the new houses. Flagellation was practiced at Monte Cassino and at Cluny, and the poet Bernard of Cluny recommended wearing lead plates next to the skin in order to repress carnal desires. The Cluniac cardinal Matthew of Albano, writing about 1132, even described the celebration of matins in winter as a great torment. 'What madmen,' he asked, taunting the critics of the allegedly easy life at Cluny, 'would dare to ascribe that to pleasure of self-glorification?'

A new ascetic value was given at that time to the practices of both poverty and manual labor in monasteries. Traditionally, monastic poverty was individual and spiritual: the monk must be personally without property and above all poor in spirit, though the monastery might be rich. Poverty in this sense was very much like humility and obedience. The eleventh and twelfth-century reformers, on the other hand, emphasized true economic poverty and institutional as well as personal divestment: the monastery as well as the monks must be poor. The *pauperes Christi* were those who had freely given up their worldly goods and fully committed themselves to God. At times they were almost obsessed by the dangers of wealth and welcomed all the more the hardships of extreme poverty. In the thirteenth century poverty became the heart and soul of the mendicant movement, and particularly of the teaching of Francis of Assisi, whose whole life was devoted to the ideals of poverty and mendicancy.

In the eleventh and twelfth centuries, however, begging was considered beneath the dignity of monks, and the corollary of poverty was not mendicancy but manual labor, which served the double purpose of economic support and physical mortification. For Bernard of Clairvaux and other spiritual writers of the twelfth century work, of various types, filled the role of the active life which for Cassian and the early monastic theorists had consisted primarily of ascetic exercises. While more research needs to be done on the emergence of the modern attitude toward work, it seems to have been above all in the twelfth century that the ancient and early medieval depreciation of manual labor was replaced by a more positive view of work as an active means of salvation and self-fulfillment.

These developments took place not only in monasteries. The fiercely individualistic, and greatly admired, hermit Gezzelin of Trier never joined a religious house. He lived alone, without any habitation or clothing, and nourished himself on grass and roots, having, as a contemporary said, 'the sky in place of a roof, the air in place of clothes, and the support of flocks in place of human food.' John of Salisbury, who was a secular cleric and no ascetic, said of himself in the *Policraticus* that:

I know a man...subjected to constant assault of diseases, though they do not exceed what he can bear, who rejoices that the lascivity of his flesh has been crushed and his spirit aroused and strengthened in the knowledge of God, contempt for the world, and exercise of virtue. He desires that while the senses of his soul and body may be preserved intact [This is a reference to I Thessalonians 5.23.] the violence of disease will not draw him away from his activities. He expects and welcomes from the hand of the Lord some flagellation, though light and tolerable to the infirm.

It is uncertain here whether the flagellation to which John referred was actual whipping or simply his ailments. There is no doubt, however, about the active mortifications of the regular canon Dodo of Hascha, in Frisia, who died in 1231. He spent his life, in the words of his biographer, 'in unremitting weeping and grieving, groaning and praying for himself and for the entire holy church of God.' He ate 'one meal a day, eating fish and beer one day and bread and water the next; on Friday he ate nothing.' As to clothing, still according to his biographer, 'First, seven iron plates girded his flesh around his sides, two around his arms; over these was a hair-shirt; after this an iron *lorica* was put on; finally he had two woolen tunics, and a scapular above, and so he remained day and night without changes.' He slept on a hard bed, with a mat for a blanket and a concave stone, with a piece of cloth in the cavity, for a pillow, 'following the example of our Lord Jesus Christ, Who was placed in a manger wrapped in rags.' He rose in the middle of the night for matins, and he then spent the rest of the night in prayer, discipline, and various sorts of genuflexions, performing 'five hundred genuflexions each day and night, and frequently more.' 'His knees were calloused like those of a camel, and since he was a true worshiper of God, the Lord therefore performed many miracles through him.'

These examples cover the period from the early eleventh to the early thirteenth century and illustrate the continuity as well as the changes in the attitudes towards self-inflicted suffering in the central Middle Ages. Behind them all lay a pervasive sense of sin, resembling what Dodds called the 'intense and wide-spread guilt-feelings' in Late Antiquity. This was nourished not only by theological teachings about the depravity of man but also by personal feelings of inadequacy and remorse among laymen as well as monks and clerics. The tender social consciences of men like Robert of Arbrissel and Stephen of Obazine were specially aroused by the sufferings of the poor, sick, and unfortunate in an age of generally growing material prosperity and social mobility, when the traditional ways of dealing with misfortune in society were proving increasingly inadequate. It is significant that many of the reformers, including Bernard of Clairvaux and Francis of Assisi, came from the ranks of the ruling and privileged classes. The *sola cruciendi voluntas* of Stephen of Obazine when he wore frozen clothing was inspired by guilt and a desire to share the sufferings of the poor. Great nobles like Boniface of Tuscany in the eleventh century and William of Aquitaine in the twelfth agreed to be whipped in order to expiate their sins. Yet more remarkable was the barefoot flight of Provost Bertulf of St. Donatien at Bruges, one of the chief conspirators in the murder of

Charles the Good, count of Flanders. In the words of the historian Galbert, Bertulf fled with bare feet, 'voluntarily (*sponte*) performing penance for his sins, in order that God might be merciful to such a sinner.' When he was captured, he was found to have left a trail of blood on the ground.

Actions such as these were not motivated by dualistic repression of the body or by love of suffering for its own sake. Real dualism was rare among orthodox Christians at this time especially owing to the condemnation by many contemporary heretics of all material things, including the eucharistic elements and the wood of the cross. The Cathars and Albigensians in particular were dualists in their avoidance of all material aspects of life. Catholics were therefore careful to limit their objections to the misuse of matter (that is, a question of the will) rather than to matter itself. There remained a strong element of practical dualism, however. John of Salisbury rejoiced that disease had crushed the lascivity of his flesh, and St. Francis considered mortification a means of controlling 'the lower nature which leads him [man] into sin.' Such an unimpeachably orthodox theologian as Hugh of St. Victor praised the new orders of monks precisely for their physical austerities. 'For while they lacerate their flesh,' he said, 'they enrich the spirit; while they weaken the flesh, they strengthen the spirit; while they take something away from the outer flesh, they add greatly to the inner spirit.'

There was a growing tendency in the twelfth century, which may be associated with crusading spirituality, to see the Christian as a soldier engaged in warfare against the powers of evil. Military metaphors had long been used in Christian spiritual writings, but in the early Middle Ages the *miles Christi* was an obedient follower or occasionally an individual warrior. Now he was increasingly seen as a knight in the service of Christ. A secular knight gave his *lorca* to the hermit Wulfric of Hazelbury 'as to a stronger soldier,' and Wulfric wore it until it slipped off his shoulders in old age. This military metaphor doubtless also encouraged the ascetic competitiveness that we have already observed among the early hermits. Dominic *Loricatus* constantly strove to beat his own records after he had outstripped all others.

This stress on the inner and emotional nature of asceticism, and its effect on the spirit, was characteristic of twelfth-century spirituality, which emphasized the motive of love both as a quasi-martyrdom and sacrifice for Christ and as a passionate desire to imitate and suffer with Him. Self-sacrifice is likewise a dominant theme in the secular love literature of the twelfth and thirteenth centuries, with which the spiritual writings have many affinities. Devotion to the human Christ was especially marked in the religious personalities of some of the fiercest ascetics, whose tears and groans increasingly expressed, as Berlière pointed out, their sympathy for the sufferings of Christ as well as their remorse for their own sins and who sought in their actions to imitate every aspect of Christ's life on earth. Peter Damiani specifically cited the example of Christ in his defense of flagellation and expressed his own fervent desire to copy Christ. 'I would like to undergo martyrdom for Christ,' he wrote in one of his letters, 'but I have no possibility for it now that the [persecuting] zeal has ceased. I show at least the desire of a fervent soul by destroying myself with beating. For if the persecutor should strike me, I would beat myself, since I would voluntarily expose myself to be beaten. ...The king of martyrs Himself, Christ, likewise was delivered not only by Judas but also by the Father and by Himself.' Dominic *Loricatus* and Stephen of Obazine were both said to have carried on their bodies the signs or stigmata of the wounds of Christ, and while these may have been symbolic, there is no question that Dodo of Hascha not only imitated the infant Christ, as has been mentioned, but also bore visible marks on his body in the places of Christ's wounds 'in order to suffer with the crucified One.' For although Francis of Assisi, so far as is known, was the first visible stigmatic whose wounds were probably not self-imposed, many people in the twelfth and thirteenth centuries, both male and female, felt the pain of Christ's sufferings, and some inflicted His wounds on themselves as evidence of their desire to suffer with Him. According to the great fifteenth-century Franciscan preacher Bernardino of Siena, St. Paul did not say that we should understand Christ Crucified 'but that we should feel within ourselves, as He felt on the cross. *Hoc enim sentite in vobis.* And this is the difference,' Bernardino continued, 'between feeling a thing from outside it, from inside it, and from partaking in it.'

The participation in and interiorization of the sufferings of Christ was a central aspect of late medieval mysticism, and a source of ineffible exaltation for those who experienced it. 'Suffering alone is sufficient preparation for God's dwelling in man's heart,' said Eckhart in one of his sermons. 'It makes man Godlike.' Likewise for Catherine of Siena, suffering was a means of progressing toward the vision of God. 'It is for me the greatest consolation, when I suffer some evil,' she said, according to the *Legenda maior,* 'because I know that through that passion I shall have a more perfect vision of God. For this reason the tribulations are not only not burdensome to me but also delectable to my mind, just as you and the others who converse with me can perceive every day.'

Catherine was a shrewd psychologist, and her reference to her sufferings as *delectabiles menti meae* brings out the element of sublimation which must not be forgotten when we consider voluntary or self-inflicted suffering either in the Middle Ages or today. Not only may the fact of abstinence have modified the needs of the body and the physical exertions of asceticism have reduced the capacity for pain, but the mind transformed what for some would literally have been a source of agony into a source of happiness and peace and a sense of being in harmony with others and with the immaterial forces that govern the universe.

I would not want to leave you with the impression that indiscriminate or purposeless suffering, either voluntary or involuntary, was admired by serious men and women in the Middle Ages, though there were doubtless people then, as now, who were impressed by, and even enjoyed, the mere act of suffering and physical violence. It may have served as a sort of vicarious release for feelings that could not be expressed directly. Likewise today, many people enjoy tales of horror and scenes of violence. The sufferings of the saints, and the stories of their lives, may have played something of the same role in medieval society.[8] Thoughtful people looked below the surface of the exterior actions, however, and tried to discern the motives, warning against flamboyant or excessive ascetic practices.

From the earliest times there was an insistence, perhaps inspired by fear of dualism, on discretion in self-imposed sufferings and an awareness of the dangers of hypocrisy. St. Paul himself warned the Corinthians against delivering the body to be burned but not having love. The story in the *Vitae patrum* about Abbot John, who decided after fasting in the wilderness for eight days to be a good man rather than an angel, was cited as an example of the temptation of extravagant asceticism, and even a rigid ascetic like Daniel the Stylite did not force his body beyond what it could endure, saying that he ate what was necessary. The author of a homily *On Perfect Monks,* written in Spain in the late sixth or early seventh century, stressed that the Devil often sent the temptation to fast or lie on the ground in order to keep monks from their proper occupations. The earliest commentaries on the Rule of Benedict, which were written in the Carolingian period, also do not stress bodily austerities and in their discussions of fasting deal with such issues as the permissibility of eating fowls.

The fear of hypocrisy was reflected in the tendency to admire austerities and mortifications that were kept secret or were revealed only in confidence. Cassian maintained that fasting should be secret as well as restrained and that it was good not in itself but only as a means toward virtue. Austerities, such as wearing a hair-shirt under comfortable clothing, were sometimes discovered only after death, as were the stigmata of Dodo of Hascha. St. Arnulf, who died as bishop of Soissons in 1087, wore a spiny branch under his clothes, according to his biographer, 'in order to extinguish entirely within himself the smile and emotion of worldly joy...while exhibiting to everyone, however, a happy and joyful countenance.' Especially in the eleventh and twelfth centuries, the sentiment against displays of asceticism seems to have grown, as a result not only of the excesses of the past but also of the new stress on interiority. Ascetic extravagance came to be regarded with suspicion. Many of the religious leaders of the time, and a number of the new monastic and canonical rules and customs, urged discretion in this regard and even forbade unauthorized or supererogatory mortifications of the flesh. According to the late eleventh-century constitutions of Camaldoli, for instance, where Dominic *Loricatus* had been a monk not long before, flagellation was to be practiced for the sake of humility, not of torment, and in imitation of the Passion. They established that in this and other mortifications, 'Each monk ought to do what he can bear and utility advises or divine grace inspires. For in such matters force does not impose but voluntary offering advises.' In some rules an increasing concern was also shown for the physical health of monks and nuns in matters such as adequate food and sleep. You will remember that John of Salisbury specified that his flagellation, though welcome, should be light and tolerable to the infirm.

Bernard of Clairvaux was an ascetic himself, who ruined his health by excessive fasting, and a fervent admirer of the hermit Gezzelin. He praised physical hardship and bodily afflictions, including regular discipline, 'by which,' he said, 'we live not by our own but by another's will,' and stressed that they must be willingly and voluntarily born. He was at the same time an experienced and sensitive spiritual advisor and acutely aware of the dangers of excessive zeal and self-will in ascetic practices. In his treatise *On the Steps of Humility,* where he described the successive vices which a monk must overcome in his ascent to God, Bernard gave under the fifth step, singularity, a classic picture of the hypocritical and loveless ascetic who, caring more for appearances than substance, fasted when the other monks ate and prayed alone in the corner filling the ears of those outside with groans and sighs. 'But although these things which he does with singularity but without sincerity raise his reputation among the more innocent, who praise the works they see without discerning whence they proceed,' Bernard concluded, 'the poor wretch is grievously deceived when they call him blessed.'

Parallel passages can be found in many twelfth- and thirteenth-century works. Robert of Arbrissel, the founder of Fontevrault, who was criticized for his own asceticism even by his admirers, urged the countess of Brittany, in a letter written probably in 1109, to use 'discretion in all matters, in abstinence, fasts, vigils, prayers' and not to kill herself, 'since whoever kills the flesh, kills its inhabitant,' that is, the spirit. The kingdom of God, he said, lies not in food and drink, but in grace and peace. Abbot Peter the

Venerable of Cluny, citing I Corinthians 13.3, said that it was useless to practice austerities without love. And the great preacher, and later cardinal, James of Vitry remarked in his biography of Mary of Oignies, after describing with admiration her ascetic devotions, including the stigmata, that, 'I say this not to commend excess but to show fervor. In these, and in many others, however, ...' he continued, 'the discreet reader will observe that the privileges of the few do not make a general rule. ...We should therefore admire rather than imitate what we read certain saints to have done at the private instigation of the Holy Spirit.'

There was agreement among serious churchmen at that time, and later, that meaningful sufferings must be an expression of devotion and that outer actions must be correlated to the inner life. The moral stress on intention in the twelfth century touched the practice of asceticism no less than the fields of theology and law. Interior devotion was as necessary in fasting as in prayer, according to the author of the Bridlington Dialogue. 'Fasts that are performed for human praise,' he said, 'do not please God.' The body should not be made to suffer more than it could reasonably bear, and moderation must be the rule. 'Let sleep be brief, food light, drink easy, clothing humble.' These words are from Petrarch's treatise *On the Solitary Life,* and they reflect the tradition of medieval monastic spirituality as well as the classical ideal of temperance. They are a reminder that many of our own ideals, though differently formulated today, were shaped in the Middle Ages. The standards and systems of values at that time were, needless to say, different from those that prevail today, but the spiritual ideals and psychological needs—to justify ourselves and, if necessary, to suffer for what we believe in—are still with us and show that the study of history can deepen our understanding not only of the past but also of the present.

Notes

1. Pierre Teilhard de Chardin, *Letters to Two Friends, 1926-1952* (New York, 1968) p. 187, writing in 1947 about Gide's *La porte étroite,* said that the 'idea of a value of sacrifice and pain for the sake of sacrifice and pain itself' was an expression of Gide's 'native Protestant education' and 'a dangerous (and very "Protestant") perversion of the "meaning of the Cross".' Dame Laurentia McLachlan, the abbess of Stanbrook, said almost the opposite: "We all know what happiness of heart can be found in the pain of mind and body that God sends us, or in the case of bodily suffering that is self-inflicted. ...We all have to suffer if God is to make anything of us.' *In a Great Tradition: The Life of Dame Laurentia McLachlan* (New York, 1956) pp. 101-2.

2. According to Jack Douglas, *The Social Meanings of Suicide* (Princeton, 1967) p. 372, citing T. Reik and S. Rado: 'Masochism led Freud and others to believe that men can and frequently do will suffering for the self, but they have seen this willing of self-suffering as being the result of expectations of "secondary gain," either through "victory through defeat" or "less defeat through preemptive punishment".'

3. Some of the material in this paragraph is derived from the *Oxford Dictionary of the Christian Church,* 2nd ed. (Oxford, 1974), which should be consulted for further details.

4. E. R. Dodds, *Pagan and Christian in an Age of Anxiety: Some Aspects of Religious Experience from Marcus Aurelius to Constantine* (Cambridge, 1965) pp. 18 and 36. This can be compared with the well-known view of J. B. Bury attributing the decline of the ancient world to 'a failure of nerve' and J. N. Cochrane's exposition of the 'moral and intellectual failure of the Greco-Roman mind' in the fourth century.

5. Edward Cuthbert Butler, *Benedictine Monachism,* 2nd ed. (London, 1924) pp. 13-14. See also Derwas J. Chitty, *The Desert a City: An Introduction to the Study of Egyptian and Palestinian Monasticism under the Christian Empire* (Oxford, 1966) pp. 32-3.

6. S. Dominic Ruegg, *Sancti Aurelii Augustini De utilitate ieiunii: A Text with a Translation, Introduction and Commentary* (Washington, D.C., 1951). The quotations are on pp. 69 and 77.

7. See Bernd Jaspert, *Die Regula Benedicti—Regula Magistri—Kontroverse* (Hildesheim, 1975), where the index of persons (pp. 508-19) is a guide to the huge bibliography on this topic.

8. See the remarks of Hippolyte Delehaye, *Les passions des martyrs et les genres littéraires* (Brussels, 1921) pp. 273-87.

Bibliographical Note

Since this paper was prepared for a general audience, I have kept the notes to a minimum and used them to elucidate points that might otherwise be unclear and to indicate my indebtedness to authors and works not specifically mentioned in the text. The following indications may be helpful, however, to those who are interested in pursuing the subject further.

The original sources for the paper are mostly the *Vitae* or biographies of saints, of which there is a useful list in the *Bibliotheca hagiographica latina* (Brussels, 1898-1901), of which a new edition is in preparation. They can also be located in any of several dictionaries of saints, such as (for Benedictine saints) Alfons M. Zimmermann, *Kalendarium benedictinum* (Metten, 1933-8). A number of the Lives cited in this paper have been translated into English: see Clarissa P. Farrar and Austin P. Evans, *Bibliography of English Translations from Medieval Sources* (New York, 1946) and the supplement by Mary A. H. Ferguson, *Bibliography of English Translations from Medieval Sources, 1943-1967* (New York and London, 1974). Two useful collections of translations, both including Lives cited here, are Elizabeth Dawes and Norman H. Baynes, *Three Byzantine Saints* (Oxford, 1948) and Clinton Albertson, *Anglo-Saxon Saints and Heroes* (New York, 1967). The essential collections for Ireland are Charles Plummer's *Vitae Sanctorum Hiberniae* (Oxford, 1910) and *Lives of the Irish Saints* (Oxford, 1922). The three saints whose lives are particularly discussed here are Dominic *Loricatus*, whose Life by Peter Damiani can be found in the *Patrologia latina*, CXLIV, 1012-24, Stephen of Obazine, of whose Life there is a new edition by M. Aubrun, *Vie de Saint Etienne d'Obazine* (Clermont, 1970), and Dodo of Hascha, whose Life is found in the great *Acta sanctorum*, edited by the Bollandists, in the volume for March, III, 848-9.

Of the non-hagiographical sources cited here, at least three are available in good recent translation: *The Lives of the Desert Fathers*, tr. Norman Russell (London and Oxford, 1980); Gregory of Tours, *The History of the Franks*, tr. Lewis Thorpe (Harmondsworth, 1974); and *Bede's Ecclesiastical History of the English People*, ed. Bertram Colgrave and R. A. B. Mynors (Oxford, 1969). Not available in English, but of great interest for the subject of this paper, are two collections of *exempla* (stories used in sermons) by James of Vitry: *The Exempla or Illustrative Stories from the Sermones Vulgares of Jacques de Vitry*, ed. Thomas F. Crane (London, 1890) and *Die Exempla aus den Sermones feriales et communes des Jakob von Vitry*, ed. Joseph Greven (Heidelberg, 1914). Most of the other non-hagiographical works from before the thirteenth century are printed in serviceable, though often antiquated, editions in the *Patrologia latina*. The translation from Bernard's *The Steps of Humility* is by George B. Burch (Cambridge, Mass., 1940). The passages from Eckhart and Bernardino of Siena are from the books of Franz Pfeiffer and Iris Origo, respectively. Full references to the sources recommending moderation, and restraint, some of which are more obscure, will be given in the article I plan to write on this subject.

Among secondary works, in addition to the three general books by Emile Durkheim, *The Elementary Forms of the Religious Life*, William James, *The Varieties of Religious Experience*, and Kenneth Kirk, *The Vision of God*, which are cited early in the paper, I have used Uta Ranke-Heinemann, *Das frühe Mönchtum. Seine Motive nach den Selbstzeugnissen* (Essen, 1964) and Peter Nagel, *Die Motivierung der Askese in der alten Kirche und der Ursprung des Mönchtums* (Berlin, 1966). On Basil and Cassian, see, respectively, David Amand (Emmanuel Amand de Mendieta), *L'ascèse monastique de Saint Basile* (Maredsous, 1949) and Owen Chadwick, *John Cassian*, 2nd ed. (Cambridge, 1968). There are several interesting articles in *Théologie de la vie monastique. Etudes sur la tradition patristique* (Paris, 1961). See also Violet MacDermot, *The Cult of the Seer in the Ancient Middle East* (London, 1971) and the article by Peter Brown, 'The Rise and Function of the Holy Man in Late Antiquity,' *Journal of Roman Studies*, LXI (1971) 80-101.

Articles on Abnegation, Abstinence, Asceticism, and other specific practices (including the ascetic kiss) can be found in the *Dictionnaire de spiritualité* (Paris, 1932 ff.) Several of these are by Louis Gougaud, whose two books on *Dévotions et pratiques ascétiques du moyen âge* (Paris and Maredsous, 1925; Eng. tr. by G.C. Bateman, 1927) and *Ermites et reclus. Etudes sur d'anciennes formes de vie religieuse* (Liguge, 1928) should also be consulted. Among general works on Christian asceticism those of Mar-cel Viller and Karl Rahner, *Aszese und Mystik in der Väterzeit* (Freiburg im Br., 1939) and Anselme Stolz, *L'ascèse chrétienne* (Chevetogne, 1948) are useful, as is the older work of Otto Zöckler, *Askese und Mönchtum*, of asceticism in the central Middle Ages. There is relevant material in Albert Dresdner, *Kultur- und Sittengeschichte der italienischen Geist-lichkeit im 10. und 11. Jahrhundert* (Breslau, 1890) and in Jean Leclercq, *La vie parfaite. Points de vue sur l'essence de l'état religieux* (Turnhout and Paris, 1948; Eng. tr., 1961). The otherwise valuable work of Ursmer Berlière, *L'ascèse bénédictine des origines à la fin du XIIe siècle* (Paris and Maredsous, 1927) devotes comparatively little attention to self-in-flicted mortifications on account of its stress on Benedictine monasticism as a moderate life of silence, prayer, and work. On fasting, see Herbert

Musurillo, 'The Problem of Ascetical Fasting in the Greek Patristic Writers,' *Traditio,* XII (1956) 1-64, and on celibacy, Bernhard Kötting, *Der Zölibat in der alten Kirche* (Münster in W., 1968). The theme of ascetic homelessness is treated in the brief work of Hans von Campenhausen, *Die asketische Heimatslosigkeit im altkirchlichen und frühmittelalterlichen Mönchtum* (Tübingen, 1930), and also in my article on 'Monachisme et pèlerinage au Moyen Age,' *Revue historique,* CCLVIII (1977) 3-27, where further references will be found. On *syneisactism* ('the chaste living together of a male and female ascetic'), see Roger Reynolds, '*Virgines subintroductae* in Celtic Christianity,' *Harvard Theological Review,* LXI (1968) 547-66. The topic of the stigmata in the eleventh and twelfth centuries will be covered in my *forthcoming article on 'Miracles and History in the Twelfth Century.' There is a large literature on flagellation, beginning with the old but still useful works of Jean Mabillon, *Annales O. S. B.,* IV (Lucca, 1739), esp. 513-15, and Edmond Martène, *De antiquis ecclesiae ritibus,* IV (Antwerp, 1738) 229-33. There is an article on flagellation by Paul Bailly in the *Dictionnaire de spiritualité,* V, 392-408, and a collection of articles entitled *Il movimento dei disciplinati nel settimo centenario dal suo inizio* (Perugia, 1962). The contributions by G. G. Meersseman and Jean Leclercq are especially valuable for the purposes of this paper.

Relatively little work has been done on the subject of moderation and restraint in ascetic practices, upon which I plan to write an article. The important article of Bernhard Schmeidler, 'Anti-asketische Äusserungen aus Deutschlands im 11. und beginnenden 12. Jahrhundert,' *Kultur und Universalgeschichte (Festschrift Walter Goetz)* (Berlin and Leipzig, 1927) 35-52, must be used with some caution owing to its stress on the Germanic character of the reaction. Some interesting indications of the growing concern for the physical health of monks and nuns can be found in Gerd Zimmermann, *Ordensleben und Lebensstandard. Die cura corporis in den Ordensvorschriften des abendländischen Hochmittelalters* (Münster in W., 1973) esp. 147, 215-6, 234-5, and 459.

X

MODERATION AND RESTRAINT IN ASCETIC PRACTICES
IN THE MIDDLE AGES

Although asceticism was generally admired in the Middle Ages, and many forms of bodily austerities and mortifications were practiced, there was a significant tradition, stemming both from the Bible and from classical Antiquity, which insisted on moderation and restraint.[1] The *via regia* by which the children of Israel passed through the lands of the king of the Amorrites (Num. 21.22) was identified with the *via media* of the ancient philosophers and the monastic *iter disciplinae regularis*.[2] Solomon said that men should be neither overly just and wise nor overly wicked and foolish (Eccl. 7.17-18), and for Cicero the middle way (*mediocritas*) was best in clothing "as in many things".[3] Paul proposed an equitable division of charitable burdens in a passage which was applied to other aspects of Christian life (2 Cor. 8.13), and his statement that "If I should deliver my body to be burned and have not charity, it profiteth me nothing" (1 Cor. 13.3) was often cited as a warning against hypocrisy and ostentation. "Bodily exercise is profitable to little", Paul said, "but godliness is profitable to all things" (1 Tim. 4.8). Cassian's decription of discretion as the mother of virtues was cited in the rule of Benedict and by many monastic writers.[4] The image of the bow which loses its strength if it is kept bent was used by Phaedrus to show that the mind should occasionally be allowed to play and was put by Cassian into the mouth of a hermit whom a hunter found doing some humble work and who explained that "unless he relieved and relaxed the rigor of exertion by some remission from time to time, his spirit would become weak from his unremitting endeavor in virtue and was unable to obey when it was necessary".[5] The story in the *Sayings of the Fathers* about

---

[1] The only work devoted exclusively to this subject is Bernhard Schmeidler, "Anti-asketische Äusserungen aus Deutschland im 11. und beginnenden 12. Jahrhundert", in *Kultur und Universalgeschichte (Festschrift Walter Goetz)* (Leipzig-Berlin, 1927) 35-52. See also my small work on *Attitudes Toward Self-Inflicted Suffering in the Middle Ages* (Brookline, Mass., 1982) 21-23, citing some of the examples which are used here. The section on "Les attaques contre l'abstinence" in F. Mugnier's article on "Abstinence" in the *Dictionnaire de spiritualité*, I (Paris, 1937) coll. 127-129, is exclusively concerned with heretical opposition, mostly in the late Middle Ages.

[2] On the *via regia* in the twelfth century, see Matthäus Bernards, *Speculum virginum. Geistigkeit und Seelenleben der Frau im Hochmittelalter*, Forschungen zur Volkskunde, 36-38 (Köln-Graz, 1955) 135, and Chrysogonus Waddell, "Sequantur IIII Collecte: A Letter to Brother Aidan about the Cistercian Prayers for the Blessing of a Monk", *Liturgy*, XII (1978) 119-121, comparing Cassian with the rule of Benedict.

[3] Cicero, *De officiis*, I, 36 (130), tr. Walter Miller, Loeb Library (London-New York, 1928) 132.

[4] Cassian, *Conlationes*, II, 4, ed. Michael Petschenig, *CSEL* XIII.2 (Vienna, 1886) 44; *Regula Benedicti*, LXIV, ed. Philibert Schmitz (Maredsous, 1955) 131. See nn. 22 (Bernard of Clairvaux) and 24 (Peter the Venerable) below.

[5] Phaedrus, *Fable*, III, 14, ed. Ben Edwin Perry, Loeb Library (Cambridge, Mass.-London, 1965) 282, and Cassian, *Conlationes*, XXIV, 21, ed. Petschenig, 697-698; see Owen Chadwick, *John Cassian* (Cambridge, 1950) 72, on Cassian's and Anthony's praise of discretion in asceticism. See n. 20 (Bruno of La Chartreuse) below.

abba John who refused to work, put off his clothing, and left his hermitage because he wanted to live like an angel and to serve God continuously, and who when he returned was denied admission until he acknowledged that he was not an angel but a man who had to work, was frequently told in the Middle Ages to show that it was better to try to be a good man than to be an angel.[6]

Basil and Chrysostom stressed the need to be moderate and temperate in ascetical fasting and to bear in mind its spiritual dimension as the avoidance of sin,[7] and even a strict ascetic like Daniel the Stylite, who died in 493, said that he ate what was necessary in order not to force his body beyond what it could endure.[8] In Persia in the late fifth century, several councils criticized the ascetic practices of monks and nuns, especially their chastity, and legislated in favor of a married clergy. This exceptional hostility to asceticism may have been the result of Zoroastrian influence, but it shows that the Christians in the East were not uniformly well-disposed towards ascetic practices.[9] The desire for extreme austerities was depicted as a temptation from the Devil in several early western sources, including Gregory of Tours, who disapproved of Winnoch and other hermits who dressed only in skins and ate uncooked wild plants,[10] and in the homily *On perfect monks* written in Spain in the late sixth or early seventh century, where the Devil was said to tempt monks "to fast on many days and to lie on the ground", so that they were too tired to join the holy offices with other members of the community.[11] When the English hermit Guthlac, who died in 714, was advised to "afflict your flesh with the whips of abstinence and crush the arrogance of your spirit with the rods of fasting", he recognized that the advice came from two devils and "began even then to eat his daily food, lest there should appear to be any sign of his consenting to them".[12] Gregory the Great said in his *Homilies on the Gospels* that spiritual were superior to physical manifestations of sanctity and that "Bodily miracles sometimes show but do not make sanctity, but spiritual [miracles], which are performed in the mind, do not show but make the virtue of life".[13]

This view was probably a minority opinion at the time these works were written, and it may have represented a reaction against the general tendency in the early

---

[6] *Vitae patrum*, V, 10, 27, in *PL*, LXXIII, coll. 916D-917A; see *The Letters and Poems of Fulbert of Chartres*, ed. and tr. Frederick Behrends, Oxford Medieval Texts (Oxford, 1976) 268 (Letter 153), also 254 (Letter 145), where Fulbert praised holding the median; *Carmina Cantabrigiensia*, XLII, 13, ed. Walther Bulst (Heidelberg, 1950) 68; and n. 20 (Bruno of La Chartreuse) below; also Schmeidler, "Anti-asketische Äusserungen", 40-42.

[7] Herbert Musurillo, "The Problem of Ascetical Fasting in the Greek Patristic Writers", *Traditio* XII (1956) 8 and 40-41.

[8] Elizabeth Dawes and Norman H. Baynes, *Three Byzantine Saints* (Oxford, 1948) 45 (ch. 62).

[9] Stephen Gero, "Die antiasketische Bewegung im persischen Christentum: Einfluss zoroastrischer Ethik?", *Orientalia Christiana Analecta*, CCXXI (1983) 187-191, who questioned the Zoroastrian influence.

[10] Gregory of Tours, *Libri historiarum*, VIII, 34, ed. Bruno Krusch and Wilhelm Levison, 2nd ed., *MGH*: Scriptores rerum Merovingicarum, I.1-2 (Hanover, 1943-51) 403-404.

[11] Manuel C. Diaz y Diaz, "La homilía 'De monachis perfectis'", *Analecta Wisigothica*, I, Acta Salmanticensia: Filosofía y letras, XII.2 (Salamanca, 1958) 86.

[12] *Felix's Life of Saint Guthlac*, XXX, ed. and tr. Bertram Colgrave (Cambridge, 1956) 98-101.

[13] Gregory the Great, *Homilia in Evangelia*, II, 29, 4, in *PL*, LXXVI, col. 1216A.

Middle Ages to judge spiritual perfection in terms of the extent of visible suffering. Most if not all monks at that time led lives of great and sometimes extreme physical hardship, and the moderation of the rule of Benedict has been exaggerated by some scholars in order to make it more acceptable to the modern world.[14] As it is increasingly seen in the tradition of early eastern monasticism, it looks more severe. But the seeds of leniency were present both in the rule of the Master, which included moderation among the qualifications required of provosts, and in the rule of Benedict, especially in its injunction that the abbot follow discretion, the mother of virtues, and temper all things in such a way as to suit the weak as well as the strong members of the community. The earliest commentators on the rule of Benedict, writing in the first half of the ninth century, regarded fasting and abstinence as the principal forms of bodily austerity and recommended the use of discretion in ascetic practices relating to material life.[15] Abbot Maiolus of Cluny was praised by his biographer Syrus for his discretion and moderation: "In all things, even good things, whatever exceeds measure is a vice".[16]

There were signs in the eleventh century of an open resistance to extreme asceticism and recognition of the need for moderation. One of the first known spokesmen for this view was a monk of St. Vincent in Urbino named Gozo, whose opposition to any additions to the rule of Benedict was described by Peter Damiani:

> This man began to complain that what saint Benedict ordered was sufficient and always enough and that the weight of no new invention should be added and that we were not holier than the ancient fathers, who judging these things to be superstitious and superfluous established the measure of psalmody and the entire rule of living for us. We should be content with this and should not by incautiously departing from it be led into error by twists and turns.[17]

Damiani strongly opposed Gozo, whom he called "a monk in habit but a man of evil life" and who was probably motivated less by a humane spirit of moderation than by a conservative and selfish dislike for the type of strict new monasticism of which Damiani was one of the leading representatives. The emergence of anti-asceticism in Germany in the eleventh and twelfth centuries has been studied by

---

[14] See Edward Cuthbert Butler, *Benedictine Monachism*, 2nd ed. (London, 1924) 24, and Herbert Thurston, "Benedictine Monachism", *The Month*, CXXXIV (July-Dec., 1919) 430-440; also my "The Study of Monastic History Today", in *Essays on the Reconstruction of Medieval History*, ed. Vaclav Mudroch and G.S. Couse (Montreal-London, 1974) 30.

[15] *Regula Magistri*, II, 4, ed. and tr. Adalbert de Vogüé, Sources Chrétiennes, 105-107 (Paris, 1964-65), II, 9; see I, 47, where de Vogüé said, "Dans son ensemble, cette observance ne semble pas particulièrement rude, en comparaison des autres règles de l'antiquité. Un réel souci de discrétion l'inspire"; and *Regula Benedicti*, LXIV, ed. Schmitz, 131. See also M. Alfred Schroll, *Benedictine Monasticism as Reflected in the Warnefrid-Hildemar Commentaries on the Rule* (New York, 1941) 173, 178, and 185.

[16] Syrus, *Vita sancti Maioli*, II, 8-9, ed. Dominique Iogna-Prat, *Agni immaculati. Recherches sur les sources hagiographiques relatives à saint Maieul de Cluny (954-994)* (Paris, 1988) 223-224; see also the *capitula* on p. 172.

[17] Peter Damiani, *Ep*. VI, 32, in *PL*, CXLIV, col. 434B; see Albert Dresdner, *Kultur- und Sittengeschichte der italienischen Geistlichkeit im 10. und 11. Jahrhundert* (Breslau, 1890) 299-300, citing this and (in 300, n. 1) other examples of opposition to the new customs, and Arnold Angenendt, "Sühne durch Blut", *Frühmittelalterliche Studien*, XVIII (1984) 462-463.

Bernhard Schmeidler, who found it in the *Proverbs* of Wipo, the Cambridge Songs, the *Lives* of Bardo of Fulda and Benno of Osnabrück, and especially in the letter written by the clergy and laity of Mainz to Archbishop Siegfried after he became a monk in 1072. The writers of these works were mostly associated with the imperial party during the Investiture Controversy, and Schmeidler saw them as evidence both of a reaction against asceticism and monasticism and of the positive appreciation in anti-papal circles of worldly and clerical values, which he related to a new stress on the inner life, going back to Gregory the Great. "The idea that outward wonders . . . do not show a man's true holiness, which depends upon inner virtues and righteousness before God more than on outward signs, was often expressed in the Middle Ages and is throughout a part of the persistent medieval thought-world."[18]

Examples of extravagant asceticism were still frequent and were admired by many people, but the new spirituality of the twelfth century was marked by spiritual inwardness and a growing distrust of conspicuous signs of holiness. The most respected religious leaders of the age, with few exceptions, were keenly aware of the danger of pride and hypocrisy in ascetic practices and of the need for moderation, balance, reason, discretion, and prudence. Physical mortifications must be inspired by pure intentions and love of God and were seen as a means towards an end rather than as an end in themselves. This view corresponded to the concern of canon lawyers like Ivo of Chartres for "royal moderation" and "a balance of piety and justice" in government, to the emphasis found in the works of Hildebert of Le Mans on compromise as the best method of personal fulfilment, and to the revival in learned circles of the classical ideal of the golden mean and the Stoic concepts of virtue and absence of passion.[19] Bruno of La Chartreuse used the image of the bow which weakens when it is kept bent in his letter to Ralph *Viridis* and cited the example of the desert father John in his commentary on the verse "Set me a law in thy way" from Psalm 26.11. The law is moderation (*moderamen*), Bruno said, and no one should either stray backwards or move to right or left, which meant, as in Eccl. 7.17, an excess of virtue on one side, "like the hermit John the little who failed when he tried to live like an angel", and an excess of vice on the other. "He

---

[18] Schmeidler, "Anti-asketische Äusserungen", 47. The letter to Archbishop Siegfried of Mainz, praising the position of a bishop more than that of a monk, recluse, cenobite, or hermit, is printed in *Monumenta Bambergensia*, ed. Philipp Jaffé, Bibliotheca rerum germanicarum, 5 (Berlin, 1869) 81-84, no. 39. On a parallel anti-ascetic reaction in Byzantium in the twelfth century, see Paul Magdalino, "The Byzantine Holy Man in the Twelfth Century", *The Byzantine Saint*, ed. Sergei Hackel (London, 1981) 59-60, citing Eustathios of Thessalonica, Balsamon, and Choniates, and the unpublished paper by Alexander Kazhdan presented at the second colloquium on Philosophy and Mysticism held at Dumbarton Oaks on 10-12 November 1985, who cited the *Vita* of Cyril Phileotos and also the *Vita*, III (15) of St. Nilus in the tenth century, who was said to have resisted the temptation to practice excessive asceticism and to have kept measure in all things: *Acta Sanctorum*, 3rd ed., Sept. VII, 271BC.

[19] Ivo of Chartres, *Ep.* 264, in *PL*, CLXII, coll. 268B-269B; see Rolf Sprandel, *Ivo von Chartres und seine Stellung in der Kirchengeschichte*, Pariser historische Studien, 1 (Stuttgart, 1962) 141-142, on Ivo's fear of *propria voluntas* and *indiscreta pietas*, and, on Hildebert's views on asceticism, Peter von Moos, *Hildebert von Lavardin, 1056-1133*, Pariser historische Studien, 3 (Stuttgart, 1965) 137 and 143.

who is deflected neither by slackening too much nor by exceeding the measure but who proceeds along the way of God by equal measure is said to go forward on the way of God . . . [which is] the common precepts without which no one will be saved."[20] Geoffrey *Grossus* wrote of Bernard of Tiron:

> Such great prudence flourished that whatever he thought [and] whatever he did was directed by the norm of reason, and he wished and did only what was right and provided for human actions just like divine judgements . . . . Temperance had so modified him that he sought nothing for which penance was necessary, and he exceeded the law of moderation in nothing; he brought all things which the use of the body required under the yoke of reason; he deferred all things [to reason] to the extent that nature permitted; and rather than repressing worldly desires he entirely obliterated them from himself by a certain oblivion.[21]

Even when allowance is made for the rhetorical and conventional references in this passage to reason, nature, prudence, temperance, and moderation, it is remarkable to find it in the *Life* of one of the leaders of the eremitical movement of the twelfth century and the founder of one of the strict new monastic orders.

Similar sentiments were expressed in many twelfth-century spiritual works, some of which were written by men and women who were themselves notable, and sometimes extreme, ascetics. Bernard of Clairvaux in his sermons on the Song of Songs repeatedly praised balance and moderation and condemned excessive abstinence and asceticism, which he considered to be a source both of personal pride and of disruption in a religious community. "It is enough that you should love your neighbor like yourself: this is out of fairness (*ex aequalitate*)", he said in one sermon, where he cited 2 Cor. 8.13 and Eccl. 7.17 as warnings against excessive zeal. "Where there is vigorous zeal, discretion is most greatly needed", he said in another sermon, defining discretion as "the ordering (*ordinatio*) of love" which imposes order on virtue and saying that "order supplies measure and beauty and also perpetuity".[22] Ailred of Rievaulx in his *Mirror of love* distinguished between the two presences, temporal and eternal, of the saints, which men desired with the same feeling but achieved in different ways.

> For we strive for the bodily presence of the saints, if they happen to be absent, by crossing some spaces of land [and] for their eternal [presence] by living justly and piously and in a holy way. If therefore the same feeling rouses us to these two actions, the latter, in so far as it concerns inner arousal, follows its impetus immediately, for there is no fear of excess in interior

---

[20] *Lettres des premiers Chartreux*, I. S. *Bruno, Guigues, S. Anthelme*, Sources Chrétiennes, 88 (Paris, 1962) 70 (and n. 1, where the editor suggested that Bruno may have used the manuscript of Phaedrus which was in the library of St. Remy at Reims) and 72, praising prudence, and *Expositio in Psalmos*, in *PL*, CLII, col. 742AB; see also his commentary on the similar passage in Ps. CXVIII, 1, *ibid.*, coll. 1268D-1269A, identifying law as moderation.

[21] Geoffrey *Grossus, Vita Bernardi Tironiensis*, XI, 103-104, in *PL*, CLXXII, col. 1428A-D; see on this *Life*, Johannes von Walter, *Die ersten Wanderprediger Frankreichs* (Leipzig, 1903-06) II, 15-16, attributing these chapters to the later redactor who put together the two earlier lives.

[22] Bernard of Clairvaux, *Serm. in Cantica*, XVIII, 4, and XLIX, 5, ed. Jean Leclercq a.o. (Rome, 1957ff.) I, 105, and II, 75-76; see also *Serm.* XXXIII, 10 (on the temptation to excessive

sanctity, but the exterior arousal of virtues, concerning which "Be not over just" is said, should be tempered by the moderation of reason.[23]

Advice of this kind was often given to hermits and recluses, who lived alone and were thought to be particularly prone to the dangers of intemperate asceticism. Peter the Venerable wrote to the hermit Gilbert of Senlis, probably in the early 1130s, urging him to follow discretion "the mother of all virtues" in his fasts, vigils, and bodily mortifications. "Wherefore it is fitting that you should moderate your life with an even balance, so that you take from your body those things which could serve its pride and give to it those things which can satisfy only the necessity of nature."[24] The Carthusian Bernard of Portes wrote to a recluse named Rainald that "Moderate food and drink and moderate sleep are well known to be best for the soul and for the body and to promote the cleanness of the heart and of the flesh". God is better pleased, and the body and soul are better served, by "a temperance of food", he continued, "than if you pursue a more robust fast and later compensate for it by an imprudent satiety".[25] In a letter written in 1184/91 to a regular canon who had become a hermit after living for forty years in a community, the canonist Stephen of Tournai recommended "the mean of Augustine" and warned against excessive praying and reading in addition to excessive fasting and austerity.

> After some modest reading, walk about your cell or go into the garden and refresh your languid sight . . . with flourishing plants, or look among the beehives which are both a comfort and an example to you. Among these varieties you will consider the harshness of your hermitage to be the pleasures of paradise.[26]

Women were no less aware than men of the need for moderation in ascetic exercises, and much advice of this sort was written by and for them. Goscelin of St. Bertin in his *Book of strength*, which was written in 1082/83, warned the recluse Eve against harming her body by excessive austerity, saying that Christ ordered us to avert our eyes, not to tear them out.[27] Robert of Arbrissel in 1109 urged Countess Ermengarde of Brittany to

> Keep discretion in all things, in abstinence, in fasts, in vigils, in prayers. Eat, drink, and sleep as much as is necessary not for your own sake but in order to bear labor for the sake of others. I do not say that you should nourish your flesh, since whoever nourishes the flesh nourishes the enemy. But I say

---

asceticism), LXIV, 4 (on conspicuous and superstitious abstinence), and LXVI, 7 (on care of the body, which is also the body of Christ and the church) *ibid.*, I, 240-241, and II, 168 and 182-183.

[23] Ailred of Rievaulx, *Speculum caritatis*, III, 24, in *PL*, CXCV, col. 597AB (also in *CCCM*, 1).

[24] Peter the Venerable, *Ep.* 20, ed. Giles Constable, Harvard Historical Studies, 78 (Cambridge, Mass., 1967) I, 40.

[25] Bernard of Portes, *Ep. ad Rainaldum inclusum*, in *PL*, CLIII, col. 895BC.

[26] Stephen of Tournai, *Ep.* 188, ed. Jules Desilve (Valenciennes-Paris, 1893) 234.

[27] C.H. Talbot, "The Liber Confortatorius of Goscelin of Saint Bertin", in *Analecta monastica*, III, Studia Anselmiana, 37 (Rome, 1955) 74.

X

that you should not intemperately kill the flesh, since whoever kills the flesh kills its inhabitant [the soul].[28]

The emphasis on measure and discretion in the *Mirror of virgins*, according to Bernards, amounted to a tendency towards anti-asceticism.[29] Elizabeth of Schönau in her *Book on the ways of God* wrote,

> The affliction of the flesh is good, since it is opposed to the uncleanness of concupiscence, but it is useless if it exceeds measure, since it smothers the devotion of contemplation and extinguishes its light. On this account be mindful of your fragility, O man, so that you may proceed with caution along the rough road which you have entered and that in your hastening you may act patiently, lest you suffer ruin.[30]

This attitude is reflected in the accounts of the lives of three women from the Low Countries and northwestern France in the late twelfth and early thirteenth centuries. Of Margaret of St. Omer, who mutilated her face in order to avoid marriage and lived as a servant caring for the sick, Herbert of Clairvaux wrote in *On miracles*, "In relating this we do not commend the possibly indiscreet zeal of the girl in laying hands on herself so that others should imitate it, but we greatly wonder at and venerate the most ardent feeling of divine love and zeal of an adolescent girl in protecting her chastity".[31] James of Vitry in his *Life* of Mary of Oignies likewise said, after describing her austerities, that

> I say this not to commend excess but to display fervor. But in these and many other matters which she performed by the privilege of grace, the discreet reader should realize that the privileges of a few people do not make the common law. We imitate her virtues, but we cannot imitate the works of her virtues without a private privilege. For although the body should be made to serve the spirit, and we should "bear the marks of our lord Jesus Christ on our body" (Gal. 6.17), we know however that "the king's honor loveth judgment" (Ps. 98.4) and that a sacrifice "from the spoil of the poor" is not pleasing to the Lord (Is. 3.14). For we should not deprive the poor flesh of what it needs, but its vices are to be repressed. We should therefore admire rather than imitate what we read certain saints to have done at the intimate counsel of the Holy Spirit.[32]

Some people were troubled by the extreme character of the miracles of a woman named Christina, who lived at St. Trond and died about 1224, according to her *Life*, and they asked God to temper the miracles of His power more "to the common

---

[28] J. de Pétigny, "Lettre inédite de Robert d'Arbrissel à la comtesse Ermengarde", *Bibliothèque de l'Ecole des Chartes*, XV, 3rd S. V (1854) 234-235; see Von Walter, *Wanderprediger*, I, 107-108.

[29] Bernards, *Speculum virginum*, 134-136.

[30] *Die Visionen der hl. Elisabeth und die Schriften der Aebte Ekbert und Emecho von Schönau*, ed. F.W.E. Roth (Brünn, 1884) 119.

[31] Herbert of Clairvaux, *De miraculis*, II, 41, in *PL*, CLXXXV, coll. 1350D-1351C.

[32] James of Vitry, *Vita Mariae Ogniacensis*, I, 1, 2 (12), in *AASS*, June IV, 639F-640A; see Joseph Greven, *Die Anfänge der Beginen*, Vorreformationsgeschichtliche Forschungen, 8 (Münster W., 1912) 60-61.

norm of human life", which He did, and "From this she behaved more moderately, and she did not henceforth repulse the odor or the company of men".[33]

This shows that the dislike for extravagant displays of saintly powers was not restricted to monastic circles. It was spread in the twelfth century not only by letters and spiritual writings but also by saints' lives, sermons, proverbs, miracle stories, and other more popular types of works. The preacher Geoffrey of St. Thierry, who was bishop of Châlons-sur-Marne from 1131 to 1142/43, listed among the temptations sent to monks by the Devil the anticipation of common vigils, the performance of too much manual labor, and the prolongation of fasts.[34] The Cistercian Galland of Rigny, who began his collection of proverbs in 1128, interpreted the proverb "That you should not want to over-burden your ass or over-work your land" to mean that a monk should not excessively tire his body "lest he be unable either to bear the burden of the order he has received or to deliver the fruit of good work".[35] Knights who became monks seem to have been especially prone to excessive asceticism, perhaps because they continued to wage against their own bodies the physical battle they had previously waged against their enemies in the world. Peter the Venerable in his *On miracles* told of a noble knight named Armannus who after he became a monk prayed all day and night and "in that zeal scarcely indulged in food or drink" and who in spite of Peter's advice "to behave more moderately in these matters, because he appeared to exceed measure, would not acquiesce owing to the excessive zeal of his spirit".[36] And Caesarius of Heisterbach described in his *Dialogue of miracles* the fate which befell a former knight named Baldwin who while he was still a novice at Riddagshausen was reprimanded by the abbot and the master on account of his strictness. "After he became a monk he was so zealous that the common activities were not sufficient for him, and he added to the common activities many special ones and preferred private ones." His extreme vigils and labor eventually dried up his brain, according to Caesarius, and made him weak-minded, and one day he almost strangled himself on the bell-rope in the church. "Thus the vice of accidia is sometimes born from indiscreet zeal."[37]

Efforts were made in some monasteries and religious orders, including some of the strictest, to control and even prohibit such practices in view of their danger and disruptive character, and also increasingly out of a concern for the health and physi-

---

[33] *Vita Christinae Mirabilis*, IV, in J. Wolters, *Notice historique sur l'ancienne abbaye noble de Milen* (Ghent, 1853) 185; see Simone Roisin, *L'hagiographie cistercienne dans le diocèse de Liège au XIIIe siècle*, Université de Louvain: Recueil de travaux d'histoire et de philologie, 3rd S., 27 (Louvain-Brussels, 1947) 51, n. 3 (dating her death 1228) and 86, n. 10, saying that Christina was not a Beguine but a pious woman who lived alone.

[34] Geoffrey of St. Thierry, *Serm.* 30, in MS Reims, Bibl. mun. 581, f. 125v; see Robert Sullivan, *The Sermons of Geoffrey of St. Thierry*, unpublished Ph.D. dissertation, Harvard Univ. (1973) 239.

[35] Jean Châtillon, "Galandi Regniacensis Libellus Proverbiorum. Le recueil de proverbes glosés du cistercien Galland de Rigny", *Revue du Moyen Age latin*, IX (1953) 56, no. 42.

[36] Peter the Venerable, *De miraculis*, I, 18, in *PL*, CLXXXIX, col. 883C, and ed. Denise Bouthillier, *CCCM*, LXXXIII (Turnhout, 1988) 55.

[37] Caesarius of Heisterbach, *Dialogus miraculorum*, IV, 45, ed. Joseph Strange (Köln-Bonn-Brussels, 1851) I, 212-213.

cal welfare of the monks and nuns. The twelfth century saw some of the earliest references to their need for adequate food and sleep, to cleanliness, and to proper care for the sick.[38] In the constitutions of Camaldoli, which were compiled in 1080, Prior Ruldolf stressed that flagellation should be "not for the sake of tormenting the body . . . but out of zeal for the divine passion and for following the examples of humility in order to confound that one [the Devil] who is the king of pride", and also that in all types of asceticism

> everyone should perform what his ability will bear or utility advises or divine grace inspires. For a voluntary offering persuades and compulsion does not impose in such matters. Each person should measure his strength in this respect, consider the costs, and moderate his feelings so that he will not presume either to over-stretch himself by indiscretion or to sink below himself from slothfulness.[39]

Ulrich in his customs of Cluny said that the monks should fast moderately in order to save their strength "for the exercise of such a life, which is active",[40] and Guigo in the customs of La Chartreuse forbade any supplementary abstinences, disciplines, vigils, or other ascetic exercises without the permission of the prior.[41] Bernard of Clairvaux in his fortieth sermon *On various matters* said that any tormenting of the flesh must be performed in private, with the permission of the superior, and with discretion, without which "we may lose salvation when we desire to flagellate excessively and kill the inhabitant while we seek to subdue the enemy. Consider your body and its possibility, observe the condition of the flesh, impose a measure on your severity. Preserve your body unharmed for the service of the creator".[42]

Bernard was concerned with privacy not only because he disapproved of overt displays of ascetic suffering but also because he realized the dangers of pride and hypocrisy, since he said that the knowledge of the suffering should be kept "in the hidden place of your heart" rather than "in the mouth of men". Bonizo of Sutri in the *Book of Christian life*, which was written in the early 1090s, criticized the self-love not only of monks who were well-fed and well-dressed but also of those who scorned their colleagues and spent their time in labors and vigils. Weeping, groaning, fasting, and afflicting the body must be judged by their results rather than their

---

[38] See Gerd Zimmermann, *Ordensleben und Lebensstandard. Die Cura corporis in den Ordensvorschriften des abendländischen Hochmittelalters*, Beiträge zur Geschichte des alten Mönchtums und des Benediktinerordens, 32 (Münster W., 1973) 147, 149, 215-216, 234-235, and 459.

[39] Rudolf of Camaldoli, *Constitutiones*, XIX and XXXV, in Giovanni-Benedetto Mittarelli, *Annales Camaldulenses* (Venice, 1755-73) III, 521 and 528.

[40] Ulrich of Cluny, *Consuetudines Cluniacenses*, I, 52, in *PL*, CXLIX, col. 697C. See also *Bernardi Cluniacensis carmina de trinitate et de fide catholica*, ed. Katarina Halvarson, Studia latina Stockholmiensia, 11 (Stockholm, 1963) 63, lines 472ff., on moderation and discretion in fasts and the limits of measure.

[41] Guigo of La Chartreuse, *Consuetudines Cartusiae*, XXXV, 1, in [Maurice Laporte], *Aux sources de la vie cartusienne* (La Grande Chartreuse, 1960-67) IV, 146, and the editor's comments in VI, 637-641.

[42] Bernard of Clairvaux, *Serm. de diversis*, XL, 7, ed. Leclercq, VI.1, 241.

extent, Bonizo said, and were useless without an internal reformation.[43] Ivo of Chartres criticized the wandering preachers "who, inflated with pharisaical passion and fattened not with the Lord's grain, gloried in the cheapness of their food and in not sparing their bodies".[44] And Guibert of Nogent wrote in *On the relics of the saints* that

> You see hypocrites abstaining from food, bearing cold, fulfilling the stations daily and almost nightly, watching at night in almost sleepless prayers, and guided by the lightest desire for empty glory. In the minds of holy men the sweetness of heavenly hope makes the daily deaths of their bodies brief and momentary.[45]

Bernard of Clairvaux gave a famous picture of a hypocritical ascetic in his treatise *On the steps of humility* under the fifth step of pride, "which is called singularity", where he described a monk who wanted to look rather than to be better and who fasted more than other members of his community, coughed and groaned alone in a corner while the others were in the cloister, and inspected his body to make sure that his face was sufficiently pale. "But although these things which he does with singularity but without utility raise his reputation among the simpler monks, who praise the works they see without discerning whence they come, they lead the poor man into error when they call him blessed."[46] An equally scathing attack on hypocrites who pretended to live for Christ alone, mortified their flesh, lead an angelic life, fasted, prayed loudly and continually, wore rough and dirty clothes, and criticized the clergy and laity is found in the *Policraticus* of John of Salisbury, who was not opposed to a moderate degree of suffering in order to crush the lasciviousness of the flesh and to rouse and strengthen the spirit but who disapproved of any ostentatious display.

> They display the pallor of their faces, are accustomed to produce deep sighs, are suddenly flooded with artificial and obsequious tears, with the head inclined to one side, closed eyes, short hair, an almost shaven head, a lowered voice, lips moving in prayer, a slow walk as with steps formed by a fixed proportion, ragged, covered-over, and in dirty clothing, they praise an affected cheapness in order to climb more easily to a place where they are more studiously seen to have thrown themselves down into a very new place and where those who have voluntarily descended may be compelled with reluctance to rise.[47]

The theme of the hypocritical ascetic began to influence hagiography and the ideal of monastic perfection in the eleventh century and became a commonplace

---

[43] Bonizo of Sutri, *Liber de vita christiana*, X, 78, ed. Ernst Perels, Texte zur Geschichte des römischen und kanonischen Rechts im Mittelalter, 1 (Berlin, 1930) 333-335.

[44] Ivo of Chartres, *Ep.* 192, in *PL*, CLXII, col. 196D.

[45] Guibert of Nogent, *De pignoribus sanctorum*, IV, 1, in *PL*, CLVI, coll. 668D-669A.

[46] Bernard of Clairvaux, *De gradibus humilitatis et superbiae*, XIV, 42, ed. Leclercq, III, 48-49; see the translation by George B. Burch (Cambridge, Mass., 1940).

[47] John of Salisbury, *Policraticus*, VII, 21 ed. C.C.J. Webb (Oxford, 1909) II, 191 and 194.

among moralists and satirists in the twelfth.[48] Walter of Pontoise made himself a whip of leather thongs with knots at the ends in order to flagellate himself but was nevertheless "cautious and circumspect in the exercise of holy works" and avoided all ostentation and hypocrisy.[49] Arnulf of Soissons after he became a monk at St. Medard likewise practiced many ascetic austerities, "manfully macerating his limbs and raising his mind to heavenly things but showing a happy and joyful face to everyone".[50] There gradually emerged a model of a saint who was restrained and unostentatious in his or her outer appearance and behavior and whose claim to sanctity lay primarily in the qualities of heart and spirit. In the treatise *On the truly apostolic life*, which dates probably from the 1120s, abstinence was said to be without merit in itself and to acquire merit only from the spirit in which it was performed. The fasting of Christ, Moses, and Elijah was praised in the Bible owing to their good spirit, and the saints who fasted won the kingdom of heaven "not on account of their fasts . . . but on account of the exertions of their good spirits".[51] Heloise in two letters written in the 1130s put a characteristically Abelardian emphasis on the importance of intention in judging the merit of physical austerities.

> What should we call the penance of sinners, however great the affliction of the body may be, if the mind still retains the same will of sinning and burns with the original desires? It is indeed easy to accuse oneself by confessing one's sins and also to afflict the body with outward satisfaction, but it is very hard to separate the soul from the desires for great pleasures.

Elsewhere she asked, "Who if he considered [only] the exhibition of exterior abstinence with his bodily eye would not rank John [the Baptist] and his disciples, who tormented themselves with excessive abstinence, above Christ Himself and His disciples in religion?" Those who strive to please Him "that searcheth the heart and the reins (Apoc. 2.23)", she continued, must pay attention not only to their exterior actions but also to their interior feelings, since what is done outwardly in the body is sinful only if the spirit is corrupted by an evil will.[52] Peter the Venerable wrote in a similar vein to Prior Theodard of La Charité-sur-Loire, also in the 1130s, criticizing the extent of his mortifications and citing 1 Cor. 13.3.

> Abstain therefore from meat, abstain from fish, abstain if you wish from everything; afflict, beat, and crush your beast [i.e. body]; give no sleep to your eyes, let not your eyelids slumber (Ps. 131.4), and pass the nights in

---

[48] See Edélestand du Méril, *Poésies inédites du Moyen Age* (Paris, 1854) 320-321, for a section on hypocrites in a poem from MS Douai, Bibl. mun. 702, dated 1173, and James of Vitry, *Vita Mariae Ogniacensis*, II, 5, 3 (62-63) in *AASS*, June IV, 653, for the story of a Cistercian monk who tried to recover the innocence of Adam and Eve by his great austerities and whom James compared to a bull-frog trying to blow himself up into a bull.

[49] *Vita Gauterii* [of Pontoise], ed. J. Depoin, *Cartulaire de l'abbaye de Saint-Martin de Pontoise* (Pontoise, 1895-1909) 194 and 196.

[50] Hariulf of Oudenburg, *Vita Arnulfi* [of St. Medard at Soissons], I, 1, 11, in *AASS*, 3rd ed., Aug. III, 232CD.

[51] *De vita vere apostolica*, II, in *Veterum scriptorum et monumentorum . . . amplissima collectio*, ed. Edmond Martène and Ursin Durand (Paris, 1724-33) IX, coll. 988-989.

vigils and the days in labors; like it or not you will listen to the apostle that even "if you deliver your body to be burned [and have not charity], it profiteth you nothing".[53]

This concentration on love, intention, and interiority was one of the hallmarks of twelfth-century spirituality and was an important factor in changing the early medieval attitude towards asceticism. The late twelfth-century heretics who rejected all works, including bodily austerities, and held that the only law of Christ was love, though they were criticized by orthodox theologians, carried to an extreme a view that was widely shared at the time.[54] The avoidance of excess was also central to the revived concern for measure and moderation, which was an important aspect of twelfth-century humanism. "Wisdom is lacking where moderation (*mezura*) is not observed. So say the ancients", sang the troubadour poet Marcabru.[55] William of St. Thierry stressed the subordination of bodily to spiritual exercises in his *Golden Letter* to the Carthusians of Mont-Dieu, which was long attributed to Bernard of Clairvaux,[56] and the master in the *Bridlington Dialogue* said that fasting and abstinence required "the fullness of proper measure" and inner devotion. "Fasts which are for human praise are not pleasing to God."[57] Asceticism remained an important part of religious life, and in the late Middle Ages various types of ascetic practices and self-imposed mortifications, in particular flagellation, spread outside religious houses into lay society. There they met deep, and still not fully understood, religious and psychological needs, but they were not regarded with the same general approval and admiration as they were in the early Middle Ages. Petrarch, who was not insensitive to the religious values of a life of retirement, warned in his treatise *On the solitary life* against "a bestial disregard for sleep and food . . . lest while fleeing the extreme of too careful a life we relapse into the opposite", and he recommended, after citing the Ciceronian ideal of *mediocritas*, that sleep should be brief, food light, drink simple, and clothing humble.[58] Thus a new ideal of temperance and unostentation replaced the heroic asceticism and

---

[52] Heloise, *Ep.* III and V, ed. J.T. Muckle, in *Mediaeval Studies*, XV (1953) 80, and XVII (1955) 249 and 251.

[53] Peter the Venerable, *Ep.* 43, ed. Constable, I, 140.

[54] P. Ilarino da Milano, *L'eresia di Ugo Speroni nella confutazione del Maestro Vacario*, Studi e testi, 115 (Vatican City, 1945) 557, citing Vacarius, *Liber contra multiplices et varios errores*, XXVII, 7, which is dated 1177/85 by Walter Wakefield and Austin Evans, *Heresies of the High Middle Ages* (New York, 1969) 152.

[55] Marcabru, "L'autrier jost'una sebissa", lines 82-84 in *Poésies complètes du troubadour Marcabru*, ed. J.M.L. Dejeanne (Toulouse, 1909). The need for measure and *compas* was stressed by Peire d'Alverna, "Be m'es plazen", lines 7, 15, 22 and 44, in *Peire d'Alvernha. Liriche*, ed. Alberto del Monte (Turin, 1955). I owe these references to Professor Margaret Switten.

[56] William of St. Thierry, *Epistola ad fratres de Monte-Dei*, 57, ed. M.-M. Davy, Etudes de philosophie médiévale, 29 (Paris, 1940) 106.

[57] Robert of Bridlington, *The Bridlington Dialogue* (London, 1960) 112; see Marvin L. Colker, "Richard of Saint Victor and the Anonymous of Bridlington", *Traditio*, XVIII (1962) 181-227.

[58] Petrarch, *De vita solitaria*, II, 11, ed. Guido Martellotti, in the volume of Petrarch's *Prose*, La letteratura italiana: Storia e testi, 7 (Milan-Naples, 1955) 516. For other references, see Angenendt, "Sühne", 463, who after commenting on earlier medieval criticisms of excessive asceticism said, "die eigentliche Abkehr aber hat sich erst im späteren Mittelalter vollzogen".

conspicuous sufferings of the early saints and prepared the way for some of the most important religious and social ideals of late medieval and modern worlds.

The Ideal of Inner Solitude in the Twelfth Century

Various scholars have remarked on the tendency in twelfth-century spirituality to transform ascetic practices from external manifestations of privation, suffering, and endurance into internal attitudes known only to the individual monk or nun and to their closest colleagues and spiritual advisors. Poverty was seen as the renunciation less of property than of self-will and was equated with humility rather than indigency ; silence consisted of inner peace and quiet more than of an avoidance of speech and noise ; stability, like obedience, was the observance not of the outer commands of a religious superior but of the inner obligations of conscience and the monastic profession. Physical mortifications had spiritual value only if they were inspired by sincere repentance and grief, and the real pilgrimage of a monk or nun was with the feelings, not with the feet [1]. « The habit does not make the monk » was a common saying among monastic writers, who emphasized, as Philip of Harvengt said, that « Religion is not in the clothes but in the heart » [2]. Even chastity was regarded as a state of mind rather than of body, and according to the *Mirror of Virgins* the physical condition of virginity was less important than its spirit [3].

These attitudes were not unknown in Antiquity and among the Church Fathers. Almost all the early commentators on the Beatitudes preferred Matthew's « Blessed are the poor in spirit » to Luke's « Blessed are the poor », which implied that lack of material possessions was virtuous in itself. The verses from the Psalms « Be still and see that I am God » and « This is my rest for ever and ever » were cited in the *Lives* of many early medieval saints as examples of inner repose [4]. Cicero's statement that it was praiseworthy not to have seen Asia but to have lived well in Asia was applied to Jerusalem by Jerome in a celebrated dictum that was cited by critics of pilgrimage throughout the Middle Ages : « Non Hierosolymis fuisse, sed Hierosolymis bene vixisse laudandum est ». The second *Hierosolymis* here is ambiguous and may have meant « in the city of Jerusalem », but the context suggests, and later writers consistently assumed, that it referred to the spiritual Jerusalem, for which men should live well at home rather than visit the earthly city [5].

The concept of inner solitude appears in the works of both Greek and Latin Fathers. Origen in his commentary on « You shall be holy, because I am holy » (Lev. 11.46) said that holy meant set apart and that « We are said to be set apart not in places but in actions, not in regions but in ways of life (*conversationibus*) [6] ». Diodore of Tarsus and his pupil Chrysostom developed the idea of ascetic solitaries who lived in the world and were devoted to virginity and poverty and yet who performed occasional apostolic work and were not therefore physically isolated, and Pseudo-Denis considered the solitude of the monk as an inner state rather than the condition of actually living alone [7]. Gregory the Great, commenting on the kings and consuls « who build themselves solitudes » (Job 3.14), said that « To build solitudes is to expel the tumults of worldly desires from the hidden place of the heart and to seek the love of innermost quiet with a single devotion to the eternal homeland... Let him seek a quiet mind in which the more fully he sees God the more alone he will find himself with Him alone » [8].

Solitude of mind and heart was emphasized in the late eleventh and twelfth centuries not only as part of the general emphasis at that time on spiritual inwardness but also in reaction against the exaltation of eremitical solitude by some of the extreme exponents of monastic reform. Ivo of Chartres addressed this issue in his letter to the monks of Coulombs, who had been urged by some wandering preachers to leave their monastery and to become hermits.

> For the hidden places of forests and the peaks of moutains do not make a man blessed unless he has with him solitude of mind, the sabbath-day of heart, tranquillity of conscience, and risings in his heart (Ps. 83.6), without which boredom (*accidia*) of the mind, curiosity, vainglory, and dangerous onslaughts of temptations accompany all solitude ; and no suitable tranquillity is given to the endangered soul unless the importunate tempest of temptations is repelled with God reproving [9].

This passage also appears in one of the sermons of Abbot Geoffrey of St Thierry of Rheims (1112-1120), who later became abbot of St Nicasius and bishop of Châlons-sur-Marne. He omitted « solitude of mind » but added at the beginning « the remote places of valleys, ...the unpassable places of rocks, the horror of caves, and the shallow places of pools » [10]. It is likewise found, with « the hidden places of forests, the remote places of valleys, and the peaks of mountains », and without « solitude of mind », in the collection of texts, many of which are associated with Bernard of Clairvaux, in manuscript Lincoln 201 [11]. The passage may therefore not be original to Ivo, although its first known appearance is in his letter, and its use both in a Benedictine sermon and in a Cistercian miscellany shows that it had a wide appeal.

The secular canon Godwin, who was precentor of the cathedral of Salisbury in the early twelfth century, wrote in the *Meditations* he addressed to the recluse Rainild (which are really a sermon on poverty of spirit or humility, which Godwin considered « the summit of virtue ») that « There are two ways of leaving this world and two ways of following and imitating the cross of Christ, of which one is in the mind and the other is at the same time in open action [12] ». Peter the Venerable, writing to his secretary Peter of Poitiers in 1134, contrasted his own location in the fields at St Martin-des-Champs in Paris with the lofty position of Peter of Poitiers, who had left him to live in a mountainous retreat. He would also like to find a cleft in the rock, he wrote, citing the Song of Songs 2.14, and to use it as both a spiritual and a bodily home. If this is impossible, he will copy the just man who among crowds of people, royal feasts, and gilded walls says with the Psalmist

> « Lo, I have gone far off, flying away, and I abode in solitude » (Ps. 54.8). And as in the enclosures of moutains, so let us build for ourselves in the hidden places of our hearts solitudes where alone a true hermitage is found by those who truly despise the world, where no outsider is admitted, where the storm and noise of worldly tumults is calmed, where the voice of the speaking God is heard without any sound of a bodily voice in « a whistling of a gentle air » (3 Kings 19.12). Let us go back constantly to this solitude « while we are in the body and are absent from the Lord » (2 Cor. 5.6), and placed in the middle of crowds, and let us find in ourselves what we seek in the uttermost borders of the world, for « the kingdom of God is within you » (Luke 17.21) [13].

This passage, up to the citation from 3 Kings, was also used by Geoffrey of St Thierry in the sermon mentioned above [14]. If it was written while Geoffrey was abbot of St Thierry, from 1112 to 1120, Peter the Venerable must have taken it either from him or from a common source, but like the previous passage, it shows the appeal of these sentiments in the early twelfth century.

Commenting on the solitude of the dove in the clefts of the rock in his sermons of the Song of Songs, Bernard of Clairvaux urged his monks to « Withdraw, therefore, but in mind, in intention, in devotion, in spirit, not in body. For the spirit before your face is the Lord Christ, the spirit which does not require solitude of body, although at times you may also separate yourself in body whithout idleness, when you can do so opportunely, especially in time of prayer » [15]. This passage reflects the preference for community life felt by Bernard and many religious reformers of his time, who feared the many opportunities for sin and spiritual pride offered by physical solitude [16]. William of St Thierry in his treatise *On the nature and dignity of love* praised the common life of religious men, who sleep, rise, pray, worship, and read together. « Is not this a heavenly rather than an earthly paradise ? They allow no one among them to be alone lest Solomon say to him « Woe to him that is alone » (Eccle. 4.10). They consider to be a solitary anyone who does not wish to have a companion in his conscience through confession or who disturbs the society of the brothers by new and solitary inventions » [17]. In the description of the life of the monks at Clairvaux in the *First Life* of Bernard, William said that

> All the people there were indeed solitaries even in a crowd. For ordered love by reason of order made that valley, which was filled with men, a solitude for each of them, since just as a single disordered man, even when he is alone, is a crowd unto himself, so in that ordered multitude

of men the very order in that place protected for each of them the
solitude of his heart in the unity of spirit and by the law of regular
silence [18].

A recruiting letter written by Bernard's secretary Nicholas of Montiéramey included a description of his writing-room at Clairvaux, which was
located between the cloister, the infirmary, and the novices' cell and was,
he said, surrounded (vallatum, perhaps a play on the name of Clairvaux)
and concealed on every side by heavenly offices : « This was given to him
for reading, writing, dictating, meditating, praying, and adoring the Lord
of majesty. Here when I am weighed down by the mass of my unhappy
conscience, I enter alone the solitude of my heart, and reason is my judge,
conscience my witness, and fear my executioner, and I stand before my
own face lest that terrible majesty into whose hands it is horrible to fall
should stand me before His face » [19]. While Nicholas is not in all respects
a trustworthy witness, this passage shows how he considered it possible to
be spiritually alone even in the midst of a crowded religious community.

Examples of this type of mental withdrawal and inner solitude can be
found in the Lives of many twelfth-century saints and holy persons. One
of the most famous instances is Alan of Auxerre's account in the Second
Life of Bernard of Clairvaux of his ride along the Lake of Geneva, when
« for the journey of a whole day, he entirely paid no attention and did
not see what he saw. For when evening came, and his companions spoke
together about the lake, he asked them where the lake was, and they were
amazed » [20]. This circumstance has been attributed by scholars both to the
depth of Bernard's cowl, which limited his vision, and to the state of his
health, and it was cited by John Addington Symonds as an illustration of
the attitude of men in the Middle Ages towards their surroundings, even
though Alan's account shows that Bernard's companions observed and
spoke about the lake [21]. The clue to its real meaning lies in the preceding
account of Bernard's failure to notice the trappings (stramentum) of the
animal on which he had travelled from Clairvaux to La Chartreuse and
which was not his but had been provided by a Cluniac monk. « Hearing
this the prior [of La Chartreuse] was greatly amazed that the abbot and
servant of God so restricted his eyes externally and concentrated his spirit
internally that he had not observed during the space of so long a journey
what he [the prior] had observed at once [22] ». The contrast here between
oculus and anima, foris and intus, and circumcidere and occupare also
applies to Bernard's journey along the lake, which shows his power to
restrict his outward vision and to concentrate his spirit internally. Similar
stories were told about Geoffrey of Chalard, who died in 1125 and who
when he was a young priest celebrating mass at the monastery of St
Martial of Limoges failed to notice an earthquake until « a vast crowd of
people congregated from all sides » [23], and the Savigniac Peter of
Avranches, who died about 1172 and who was said to have made an
agreement with his eye « that it would notice no earthly thing with
pleasure, annoyance, or excessive curiosity » [24]. While these are not
examples of inner solitude, they show the power of these men to cut

themselves off from the surrounding world and to concentrate internally as if they were alone.

Many writers in the second half of the twelfth century referred to solitude of mind or heart. Garner of St Victor followed Gregory the Great in commenting on Job 3.14, saying that solitude was the expulsion of worldly desires from the heart and the search for inner quiet, and on Job 39.6 — « To whom I have given a house in solitude, and his dwellings in the barren land » —, saying that « But of what use is solitude of the body if solitude of the heart is lacking ? For he who lives far away in the body but involves himself in the tumults of human life by his thought of worldly desires is not in solitude. But he who is physically oppressed by crowds of people and yet who suffers in his heart no tumults of secular cares, he is not in the city » [25]. A Victorine preacher, possibly Hugh but more likely Richard of St Victor, said that

> Not only contemplative men but also active men live alone when they have nothing to do with the deeds of reprobates. Since it is therefore fitting for all faithful men to live alone with regard not to the housing of their bodies but to the unanimity of their hearts, it most greatly fits those who are enclosed by the habit of religion and have professed the religious life that they should live alone not only by the singularity of their good works but also as much as possible by the housing of their bodies.

Those who lead religious lives should therefore live apart even more than other men, who have to find solitude in their hearts rather than in their bodies [26]. The Cistercian Geoffrey of Auxerre said in his commentary on the Song of Songs, which was written probably in the early 1190s, after he retired to Clairvaux, that

> Since the tribe of men has multiplied so greatly that solitudes can be found in almost no habitable region, but those who wish or seem to wish to seclude themselves either tolerate a crowd of frequent visitors or attract a greater one, the solitude of the cloister was invented by a truly ingenious and very lofty counsel. For is it not a solitude where there is no sollicitude of any sort even of human necessity ? Or what anchorite was formerly as foreign to the world or so immune from all business as the true cenobite is today ?[27]

Peter of Blois wrote to the new abbot of St Mary at Blois in 1196 that « You should therefore constantly surround yourself with a certain inner solitude, so that your spirit is collected in itself and does not flow toward external things nor attend to what appears outside or what is heard externally » [28]. The contrast here between *interior* on one side and *exterior* and *foris* on the other resembles that in the *Second Life* of Bernard of Clairvaux. The Cistercian Adam of Perseigne used the terms *interna vacatio* and *interna solitudo* in a letter written about 1210 to a monk of St Martin at Séez : « This solitude makes a monk and makes of one spirit with God he who passes the day of internal freedom while he adheres to a community in which he rests singularly and alone divided from many men. He seeks for himself the secret of this internal solitude and the joy of divine love, while he who is busy with many things is unaccustomed to spiritual quiet and cannot rest and see how sweet is the Lord » [29].

From these and other spiritual writings of the twelfth century the ideal of inner solitude and freedom passed to the later Middle Ages and modern times. Petrarch in his treatise *On the solitary life* defined the three types of solitude of place, time, and spirit, which he identified with « those men who, abstracted most profoundly by the force of contemplation, are unaware of what is going on in broad daylight and in the bustling market-place [and] who are alone as often as and wherever they wish ». He said that he could himself create his own solitude when he was in the city « by an artifice not known to all men of controlling the senses so that they do not feel what they feel » [30]. This was evidently a form of mental abstraction which is known not only to religious mystics but also to scholars and others who have learned to concentrate even when they are surrounded by other people and many distractions. It also became a sort of spiritual and emotional individualism, and Shelley in his essay « On Love » referred to the love of natural things felt by men « in solitude, or in that deserted state when we are surrounded by human beings, and yet they sympathize not with us ». The so-called cult of solitude in the eighteenth and nineteenth centuries was marked not only by a desire for physical isolation but also by the cultivation of powers of inner concentration which resembled those that were praised by the spiritual writers of the twelfth century.

NOTES

1. On these and other spiritual practices that were interiorized in the twelfth century, see
   Jean Leclercq, *Otia monastica* (*Studia Anselmiana*, 51 ; Rome, 1963), pp. 70-76 (« Silence
   intérieur »), and « "Eremus" et "Eremita" . Pour l'histoire du vocabulaire de la vie
   solitaire », *Collectanea O.C.R.*, XXV (1963), 29 ; and my own articles on « Opposition
   to Pilgrimage in the Middle Ages », *Studia Gratiana*, XIX (1976 = Mélanges G. Fransen,
   1), 125-146, esp. 137, and « Liberty and Free Choice in Monastic Life and Thought », in
   La notion de liberté au moyen âge. Islam, Byzance, Occident, ed. G. Makdisi, D. Sourdel, and J.
   Sourdel-Thomine (Pennsylvania-Paris-Dumbarton Oaks Colloquia, IV; Paris, 1985), 99–118.

2. Philip of Harvengt, *De institutione clericorum*, IV : *De continentia clericorum*, 127, in
   Patrologia latina, CCIII, col. 838D.

3. Matthäus Bernards, *Speculum virginum. Geistigkeit und Seelenleben der Frau im Hochmittelalter* (Forschungen zur Volkskunde, 36-38 ; Cologne-Graz, 1955), p.51. On this
   idea in the patristic period, see Jo Ann McNamara, *A New Song : Celibate Women in the
   First Three Christian Centuries* (New York, 1983), p. 109.

4. Leclercq, *Otia*, p. 75.

5. Jerome, *Epistulae*, 58.2, ed. Isidor Hilberg, I (Corpus scriptorum ecclesiasticorum latinorum, 54 ; Vienna-Leipzig, 1910), p. 529 ; see Constable, « Opposition to Pilgrimage », p.
   126, and Joshua Prawer, « Jerusalem in the Christian and Jewish Perspectives of the
   Early Middle Ages », *Gli Ebrei nell'Alto Medioevo* (Settimane di studio del Centro di
   studi sull'Alto Medioevo, 26 ; Spoleto, 1980), p. 763, who translated the second *Hierosolymis* as « in Jerusalem ».

6. Origen, *In Leviticum homilia XI*, in *Origines Werke*, VI : *Homilien zum Hexateuch in
   Rufins Übersetzung*, ed. W. A. Baehrens (Die griechischen christlichen Schriftsteller der
   ersten drei Jahrhunderte, 29 ; Leipzig, 1920), p. 448.

7. *Théologie de la vie monastique* (Théologie : Etudes publiées sous la direction de la
   Faculté de Théologie S.J. de Lyon-Fourvière, 49 ; Paris, 1961), pp. 149-150 (Jean-Marie
   Leroux on Diodore and Chrysostom) and 306 (René Roques on Pseudo-Denis).

8. Gregory the Great, *Moralia in Job*, IV, 30 (58), in *Pat. lat.*, LXXV, coll. 668C-669A.

9. Ivo of Chartres, *Ep.* 192, in *Pat. lat.*, CLXII, coll. 201D-202A.

10. Geoffrey of St Thierry, *Serm.* 28, in MS Rheims, Bibl. mun., 581, f. 114v A. Later he remarked,
    «*Locum tantum quietis est secretum interne solitudinis, luminis serenum, pacis
    habitaculum* » (f. 114v B), and see n. 14 below. In his *Serm.* 6, in MS Paris, Bibl. nat.,
    Lat. 3563, f. 7r A, and Lat. 13586, p. 15, Geoffrey referred to the just man « *quem
    solitudo non tam corporis quam cordis ab amore carnali per contemplationem abscondit* » ;
    see Barthélemy Hauréau, *Notices et extraits de quelques manuscrits latins de la Bibliothè-
    que nationale* (Paris 1890-1893), II, 302. I owe the manuscript references to the Rev. Dr.
    Robert Sullivan, but neither of these sermons were included in his Harvard Ph. D.
    dissertation.

11. H.-M. Rochais and R. M. Irène Binont, « La collection de textes divers du manuscrit
    Lincoln 201 et Saint Bernard », *Sacris Erudiri*, XV (1964), 201.

12. *Meditationes Godwini cantoris Salesberie ad Rainildam reclusam*, in MS Oxford, Bodleian
    Library, Digby 96, ff. 8r and 13r ; see Charles Dereine, « La spiritualité " apostolique "
    des premiers fondateurs d'Afflighem (1083-1100) ». *Revue d'histoire ecclésiastique*, LIV
    (1959), 43, n. 1 (saying that he was preparing an edition), and, on Godwin, Kathleen
    Edwards, *The English Secular Cathedrals in the Middle Ages*, 2nd ed. (Manchester-New
    York, 1967), pp. 4, 7, and 183 n. A transcript of the text was made by Charles Talbot,
    who informed me in a letter dated 30 december 1964 that it consisted essentially of
    sermons addressed to men.

13. Peter the Venerable, *Ep.* 58, in *The Letters of Peter the Venerable*, ed. Giles Constable
    (Harvard Historical Studies, 78 ; Cambridge, Mass., 1967), I, 188 ; see II, 338-341. In the
    passage from Psalm 54, I have translated *solitudo* as « solitude » rather than « wilder-
    ness », as in the Douai Bible.

14. Geoffrey of St Thierry, *Serm.* 28, in MS Rheims, Bibl. mun., 581, f. 118r B ; see n. 10 above. Jean Leclercq in a letter dated 17 January 1972 suggested that this passage may derive from Peter Damiani or John of Fécamp, elaborating on Gregory the Great, *Moralia in Job*, IV, 30, but I have not located it.

15. Bernard of Clairvaux, *Serm. in Cantica*, XL, 4, in *Sancti Bernardi opera*, ed. Jean Leclercq a.o. (Rome, 1957 ff.), II, 27.

16. Giles Constable, « Eremitical Forms of Monastic Life », *Istituzioni monastiche e istituzioni canonicali in Occidente, 1123-1215* (Atti della settima Settimana internazionale di studi medioevali, Mendola, 28 agosto-3 settembre 1977 ; Milan, 1980), p. 250.

17. William of St Thierry, *De natura et dignitate amoris*, IX, 24-25, in *Pat. lat.*, CLXXXIV, coll. 395C-396C.

18. William of St Thierry, *Vita prima* of Bernard of Clairvaux, VII, 35, in *Pat. lat.*, CLXXXV. 1, col. 248 B ; see Jean Leclercq, « *Eremus* », pp. 28-29, and *Aux sources de la spiritualité occidentale* (Paris, 1964), pp. 248-249.

19. Nicholas of Montiéramey, *Ep.* 35, in *Pat. lat.*, CXCVI, coll. 1696D-1697C ; see also his letter to Peter of Celle, among Peter's letters, I, 65, in *Pat. lat.*, CCII, col. 499AB.

* 20. Alan of Auxerre, *Vita secunda* of Bernard of Clairvaux, XVI, 45, in *Pat. lat.*, CLXXXV. 1, col. 496BC.
Bernard's example was cited, together with that of Martin of Tours, who was said to have travelled with his eyes fixed on the heavens, in the Life of Hugh of Lincoln, who behaved with his mental eyes « *ut iter semper faciens ultra crinem equi cui insedisset rem prorsus aliquam corporeis oculis fere nunquam uideret* » : *Magna vita sancti Hugonis*, V, 17, ed. Decima Douai and David H. Farmer, 2nd printing (Oxford Medieval Texts ; Oxford, 1985), II, pp. 201-202.

* 21. John Addington Symonds, *Renaissance in Italy* [I] : *The Age of the Despots* (London, 1875), p. 14 ; see John F. Benton, « Consciousness of Self and Perceptions of Individuality », in *Renaissance and Renewal in the Twelfth Century*, ed. Robert L. Benson and Giles Constable (Cambridge, Mass., 1982), pp. 268-269. When Symonds wrote, « During the middle ages man had lived enveloped in a cowl . He had not seen the beauty of the world, » he was, I think, using the term cowl metaphorically rather than literally.

22. See n. 20 above.

23. *Vita beati Gaufredi Castaliensis*, I, 1, ed. A. Bosvieux, in *Mémoires de la Société des sciences naturelles et archéologiques de la Creuse*, III (1862), 77.

24. *Vitae B. Petri Abrincensis et B. Hamonis monachorum coenobii Saviniacensis*, ed. E. P. Sauvage (offprint from *Analecta Bollandiana* ; Brussels, 1883), p. 13.

25. Garner of St Victor, *Gregorianum*, VI, 17, in *Pat. lat.*, CXCIII, coll. 269D-270C ; see Constable, « *Eremitical Forms* », pp. 249-250, where I translated the passages somewhat differently and missed the citation from Gregory the Great (see n. 8 above).

26. Published as Hugh of St Victor, *Serm.* LXXVI, in *Pat. lat.*, CLXXVII, col. 1141AB.

27. Geoffrey of Auxerre, *Expositio in Cantica canticorum*, ed. Ferruccio Gastaldelli (Temi e testi, 19 ; Rome, 1974), p. 460. This passage was also published, with a few different readings (some of which I have followed here), by Jean Leclercq, « Le témoignage de Geoffroy d'Auxerre sur la vie cistercienne », in *Analecta monastica*, II (*Studia Anselmiana*, 31 ; Rome, 1953), p. 180.

28. Peter of Blois, *Ep.* 134, in *Opera omnia*, ed. J. G. Giles (Oxford, 1847), II, 9.

29. *Correspondance d'Adam, abbé de Perseigne (1188-1221)*, ed. J. Bouvet (Archives historiques du Maine, 13 ; Le Mans, 1951-1962), p. 271.

30. Petrarch, *De vita solitaria*, I, 4, and II, 6, ed. Guido Martellotti, in Petrarch, *Prose* (La letteratura italiana : Storia e testi, 7 ; Milan-Naples, 1955), pp. 336 and 454 ; see Giles Constable, « Petrarch and Monasticism », *Francesco Petrarca : Citizen of the World. Proceedings of the World Petrarch Congress, Washington, D.C., April 3-13, 1974* (Ente nazionale Francesco Petrarca. Studi sul Petrarca, 8 ; Padua-Albany, 1980), pp. 64-65, where I discuss these passages and relate them to earlier monastic spirituality.

XII

The Concern for Sincerity and Understanding in Liturgical Prayer, Especially in the Twelfth Century

A fear of hypocrisy and misunderstanding in worship, and a corresponding desire for sincerity and accuracy, were deeply rooted in Christian thought and tradition. They were often expressed as a dichotemy or a search for harmony between two associated aspects of the act of worship or prayer, one internal, such as the soul, spirit, heart, mind, thought, meaning, or sense, and the other external, such as the voice, tongue, lips, breath, words, or sound. "They blessed with their mouth, but cursed with their heart," according to Psalm 61.5. The Lord's complaint in Isaiah 29.13 that the people "with their lips glorify me, but their heart is far from me" was repeated in Matthew 15.8, and Ezechiel in his judgment on the Jews said that they "hear thy words and do them not: for they turn them into a song of their mouth, and their heart goeth after their covetousness" (Ezech. 33.31). Paul in 1 Corinthians 14.14–19 spoke of the need for understanding (*mens* and *sensus*) in prayer, saying that he would sing and pray both with the spirit (here meaning breath) and with the understanding and that "In the church I had rather speak five words with my understanding, that I may instruct others also, than ten thousand words in a tongue."[1]

The importance of inner attention in prayer was also emphasized in ancient religion, especially by the Stoics. Cicero wrote in *On the nature of the gods* that "The worship *(cultus)* of the gods is best and at the same time most holy and sacred in piety, so that we should venerate them in both mind and voice *(et mente et voce)* that is pure, complete, and uncorrupted," where *vox*, according to Arthur Pease, probably referred not to hymn-singing but to prayers, "which were regularly spoken aloud rather than secretly."[2] The younger Seneca in one of his letters to Lucilius said, "Let us speak what we feel *(sentimus)*, let us feel what we speak: speech should be in agreement with life *(concordet sermo cum vita)*."[3]

From these works the idea and sometimes the words passed into the writings of the church fathers and early monks, which have been closely examined by scholars particularly in order to discover the source of the injunction in the rule of Benedict that monks should recite the psalms in such a way "that our mind may be in agreement with our voice *(ut mens nostra concordet voci nostrae)*."[4] Cyprian at several places in his works associated the voice with the heart or breast, and in his commentary on the Lord's Prayer he wrote,

> When we are worshipping we ought to be intent and pay attention to the prayers with our whole heart ... so that nothing may distract our prayers from God in such a way that we have one thing in our heart and another thing in our voice *(aliud in corde ... aliud in voce)*, when not the sound of the voice but the soul and the understanding should worship the Lord with a sincere intention.[5]

Ambrose in his commentary on "I will open my proposition on the psaltery" (Ps. 48.5) said that Paul in his prayers sounded the interior and exterior chords "so that he worshiped both with the tongue and with the mind *(et lingua oraret et mente)*";[6] and Jerome, commenting on "singing and making melody in your hearts to the Lord" (Eph. 5.19), wrote, "We ought to sing and recite the psalms and praise the Lord more in spirit than in voice *(magis animo quam voce)*."[7] Nicetas of Remesiana specifically associated this passage with Romans 8.27 and 1 Corinthians 14.15, where to sing with the spirit and to sing with the mind, he said, meant "with voice and thougth *(voce et cogitatione)*." "We should sing the psalms, dearly beloved, with eager sense and watchful mind ... so that the psalm is said not only with the spirit, that is by the sound of the voice, but also with understanding *(non solum spiritu, hoc est sono uocis, sed et mente)*, and that we think about what we sing."[8]

Augustine particularly stressed the concordance of word and action in his Sermon CCLVI, where he said,

> Let us praise the Lord, brothers, in life and tongue, in heart and mouth, in voices and behavior. ... First let the tongue agree with life, the mouth with the conscience in ourselves. Let the voices, I say, agree with behavior, so that good voices may not perchance bear witness against bad behavior.[9]

The term *concordare* was also used in a sermon attributed to Augustine calling on the listener to open the eyes of his heart and to imbibe what he heard and to let his tongue agree with his heart *(concorda lingua cum corde tuo)*.[10] In another sermon Augustine warned his hearers "lest by contempt of the words of God as by the scorn of manna your hearts become foolish like internal mouths" and told them not "to imitate Christians in name [who are] empty in works."[11] In Letter 211, which was the basis of the rule later associated with Augustine's name, he wrote, "When you worship God in psalms and hymns, consider in your heart what you pronounce with your voice, and do not sing unless those things which you read ought to be sung."[12]

These words were addressed to the members of a religious community. Cassian in his *On the institutes of cenobites* also stressed the community aspect of prayer but made allowance (in an interesting passage contrasting the mouth with the mind, heart, and spirit) for prayers "which escape the enclosure of the mouth by overflowing from the mind and insensibly come upon the heart when an immoderate and unbearable fervor of spirit has arisen."[13] In the rule of the Master the chapter "On the discpline of psalmody" cited 1 Corinthians 14.15 and said, referring to God, that "He who sounds in the voice should also be in the mind of the singer. Let us therefore sing together in voice and in mind *(uoce et mente)*, since the apostle says, 'I will sing with the spirit, I will sing also with the understanding,'" and the following chapter "On reverence in worship" cited Cyprian that, "There ought to be no duplicity in worship. One thing should not be found in the mouth, another thing in the heart."[14]

The idea that "our mind should agree with our voice'" in singing the psalms was therefore familiar at the time the rule of Benedict was written, and it is impossible to establish with certainty its source. It may have derived, as Cramer argued, from Stoic sources, but the term *mens* (together with either *vox* or *lingua*) was used by Ambrose and Nicetas and in the rule of the Master as well as by Cicero.[15] *Concordare* was used in this connection not only by Seneca but also by Augustine and Caesarius of Arles,[16] who said in his Sermon LXXV:

> Above all strive not only in your prayers but also in your holy thoughts to fulfill in your prayers what you sing in the words of the psalms, and the Holy Spirit who sounds in your mouth may also deign to live in your heart. It is good and pleasing to God when the tongue faithfully sings, but it is truly good if the tongue is also in agreement with life *(lingua concordet vita)*. Let the voices and the behavior be in one accord together *(Consentiant simul voces et mores)*.

And he went on to discuss the consonance of mouth and deed, voice and meaning, and ear and heart.[17]

The formulation in the rule of Benedict, therefore, although exceptionally ✳ influential owing to its source and widely cited in the Middle Ages, was not exceptional in its meaning and is less enigmatic than has been suggested by some scholars, especially those who are interested in the shift to the formulation of Francis of Assisi that "the voice should be in agreement with the mind *(vox concordet menti)*,"[18] which is closer to the spirit of late medieval and modern Christianity. Warnach was at pains to argue that *vox* in the rule of Benedict meant community prayer and symbolized the word of God and divine Logos with which the mind of the individual monk should be in agreement;[19] and de Boer distinguished three categories of the dichotemy between *mens* and *vox,* of which the first was negative, saying (as in Cyprian and the rule of the Master) that there should be no duplicity in prayer, and the others positive, one stressing that prayer involves both interior and exterior activities and the second using the theme of agreement, and the verbs *concordare, consonare,* and *convenire* and the associated nouns and adjectives.[20] The overlap among the writers who used these various forms shows that there was no basic difference in meaning between them, and they were all consistent with the importance placed in ancient and early medieval religious thought on the memorization and recitation of texts, especially from Scripture.[21] For the early Christians meditation was, like digestion and rumination, an activity which involved all aspects, internal and external, of the body, since a text had to be spoken or heard before it could be memorized, understood, and put into practice.[22] This is what was intended in the rule of Benedict when it said that in psalmody the mind should be in agreement with the voice, which provided the material for the formation of the monk's inner *persona,* his heart, mind, soul, and spirit. Although the balance and priority of these activities shifted as the Middle Ages progressed, and relatively greater attention was given to the interior aspects of prayer as confidence in the outer aspects waned, the ideal of harmony between the two remained close to the hearts of liturgical reformers, who sought to make every aspect of the liturgy harmonious and meaningful.

Early in the reign of Louis the Pious, in about 820, the arch-chancellor Abbot Helisachar wrote to his friend the archbishop of Narbonne:

> I believe that your paternity remembers that some time ago, when by the emperor's order I was bound to an official position in the palace at Aachen and you were obliged [to be there] for settling some ecclesiastical affairs, we often came together in the night hours to celebrate the divine office, and the reading of sacred scripture made our soul serene, but, as you used to say, the responsories, which were lacking in authority and reason, and the verses, which in some responsories were unsuitably fitted by our singers [at the palace] and yours [from Narbonne], greatly bewildered your soul, [and] you instructed me by ordering that I should hunt through the fields of divine writings for suitable verses, taking care to catch their special character and to fit them in proper places into the responsories, which would be filled with authority and reason.[23]

The changes which Helisachar made did not meet with universal approval, among others from Amalarius of Metz,[24] but the reasons he gave in this letter for making them show the desire of two influential Carolingian churchmen to replace the responsories and versets which they considered unsuitable and confusing by others which were both authoritative and reasonable.[25]

The concern for liturgical authenticity in the twelfth century was studied by Joseph Szövérffy in an article entitled "'False' Use of 'Unfitting' Hymns: Some Ideas Shared by Peter the Venerable, Peter Abelard and Heloise," where he argued on the basis of parallels of ideas and words that Abelard composed his "innovative venture in twelfth century history of hymnody," the hymnal of the Paraclete, before Peter the Venerable's Statute 61 and Letter 124 but wrote his hymn for Benedict after Peter's Benedict hymn.[26] In Letter 124, which Peter sent to his secretary Peter of Poitiers together with his Benedict hymn, probably in 1139/41, he wrote, "You know how greatly false songs in the church of God displease me, and how hateful melodious nonsenses are to me."[27] He gave similar reasons for changing the liturgy at Cluny in the *causae* or reasons which he appended to each of his statutes. The sequence *Nostra tuba nunc* was no longer used at the second or dawn mass at Christmas because it was "an inelegant series of words and had almost nothing to do with the Nativity of Christ"; the antiphons on the first four Sundays of Lent were changed because they were used at other times; a pause was introduced between the celebration of Lauds, which was in the dark, and that of the regular Prime and Prime of the Virgin, at daybreak, in winter in the infirmary chapel in order not to disturb the inmates of the infirmary and not to sing the hymn *Iam lucis orto sidere* in the middle of the night:

> Wherefore it [the pause] was instituted so that the children of light should no longer proclaim so great a lie in the presence of God and so that the words of those who pray to and praise the Lord should not be at variance with the facts.

The cross presented to a dying monk was to be made of wood rather than gold or silver because the cross of Christ was of wood and the usual hymn sung at the adoration of the cross was *Ecce lignum crucis*, and "in these words which are customarily sung while it is adored, no note of falsity, or a small one, should be observed."[28] Peter the Venerable's purpose in these and other statutes, as Szövérffy described it, was "to eliminate incongruity and discrepancies which may have disturbing effect, rendering liturgy 'senseless' and 'imbalanced.'"[29]

The reasons for these changes, and especially those for introducing a pause between Lauds and Prime in the infirmary chapel, resembled those in the first preface to the Paraclete hymnal, which was written by Abelard in the name of Heloise. "Both passages list a number of hymns which are incongruous with the time at which they are sung ... and both use words such as 'mentiri,' 'mendacium' ('mendacii'), 'mendaces' ... in identical contexts."[30] Abelard and Heloise were also concerned by the confusion of the hymns which were customarily used, and of which the titles rarely indicated their source, and by the manner in which they were sung, especially "the unequal number of syllables, so that the song-texts can scarcely receive a melody." This referred to the refusal by some liturgical reformers, including the Cistercians, to elide the extra syllables in lines with more than the proper number of syllables to be sung regularly. Abelard himself in his hymns was careful to avoid lines with additional syllables, but the

Cistercians put such emphasis on the integrity of each word, according to Waddell, "that not even for the sake of literary convention would they agree to its 'distortion'" and the "principle of the primacy of the word reigned supreme over all musical considerations." The consequent need to fit the melody to irregular lines rather than, as was customary, the lines to the melody, gave rise to the objections of Abelard and Heloise.[31]

Authority and authenticity were the touchstones of liturgical reform in the twelfth century, especially for the Cistercians, who based their revisions of the Bible and of their hymnal and liturgical books on the standard of truth as embodied in antiquity and reason.[32] In the manuscript of the Bible made for Stephen Harding, there is a note in the margin next to Acts 10.6 saying, "In the two oldest and most truthful accounts we do not find this verse: 'He will tell thee what thou must do.'"[33] For the Cistercians the "recovery of a likeness lost by sin" was central not only in individuals, who could thus recover their true nature, but also in architecture, economy, and the liturgy, each of which had "its own nature which must be respected."[34] Bernard of Clairvaux in his letter to the monks of Montiéramey, written after 1137, said, "In the solemn assembly [in church] it is fitting to hear nothing new or frivolous but things that are certainly authentic and ancient, which both build the church and diffuse ecclesiastical gravity"; and in his introductory letter to the treatise on the hymnal reform of 1147 he stressed that the early Cistercians wanted to use the chant "that is found to be the most authentic."[35] In the treatise itself, which was probably written by Guy of Cherlieu, the desire for "the truth of the rule" was linked to "the correct knowledge of chanting," and he rejected the presumptions of people "who pay more attention to imitation (similitudo) than to nature in chants." The reformers found among the old antiphons many false and apocryphal passages which were boring and repellant and replaced them with "customary (usitata) and authentic responsaries." He said in the conclusion that in their corrections they had sought nature more than custom (usum) and that reason rather than chance made their antiphonary different from others.[36] Like Abbot Helisachar three centuries before, the Cistercians tried to make the liturgical prayer into a rational whole; like him they used the terms auctoritas and ratio, and his phrase pro captu ingenii (which I translated "to catch their special character") may have been intended to convey something of sense of natura which the Cistercians contrasted to similitudo and usus.

Many churchmen in the twelfth century, both conservatives and reformers, were sensitive to the need for thoughtful attention and understanding in the liturgy, even by people who did not participate actively. Peter the Venerable established in his first statute that there should be "a single and moderate pause" between the versets of the regular hours and that all the singers should begin and end together in order, as he explained in the causa, to abolish the confusion created by the singers beginning and ending at different times and to allow them to re-form "the understanding itself *(intellectus ipse)* ... by pausing together as in a certain common silence."[37] Peter was here more in agreement with some of the critics of Cluny than with his old friend and ally Cardinal Matthew of Albano, who poured scorn on the abbots gathered at Rheims in 1131 when they proposed to change the manner of chanting:

> Perhaps you will reply to me, "We have curtailed the psalmody because we sing more slowly and more attentively those psalms which we now say." How splendid, brothers! This is indeed a great thing, since they are said in your monasteries too confusedly and too negligently.

The abbots, meeting again at Soissons the following year, replied in the words of Paul that, "'In the church I had rather speak five words with my understanding, that I may instruct others also, than ten thousand words in a tongue,' that is, without intelligence."[38] This letter may have been written by William of St Thierry, who in his Golden Letter to the Carthusians of Mont-Dieu cited the same passage form 1 Corinthians, together with Paul's foregoing remarks on praying and singing without fruit to his understanding, and said, speaking of the night offices,

> For then their fruits in understanding and in spirit should be enlarged so that then either we may be cheered in the abundance of the blessing of God in the quiet of the night or, when we rise for the praises of God [Lauds], the whole course of our labor in his praises may then be formed and enlivened. For this reason it is not advantageous in the foregoing nocturnal vigils to overwhelm the mind and to exhaust or overwhelm the spirit by a multitude of psalms.[39]

Rupert of Deutz in the preface to his *Book on the divine offices* cited 1 Corinthians 14.14, where Paul said, "If I pray in a tongue my spirit prayeth; but my understanding is without fruit," and commented,

> People, who frequent the mysteries and signs of the church faithfully and piously, although they cannot know their causes, are not however without fruit. For these are indeed instituted in order that the secrets of God, which can be understood by few people, can in a wonderful way be performed by almost everyone. Because only the eyes see in their working, are the other members, which do not see but none the less work, without fruit? But each member has its dignity.[40]

The precise sense of this passage is uncertain, but taken in the context of Paul's reference to praying with the tongue and breath as fruitless for the understanding, it suggests that in order to achieve some advantage in prayer people should participate in ecclesiastical ceremonies with all their faculties.

Bernard of Clairvaux in his forty-seventh sermon on the Song of Songs, after citing the precept in the rule of Benedict that nothing should be preferred to the work of God, said,

> I therefore advise you, dearly beloved, always to participate single-mindedly *(pure)* and actively *(strenue)* in the divine praises: [participate] actively, indeed, so that you may stand before the Lord no less eagerly than reverently, not lazy, not sleepy, not listless, not sparing your voices, not breaking-off in half-words, not skipping-over entire words, not producing broken and negligent noises through the nose like a stammering woman, but manfully, as is proper, bringing forth the voices of the Holy Spirit both in sound and in feeling; and [participate] single-mindedly, so that while you are singing the psalms you are thinking only about what you are singing.[41]

In his letter to the abbot and monks of Montiéramey, Bernard wrote in a similar vein:

> The undoubted meanings should shine with truth, sound justice, urge humility, teach equity; and they should bring a light to the mind, a form to behavior, a cross to the vices, devotion to the feelings, [and] discipline to the senses. If there is a melody, let it be filled with gravity, and let it not sound of lewdness or of rusticity. ... Let it lighten sadness, calm anger, and nourish rather than empty the sense of the letter.[42]

Bernard's attitude toward participation in singing the psalms is illustrated by the story of his vision of the angels observing and writing down how each monk sang in church, of which there are three slightly different versions, one in the *Book of visions and miracles* compiled at Clairvaux in the 1170s, another in the so-called Beaupré collection of about 1200, and the third and best-known in Conrad of Ebersbach's *Great beginning of Cîteaux*, which dates from between 1190 and 1210.[43] In this vision Bernard saw the angels writing in gold, silver, ink, water, or nothing depending on the attitude of the monks who were singing. Gold stood for the pure or sole love of God in the *Book of visions* and the Beaupré collection and for "the most fervent zeal in the service of God and application of heart" in the *Great beginning*. Silver stood respectively in the three collections for chanting for the sake of the saints, out of love for the saints, and with pure devotion but less fervor than was recorded in gold; ink for the custom and pleasure of singing in the first two collectons and for the continuous use of good will but not much devotion in the *Great beginning;* water for complaining and reluctance in the first two collections and for the sleepiness and laziness which gives rise to vain thoughts in the third; and nothing for false things or words sung out of negligence or frivolity in the *Book of visions* and Beaupré collection and for hardness of heart in the *Great beginning*. The differences between the three versions are interesting and show the efforts of Conrad of Ebersbach, who probably took the story from the *Book of visions,* to make it theologically more precise, but they all show the priority given in chanting to love of God and the saints, which Conrad defined as fervent zeal, application of heart, and devotion. As the devotion decreased, so did the merit, down to singing negligently and frivolously with false words, which Conrad changed to hardness of heart.

This emphasis on the inner quality of devotion was characteristic of spirituality in the twelfth century. Robert of Arbrissel wrote to Countess Ermengard of Brittany early in the century:

> Brief prayer is useful, prayer of the heart not of the lips is agreeable to God. God pays attention not to the words but to the heart of the person who prays. All the works of the just [and] good man is prayer. We can always pray with the heart, not always with the voice.[44]

Robert here contrasted the heart in three places respectively with the lips, words, and the voice, and in his almost exclusive exphasis on the heart he anticipated some future attitudes toward prayer. Not all his contemporaries agreed with him in deprecating the value of words, as the concern of the Cistercians for verbal accuracy shows. Bernard insisted that a liturgical melody must serve to make the letter more meaningful, and in the two earlier versions of his vision of angels in the choir the worst fault was the use of false words. Honorius of Augsburg in the general sermon in his *Mirror of the church* stressed the importance of words, to which his hearers were told to pay more attention than to his works, "just as if the emperor sent you an order, you would pay attention not to the bearer's deeds but to the sender's orders, by which you can serve his grace."[45] Honorius was referring here to God's words, which according to traditional teaching should shape the attitudes and actions of the hearer. The established view of making the mind agree with the voice was still found even in religious houses which did not observe the rule of Benedict. "When you stand in the presence of the Lord singing the psalms," wrote the Carthusian Bernard of Portes to a recluse named Rainald, "apply all your zeal and all your attention so that the mind may come together with the tongue *(mens cum lingua conveniat)*."[46] One of the prayers for the profession of regular canons at St Rufus, Marbach, and Prémontré in the twelfth century asked that "their life may agree with their name *(concordet ... vita cum nomine)*, so that their profession may be felt in their works."[47]

These sources echo the ancient formulas which dated back to the early church and were embalmed in the rules of Benedict and Augustine, but the emphasis was changing and preparing the way for the Franciscan formula "that the voice should be in agreement with the mind." Adam of Dryburgh, who was a Premonstratensian canon before he became a Carthusian monk and who died in 1212, wrote in his *On the four-part exercise of the will*, which was long attributed to Guigo of La Chartreuse, that when praying the reader should

> Pay attention in these matters and in the very words of your petition ... that you

experience in your heart what you say with your mouth, so that your voice may be in agreement with your mind, and the latter may think about what the former sounds *(quod dicis ore, revolvas in corde, ut concordet vox tua cum mente tua, et hoc cogitet illa quod sonet ista)*.

He should pay close attention, Adam continued, both to whom he worships and to what he says "so that the soul may understand what the tongue sounds *(ut quod lingua sonat, animus intelligat)*" and should when he worships God "apply the heart to those things which you sound with the mouth *(appone cor iis quae ore sonas)*." Some people can make "the exterior proclamation of words" but not "the interior understanding of the meaning which lies in the words," owing both to the instability of their minds and to their ignorance of letters, but when Adam's reader hears, sings, or reads anything in choir, "Whatever you proclaim externally by sound in your mouth should be considered within yourself by understanding in your heart," and when he hears other recite, sing, or read the psalms, he should through his ear apply his heart by intelligence to what he hears them saying.[48]

In these few phrases Adam constrasted not only, on one side, the heart, mind, spirit, intellect, attention, intelligence, and meaning with, on the other, the mouth, voice, tongue, ear, and words but also the interior activities of thinking, meditating, considering, and understanding *(cogitare, revolvere, intelligere, versare)* with the exterior activities of speaking, sounding, proclaiming, and hearing, and he insisted upon the subordination of the external to the internal activities. In writing that the voice should agree with the mind, he may not have been fully aware that he was reversing for the first known time the formula in the rule of Benedict, since he went on immediately to say that the mind should consider what the voice says, and throughout the passage his principal concern was that worshippers should think about and try to understand what they said, not that they should put into words what was in their minds. The reversal reflected an important tendency in contemporary spirituality, however, and pointed the way towards the time when more attention was given in prayer to what was thought than what was said. For Robert of Arbrissel, and for many who came after him, true prayer came from the heart and was expressed in works rather than in words, but although their priorities differed from those in the early Middle Ages, they were equally concerned for harmony between the inner and outer aspects of prayer and insisted no less strongly than the fathers of the church and the early monastic writers that Christians should understand the meaning and intend the consequences of their words and actions in prayer.

NOTES

Note: The language of medieval liturgical and spiritual texts is difficult to translate into clear and consistent English. In this article *canere, cantare,* and *psallere* are all translated "to sing" or "to chant [the psalms]"; *laudare* as "to praise"; and *precari* as "to pray." *Orare* and *oratio* present more difficulty and are translated here as both "to pray" ("prayer") and "to worship" ("worship"). It is often hard to distinguish between *anima, intellectus, mens, sensus,* and *spiritus,* which are generally translated as "soul," "intellect," "mind," "sense," and "spirit," but in the famous text of Paul cited below *spiritus* means "breath" or "voice" in contrast to *mens* and *sensus,* which are both translated in the Douai Bible as "understanding."

1. Paul had in mind here the understanding of those to whom he was speaking, but the text was usually taken in a personal sense as referring to the understanding of the worshipper. See also Romans 8.27 and Ephesians 5.19, where Paul referred to God's searching the hearts of men and to singing "in your hearts to the Lord," which were later cited as evidence of the primacy of the heart, or interiority, in prayer.

2. Cicero, *De natura deorum,* II, 71, ed. Arthur Stanley Pease (Cambridge, Mass., 1955—58), II, p. 737.

3. Seneca, *Ep.,* LXXV, 4, ed. Otto Hense (= *Opera,* III; Leipzig, 1898), p. 256.

4. *Regula Benedicti,* XIX, ed. Philibert Schmitz (Maredsous, 1955), p. 83. On this passage see, in addition to the references below, Viktor Warnach, "Mens concordet voci. Zur Lehre des heiligen Benedikt über die geistige Haltung beim Chorgebet nach dem 19. Kapitel seiner Klosterregel," *Liturgisches Leben,* V (1938), pp. 169—90; Bertilo de Boer, "La soi-disant opposition de saint François d'Assise à saint Benoît," *Études franciscaines,* N.S. VIII (1957), pp. 181—94, and IX (1958), pp. 57—65 (I have not found the indicated continuation); Gloria-Maria Widhalm, *Die rhetorischen Elemente in der Regula Benedicti* (Regulae Benedicti Studia. Supplementa, 2; Hildesheim, 1974), pp. 192—93; and Winfrid Cramer, "Mens concordet voci. Zum Fortleben einer stoischen Gebetsmaxime in der Regula Benedicti," in *Pietas. Festschrift für Bernhard Kötting,* ed. Ernst Dassmann and K. Suso Frank (*Jahrbuch für Antike und Christentum.* Ergänzungsband, 8; Münster W., 1980), pp. 447—57. I have not seen C. Baraut, "Sic stemus ad psallendum, ut mens nostra concordet voci nostrae," in *Actas del Congreso Nacional de Perfección y Apostolado,* III (Madrid, 1958), pp. 505—14, cited by Cramer, "Mens," p. 447, n. 3.

5. This and other relevant texts by Cyprian are cited by André Borias, "L'influence de saint Cyprien sur saint Benoît," *Revue bénédictine,* LXXIV (1964), p. 75. See also Warnach, "Mens," pp. 182—83; de Boer, "Opposition," p. 183; and Cramer, "Mens," p. 448, n. 11, and p. 455, n. 70, arguing that the *Reg. Ben.* owed more to Lactantius than to Cyprian.

6. Ambrose, *Enarratio in psalmum XLVIII,* VII, in *PL,* XIV, col. 1158AB; see de Boer, "Opposition," pp. 184—85.

7. Jerome, *Commentariorum in epistolam ad Ephesos libri tres,* ad 5.19, in *PL,* XXVI, coll. 561D—62A.

8. C. H. Turner, "Niceta of Remesiana II: Introduction and Text of *De psalmodiae bono,"* *Journal of Theological Studies,* XXIV (1923), pp. 234 and 239 (cc. 1 and 13).

9. Augustine, *Serm.,* CCLVI, 1, in *PL,* XXXVIII, col. 1190.

10. Augustine, *Serm.* X, 1 (from MS. Vat. 5758, p. 98), in *Nova patrum bibliotheca,* ed. Angelo Mai, I (Rome, 1852), p. 19.

11. Augustine, *Serm.,* CCCLIII, 4, in *PL,* XXXIX, col. 1562.

12. Augustine, *Ep.,* CCXI, 7, ed. Al. Goldbacher (Corpus scriptorum ecclesiasticorum latinorum, 57; Vienna-Leipzig, 1911), p. 361; see L. M. J. Verheijen, *La règle de saint Augustine* (Paris,

1967) and the review by A. Sage, in *Revue des études augustiniennes*, XIV (1968), pp. 123—32, on the importance of this letter in the formation of the so-called rule of Augustine. See also de Boer, "Opposition," p. 185, and Cramer, "Mens," p. 448, n. 11.

13. Cassian, *De institutis coenobiorum*, II, 10, ed. Michael Petschenig (Corpus scriptorum ecclesiasticorum latinorum, 17; Prague-Vienna-Leipzig, 1888), p. 25.

14. *Regula Magistri*, XLVII, 18—20, and XLVIII, 3—4, ed. Adalbert de Vogüé (Sources chrétiennes 105—7: Textes monastiques d'Occident, 14—16; Paris, 1964—65), II, pp. 216—18; see Cramer, "Mens," p. 448, and the refs. in n. 6.

15. Cramer, "Mens," p. 450, stressed the parallel between the uses of *mens* and *vox* by Cicero and in the rules of the Master and Benedict and sharply criticized Widhalm, *Rhetorischen Elemente*, pp. 192—93, for saying that the antithesis of *mens* and *vox* (like that of *cor* and *vox*) was a topos in Christian literature (p. 449, n. 14). For Warnach, "Mens," pp. 172 and 174—76, *mens nostra* was the key to this chapter of the rule and involved the entire inner man (= *anima, cor, intellectus, spiritus*).

16. Warnach, "Mens," pp. 178—79, linked *concordet* in the rule with the Stoic concept of *concordia* (*homologia*), and Cramer, "Mens," p. 454, n. 50, cited examples of the use of *concordare* by Stoic writers. Of the examples cited in the *Thesaurus linguae latinae*, s.v., those by Seneca and Ps-Augustine come closest to the rule of Benedict.

17. Caesarius of Arles, *Serm.*, LXXV, 2, ed. Germain Morin, 2nd ed. (Corpus Christianorum, 103; Turnhout, 1953), p. 314.

18. See Warnach, "Mens," p. 172, and esp. de Boer, "Opposition," both with references to previous literature.

19. Warnach, "Mens," pp. 181—86.

20. De Boer, "Opposition," pp. 182—87, cited (1) for the negative form Cyprian, Augustine, Isidore, Hugh of St. Victor, Bernard of Clairvaux, and Thomas of Froidmont, (2) for the first positive form Nicetas, Caesarius of Arles, Cassiodorus, Isidore, Smaragdus, Hugh of St Victor, and the rule of Tarnat, and (3) for the second positive form Nicetas, the rule of Paul and Stephen, Smaragdus, Bruno of La Chartreuse, Bernard of Portes, and Hugh of St Victor.

21. See Cramer, "Mens," pp. 454—56.

22. See Emmanuel von Severus, "Das Wort 'Meditari' im Sprachgebrauch der Heiligen Schrift," *Geist und Leben*, XXVI (1953), pp. 365—75, esp. 366—67; Jean Leclercq, *L'amour des lettres et le désir de Dieu* (Paris, 1957), pp. 22—23 and 72—73; idem, "Meditation as a Biblical Reading," *Worship*, XXXIII (1958—59), pp. 562—69; and Heinrich Bacht, "'Meditatio' in den ältesten Mönchsquellen," *Geist und Leben*, XXVIII (1955), pp. 360—73, revised in his *Das Vermächtnis des Ursprungs. Studien zum frühen Mönchtum*, I (Studien zur Theologie des geistlichen Lebens, 5; Würzburg, 1972), pp. 244—64. I owe these references to William Graham, who remarks in his forthcoming book on *Scripture as Spoken Word* that the early monks meditated with their mouths and ears as well as with their minds and hearts.

23. Edmund Bishop, "A Letter of Abbot Helisachar," in *Liturgica historica* (Oxford, 1918), p. 337, with a partial translation on p. 335. I am indebted to the Rev. Chrysogonus Waddell for drawing this text to my attention.

24. R. Le Roux, "Les répons de *Psalmis* pour les Matines, de l'Épiphanie à la Septuagésime," *Études grégoriennes*, VI (1963), pp. 130—32, who was apparently unaware of Bishop's publication and commentary.

25. The phrase *auctoritate et ratione* is used twice in the text.

26. Joseph Szövérffy, "'False' Use of 'Unfitting' Hymns: Some Ideas Shared by Peter the Venerable, Peter Abelard and Heloise," *Revue bénédictine*, LXXXIX (1979), pp. 187—99.

27. Peter the Venerable, *Ep.*, 124, ed. Giles Constable (Harvard Historical Studies, 78; Cambridge, Mass., 1967), I, p. 318.

28. Peter the Venerable, *Stat.*, 58, 59, 61, and 62, in *Consuetudines benedictinae variae*, ed. Giles Constable (Corpus Consuetudinum Monasticarum, 6; Siegburg, 1975), pp. 88, 90, 93, and 94. Szövérffy cited in addition *Stat.* 68 and 74—76, pp. 99 and 103—5, which are concerned with the congruity and suitability of hymns, the Kyrie, and *Salve regina*.

29. Szövérffy, "'False' Use," p. 190.

30. *Ibid.*, p. 191, to which can be added the use of *falsitas* by Peter the Venerable in Statute 62.

31. See the edition by Chrysogonus Waddell in *The Twelfth-Century Cistercian Missal*, II: *The Milanese-Cistercian Recension and the Bernardine Recension* (Cistercian Liturgy Series, 2; Trappist, Ky., 1984) p. 8, with references to previous editions of the entire text, including that of Szövérffy, on p. 7, and Waddell's valuable commentary in *The Twelfth-Century Cistercian Hymnal*, I: *Introduction and Commentary* (Cistercian Liturgy Series, 1; Trappist, Ky., 1984), pp. 67—69.

32. On the concept of authenticity, see Marie-Dominique Chenu, *Introduction à l'étude de saint Thomas d'Aquin* (Publications de l'Institut d'études médiévales, 11; Montreal, 1950), pp. 110 f., and *La théologie au douzième siècle* (Études de philosophie médiévale, 45; Paris, 1957), pp. 351—65; on authority and tradition, see Klaus Schreiner, "'Discrimen veri ac falsi.' Ansätze und Formen der Kritik in der Heiligen- und Reliquienverehrung des Mittelalters," *Archiv für Kulturgeschichte*, XLVIII (1966), pp. 19—20, and on antiquity, idem, "Zur Wahrheitsverständnis im Heiligen- und Reliquienwesen des Mittelalters," *Saeculum*, XVII (1966), pp. 157—58.

33. MS Dijon, Bibl. mun., 15, f. 73ᵛ: "In duobus uetustissimis et multum ueracibus hystoriis non inuenimus hunc uersum. hic dicet tibi quid te oporteat facere."

34. Chrysogonus Waddell, "An Aspect of the Chant Reform Called Bernardine," *Liturgy*, VI (1972), p. 92.

35. Bernard of Clairvaux, *Ep.*, CCCXCVIII, 2, ed. Jean Leclercq, a.o. (Rome, 1957 ff.), VIII, p. 378; and n. 36 below for the introductory letter.

36. This treatise is edited together with Bernard's introductory letter under the title *Cantum quem Cisterciensis ordinis ecclesiae cantare consueuerant* by Francis J. Guentner (Corpus scriptorum de musica, 24; n. p. [American Institute of Musicology], 1974), pp. 22—24 and 40; see Waddell, "Chant Reform," p. 89, on the responsory versets; his article on "The Reform of the Liturgy from a Renaissance Perspective," in *Renaissance and Renewal in the Twelfth Century*, ed. Robert L. Benson and Giles Constable (Cambridge, Mass., 1982), pp. 106—7; and in *Cistercian Hymnal*, I, pp. 73—75.

37. Peter the Venerable, *Stat.*, 1, ed. Constable, p. 42.

38. The documents concerning the meetings of the abbots in the province of Rheims were published by Ursmer Berlière, *Documents inédits pour servir à l'histoire ecclésiastique de la Belgique*, I (Maredsous, 1894), pp. 91—110, and again by Stanislaus Ceglar, "Guillaume de Saint-Thierry et son rôle directeur aux premiers chapîtres des abbés bénédictins, Reims 1131 et Soissons 1132," in *Saint Thierry. Une abbaye du VIᵉ aus XXᵉ siècle* (St Thierry, 1979), pp. 312—50 (quotations on pp. 330 and 346).

39. William of St Thierry, *Epistola ad fratres de Monte Dei*, I, 10, 29, in *PL*, CLXXXIV, col. 326CD, and ed. M.-M. Davy (Études de philosophie médiévale, 29; Paris, 1940).

40. Rupert of Deutz, *Liber de divinis officiis*, prol., ed. Hrabanus Haacke (Corpus Christianorum: Continuatio mediaeualis, 7; Turnhout, 1967), p. 6.

41. Bernard of Clairvaux, *Serm. super Cantica*, XLVII, 8, ed. Leclercq, II, p. 66.

42. Bernard, *Ep.*, CCCXCVIII, 2, ed. Leclercq, VIII, p. 378.

43. These three versions are found respectively in MSS Troyes, Bibl. mun., 946, f. 134ᵛ, and Paris, Bibl. nat., Lat. 15912, f. 35ʳ A, and edited by Bruno Griesser (Series scriptorum S. Ordinis Cisterciensis, 2; Rome, 1961), p. 100 (II, 3); see the two articles by Brian P. McGuire, "A Lost

Clairvaux Exemplum Collection Found: The *Liber visionum et miraculorum* compiled under Prior John of Clairvaux (1171—79)," *Analecta Cisterciensia*, XXXIX (1983), pp. 44—45, and "The Cistercians and the Rise of the Exemplum in Early Thirteenth Century France: A Reevaluation of Paris BN MS lat. 15912," *Classica et Mediaevalia*, XXXIV (1983), pp. 239—40.

44.   J. de Petigny, "Lettre inédite de Robert d'Arbrissel à la comtesse Ermengarde," *Bibliothèque de l'École des Chartes*, XV (3rd S., V; 1854), p. 232.

45.   Honorius of Augsburg, *Speculum ecclesiae: Sermo generalis*, in *PL*, CLXXII, col. 869A.

46.   Bernard of Portes, *Ep. ad Rainaldum inclusum*, in *PL*, CLIII, col. 896C.

47.   Josef Siegwart, *Die Consuetudines des Augustiner-Chorherrenstiftes Marbach im Elsass* (Spicilegium Friburgense, 10; Fribourg S., 1965), p. 170, no. 143, with references to the customaries of St Rufus and Prémontré, and note on p. 320 pointing out the parallels with the sermons of Augustine and Caesarius of Arles cited nn. 11 and 17 above.

48.   Adam of Dryburgh, *De quadripartito exercitio cellae*, XXXV, in *PL*, CLIII, coll. 878C—79B, reprinted by de Boer, "Opposition," pp. 61—62, with a note on the authorship on p. 61, n. 35.

ADDENDA

To Article I:

p. 31: On Theophilus, see John Van Engen, 'Theophilus Presbyter and Rupert of Deutz: The Manual Arts and Benedictine Theology in the Early Twelfth Century', *Viator*, 11 (1980), pp. 147–63, who argued that Theophilus was a monk and priest writing in the Rhineland in the mid- or late 1120s, and Virginia Roehrig Kaufmann, 'Malanleitungen im Buch I *De diversis artibus* des Theophilus und ihrer Anwendung im Evangeliar Heinrichs des Löwen', in *Heinrich der Löwe und seine Zeit. Katalog zur Ausstellung Braunschweig Herzog Anton Ulrich-Museum*, II (Munich, 1995), pp. 301–11, who proposed that 'Theophilus' was a composite work, revised and put together over a period of time.

To Article II:

p. 32: The letter of Siboto IV was the subject of a full analysis, which grew out of a discussion in the medieval seminar at the Institute for Advanced Study, by Patrick Geary and John B. Freed, 'Literacy and Violence in Twelfth-Century Bavaria: The "Murder Letter" of Count Siboto IV', *Viator*, 25 (1994), pp. 115–29.

To Article IV:

André Gouron sent me a relevant passage from the preface to the *Liber instrumentorum memorialium. Cartulaire des Guillems de Montpellier* (Montpellier, 1884–1886), p. 1: 'Quod utique cognicionis genus non habet homo prestancius, quam si ea quorum recoli mavult, ac reminisci desiderat, stilo commendaverit, ne labefactante memoria, quod facile adinvenit facilius evanescat, et ab ipsius collabatur memoria. Unde est ut donationes, hemptiones, permutaciones, ac reliquos adquirendi contractus scriptura teste notificet, quo possit securius contra calumpiantes rationes suas exponere, et certis possidendi titulis causam suam defendere.' This was written, according to Professor Gouron, in 1202 or 1203, possibly by a friend of Alan of Lille, who was in Montpellier in 1200.

p. 135 and 157 n. 109: The 'separate paper' and 'the article, mentioned above, on *A Living Past*' was published in the *Harvard Library Bulletin*, N.S. 1.3 (1990), pp. 49–70, and is reprinted as article V here.

p. 145 n. 48: To the works on time cited there can be added G.J. Whitrow, *Time in History: Views of Time from Prehistory to the Present Day* (Oxford, 1988), esp. pp. 43–57 on the linear, non-cyclical concept of time in Late Antiquity. On 'the Chartrian preoccupation with correct talk about time', see *The 'Glosae super Platonem' of Bernard of Chartres*, ed. Paul Edward Dutton ([Pontifical Institute of Mediaeval Studies] Studies and Texts, 107; Toronto, 1991), pp. 92–4, with references in 93 n. 266.

p. 161 n. 134: See also Karl Morrison, *Understanding Conversion* (Charlottesville and London, 1992) and *Conversion and Text* (Charlottesville and London, 1992).

To Article V:

On the visualisation of the past, especially in historical works of the twelfth century, see Karl Morrison, *History as a Visual Art in the Twelfth-Century Renaissance* (Princeton, 1990), who said (p. 78) that 'Reading history therefore became an event by which what happened in the theater of the world ... was recreated and restored to wholeness in the theater of the mind' and (p. 85) that for John of Salisbury 'to imagine was specifically to visualize'.

p. 49, introductory note: The proceedings of the Fifth Penn-Paris-Dumbarton Oaks Colloquium were never published.

p. 50 at n. 10: on the view that the eyes were more reliable than the ears, with citations to Josephus, Aulus Gellius, and Gregory of Tours, see Walter Goffart, *The Narrators of Barbarian History (A.D. 550–800)* (Princeton, 1988), p. 119; cf. 145: 'Only experience, not words, commanded credence'.

pp. 63ff: on anachronism in art, see Morrison, *History as a Visual Art*, p. 161.

To Article VI:

I might have said something in this paper, though it is not strictly relevant to the language of preaching, about the concept of the *taciturnus* or *tacitus praedicator*, on which see *The Letters of Peter the Venerable* (Harvard Historical Studies, 78; Cambridge, Mass., 1967), I, 38–9, and II, 107, and the *Dialogus de mundi contemptu vel amore*, ed. Robert Bultot (Analecta mediaevalia Namurcensia, 19; Louvain-Lille, 1966), pp. 72–3, which is attributed to Conrad of Hirsau, who wrote 'Sicut enim clamosis, sic tacitis praedicatoribus christus ecclesiam per hoc idumeę desertum transducit, ut quod alter in uerbo, alter ad profectum proximi clamet in exemplo'.

p.133: Mary Rouse drew to my attention an interesting example of distrust of vernacular preaching in the second half of the thirteenth century, when Gilbert of Tournai in his *Collectio de scandalis ecclesiae*, 25, ed. A. Stroick, in *Archivum franciscanum historicum*, 24 (1931), pp. 61–2, recommended that copies of the *biblia gallicata* be destroyed 'ne sermo divinus a dictione uulgari uilescat', where *sermo divinus* may mean either the holy word of Scripture or preaching.

p. 145: On Peter of Cornwall, see Richard H. Rouse and Mary A. Rouse 'Statim invenire: Schools, Preachers, and New Attitudes to the Page', in *Renaissance and Renewal in the Twelfth Century*, ed. Robert L. Benson and Giles Constable with Carol D. Lanham (Cambridge, Mass., 1982), pp. 215–16, where he explained that his collection was fashioned so that sermon-makers (*sermonem facientes*) needed not to make sermons but to form sermons already made for them ('non tam sermonem facere quam iam factum formare'), that is, to crib them.

pp. 146–7: In the mid-twelfth century archbishop Albero of Trier could barely explain his material 'when he gave a sermon to the people, in part because he spoke slowly, in part because having been born in the French tongue he was not skilled in German, and in part because he treated very deep matters': Baldric, *Gesta Alberonis Trevirorum archiepiscopi*, 26, in *Monumenta Germaniae historica: Scriptores* in fol., VIII, 257.

To Article VII:

p. 824, n. 169: The letter of Hugh Farsit has been edited in *Cristianità ed Europa. Miscellanea di studi in onore di Luigi Prosdocimi*, ed. Cesare Alzati (Rome-Freiburg-Vienna, 1994), I.1, 249–63.

To Article VIII:

p. 45: Peter of Blois wrote to pope Innocent III in 1206/8, defending the various customs of the church in England, 'absit autem ut sponsa Christi amicta varietatibus, clericali, monacali, albi et nigri, linei et lanei, pro unius ambitione sustineat pallium Joseph aut Christi tunicam ita scindi': *The Later Letters of Peter of Blois*, ed. Elizabeth Revell (Auctores Britannici Medii Aevi, 13; Oxford, 1993), p. 66.

To Article IX:

Mircea Eliade stressed the normality and inevitability of suffering in his *Myth of the Eternal Reform or, Cosmos and History*, tr. Willard Trask (Bollingen Series, 46; Princeton, 1954; corrected reprint 1965), pp. 95–102.

p. 9: Ammianus Marcellinus, *Res gestae*, 22, 16, 23, ed. Wolfgang Seyforth, I (Bibliotheca ...Teubneriana; Leipzig, 1978), pp. 292–3, said that the Egyptians were ashamed if they did not show 'many stripes on the body (*plurimas in corpore uibices*)' for not paying tribute.

p. 27: The material on the stigmata in the eleventh and twelfth centuries was published in *Three Studies in Medieval Religious and Social Thought* (Cambridge, 1995), pp. 194–217, and on moderation and restraint in ascetic practices in *From Athens to Chartres: Neoplatonism and Medieval Thought. Studies in Honour of Edouard Jeauneau*, ed. Haijo Jan Westra (Leiden-New York-Cologne, 1992), pp. 315–27, reprinted as article X here.

To Article XI:

pp. 30 and n. 20: In William of St Thierry, *Vita prima Bernardi*, I, IV, 20, in *Pat. lat.*, CLXXXV, 238D, Bernard was said to have been unaware of the roof after a year in the novices' cell: cf. *Verba seniorum*, IV, 16, and VII, 19, in *Pat. lat.*, LXXIII, 866C and 896D–7A.

p. 33 n. 1: The article on 'Liberty and Free Choice' was published in *La notion de liberté au moyen âge. Islam, Byzance, Occident*, ed. George Makdisi, Dominique Sourdel, and Janine Sourdel-Thomine (Pennsylvania-Paris-Dumbarton Oaks Colloquia, 4; Paris, 1985), pp. 99–118, and reprinted in my *Monks, Hermits and Crusaders in Medieval Europe* (Variorum Reprint, CS273; London, 1988), article IV.

p. 34 n. 21: For other views on Bernard's ride beside the lake of Geneva, see Georges Duby, *Saint Bernard. L'art cistercien* (Paris, 1979), p. 88, who said that in spite of this and other parallel anecdotes Bernard was 'fort capable de percevoir les valeurs visuelles'; A.J. Gurevich, *Categories of Medieval Culture*, tr. G.L. Campbell (London, 1985), pp. 61–2, for whom Bernard's lack of appreciation for nature was not characteristic of the period; Jacques Dalarun, *L'impossible sainteté. La vie retrouvée de Robert d'Arbrissel (v. 1045–1116) fondateur de Fontevraud* (Paris, 1985), p. 237, who considered it a hagiographical topos; C.N.L. Brooke, 'St Bernard, the patrons and monastic planning', in *Cistercian Art and Architecture in the British Isles*, ed. Christopher Norton and David Park (Cambridge, 1986), p. 19, citing various interpretations of the episode; and Conrad Rudolph, *The 'Things of Greater Importance': Bernard of Clairvaux's 'Apologia' and the Medieval Attitude toward Art* (Philadelphia, 1990), p. 112, who called this and parallel episodes 'hagiographical devices'. Logan Pearsall Smith, *Reperusals and Re-collections* (London, 1936), p. 27, cited Gibbon's view of the 'holy apathy' of Bernard.

To Article XII:

p. 18 at n. 9: The rhetorical character of this passage was emphasized by Erich Auerbach, *Literary Language and Its Public in Late Latin Antiquity and in the Middle Ages*, tr. Ralph Manheim (Bollingen Series, 74; New York, 1965), p. 31.

p. 18: Egeria in her *Itinerarium*, XLVII, 5, in *Corpus Christianorum*, CLXXV, 89, wrote 'Illud autem hic ante omnia ualde gratum fit et ualde admirabile, ut semper tam ymni quam antiphonae et lectiones nec non etiam et orationes, quas dicet episcopus tales pronuntiationes habeant, ut et dici, qui celebretur, et loco, in quo agitur, aptae et conuenientes sint semper'.

p. 19: Benedictus Van Haeften in his commentary on the rule of Benedict, *S Benedictus illustratus sive disquisitionum monasticarum libri XII* (Antwerp, 1644), pp. 720–1 (VII, 4, 7), cited various early sources on the need for attention in the psalmody.

pp. 19–20: Odo of Cluny in his *Vita Geraldi Auriliacensis*, II, 9, said 'Et cum debeat voci mentis intelligentia convenire, nos facimus currere vocem post levitatem mentis', in *Pat. lat.*, CXXXIII, 676BC.

INDEX

This index is limited to significant proper names. 'St' before a name indicates a place; after a name, a saint. The following abbreviations are used: abp = archbishop; abt = abbot; bp = bishop; card = cardinal; ct = count; emp = emperor; k = king. 'Add' indicates a reference in the Addenda.